Annuities and Other Retirement Products

Annuities and Other Retirement Products

Designing the Payout Phase

Roberto Rocha
Dimitri Vittas
Heinz P. Rudolph

THE WORLD BANK
Washington, D.C.

ISBN: 978-0-8213-8573-9
eISBN: 978-0-8213-8574-6
DOI: 10.1596/978-0-8213-8573-9

Library of Congress Cataloging-in-Publication Data

Rocha, Roberto Rezende.
  Annuities and other retirement products : designing the payout phase / Roberto Rocha, Dimitri Vittas, Heinz P. Rudolph.
    p. cm. — (Directions in development)
  Includes bibliographical references and index.
  ISBN 978-0-8213-8573-9 (alk. paper) — ISBN 978-0-8213-8574-6
  1. Pensions. 2. Annuities. 3. Old age pensions. 4. Pensions—Government policy.
  5. Annuities—Government policy. 6. Old age pensions—Government policy. I. Vittas, Dimitri. II. Rudolph, Heinz P. III. Title.
  HD7091.R63 2010
  331.25'24—dc22

                                                                        2010036026

Cover photo: © iStockphoto.com/ozgurdonmaz
Cover design: Quantum Think

Contents

Figures

Tables

Preface

Many countries that have implemented systemic pension reforms and introduced private pension systems are now facing the challenge of organizing the payout phase for retiring workers. This effort entails introducing a well-regulated market for retirement products, covering their effective regulation and supervision, marketing activities, providers, and intermediaries. However, the literature on the payout phase is generally focused on a few countries and topics, and it does not address in sufficient detail the institutional and regulatory issues faced by policy makers in reforming countries.

Annuities and Other Retirement Products: Designing the Payout Phase aims to fill this gap by reviewing in detail five representative country cases: Australia, Chile, Denmark, Sweden, and Switzerland. All these countries have large mandatory or quasi-mandatory private pension systems operating primarily on a defined contribution basis, and they have already entered the payout phase. But their institutional and regulatory arrangements for the payout phase differ in many aspects, including decentralized and centralized arrangements for the provision of life and term annuities, different menus of retirement products, different approaches to price regulation and risk sharing, different marketing rules, and different capital rules for providers. Therefore, these countries provide a rich variety of experiences and policy lessons for other reforming countries.

Studies covering each of these five countries were commissioned and completed over the past few years (Andersen and Skjodt 2007; Brunner and Thorburn 2008; Bütler and Ruesch 2007; Palmer 2008; Rocha and Thorburn 2007). This book contains edited summaries of these country studies as well as a detailed discussion of policy issues, constraints, and options and a comparative analysis of the main similarities and differences between the five countries.

We hope that the analysis contained in this book will be useful to policy makers in reforming countries around the world. We are greatly indebted to Carsten Andersen, Gregory Gordon Brunner, Monika Bütler, Edward Palmer, Martin Ruesch, Peter Skjodt, and Craig Thorburn, the country experts who prepared the individual studies and collaborated with us in the development of the manuscript for this book. We are also grateful to Loic Chiquier, Augusto de la Torre, Gregorio Impavido, Estelle James, John Pollner, and Anita Schwarz for their extensive comments and insights on various parts of the manuscript.

References

Andersen, Carsten, and Peter Skjodt. 2007. "Pension Institutions and Annuities in Denmark." Policy Research Working Paper 4437, World Bank, Washington, DC.

Brunner, Gregory Gordon, and Craig Thorburn. 2008. "The Market for Retirement Products in Australia." Policy Research Working Paper 4749, World Bank, Washington, DC.

Bütler, Monika, and Martin Ruesch. 2007. "Annuities in Switzerland." Policy Research Working Paper 4438, World Bank, Washington, DC.

Palmer, Edward. 2008. "The Market for Retirement Products in Sweden." Policy Research Working Paper 4748, World Bank, Washington, DC.

Rocha, Roberto, and Craig Thorburn. 2007. *Developing Annuities Markets: The Experience of Chile.* Washington, DC: World Bank.

Abbreviations

$A	Australian dollars
ABI	accrued benefits index
ABM	automatic balancing mechanism
ACF	annuity conversion factor
AFP	*administrador de fondo de pensión,* or pension fund administrator (Chile)
AP	*allmänna pension,* or national pension (Sweden)
APRA	Australian Prudential Regulation Authority
APS	*aporte previsional solidario,* or pension solidarity supplement (Chile)
ATP	Arbejdsmarkedets Tillaegspension, or Labor Market Supplementary Pension (Denmark)
BCU	Banco Central de Chile bonds in UF
Ch$	Chilean pesos
CPI	consumer price index
DB	defined benefit
DC	defined contribution
DKr	Danish kroner
EU	European Union
FDC	financial defined contribution

FIF	Federal Insurance Fund (Switzerland)
FSA	Finansinspektionen, or Financial Supervisory Authority (Sweden)
GDP	gross domestic product
ITP-ITPK	Industrins och handelns tilläggspension–Individuellt styrd komplettering till ITP, or Industry and Commerce Supplementary Pension–Individually Controlled Supplement to the ITP (Sweden)
KAP-KL	KollektivAvtalad Pension–Kommuner och Landsting, or Collective Pension–Municipalities and Regions (Sweden)
LD	Lønmodtagernes Dyrtidsfond, or Employees' Capital Fund (Denmark)
LO	Landsorganisationen, or Swedish Trade Union
MBI	minimum benefit index
MIR	minimum interest rate
MPG	minimum pension guarantee
MTAWE	male total average weekly earnings
MWR	money's worth ratio
NDC	notional defined contribution
OECD	Organisation for Economic Co-operation and Development
OFAS	Office Fédéral des Assurances Sociales, or Federal Office for Social Insurance (Switzerland)
PAIRS	Probability and Impact Rating System (Australia)
PASIS	Pensión Asistencial de Ancianidad, or Care of Elderly Pension (Chile)
PAYG	pay-as-you-go
PBS	*pensión básica solidaria*, or basic solidarity pension (Chile)
PMAS	*pensión máxima con aporte solidario*, or maximum pension with solidarity support (Chile)
PPM	Premiumpensionsmyndigheten, or Premium Pension Authority (Sweden)
PW	phased withdrawal
RIM	Retirement and Income Modelling (Unit) (Australia)
ROE	return on equity
RSA	retirement savings account
SAF	Svenska Arbetsgivareföreningen, or Swedish Employers' Association

SCOMP	Sistema de Consultas y Ofertas de Montos de Pensión, or Pension Consultations and Offers System (Chile)
SEQUAL	Senior Australians Equity Release Association of Lenders
SG	superannuation guarantee
SKr	Swedish kronor
SOARS	Supervisory Oversight and Response System (Australia)
SP	Særlige Pensionsopsparing, or Special Pension Savings Scheme (Denmark)
SUPP	Supplerende arbejdsmarkedspension, or Supplementary Labor Market Pension Scheme for Disability Pensioners (Denmark)
Sw F	Swiss francs
TW	temporary withdrawal
UF	*unidad de fomento*, a unit of account that is indexed to prices and is widely used in Chile
US$	U.S. dollars
VBI	vested benefits index

CHAPTER 1

Introduction and Overview

The demand for voluntary annuities has been weak in most countries around the world. The main reason for this weak demand has probably been—at least in member countries of the Organisation for Economic Co-operation and Development—the payment of social security pensions to nearly the whole population and the offer of company pensions to most middle- and high-income individuals.

Historically, social security and company pensions were introduced at a time when financial and insurance markets were unstable and poorly regulated. The demand for annuities was weakened by the lack of trust in the long-term solvency and integrity of insurance companies and the exposure of nominal annuities to inflation risk. The offer of social security and company pensions filled a gap in the provision of financial services that financial and insurance markets were unable to satisfy.

Recent years have witnessed, however, far-reaching changes in the landscape of annuity markets. Under the growing strain of demographic aging, social security systems have been restructured and effectively downsized in a large number of countries. In addition, for competitive and other reasons, traditional defined benefit (DB) company pension schemes have been closed and have been replaced by defined contribution (DC) plans. At the same time, financial and insurance markets have become better regulated and thus more robust. Financial innovation has expanded the range of products and choices that could stimulate the growth of private annuity markets.

The global financial crisis of 2008 has demonstrated that despite the significant progress in financial regulation, financial markets and institutions continue to suffer from bouts of excessive risk taking that threaten the survival of individual institutions and undermine confidence in the sustainability of long-term financial contracts. Although the growth of DC pension plans is likely to stimulate the demand for life annuities, successful development of the annuity market will necessitate a significant strengthening of financial regulation and supervision to instill greater trust in the long-term solvency and integrity of annuity providers.

Much of the early research on pension systems has focused on the policy challenges of the accumulation phase. As pension systems have moved away from the traditional unfunded social security systems and funded DB occupational pension schemes, the main emphasis has been placed on the structure, performance, and regulation of DC pension funds in both the public and the private sectors and in both developed and emerging countries. This emphasis has been fully understandable given the paramount importance of ensuring the safety and efficiency of the accumulation phase.

With the growing maturity of pension reforms in terms of performance and regulation as well as in terms of size and age, the issues and challenges of the payout phase have started to attract attention. The policy and regulatory issues that will confront the conversion of accumulated account balances in DC plans into streams of retirement income, such as life annuities and phased withdrawals (PWs), have been underscored in a fast-growing volume of theoretical and empirical research.

However, despite its significant expansion, this research has remained focused on specific issues and countries. Researchers have examined the adverse selection problem that may hinder the growth of annuity markets; documented the thinness of voluntary annuity markets; calculated the implicit returns to annuitants; identified some of the major risks facing workers, retirees, and providers; and offered some solutions designed to deal with these risks. Nevertheless, a wide range of issues in the regulation of products and intermediaries has not been properly examined. Moreover, the bulk of the empirical research has been restricted to very few developed countries, primarily the United Kingdom and the United States. Research on other countries has usually been limited to a general overview of the institutional and regulatory framework (see, for example, Blake 1999; Brown, Mitchell, and Poterba 2001; Cardinale, Findlater, and Orszag 2002; Davis 2000; Fornero and Luciano 2004; Impavido, Thorburn, and Wadsworth 2003; James, Song, and Vittas 2001; Mitchell and others 2001; Palacios and Rofman 2001; Valdés-Prieto 1998).

Policy Issues in the Design of Payout Phases in Emerging Countries

Although the existing body of research has produced useful insights, it has failed to address many questions that are critical for policy makers in emerging countries. The need for answers is particularly strong in the many countries in Eastern Europe and Latin America that have undergone systemic pension reforms, entailing an important role for the private sector, and in countries where regulatory restrictions on lump sums imply that PWs and life annuities will become important vehicles of retirement income. A central question faced by policy makers in these countries is whether the insurance sector can effectively deliver relatively complex products, such as life annuities, and honor contracts that may span 40 years or longer. This question is not trivial given the lack of reliable mortality data in many emerging countries, their less-developed institutional and regulatory frameworks, and their less-developed capital markets.

The fundamental question facing policy makers in many countries in the new emerging landscape is whether product innovation will respond to the preferences and constraints of prospective annuitants without policy support or whether the development of annuity markets will require supportive policy measures, such as tax incentives, restrictions on payout options, and even compulsory annuitization.

In the case of saving for retirement, most countries around the world use tax incentives to encourage workers to accumulate financial wealth during their active lives, while several countries impose mandatory (or quasi-mandatory) participation rules. This approach is predicated on the argument that absent such policy measures, a large number of workers—perhaps a significant plurality, though not necessarily the majority—would make insufficient provision for their financial needs in retirement. This problem is attributed to myopic behavior by workers, a difficulty in estimating their retirement needs, and an underestimation of their longevity.

If supportive measures are deemed necessary during the accumulation phase, it is difficult to argue that they would be completely redundant during the payout phase. If this premise is accepted, then the more practical questions concern the desired level and conditions of annuitization and the relative role of tax incentives, payout restrictions, and compulsion.

Scope and Structure of the Book

Policy makers and regulators in many countries would benefit from a more in-depth analysis of the markets for retirement products across a greater number of countries because such an analysis would enable them to identify best practices in the regulation of products and intermediaries and to formulate institutional arrangements that might work better, particularly in less-sophisticated environments.

This book examines recent changes in the landscape of retirement products and annuity markets in five countries. All the selected countries (Australia, Chile, Denmark, Sweden, and Switzerland) have mandatory or quasi-mandatory savings schemes. But they also exhibit significant differences in the structure of their pension systems, the relative importance of public pillars, the role and structure of private provision, the level of annuitization, and the structure and focus of their regulatory frameworks. Five studies have been commissioned to examine the state of annuity markets in each of these countries. The findings of these studies are summarized in the last five chapters of this book.

The structure of the book is as follows. Chapter 2 focuses on the policy issues and constraints facing the design of the payout phase. It discusses the various risks faced by pensioners and the risk characteristics of alternative retirement products, and it reviews the risks faced by providers of retirement products and the management and regulatory challenges of dealing with those risks. The chapter focuses on policies that could be adopted in countries where financial and insurance markets are not well developed.

Chapter 2 notes that because pensioner risks often pull in opposite directions, policy makers should target an adequate level of annuitization but should be wary of causing overannuitization. It also highlights the important shortcomings of all types of retirement products and argues for policies that favor a combination of payout options, covering different products at a particular point in time as well as different payout options over time.

This discussion is linked to the case for mandating a minimum level of compulsory annuitization and the related question of the types of restrictions that should be applied to payout options. The chapter then discusses the risks faced by providers and reviews the challenges of various regulatory issues, ranging from the institutional organization of the market for retirement products to the regulation of marketing and pricing policies and the regulation of risk management. The chapter concludes with a brief summary of main points and conclusions.

Chapter 3 offers a comparative summary of the experience of the five countries for which detailed studies have been commissioned. It starts by comparing the overall structure of the pension systems of the five countries, focusing on the relative role of different pillars. It then reviews the regulation of payout options of different retirement products. This review is followed by a discussion of the regulation of marketing policies and an examination of differences in the level of annuitization across the five countries. The chapter then reviews the five countries' approaches to regulation of providers of retirement products, covering in turn differences in institutional structure, capital and prudential regulations, risk management, and risk-sharing arrangements. The chapter concludes by summarizing the lessons for other countries.

The last five chapters are devoted to country summaries of the experiences of the five individual countries covered in this project. The country chapters follow a broadly similar structure and review the evolution of pension systems and annuity markets in each country.

Overview of Country Findings

This section presents a brief overview of the findings of the five country chapters. A more-detailed comparison of different features of retirement systems is provided in chapter 3. The first two countries, Australia and Switzerland, have one important feature in common but stand at opposite ends in terms of outcomes. The common feature is that neither country imposes any restrictions on lump-sum withdrawals. But underscoring the complexity of retirement systems and the effects of other factors, the two countries report extreme levels of annuitization: very low use of life annuities in Australia and very high use in Switzerland. Sweden and Denmark, which are discussed next, have more similarities than differences, especially following the relatively recent conversion of the Swedish public and private pillars from DB to DC plans. The last country, Chile, is in many respects a unique case, not least because it has been a reform-oriented developing country.

It is, however, important to note that in none of these five countries, or in any other country in any region of the world, have the new pension systems reached maturity. The original major pension reform in Chile was implemented nearly 30 years ago, which is probably half the time needed for a pension system to reach maturity. Major changes and reforms in the other countries date from the mid-1980s (Denmark and Switzerland) to the mid-1990s (Australia and Sweden). Moreover, reform programs have often been subject to gradual implementation, whereas subsequent major changes have attempted to fill important gaps or to correct inefficiencies and inconsistencies. The 2008 Chilean changes offer a good example of this approach, but all countries have experienced greater or fewer changes in recent years.

Australia

The market for lifetime retirement products is not well developed in Australia. This lack of development is not attributed to any major supply constraints but largely reflects the presence of a modest means-tested universal age pension, the strong preference of Australians for lump-sum withdrawals and term annuities, and their effective reliance on self-annuitization.

The Australian system mandates lifetime saving for retirement through occupational plans, but it does not impose any restrictions on investment choices or on payout options. Both active and retired workers are allowed great flexibility and personal choice regarding how they invest their retirement assets. A range of mild tax incentives is provided to encourage retirees to take up retirement products that offer regular income streams, but no policy measures require or even promote the use of life annuities. Unlimited lump-sum withdrawals, term and life annuities of various kinds, and PWs (known in Australia as *allocated annuities*) are all permitted.

A long-standing and relatively generous public pillar offers a noncontributory universal pension to all elderly residents. This pension provides some insurance of longevity risk but is subject to large clawback provisions that aim at containing its cost. Management of the second pillar is left to the private sector. No strict rules apply to asset allocation strategies, product design, and pricing policies.

A comprehensive prudential regulatory and supervisory framework supports the second pillar during both the accumulation and payout phases. A formal risk-based model provides both a risk rating for pension funds and life insurance companies and a matrix of supervisory responses. Providers who offer guaranteed income streams are subject to capital requirements to ensure that their commitments can be honored.

The Australian mandatory system has stimulated a large and rapid accumulation of retirement assets that reached 110 percent of gross domestic product (GDP) in 2007 (but fell to 85 percent in 2009 following the 2008 global financial crisis). Use of term and allocated annuities, which generate regular income streams but do not provide protection against longevity risk, is growing. Also, lump-sum withdrawals continue to be used. At present, there do not appear to be any significant concerns about exposure to longevity risk, and demand for life annuities is very low. The expectation is that the majority of retirees will have sufficient assets, with home ownership providing an additional buffer, to ensure a comfortable retirement. Those who do not will rely on the age pension.

Switzerland

Like Australia, Switzerland has a mandatory occupational pillar. It also has a contributory pay-as-you-go (PAYG) public pillar that offers higher benefits than the Australian public pillar to the average worker and is not subject to clawback provisions. Although there are no restrictions on lump-sum withdrawals, restrictions on other payout options—as well as on investment choices, pricing policies, and product design—are pervasive. Only fixed nominal joint life annuities are provided under the mandatory system. Pension funds are encouraged to make cost-of-living adjustments if their financial situation permits. Variable annuities as well as term annuities and PWs are not allowed.

The stipulation of minimum contribution rates, interest rates, and annuity conversion factors for the mandated benefits has aimed at achieving targeted replacement rates while protecting individual workers from the vicissitudes of financial markets. However, pension funds that offer super-mandatory benefits are granted greater flexibility. The mandatory pillar has suffered from a regulatory failure to adjust over the first 17 years of its operation both the minimum interest rate and the minimum annuity conversion factor despite a significant fall in the level of financial market returns and a significant increase in longevity. Both of these regulated prices have been lowered in recent years, but questions remain regarding the ability to adjust flexibly to changing market conditions.

The regulations have also caused distortions and redistribution among different groups of workers, raising questions about the need for a more-fundamental restructuring of the second pillar. Insurance companies are subject to risk-based solvency requirements and supervision, but the supervision of pension funds is impeded by the institutional fragmentation of both the pension funds and the supervisory authorities. The system has experienced a gradual conversion of former DB plans into DC plans.

The Swiss system has accumulated large retirement savings that corresponded to 99 percent of GDP in 2008 (after reaching 117 percent in

2005). Including third-pillar assets, the total amounted to 122 percent of GDP in 2008. The second pillar is characterized by a very high level of life annuitization, which is estimated at 80 percent of the available balances of retiring workers. This high level reflects a pension mentality that evolved during the past reliance on traditional DB plans but may also be explained by the stipulation of a very high annuity conversion factor. Although the latter compensated retiring workers for the stipulated low minimum interest rate during the accumulation phase, it has led to very high money worth's ratios for life annuities, exacerbating the strains caused by the rigid application of these rules.

Sweden

The Swedish retirement system underwent a major transformation over the past decade or so. The old DB public pillar was converted into a notional (or nonfinancial) defined contribution (NDC) plan, and a new funded DC public component (known as the *premium pension*) was created with centralized administration but decentralized asset management. Meanwhile, the main private multiemployer pension plans followed suit by adopting a similar funded DC structure for younger workers. The reforms placed an upper limit on the cost of the unfunded public pillar and also created a new landscape for the development of retirement products. At the same time, the regulation of the whole financial system was transformed. Quantitative restrictions and direct controls were replaced by indirect market-based rules.

The benefits that workers receive from the two components of the public pillar take the form of life annuities, the value of which depends on individual account balances and cohort life expectancy at retirement. Occupational plans allow a choice between life and term annuities. However, lump-sum withdrawals are not permitted under either the public or occupational plans. Term annuities from the occupational pension plans for 5 or 10 years have been popular with workers who wish to have higher levels of income in the early stages of retirement.

Life and term annuities in the funded schemes are in the form of either (a) with-profits annuities with minimum guaranteed benefits and annual bonuses or (b) unit-linked annuities. These forms imply that providers assume the investment and longevity risks up to the level of guaranteed benefits, but beyond that level participants share in those risks on the basis of investment performance and longevity experience. The presence of a public entity, the Premium Pension Authority (Premiumpensionsmyndigheten, or PPM), and the operation of private occupational plans under collective labor agreements ensure that the interests of workers and retirees are well protected.

The conversion to financial DC schemes led to a considerable injection of long-term financial savings into the Swedish financial market. The total assets of life insurance companies, private pension funds, and the funded component of the public pillar (PPM) amounted to 87 percent of GDP in 2009. Adding the resources of the five AP (*allmänna pension,* or national pension) buffer funds for the unfunded pillar brings the total to 113 percent of GDP. The new pension system underscored the continuing strong commitment to public welfare but also emphasized personal responsibility in key aspects of the functioning of the system, such as the decision to retire and the choice of investment and retirement products. The overall regulatory and supervisory framework has also been significantly strengthened with increasing emphasis on risk-based solvency requirements, supervision, and greater transparency.

Denmark

The Danish pension system includes a modest universal social pension with a supplement for low-income pensioners (both of which are subject to clawback provisions); a mandatory funded component of the public pillar, the Labor Market Supplementary Pension (known as Arbejdsmarkedets Tillaegspension, or ATP), which was established in 1964 and operates on a DC basis; and near-universal participation in occupational and personal pensions that are also primarily based on DC plans. Coverage of occupational pension plans experienced a major expansion in the late 1980s and early 1990s as a result of collective bargaining and political support through the offer of tax incentives. Plans exhibit a wide variety of terms and conditions, often reflecting industry- or sector-specific factors, but adding to the complexity of the Danish pension system.

Distinct features of the Danish pension system include the widespread use of profit-participating contracts, with minimum guaranteed benefits and regular declaration of bonuses, covering both the accumulation and payout phases, and extensive use of group deferred annuity contracts. Risk-sharing arrangements aim at distributing the investment and insurance risks between the pension institutions and their members, covering both active and retired workers, while avoiding transfers across different cohorts of members.

The annuity market is well developed: 40 percent of annual contributions are allocated to the purchase of deferred life annuities, while immediate life annuities are also purchased at or even after retirement. Term annuities are also widely used. However, detailed comprehensive data on the rate of annuitization are lacking. In addition, calculation of money's worth ratios for the different types of annuities is impeded by the lack of detailed data on both projected (ex ante) and declared (ex post) bonuses.

In recent years, the Danish pension industry has adopted fair value accounting of both assets and liabilities, decomposition of technical provisions between different types of guaranteed benefits and bonus potential, and use of a market-based zero-coupon yield curve to determine their value. Although the regulatory framework is not yet formally risk based, implementation of risk-based supervision is well advanced, following the introduction of the traffic light system with regular periodic stress testing. The new approach has resulted in greater emphasis on asset liability matching and the use of long-term hedging strategies by pension institutions as well as a shift in investment policies in favor of foreign bonds and long-term interest rate swap contracts.

The offer of contracts with minimum guaranteed benefits has come under strain in the past 15 years or so as a result of declining interest rates and the high volatility of global equity markets. Private pension funds have been forced to lower their guaranteed benefits, thereby stimulating an increasing demand for unit-linked plans and greater personal choice for participating members. However, the public ATP and some private funds have also emphasized the benefits of long-term hedging.

In general, detailed information on the performance of different plans is lacking. No attempt has been made so far to create a central register with a systematic compilation of performance data on different providers, perhaps because pension plans are governed by collective labor agreements, and representatives of employers and workers are expected to monitor the performance of providers and protect the interests of workers.

Expanding coverage and rising contribution rates have resulted in a large accumulation of long-term assets. These assets amounted to 146 percent of GDP in 2008, with the ATP alone accounting for more than a fifth of the total. Annual contributions to occupational pension plans amounted to 5.2 percent of GDP in 2008, but adding the contributions to the ATP and third-pillar personal pension plans brings total contributions to 6.9 percent of GDP.

Chile

The rapid growth of the market for retirement products in Chile has its origins in the pension reform that was implemented in 1981. This reform involved the gradual replacement of the old public PAYG system with a new private and fully funded system operating on a DC basis. However, the pension reform was a necessary but insufficient condition for the development of this market. Restrictions on lump-sum distributions, which were justified by the absence of an adequate public pension for middle- and high-income workers, were important factors.

Chile mandated the use of fixed inflation-indexed annuities or lifetime PWs to protect pensioners from inflation risk. Requiring the use of joint life annuities initially for married males and, more recently, for married couples provided protection to surviving spouses, while allowing use of guaranteed life annuities for 10 or 15 years addressed the bequest motive. As the market matured, the rules were adapted and allowed the use of combinations of minimum fixed real annuities with either PWs or variable annuities.

Chile created a rigorous regulatory regime for providers of retirement products to minimize the bankruptcy risk faced by pensioners. It also promoted the offer of inflation-indexed products and financial instruments to support the efficient operation of providers of retirement products, and it introduced state guarantees to protect pensioners against provider insolvency as well as aberrant behavior.

The Chilean system and its regulatory framework underwent considerable change over time. Major reforms were enacted in 2004 and 2008. In 2004, the range of retirement products was expanded, the regulation of marketing was strengthened, and the conditions for early retirement were tightened. In 2008, a new public solidarity pillar was created to provide a basic pension to uncovered workers, while new measures were taken to encourage greater participation by self-employed workers and to contain the exposure of the government pension guarantee.

The level of annuitization is estimated at 70 percent of accumulated balances. Before 2004, it was strongly associated with early retirement. This association is likely to weaken after the recent reforms, but the tighter rules on PWs will likely increase annuitization among normal old-age retirees. Annuitization was also stimulated by the strong marketing push of insurance companies and their brokers. A centralized electronic quotation system, known as the Pension Consultations and Offers System (Sistema de Consultas y Ofertas de Montos de Pensión, or SCOMP), was created in 2004. SCOMP compiles and validates individual data on retiring workers and solicits quotes from participating institutions. It aims at reducing the influence of brokers, lowering search costs for retiring workers, enhancing the quality of information available to them, and ensuring broad access to competitively priced annuities.

The pension system has contributed to the accumulation of large long-term financial resources. The total assets of the pension funds amounted to 53 percent of GDP in 2008, after reaching 65 percent in 2007, while those of life insurance companies, which mainly cover their annuity business, amounted to an additional 20 percent of GDP. Annual contributions to the pension system are close to 4 percent of GDP. This figure is lower than in the other countries covered in this book, mainly because of the relatively large size of the informal labor market in Chile.

The experience of Chile confirms the feasibility of developing a sound market for retirement products from a very low initial base. When Chile implemented its 1981 pension reform, the market for retirement products did not exist. Twenty-nine years later, Chile has a well-developed and rapidly growing market for life annuities and lifetime PWs.

Summary of Policy Recommendations

A first recommendation is that policy makers should target an adequate level of annuitization but be wary of causing excessive annuitization. Some of the risks faced by pensioners might not be properly managed with excessive levels of annuitization. For example, purchasing life annuities protects against longevity risk but eliminates the possibility of bequests, while investing in long-term assets addresses the investment risk but exposes holders to liquidity risk.

A second policy conclusion is that policy makers should favor a combination of payout options, covering different products at a particular point in time as well as different payout options over time, rather than mandate use of a single product by all. This recommendation is made because the various types of retirement products have their own features and risk characteristics, and they all suffer from important shortcomings.

Mandating complete reliance on fixed real (inflation-protected) annuities should be avoided for two reasons: (a) fixed real annuities may be costly in terms of low real returns, especially if inflation-linked private sector securities are not offered, and (b) they require access to an ample supply of long-duration inflation-indexed bonds, which are lacking in most countries. However, it is essential to require a minimum level of annuitization through fixed real annuities, which the public sector is best equipped to provide.

Fixed nominal annuities should not be mandated or even encouraged because they fail to provide protection against inflation, especially for long-lived individuals. If use of fixed real or variable annuities is not feasible or advisable, escalating nominal annuities represent an attractive alternative.

The use of joint life annuities with guaranteed periods of payment deserves public policy support. These products address the bequest motive and the fear of capital loss in case of early death. They also help overcome the problems caused by impaired health and adverse selection. In addition, joint life annuities mitigate the distorting effects of the use of unisex life tables, which is compulsory in European Union countries. Annuities with guaranteed periods of payment are very popular when they are offered, but they do not need to be mandated.

Term annuities appeal to pensioners who wish to have higher incomes during the first years of their retirement life. They do not provide protection against longevity risk, but they may appeal to workers with impaired health. PWs also do not provide full protection against longevity risk, but because of limits on annual withdrawals, they stretch balances over a longer period. PWs allow for bequests but are exposed to investment and inflation risks. Unlike life and term annuities, they are portable and can be transferred to other financial institutions. Like term annuities, they have advantages for workers with impaired health and a short life expectancy.

A combination of a minimum level fixed real annuity (preferably but not exclusively provided through the public sector) and a life expectancy PW merits serious consideration in any country. This combination provides minimum security in old age while allowing participation in the higher returns of market investments. And in contrast to variable annuities, it does not require a major strengthening of regulation and supervision.

Variable payout annuities—profit participating or unit linked, with or without minimum guaranteed benefits—have their own merits and attractions. They appeal to pensioners who want to participate in the upside potential of investments in equities and real estate. But their offer requires a robust regulatory framework and a high level of transparency and integrity on the part of providers.

Variable annuities are exposed to investment risk, and complete reliance on them would not be advisable. Like term annuities and PWs, they may be included in product combinations once minimum levels of inflation-protected life annuitization are secured and the regulatory framework is sufficiently robust.

Deferred annuities (with or without refunds), which are purchased at the time of retirement and are payable 10, 15, or 20 years later, are an attractive option in most countries. Because they have greater exposure to the tail end of the age distribution, they are more difficult to price than are immediate annuities. In countries with sophisticated insurance markets and reliable mortality data, they may be used in combination with term annuities, PWs, or even self-annuitization during the deferment period.

Countries that offer a constrained choice to retiring workers and do not mandate the use of a single retirement product for all should also specify the product that will be used as the default option. Having a default will help workers who are unable or unwilling to make a decision on their own and will protect them from abusive selling practices of brokers and selling agents of providers. The use of centralized electronic quotation systems and offer of guidance and advice by regulatory agencies will also contribute to greater consumer protection.

Centralized provision of some services linked to retirement products, such as account administration, benefit payment, and risk pooling, has several potential advantages, including a larger base for risk pooling, economies of scale, and avoidance of heavy marketing costs. The disadvantages are potentially weaker incentives for operational efficiency and product innovation.

Countries that favor a decentralized competitive market structure need to monitor closely trends toward growing market consolidation. They need to ensure that profit margins are not excessive and that the benefits of greater competition and innovation are not eroded by increasingly oligopolistic and wasteful marketing practices.

Adopting a centralized electronic quotation system to lower search costs and improve the marketing of fixed nominal and real annuities as well as escalating annuities is a high priority. However, the marketing of "guarantee and bonus" or "unit-linked" variable annuities through a decentralized competitive market raises major regulatory and supervisory challenges. It is preferable to offer variable annuities through a centralized provider but with decentralized asset management.

Regulation of risk management needs to focus on maintenance of adequate levels of technical reserves and risk capital. Institutions that offer PWs and unit-linked products without any guaranteed benefits do not present complex risk management issues. But for providers of products with guaranteed benefits, the regulatory framework needs to be more complex and robust. There should be requirements for the use of fair value accounting and market-based maturity-dependent discount rates, and the application of stress tests to assess the vulnerability of individual institutions to specified external shocks should also be mandated.

The risk-sharing arrangements of some types of variable annuities whereby longevity risk is shared among annuitants offer several advantages.

However, the offer of such annuities requires a high level of transparency and integrity on the part of providers and is best organized through a centralized structure.

The introduction of government guarantee schemes covering all types of retirement products merits serious consideration. The government guarantees could emulate evolving practice in deposit insurance schemes, including upper limits on the amounts insured and a reasonable amount of coinsurance by pensioners to minimize the possible loss of market discipline at the point of purchase. The potential cost of government guarantees should be estimated, and such estimates should be used to determine risk-based premiums on annuity providers.

In addition, the authorities should compile a comprehensive database of retirement products and should undertake educational programs to expand financial literacy and improve understanding of the main features, cost, and performance of different retirement products.

In conclusion, the degree of annuitization observed in different countries is largely explained by regulatory or plan restrictions on payout options. If a high degree of annuitization is a policy objective, the menu of retirement products and payout options must be regulated accordingly. However, it is important to avoid overannuitization. Doing so implies taking into account other conditions prevailing in different countries—in particular the presence and relative importance of the zero and first public pension pillars. The optimal policy on payout options is bound to be country specific.

The Chilean approach to product regulation is appropriate for countries that expect the new second pillar to play a major role in retirement provision and social protection. The restrictions on lump sums increase the potential demand for all retirement products, including life annuities. A PW formula that is based on life expectancy prevents a premature exhaustion of funds. The imposition of fixed annuities indexed to inflation and joint annuities for married couples helps to prevent an early exhaustion of funds and poverty in old age. The introduction of new products, such as variable and adjustable annuities, should require a minimum fixed annuity component providing a minimum level of investment and longevity insurance. This requirement is very important in countries where the public social security system is either closed down or reduced to a subsistence level.

Countries with larger zero or first public pillars could adopt a more liberal approach to the regulation of payout options, because in those cases the exposure of retiring workers to investment and longevity risk is more limited. Fewer restrictions would need to be imposed on lump-sum withdrawals, although very liberal rules for lump sums can hinder significantly the development of the market for retirement products, especially life annuities.

The appropriate policies in this area will vary significantly from country to country. In some cases, it may be appropriate to continue restricting lump sums but to adopt a more liberal approach to the design of retirement products. For example, the regulation of PWs and term annuities may be more liberal, allowing designs that enable a faster withdrawal of funds. Term annuities play an important part in Denmark and Sweden and have a rapidly growing presence in Australia. Likewise, variable and adjustable annuities may be introduced without the obligation of a minimum fixed annuity component.

Increasing longevity, globalized competition, and market fluidity have created a new landscape for the development of retirement products in most countries. Complete reliance on traditional social security systems and DB company pensions is no longer feasible anywhere in the world. As the development of robust systems of retirement savings during both the accumulation and the payout phases attracts increasing attention from policy makers, valuable lessons can be gleaned from the experiences of countries that are ahead in the reform process.

References

Blake, David. 1999. "Annuity Markets: Problems and Solutions." *Geneva Papers on Risk and Insurance* 24 (3): 358–75.

Brown, Jeffrey R., Olivia S. Mitchell, and James M. Poterba. 2001. "The Role of Real Annuities and Indexed Bonds in an Individual Accounts Retirement Program." In *The Role of Annuity Markets in Financing Retirement*, ed. Jeffrey R. Brown, Olivia S. Mitchell, James M. Poterba, and Mark J. Warshawsky, 107–52. Cambridge, MA: MIT Press.

Cardinale, Mirko, Alex Findlater, and Mike Orszag. 2002. "Paying Out Pensions: A Review of International Annuities Markets." Research Report 2002-RU07, Watson Wyatt, Arlington, VA.

Davis, E. Philip. 2000. "Issues in the Regulation of Annuities Markets." CeRP Working Paper 26/02, Center for Research on Pensions and Welfare Policies, Turin, Italy.

Fornero, Elsa, and Elisa Luciano, eds. 2004. *Developing an Annuity Market in Europe.* Cheltenham, U.K.: Edward Elgar.

Impavido, Gregorio, Craig W. Thorburn, and Mike Wadsworth. 2003. "A Conceptual Framework for Retirement Products: Risk Sharing Arrangements between Providers and Retirees." Policy Research Working Paper 3208, World Bank, Washington, DC.

James, Estelle, Xue Song, and Dimitri Vittas. 2001. "Annuity Markets around the World: Money's Worth to Annuitants and How Do Insurance Companies Cover It?" CeRP Working Paper 16/01, Center for Research on Pensions and Welfare Policies, Turin, Italy.

Mitchell, Olivia S., James M. Poterba, Mark J. Warshawsky, and Jeffrey R. Brown. 2001. "New Evidence on the Money's Worth of Individual Annuities." In *The Role of Annuity Markets in Financing Retirement*, ed. Jeffrey R. Brown, Olivia S. Mitchell, James M. Poterba, and Mark J. Warshawsky, 71–106. Cambridge, MA: MIT Press.

Palacios, Robert, and Rafael Rofman. 2001. "Annuity Markets and Benefit Design in Multipillar Pension Schemes: Experience and Lessons of Four Latin American Countries." Pension Reform Primer Paper 107, World Bank, Washington, DC.

Valdés-Prieto, Salvador. 1998. "Risks in Pensions and Annuities: Efficient Designs." Social Protection Discussion Paper 9804, World Bank, Washington, DC.

CHAPTER 2

Designing the Payout Phase of Pension Systems

Policy Issues, Constraints, and Options

Many countries have undertaken systemic reforms of their pension systems. Reform programs have in general entailed a significant downsizing of public pension pillars and an expansion of private provision, mainly in the form of individual accounts in defined contribution (DC) plans. Much of the early research on pension systems has focused on the policy challenges of the new systems during the accumulation phase, placing particular emphasis on the structure, performance, and regulation of DC pension funds in both the public and the private sectors and in both developed and emerging countries. This emphasis has been fully understandable given the paramount importance of ensuring the safety and efficiency of the accumulation phase.

However, as systemic pension reforms reach maturity, the issues and challenges of the payout phase have started to attract attention. This chapter addresses the policy issues, constraints, and options that policy makers face in designing the payout phase of pension systems and in facilitating the conversion of accumulated balances in DC plans into streams of retirement income, such as life annuities and phased withdrawals (PWs). The chapter focuses on policies that could be adopted

---

This chapter is a slightly revised version of Rocha and Vittas (2010).

in developing and transitioning countries where financial and insurance markets are not well developed.[1]

The chapter starts by discussing the various risks faced by pensioners and the risk characteristics of alternative retirement products. It notes that pensioner risks often pull in opposite directions, requiring caution on the part of policy makers to target an adequate level of annuitization but at the same time to be wary of causing excessive annuitization. The chapter also highlights the important shortcomings of all types of retirement products and argues for policies that favor a combination of payout options, covering different products at a particular point in time as well as different payout options over time.

The next section reviews the risks faced by providers of retirement products and discusses the different ways in which providers can cope with these risks. The risks faced by governments in operating guarantee schemes to cover minimum levels of benefits and to protect pensioners from provider insolvency are also discussed.

The chapter then examines the policy options faced by policy makers in developing countries. It first addresses the regulation of payout options in the context of a desired level of annuitization to ensure not only that pensioners do not suffer from abject poverty in old age but also that they maintain a reasonable standard of living in retirement compared with their preretirement levels of consumption. This examination is followed by a discussion of the regulation of providers of retirement products, ranging from the institutional organization of markets to the regulation of marketing and pricing policies and the regulation of risk management. The chapter concludes with a summary of the main findings and policy recommendations.

This book does not address the so-called annuity puzzle. It accepts the view that the historically weak demand for voluntary annuities should primarily be attributed to the presence of social security and company pensions. Other possible factors include the strength of the bequest motive, the tendency of most individuals to underestimate their longevity, the lack of liquidity and flexibility of annuity products, and the irreversibility of annuity decisions. Life insurance business has been able to flourish in countries with well-regulated markets, partly because when consumers purchase life insurance policies, they agree to make small periodic payments and receive the accumulated capital when policies mature or their families are protected in case of premature death. But in the case of annuities, consumers have to part with large capital sums for a stream of uncertain future income. This decision is more difficult and requires much greater confidence that the decision is correct.[2] Because most annuity contracts, especially fixed nominal or real life annuities, are long-term contracts that are neither revocable nor transferable by the annuitants, sufficient trust in the integrity and solvency of the chosen company becomes far more important than in the case of life insurance.

Another reason for weak demand that is often underscored in economic studies of annuity markets is the possibility of adverse selection, whereby people with impaired health withdraw from the annuity market, resulting in more expensive annuities for healthy annuitants. The increase in the cost of annuities causes more people to withdraw from the market, resulting in a further increase in annuity prices and eventual market failure.

However, the role of adverse selection in explaining the underdevelopment of voluntary annuity markets is often overstated. After all, risk classification and risk-based insurance premiums are widely used and have been fully accepted in several lines of insurance business, such as home, motor, and especially life insurance, where people with impaired health are charged higher premiums. There is no reason risk-based premiums should not or would not also be accepted in the annuity business. In fact, insurance companies in several countries have already started to offer special annuities with lower risk premiums that are targeted to people with impaired health.[3]

The view embraced in this book is that as the level of social security and company pensions is reduced, the demand for life annuities and PWs will increase. Policy makers need to recognize the shortcomings of current products, address the challenging regulatory issues of organizing robust and transparent annuity markets, and promote combinations of products and payout options.

Pensioner Risks and Retirement Products

Pensioners face a number of risks, and various retirement products have been developed to address those risks.

Pensioner Risks

The main risk faced by pensioners is the risk of outliving their savings, which is often defined as longevity risk, although the two risks are not identical, as will be explained shortly.[4] Depending on how their savings are invested, pensioners are exposed to investment and inflation risks as well as liquidity and bequest risks. Bankruptcy risk, which relates to the fate of the institution providing a particular product rather than to the product itself, is also an important risk that requires regulatory action to ensure that providers are financially sound.

Bankruptcy risk is present in all types of financial products but is particularly important in the case of life annuities, which in principle are long-term contracts that are neither revocable nor portable. In recent years, transfer of fixed life annuities among providers has become increasingly possible, magnifying the risk exposure of annuitants, who have no control over the transfer process. This situation places a clear responsibility on the regulatory authorities to adopt an effective and robust system of prudential regulation and supervision.

Except for the bequest risk and to a lesser extent liquidity risk,[5] all the other risks relate to the risk of pensioners outliving their savings. This last risk is not identical to longevity risk because retirees may outlive their savings for several reasons even at a relatively young age. Their savings at the time of retirement may be too low, their rate of consumption in retirement may be too high, they may incur large medical costs, their savings may be exposed to a high investment risk, or high inflation may deplete their savings. Longevity risk is the risk of living longer than anticipated at the time of retirement. In such cases, even very large savings may be exhausted and prove inadequate. Linked to the risk of outliving savings is the risk of a substantial decline in consumption and living standard, because retirees experiencing a significant erosion of their savings will take action to cut their consumption spending to delay the moment of crisis when their savings are fully depleted.

Retiring workers also face annuitization risk—that is, the risk that at the time of their retirement financial markets may be depressed, lowering the value of accumulated balances, especially those invested in equities and real estate, while long-term interest rates may be low, implying a high cost of fixed annuities.

An important characteristic of the risks faced by pensioners is that such risks often pull in opposite directions. Thus, the bequest risk works counter to the longevity risk and the risk of outliving one's savings. In a similar vein, the investment risk points in an opposite direction in terms of desirable financial instruments to the liquidity risk. Bearing in mind these opposing implications, policy makers should adopt a cautious approach, favoring a reasonable level of annuitization but avoiding excessive annuitization.

Retirement Products

The main retirement products address the various risks faced by pensioners in different ways. They have their own risk characteristics and have advantages and disadvantages that shape their appeal to different groups of pensioners. Table 2.1 summarizes the risk characteristics of different products.

Fixed and escalating life annuities. The common feature of fixed and escalating annuities is that either their regular payments are fixed in nominal or real terms or they grow at a predetermined rate of increase. They avoid the fluctuations in regular payments that characterize variable annuities.

Fixed real life annuities provide protection against longevity, investment, and inflation risks. Their offer requires access to long-term inflation-linked securities. In the absence of such instruments, insurance companies charge an inflation risk premium that raises the cost of fixed real annuities.

Real annuities start with lower payments than nominal annuities but exceed nominal annuity payments in later years. For this reason, they appeal to people with longer life expectancies. This self-selection bias is taken into account by insurance companies in setting their premiums and explains further the higher load they charged in offering these products.

Table 2.1   Risk Characteristics of Retirement Products for Pensioners

	Protections offered			Benefits provided	
Retirement product	Longevity risk	Investment risk	Inflation risk	Bequest	Liquidity
Fixed real life annuities	Yes	Yes	Yes	Limited	No
Fixed nominal life annuities	Yes	Yes	No	Limited	No
Escalating real life annuities	Yes	Yes	Yes plus	Limited	No
Escalating nominal life annuities	Yes	Yes	Partial	Limited	No
Variable life annuities, guaranteed benefits	Yes	Yes	Possible	Limited	No
Variable life annuities, bonus payments	Shared	Shared	Shared	Limited	No
Variable life annuities, unit linked	Shared	No	No	Limited	No
Lifetime phased withdrawals	No	No	Possible	Yes	No
Term annuities	No	Possible	Possible	Yes	No
Lump sums	No	Possible	Possible	Yes	Yes
Self-annuitization	No	Possible	Possible	Yes	Yes

Source: Authors' compilation.
Note: Annuitization risk is present in all fixed and escalating annuities but does not affect variable annuities. Bankruptcy risk affects all types of retirement products but is particularly important in life annuities.

Like all types of life annuities, fixed real annuities face liquidity and bankruptcy risks, but their main shortcoming is that they suffer from relatively low returns. In most advanced countries, inflation-protected bonds earn on average lower real rates of return than do nominal bonds, equities, or other real assets, although their returns suffer from lower volatility.

Fixed real annuities may earn a lower real rate of return than do fixed nominal annuities for two reasons. First, real returns on inflation-linked bonds may be lower than those on nominal bonds because of the inflation protection that is provided to investors. The real return differential between nominal and real bonds can be seen as a premium for insuring against uncertain future inflation. Empirical evidence on this point is inconclusive, probably because the inflation risk premium on nominal bonds has been offset by the liquidity premium that has burdened the less liquid inflation-linked bonds. However, as the market for inflation-linked bonds becomes more liquid, the real return differential should favor nominal bonds.

A second reason fixed real annuities may be more expensive relates to the absence in most countries of inflation-linked corporate and mortgage bonds.[6] In contrast, nominal annuities benefit from the ability of annuity providers to invest in corporate and mortgage bonds that offer higher returns than do government bonds.

Fixed nominal annuities provide protection against longevity and investment risks but are exposed to inflation and liquidity risks as well as bankruptcy risk. Their exposure to inflation risk undermines their longevity protection since even a moderate rate of inflation causes significant erosion in the real value of annuity payments over a long period.[7] Because early payments are relatively higher than payments from other types of annuities, people who have shorter life expectancies or who tend to underestimate their longevity favor them.

Escalating nominal annuities provide partial protection against inflation, depending on the rate of escalation (which is usually set at 3 or 5 percent) and the rate of inflation. If they increase at a rate that is higher than the rate of inflation, they entail an increase in the real value of annuity payments and thus contribute to preserving the value of pensions relative to wages. However, escalating nominal annuities are exposed to inflation risk if the inflation rate is higher than the escalation rate. Escalating nominal annuities also start with lower initial payments and are exposed to a selection bias like real life annuities.

Escalating real annuities provide full protection against inflation and also allow for a gradual increase in the real value of pensions. Their main disadvantage is that early payments are further reduced compared with fixed real or nominal annuities and are therefore even less attractive to people with a short life expectancy.

Annuities denominated in, or linked to, a reserve currency (either the U.S. dollar or the euro) also provide some protection against inflation and are often recommended when the supply of domestic inflation-linked bonds is limited. However, reserve currency annuities are fixed annuities that provide protection against runaway domestic inflation and domestic currency depreciation but not against global inflation. In addition, persistent deviations from purchasing power parity imply that for prolonged periods reserve currency annuities do not provide full protection even against domestic inflation. This situation is corrected when large devaluations take place.

All types of fixed and escalating annuities are exposed to annuitization risk, which is the risk of retiring and purchasing annuities at an inopportune time when financial markets are depressed and the cost of fixed annuities is high. They are also exposed to deceptive practices by selling agents, who may not promote the products that offer the best prices and returns to annuitants. Moreover, they suffer from a wide dispersion of annuity prices.[8]

Variable annuities. An important shortcoming of fixed and escalating annuities, whether real or nominal, is that they prevent pensioners from participating in the normally higher investment returns of equities and real assets. Thus, the protection against investment and inflation risks comes at a high cost.

Participation in equity and real asset returns is possible with variable annuities.[9] These products involve a risk-sharing arrangement with annuitants that may cover both investment and longevity risks.[10] In some variable payout annuities, the providers bear the longevity risk. However, variable annuities in which the annuitants assume or share the investment and longevity risks are the more interesting type. Because providers bear neither of these risks, they do not need to charge high upfront loads on such annuities. But they need to adopt transparent and reliable methods of measuring investment performance and calculating the effect of longevity experience.

Another advantage of variable annuities is that their holders do not face annuitization risk. Because annuity payments are not fixed but vary with the investment performance of annuity assets, the financial market conditions that prevail at the time of retirement do not have long-term implications.

Variable annuities can be profit participating or unit linked. The former may combine minimum guaranteed benefits with annual bonuses that target the preservation of the real value of annuity payments. In this way, they aim to provide some protection against inflation risk with some potential participation in high investment returns. In these products, which are also known as *guarantee and bonus annuities,* annuity providers assume the longevity and investment risks up to the level of guaranteed benefits but share these risks among participants for bonus-based benefits.

In guarantee and bonus annuities, providers face the problem of bonus reversibility. So that declining bonuses can be avoided, the first annuity payments are often based on conservative estimates of investment returns and defensive projections of longevity experience. Subsequent payments are adjusted to reflect realized results relative to initial projections. Under this approach, initial payments may be even lower than in fixed real annuities, giving rise to a selection bias that may be further heightened by the prevalence of more wealthy people among their users. This approach entails the creation of a large reserve to cover future bonuses. Unless special measures are taken, such as partially funding the bonus reserve with long-term debt, such an approach may give rise to involuntary transfers from older to younger cohorts.

In unit-linked variable annuities, individual pensioners bear the investment risk, which reflects the investment risk of the portfolios of their choice. But longevity risk is subject to risk-sharing arrangements either among all annuitants or among particular cohorts of annuitants. Unit-linked annuities are increasingly offered with some minimum guaranteed benefits, such that benefits may decline in a year when financial returns are negative—but subject to a floor. The floor may be calculated on the basis of a zero real rate of interest, which would provide protection against inflation. This guarantee is offered at a price, which usually involves the application of a cap when financial returns are positive. Unit-linked annuities with minimum guaranteed benefits are very similar to guarantee and bonus annuities. They have a comparative advantage over guarantee and bonus annuities in their greater transparency and objectivity, but they are more difficult to price and require more complex reserving policies.

Variable annuities suffer from several shortcomings. Their holders are exposed to investment risk and to the nondiversifiable part of longevity risk. The offer of minimum guaranteed benefits mitigates the exposure of pensioners to these risks. But holders of variable annuities may also suffer from the effects of perverse marketing campaigns by annuity providers and from opportunistic profit-distribution and transfer-pricing policies, as will be discussed later. The biggest challenge of variable annuities is the creation of a robust system of regulation and supervision to provide effective protection to annuitants.

Variable annuities, especially unit-linked annuities that are heavily invested in equities, are often criticized for exposing pensioners to large potential investment losses and to the risk of financial ruin. Concern exists that in a large and prolonged decline of equity prices, available balances may suffer significant depletion, undermining the provision of income security in old age. However, the historical mean reverting pattern of equity returns and the dollar-averaging process that is involved when retirement balances are accumulated over a long period of time act as mitigating factors to this possible adversity.[11]

Another criticism is that the large fluctuation in benefit payments from year to year may cause large changes in annual consumption patterns. However, this criticism also tends to be overstated. Pensioners do not have to consume all their annuity income when they receive it. They may well save some of their retirement income in years in which annuity payments are higher than average.

These criticisms also assume that available funds are invested in volatile financial instruments, whereas pensioners may opt for more stable asset allocations and may also be protected by the offer of minimum guaranteed benefits. Nevertheless, because variable annuities have a larger exposure to equities than do other types of retirement products and because mean reversion is subject to considerable deviations from its historical pattern, a more sanguine conclusion is to advocate partial use of variable annuities in combination with some other type of retirement products that are less volatile and more predictable.

The pooling of longevity risk also raises important policy issues. If only one pool covering all retirees is created, unintended transfers will take place from people of impaired health and short life expectancy to those of strong health and long life expectancy. This issue is complicated by the observed correlation between short life expectancy and low socioeconomic status. The problems created by socioeconomic differences in risk patterns are difficult to resolve, but people of impaired health can be placed in a special pool and encouraged to purchase fixed real or escalating nominal annuities or to use PWs.

Other types of life annuities. All types of life annuities suffer from lack of liquidity and flexibility and are exposed to bequest and bankruptcy risks. Joint life annuities and annuities with guaranteed periods of payment allow limited bequests, protecting the dependents of annuitants in the event of early death. Annuities with guaranteed periods of payment entail very small decreases in monthly payments, at least for periods up to 10 years, because in the early years of retirement, survival probabilities are very close to unity.

A useful contribution of joint life annuities is that they mitigate the distorting effects of adopting unisex mortality tables. The distortions emanate from the significant difference in the life expectancy of men and women. Countries in which the use of unisex mortality tables is compulsory should also impose on both working spouses the requirement to use joint life annuities, thus limiting the tendency of annuity providers to target male retirees.

Traditionally, most countries did not mandate the use of joint life annuities. Countries with notional defined contribution systems do not require the use of joint life annuities in these pillars, although this approach is being reconsidered in Sweden. Denmark and Sweden also do not impose any requirement for joint life annuities in their second pillars. Chile used to require married men to purchase joint life annuities but allowed working women the freedom to choose between single and joint annuities. This dichotomy reflected the traditionally lower labor force participation of women and their lower earnings. However, a recent change in the rules mandates the purchase of joint life annuities by both spouses.

The reversion rate—that is, the pension benefit of the surviving spouse—should not be lower than 60 percent of the original pension. It should be higher than 50 percent because of significant economies of scale in household living expenses. Some countries have considered imposing a low reversion rate of 30 percent, which would limit the financial protection provided to widows. Such a low reversion rate was proposed, for example, in Hungary (Vittas, Rudolph, and Pollner 2010).

Countries that impose the compulsory use of unisex mortality tables should consider the adoption of a compensation mechanism to cope with its adverse effects on insurance company marketing and profitability. Under such a mechanism, companies with a disproportionate share of male annuitants would be required to make compensating transfers to companies with a disproportionate share of female annuitants. Such a mechanism was contemplated in Poland in 2009 (Vittas, Rudolph, and Pollner 2010).

Deferred annuities, which start paying benefits a specified number of years after purchase, are an attractive option. They are less costly than immediate life annuities and could provide financial protection in old age when reliance on self-annuitization would be inadvisable.[12] The cost of deferred life annuities depends on whether refunds are allowed in case of death before the expiration of the deferment period. The greater uncertainty faced by insurance companies in projecting long-term longevity trends, especially as they affect the tail end of the age distribution, also affects costs.[13] Deferred annuities can be combined with reliance on self-annuitization and PWs in the first years after retirement or with the use of fixed-term annuities. Such combinations represent an attractive mix of retirement products, with the potential to achieve better management of the different risks facing retiring workers.

Joint life annuities with guaranteed periods of payment, which have proved very popular in Chile, are effectively combinations of term and deferred annuities, the former involving a series of certain dated payments during the guaranteed period and the latter starting to pay benefits at the end of the guaranteed period. Their wide popularity suggests that the operation of deferred annuities, which is advocated by a growing number of observers (Antolín 2008; Milevsky 2005), will not face insuperable problems. Offering deferred annuities will deprive annuity providers of the profits they would make on the term annuity part of traditional products. This situation will imply a need for adding a margin in their pricing and underwriting models but will not weaken the case for promoting deferred annuities to provide protection to pensioners in advanced old age.

Reverse mortgages are annuity products linked to the equity in owner-occupied houses. They provide regular income to pensioners in the form of interest-bearing loan advances that accumulate over time and are ultimately repaid from the proceeds of the sale of the mortgaged property. They have attractive features for pensioners who have a significant proportion of their wealth in owner-occupied housing and allow them to receive regular advances from their house without having to sell and move out. However, reverse mortgages are fraught with important regulatory issues, such as the need for a high level of transparency and integrity on the part of providers and adequate protection of owner-occupiers. Reverse mortgages have experienced limited growth in countries such as Australia and the United States. They also suffer from all the shortcomings of fixed life annuities.

Future innovations could develop new annuity products, offering more options to pensioners in coping with the various risks they face. Adjustable annuities would be an example of product innovation.[14] They would allow annuity payments to be adjusted periodically (for example, every 3, 5, or even 10 years) in line with the evolution of market interest rates and annuity prices. They would avoid excessive annuitization risk and would be attractive at times of low interest rates. Annuitants using such products would face a risk of future unanticipated declines in interest rates that would cause a reduction rather than an increase in annuity payments, but this risk could be contained by applying appropriate and transparent caps on permissible adjustments. Adjustable annuities could also convert to fixed annuities after 5 or 10 years.

Extendable annuities could be another innovation. They would combine in one product features of fixed and variable annuities but varying over time. In extendable annuities, the schedule of payments over 10 years would be determined by using the prevailing nominal yield curve and cohort life tables with conservative estimates of future longevity improvements. The account of the annuitant would be debited with the present value of the projected actuarial payments over the first 10 years of the annuity contract. The remaining balance would be invested in investment funds according to the asset allocation decision of each annuitant. Each year the predetermined payments would be extended for one more year, and the account of the annuitant would be charged with the present value of payments for the additional year. If interest rates suffered a major decline, annuitants would have two main options: (a) maintain the level of annuity payments and transfer a proportionally larger capital sum to the annuity provider or (b) accept an adjustment in the level of the annuity payments for the ensuing 10 years and transfer a proportionately smaller capital sum. Annuitants could also select a combination of the two options. If interest rates increased, annuity payments could rise, but within prespecified prudent upper limits. Extendable annuities would have several advantages: they would make it easier for annuity providers to match fully the assets and liabilities of the providers' annuity business; they would allow annuitants to benefit from the higher returns on equities and other real assets on part of the annuitants' accumulated capital; and they would avoid the large fluctuations in annuity payments that may occur with variable annuities. Longevity risk would be shared among all users of these annuities. As in the case of adjustable annuities, extendable annuities could be converted into fixed or escalating, nominal or real annuities.

Term annuities and phased withdrawals. Term annuities consist of a series of payments made to their beneficiaries over a specified period of time. They are in fact quite similar to PWs but with a fixed term that may reach up to 25 years but that normally runs for 5 or 10 years. They do not offer protection against longevity risk. Their treatment of investment and inflation risks depends on their features. They lack liquidity during their term, but they allow bequests and also permit a faster use of accumulated balances. They appeal to workers with impaired health and a short life expectancy.

Term annuities can be for fixed terms and fixed benefits calculated at the prevailing rate of interest or for fixed terms but variable benefits, with the latter consisting of guaranteed and bonus components. Term annuities are favored by pensioners who wish to have higher levels of income and spending during their early years of retirement relative to later years. The demand for term annuities is stronger when pensioners have access to universal health care services.[15]

PWs consist of a series of fixed or variable payments whereby pensioners withdraw a fraction of their accumulated capital. PWs do not provide full protection against longevity risk, but by placing limits on annual withdrawals, they stretch balances over a longer period. PWs allow bequests but are exposed to investment and inflation risks. Unlike term and life annuities, they are portable and can be transferred to other financial institutions. Like term annuities, they appeal to workers with impaired health and a short life expectancy.

PWs can be classified by the special rules covering the pace of withdrawals, including a fixed benefit rule and a fixed-percentage benefit rule.[16] The most important type is the life expectancy PW, in which the withdrawal fraction is set each year equal to the inverse of the remaining life expectancy of the account holder.

The account balance of PWs that follow the remaining life expectancy rule may increase initially if the rate of investment returns exceeds the withdrawal fraction. However, as pensioners grow old and their remaining life expectancy decreases, the withdrawal fraction is bound to surpass the rate of return and thus both the account balance and the annual benefit will start falling and will eventually become too small for long-lived individuals.

In Chile, before the 2008 changes, the monthly benefit from PWs could not fall below the minimum pension guarantee (MPG) level. When the account balance was exhausted, the government assumed the payment responsibility. Thus, longevity risk was covered at the level of the MPG. After 2008, the MPG was replaced by the basic solidarity pension (*pensión básica solidaria*, or PBS), which is now the level at which longevity risk is covered. In addition, the monthly benefit is no longer calculated by using the average remaining life expectancy but instead at a higher life expectancy that limits the probability of workers outliving their savings to 5 percent.

Because of the exposure to longevity, inflation, and investment risks, total reliance on term annuities and PWs is not advisable. However, these products can play a part in combinations of retirement products, especially in countries with strong first pillars. They also have several advantages for people with impaired health, who end up subsidizing healthy people if they are forced to purchase life annuities from a single longevity pool.

Lump sums and self-annuitization. Lump sums do not provide any protection against longevity risk but allow bequests. Their handling of investment, inflation, and liquidity risks depends on how they are invested. A major advantage of lump sums is that they may be used to repay existing debt or even to finance small business ventures. Their greater risk is that they may be wasted in frivolous consumption spending, causing an early depletion of available assets and increasing exposure to longevity risk.

Lump sums allow reliance on self-annuitization whereby accumulated balances are invested in various types of investments, primarily combinations of mutual funds, and their holders are advised to withdraw a fixed-percentage fraction each year from their accounts to cover their living expenses. This approach has many advantages, including greater liquidity and flexibility, the right of bequest, and participation in the higher returns of equities and other real assets. But it also has significant disadvantages.

This form of self-annuitization implies that average workers have several attributes of investment savvy and foresight that they usually lack. First, it assumes that retiring workers have the knowledge to manage their retirement accounts efficiently and are able to allocate wisely their balances between short-term money market instruments, long-term bonds, and real assets. It also assumes that workers have the wisdom to set their withdrawal fraction at a sufficiently low level to ensure that they will not outlive their savings. This outcome requires an ability to estimate accurately their life expectancy and their needs in retirement. Self-annuitization also implies that workers have the strength to maintain a long-term commitment to whatever withdrawal rule they adopt. Self-annuitization may generate disastrous results if pensioners adopt either overly conservative investment policies or, at the other extreme, overly aggressive ones, while at the same time breaching their withdrawal rule. In addition, self-annuitization is very difficult to manage in advanced old age when a fixed-percentage rule would probably not be appropriate.[17]

Product Shortcomings and Policy Objectives

The fundamental objective of pension systems is not to accumulate retirement capital but to provide to pensioners a regular income that is sufficient to meet their retirement needs. Traditional defined benefit (DB) social security systems and corporate pension schemes emphasized the offer of lifetime pensions to replace preretirement employment income. This system contributed to a high level of annuitization of covered workers, especially those with long contribution histories.

Corporate pension schemes often allowed a partial lump-sum commutation as a means of avoiding excessive annuitization. However, the replacement rate of preretirement employment income for those who were privileged to be covered by traditional DB schemes tended to be high.

Historically, targeted gross replacement rates from the integrated offer of social security and corporate pensions amounted to between 60 and 70 percent for workers with full contribution records. If pension contributions by workers ceased after retirement, these gross rates translated into net replacement rates of between 75 and 90 percent.[18]

The downsizing of social security systems and the growing adoption of DC plans in the private sector have shifted the decision on targeted replacement rates to individual workers. Restrictions on payout options encourage retiring workers to target a satisfactory replacement rate over the whole of their retirement life.

The preceding analysis makes clear that all types of retirement products suffer from significant shortcomings. Fixed nominal annuities provide protection against longevity and investment risks but expose their buyers to inflation risk and prevent pensioners from participating in higher returns from equities and real estate.

Fixed real annuities protect against inflation as well as longevity and investment risks but lock their holders into low real rates of return. In countries where inflation-protected securities are not widely available, fixed real annuities also suffer from relatively high inflation risk premiums charged by insurance companies.

Although fixed nominal and real annuities provide protection against longevity risk, the protection often comes at a high risk premium, especially when insurance companies adopt conservative policies and allow for significant improvements in longevity.

It is often argued (see, for example, Antolín 2008) that insurance companies underestimate improvements in longevity. However, it is never clarified whether the alleged underestimation affects both their reserving and pricing policies. Insurance companies may well overestimate longevity improvements in their pricing decisions but underestimate them in their reserving policies.[19]

In addition, retiring workers purchasing fixed or escalating annuities face annuitization risk. This risk can be reduced by gradually increasing the share of long-duration bonds in the investment portfolios of workers who are near retirement or by gradually purchasing deferred annuities a few years before and after retirement.

Variable annuities, whether they are market linked or bonus based, avoid annuitization risk and are able to benefit from the higher long-term returns of equities and other real assets. However, they expose their holders to the investment risk associated with the high volatility of equity returns. In the case of bonus-based annuities, they depend not only on the investment performance of their providers but also on their providers' integrity.

In general, annual bonuses on variable annuities reflect both investment performance and longevity experience. Thus, holders of variable annuities share in the longevity risk and are exposed to the financial effect of increasing longevity. Such products provide less protection than fixed annuities, but the greater exposure to risk is mitigated by the slow and gradual effect of longevity improvements. In addition, the greater exposure is more apparent than real because insurers incorporate projected longevity improvements in their pricing of fixed annuities.

Unless they take the form of joint life annuities with guaranteed periods of payment, all types of life annuities suffer from significant bequest risk. For this reason, joint life annuities with guaranteed periods of payment are highly recommended. These types of products mitigate the adverse impact of unisex mortality tables and are therefore particularly attractive in countries that compel the use of such tables. Compensating transfers to annuity providers with a disproportionate share of female annuities may also be used.

All types of life annuities suffer from lack of liquidity and flexibility. This shortcoming can be addressed by using a combination of retirement products.

PWs and term annuities also have shortcomings, especially the failure to protect against longevity risk. Depending on the withdrawal rule and investment performance, the holders of PWs run either a high risk of exhausting the balance and outliving their savings (for example, if an imprudent fixed benefit or fixed-percentage benefit rule is retained) or a high risk of a significant decline in the level of the withdrawn amounts (for example, in cases where the withdrawal rule is based on the remaining life expectancy).

Given all these shortcomings, in countries with no restrictions on payout options, retiring workers and financial planners not surprisingly show a preference for a policy of self-annuitization with some form of fixed withdrawal rule. Self-annuitization confers greater liquidity and flexibility, the right of bequest, and participation in the higher returns of equities and other real assets. However, it also implies possession of financial management savvy by ordinary workers and ability to maintain strong long-term commitments in the face of potentially growing financial pressures. Self-annuitization is very difficult to manage in advanced old age and is thus unsuitable as the sole product to be used throughout a person's life in retirement.

Complete reliance on self-annuitization is incompatible with a mandatory pension pillar. Imposition of compulsory saving for retirement is predicated on the argument that workers fail to make adequate provision for their retirement needs. One cannot then easily argue that retiring workers are able to make accurate estimates of their life expectancy and their needs in retirement and should not, therefore, be constrained in their payout options.

If self-annuitization cannot provide the answer of how to organize the payout phase, then although all retirement products suffer from significant shortcomings, the conclusion that emerges is that the payout phase should be based on a combination of options. Lump sums and self-annuitization can play a part, but the combination should also promote use of some types of life annuities and PWs.

This conclusion implies a judicious use of restrictions on payout options, imposing some minimum level of annuitization to protect retired workers against longevity, investment, and inflation risks but allowing for the possibility of benefiting from higher equity and real asset returns as well as for greater flexibility and liquidity. The various policy options are reviewed later in this chapter, after a discussion of risks faced by providers of retirement products and by governments.

Countries that do not mandate the use of a single retirement product by all but that offer a constrained choice to retiring workers also need to specify the product that will be used as the default option. The lack of financial savvy by most workers and the considerable complexity of most retirement products imply a strong need for guidance and impartial advice. Specifying the default option will help workers who have difficulty dealing effectively with complex financial decisions.

Risks of Retirement Products for Providers and Governments

This section discusses the risks faced by providers of retirement products and by governments in offering a safety net in retirement. It first reviews the main types of provider risks, follows with a discussion of policies to cope with these risks, and then discusses the risks faced by governments.

Main Types of Provider Risks

The main types of risks faced by providers of retirement products—investment, inflation, and longevity risks—are similar but inverse to those faced by pensioners. Other risks faced by insurance companies and pension funds include underwriting, credit or counterparty, liquidity, and operational risks.[20]

Operational risk is the risk of losses resulting from administrative failure or fraud caused by inadequate internal controls. Like any other type of financial institution, life insurance companies and pension funds are subject to operational risk. Their vulnerability may be greater because of the long-term nature of some of the products they offer. Failure to maintain effective internal controls may lead to improper portfolio decisions or transactions involving conflicts of interest and may ultimately result in low returns or losses, as well as fines or other impositions by the supervisor. Providers may also suffer from larger costs than necessary caused by the use of outdated technology and greater exposure to losses arising from fraud committed by clients and employees.

Liquidity risk is the risk of losses resulting from insufficient liquid assets for the cash flow requirements associated with underwritten policies. Providers of retirement products are generally less exposed to liquidity risk. Their cash outflows are easily predictable because they are not exposed to a sudden large increase in claims or to early and voluntary termination of contracts. Nevertheless, they still require accurate forecasts of future cash outlays and need to build an asset portfolio capable of generating the necessary liquidity.

Credit or *counterparty risk* is the risk of losses arising from the deterioration of the credit quality of issuers of instruments and counterparties, especially the risk of default. This risk is most visible in the case of instruments, such as corporate bonds, that may suffer a downgrading of credit rating, but it is also present in reinsurance arrangements and derivative agreements. It is of major importance in the case of long-term interest rate swaps.[21]

Providers of retirement products may also face credit risk in their arrangements with agents and brokers with regard to premiums receivable. Other types of counterparty risks include settlement risk (arising from time lags between the trading and settlement dates of securities transactions), documentation and custody risk (arising from failures in the legal documentation or custody of instruments in the portfolio), and concentration risk (arising from excessive concentration of investments in an individual entity, a sector, or a geographic area).

Underwriting risk is the risk of mispricing annuities because of improper assumptions about future mortality rates, investment returns, and operating costs. In the case of fixed life annuities (as well as variable annuities in which the providers assume the longevity risk), one of the major sources of underwriting risk is longevity risk, or the risk that the annuitant will live longer than was anticipated when the contract is underwritten. This risk may arise because of a variety of factors, including insufficient or poor mortality data; difficulties in assessing future improvements in longevity (caused, for example, by unanticipated medical advances and lifestyle improvements); the greater uncertainty of the tail end of the age distribution; or failure to differentiate annuitants according to their level of risk.

Annuity contracts may also be mispriced because of unrealistic assumptions about future reinvestment rates or about the company's capacity to manage its operating costs (for example, overestimating the effect of improvements in technological advances or the effect of gains in market share and increased economies of scale). Underwriting risk is often increased by the intensity of competition in decentralized markets, the incurrence of unduly high marketing costs, and the adoption of aggressive selling campaigns.

Investment risk relates to losses arising from the volatility of asset and liability prices, which are affected by changes in interest rates, exchange rates, equity prices, and property values. It reflects the extent of mismatching between assets and liabilities. Providers that offer life annuities usually suffer from mismatched positions. Typically, the duration of assets is substantially shorter than the duration of liabilities. The provider's risk then becomes reinvestment risk and relates to the risk that the returns on the funds to be reinvested will fall below anticipated levels.

Investment risk is increased by exposure to *prepayment risk*, which is the risk that issuers of debt instruments will use their right to pay their obligations before the contracted maturity. This risk is present in the case of mortgage bonds or mortgage-backed securities, where the underlying mortgages have refinancing options, or in the case of callable corporate bonds.

Investment risk can be subdivided into interest rate, equity, currency, and inflation risks. Interest rate risk results from fluctuations in the general level as well as the term structure of interest rates. The exposure to this risk is greater when the mismatch between the duration of assets and liabilities is larger. This risk is one of the most important faced by providers of fixed life annuities, because they tend to invest heavily in fixed interest assets but are unable to maintain completely matched positions.

Equity risk arises from the exposure to fluctuations in equity prices and is greater when the mismatch between the size of the equity portfolio and the size of annuity contracts linked to equity prices is larger. Likewise, currency risk occurs when the provider issues annuities denominated in one currency but holds assets denominated in another currency. Providers of retirement products face inflation risk when they issue life or term annuities indexed to prices but do not hold sufficient inflation-indexed financial instruments.

Coping with Provider Risks

Coping with operational, liquidity, and credit risks depends on the internal risk management systems of individual institutions. Thus, dealing with operational risks requires the creation of effective internal controls that emphasize deterrence and early detection of fraud and administrative failures. Regulators play an important role by requiring providers to develop risk mitigation and control policies and to ensure segregation of duties and avoidance of conflicts of interest in assigning managerial responsibilities.

To manage liquidity risk, providers need to maintain an adequate cushion of liquid assets and to take into account the level of liquidity of marketable financial instruments. Access to money market instruments and derivative products enhances the efficiency of liquidity management. In contrast, imprudent reliance on short-term money market instruments for funding purposes magnifies the risk exposure of individual institutions.

Management of credit risk entails careful consideration of the risk of deterioration of the credit quality and default of different issuers as well as close monitoring of exposure to risk concentrations. Regulators promote the sound management of credit risk by imposing limits on exposure to low-grade investments and to risk concentrations.

Use of credit derivatives facilitates the efficient hedging of credit risks, although it raises the issue of the quality of counterparty risk, which is particularly important in the case of customized derivative instruments and reinsurance arrangements. However, all these risks are no different from similar risks faced by all types of financial institutions and require the development of efficient and effective internal risk management systems supported by sound systems of prudential regulation.

Dealing effectively with underwriting risk is a complex undertaking and requires the development of sophisticated models that allow for future medical advances in lowering mortality, the likely future evolution of investment returns, and the likely future evolution of operating costs. The projection of future investment returns must allow for the possible effect of credit and prepayment risks, whereas the projection of operating costs must take into account improvements in efficiency and the effect of achieving a larger scale of operations. However, underwriting risk is often increased as a result of aggressive pricing and marketing campaigns that may result in thin financial margins. Close monitoring of underwriting results, by product and by cohort, is required.

Depending on the types of products offered by providers, underwriting risk may encompass longevity, investment, and inflation risks. There is no underwriting risk in lump-sum withdrawals, PWs, and unit-linked annuities, because with these products providers do not assume any longevity, investment, or inflation risks. In contrast, fixed real life annuities expose providers to all three of these risks. Other products, such as fixed nominal life annuities, traditional profit-participating life annuities with minimum guaranteed benefits, and term annuities, create exposure to some of these risks. The pattern of risk exposure of providers of retirement products is the reverse of that of pensioners (table 2.2).

Coping with investment and inflation risks requires the adoption of sophisticated asset and liability management techniques. These techniques emphasize the maintenance of matched positions between assets and liabilities, the use of derivative products for portfolio immunization, and the provision of capital backing to absorb financial losses from mismatched positions and adverse movements in market prices.

Close monitoring of the risk exposure of insurance companies and pension funds is essential. Regulators can play an important role by requiring the use of regular stress testing to measure the impact of

Table 2.2   Risk Characteristics of Retirement Products for Providers

Retirement product	Exposures		
	Longevity risk	Investment risk	Inflation risk
Fixed real life annuities	Yes	Yes	Yes
Fixed nominal life annuities	Yes	Yes	No
Escalating real life annuities	Yes	Yes	Yes plus
Escalating nominal life annuities	Yes	Yes	Partial
Variable life annuities, guaranteed benefits	Yes	Yes	Possible
Variable life annuities, bonus payments	No	No	No
Variable life annuities, unit linked	No	No	No
Lifetime phased withdrawals	No	No	Possible
Term annuities	No	Possible	Possible
Lump sums	No	Possible	Possible
Self-annuitization	No	Possible	Possible

Source: Authors' compilation.

adverse developments on the financial soundness of individual institutions. However, stress-testing exercises still continue to be formulated in rather static terms. The 2008 global financial crisis and the huge losses suffered by major financial institutions in subprime mortgages and credit default swaps underscore the unsatisfactory state of risk management in even the largest and most sophisticated financial institutions.

Maintaining fully matched positions between assets and liabilities minimizes exposure to investment and inflation risks. However, this approach has three major problems. First, it is not totally feasible because in most countries an adequate supply of fixed-term, fixed-rate instruments is not available to match the potential demand from fixed-rate life annuities, the liabilities of which can span 40 years or longer. Second, the policy is expensive in terms of the relatively low returns that are available on risk-free government bonds, especially inflation-protected government bonds. Third, the liabilities of providers of life annuities can be ascertained only in actuarial terms on the basis of projections of future longevity. This limitation prevents a complete matching of assets and liabilities, although the mismatching that may materialize from underestimating (or overestimating) future longevity and thus understating (or overstating) the true duration of liabilities is not usually so large as to invalidate the benefits of asset and liability management techniques. However, having access to long-term fixed-rate debt instruments and, in the case of fixed real annuities, to long-term inflation-indexed instruments is paramount.

To enhance investment returns and thus offer better terms on their annuity products, insurance companies invest in corporate and mortgage bonds that offer higher yields, although such bonds are exposed to credit risk and often prepayment risk. This exposure needs to be closely monitored and taken into account in determining the capital requirement of providers of retirement products.

Prepayment risk can be effectively managed by access to interest rate options, bond futures, swaptions, and callable debt, but most of these instruments are not usually available in developing countries. The lack of hedging facilities suggests a moderate use of callable debt instruments despite their higher yields.

Extensive use of corporate and mortgage bonds raises the question of the appropriate rate of interest for calculating the value of annuity contracts. If the government guarantees annuity payments in cases of provider insolvency, the correct rate to use is the yield curve on risk-free government bonds for the guaranteed amounts and the corporate and mortgage bond yield curves for amounts in excess of the guarantees. Use of risk-free rates when providers of annuities invest heavily in corporate and mortgage bonds overstates the value of annuities by a significant factor.

Recent years have seen the growing use of long-term interest rate swaps and swaptions in some advanced countries for hedging the liabilities of life annuities. This approach is promising, although it raises important questions about the credit quality and adequate availability of trustworthy counterparties. The widespread use of customized over-the-counter products rather than standardized exchange-traded contracts enhances the flexibility and efficiency of these hedging facilities but increases exposure to the creditworthiness of counterparties, which may be difficult to ensure over the very long duration of these contracts.

Dealing with longevity risk requires reliable projections of the expected future survivorship of annuitants, taking into account various personal characteristics as well as expected health improvements. Estimating future improvements in longevity is one of the most challenging tasks faced by annuity providers. The sharp advances in medical technology and the stricter health standards that have been introduced may result in significant differences in the future evolution of longevity. Faced with these difficulties, annuity providers use conservative assumptions about future improvements in longevity and tend to apply higher margins on younger annuitants and on deferred annuities.

Adverse regulations may also complicate the management of longevity risk. For instance, insurers may be required to use outdated mortality tables, which would be particularly detrimental in annuity pricing but would also cause problems for reserving policies. The use of outdated mortality tables is more prevalent in developing countries because of the lack of comprehensive local data and extensive reliance on mortality data from foreign countries. The compulsory use of unisex life tables, which is imposed in European Union countries, also complicates the management of longevity risk, although the impact of unisex tables may be mitigated by the widespread use of joint life annuities.

Longevity risk, especially at the more uncertain tail end of the age distribution, may be addressed by the use of reinsurance with global reinsurers. However, regulatory restrictions, such as a requirement for the localization of insurance assets, discourage foreign reinsurers from participating in the local market and hinder access to global reinsurance. Other possibilities include the use of longevity bonds and longevity derivatives. The supply and pricing of these instruments are at an early stage of development, and their use has yet to take hold even in the most advanced countries.

Another solution that is used extensively in some countries is the sharing of the longevity risk with annuitants. Risk sharing can occur either with unit-linked annuities or with traditional profit-participating guarantee and bonus annuities. In the case of guarantee and bonus annuities, insurers assume the investment and longevity risks up to the level of guaranteed benefits but share these risks among annuitants beyond that level. Effectively, improvements in longevity as well as changes in investment returns are reflected in annual bonuses. Risk-sharing arrangements have many potential advantages but require a high level of transparency and integrity on the part of annuity providers and a robust and effective system of regulation and supervision.

Risks Faced by Governments

Governments face three main risks in providing a safety net in retirement. The first emanates from the provision of public pillar benefits. The second is linked to the offer of government guarantees on accumulated balances in retirement savings accounts. The third stems from the offer of government guarantees of annuity payments in case of provider insolvency.

Public pillar benefits may be financed from general tax revenues or from unfunded (or partially funded) contributory pillars. The first type of benefits may involve universal pension benefits that are likely to be subject to clawback provisions or the offer of minimum pension guarantees that ensure that benefits from the first or second pillars do not fall below specified minimum levels. In both cases, policy makers must avoid adopting rules that distort incentives and that encourage workers to rely on public benefits for their income security in retirement. This policy requires careful stipulation of both clawback provisions in the case of universal benefits and conditions of retirement and access to government support in the case of minimum public pensions.

Benefits from unfunded (or partially funded) contributory pillars may increase pressures on government budgets as a result of deteriorating system dependency ratios when the number of beneficiaries rises much faster than the number of contributors. Changes in the rules of these pillars may be adopted to contain their cost and reduce their budgetary impact.

The second risk is linked to the performance of accumulated assets on retirement savings accounts and the considerable annuitization risk to which workers are exposed at the time of their retirement. The 2008 global financial crisis has underscored the high financial risk faced by retiring workers, especially if they have a heavy exposure to equities and other assets with volatile prices. In addressing this risk, governments may promote the use of life-cycle funds, which increase their allocations into long-term bonds as workers approach retirement. They may combine the use of life-cycle funds with the offer of a government undertaking to raise accumulated balances to the level that would reflect a specified minimum lifetime real rate of return (this rate could range between 0 and 2 percent).

The other major risk is the risk of large expenditures associated with the failure of providers of annuity products to meet their obligations. Governments provide guarantees to annuitants that they will assume the responsibility for annuity payments if a provider becomes insolvent. The terms of the guarantees need to be carefully formulated to lower the risk of moral hazard, involve an element of coinsurance, and apply risk-based premiums for the guarantee. The government risk may increase if providers adopt aggressive pricing policies and pursue imprudent investment policies. The presence of the government guarantee may weaken market discipline. Governments need to impose sound capital and reserve regulations and to implement effective risk-based supervision to reduce the risk of provider insolvency. Developing well-designed and speedy resolution mechanisms helps contain the cost of the government guarantees.

Policy Options

The preceding discussion shows that organizing the market for retirement products and ensuring an adequate level of income for retired workers and their families confront policy makers with major challenges, even in countries with well-developed financial and insurance markets. The challenges are far greater in developing countries, where financial and insurance markets are less well established.

This section discusses the policy options faced by policy makers in developing countries. It first addresses the regulation of payout options in the context of a desired level of annuitization to ensure not only that pensioners do not suffer from abject poverty in old age but also that they maintain a reasonable standard of living in retirement compared to their preretirement levels of consumption. The section then discusses the regulation of providers of retirement products, focusing on the overall organization of the market; the regulation of pricing and marketing policies; and last but by no means least, the prudential regulation of providers of retirement products in conjunction with the types of risk they assume.

The preceding discussion emphasized two important aspects of the markets for retirement products. First, the risks facing pensioners and providers are complex and difficult to manage. Second, all types of retirement products suffer from serious shortcomings. In addition, initial country conditions vary significantly and reflect historical factors as well as differences in social structure, economic development, and financial sophistication. Although this section draws on the lessons suggested by the experience of the five countries covered in this book, it avoids making prescriptive policy recommendations. Rather, this section highlights the importance of taking into account the significant differences in initial country conditions.

The Regulation of Payout Options

The first policy issue confronted by policy makers in designing the payout phase of pension systems is whether, and at what level, to make annuitization compulsory by mandating the use of life annuities. Additional issues concern the types of annuities that should be mandated:

- Should annuities cover single or joint lives?
- Should they be fixed in real or nominal terms?
- Should variable payout annuities be allowed?

In answering these questions, policy makers need to bear in mind the two main points that have emerged from the discussion of pensioner risks and the shortcomings of different annuity products. The first is that although there is a need to ensure that retiring workers opt for an adequate level of annuitization, care must be taken to avoid forcing an excessive level of annuitization. The second is that because of the serious shortcomings of all types of retirement products, ideally, a combination of payout options should be favored, covering different products as well as different payout options over time.

Policy decisions are bound to be country specific and should take into account prevailing conditions in each country, specifically the presence and relative importance of public pensions and the public provision of health care. Two limiting cases can be identified: (a) countries where public pensions continue to play a significant part in the overall system and (b) countries in which public pensions have been eliminated or substantially curtailed and a mandatory second pillar based on individual capitalization accounts is expected to play a major role in providing retirement incomes.

The Chilean approach seems appropriate for the second group of countries. It has entailed tight restrictions on lump-sum distributions and a requirement to use either fixed real annuities or life expectancy PWs. In Chile, the use of fixed real annuities has been supported by the ample supply of inflation-indexed government and private sector long-term debt. The use of joint life annuities has been imposed on married persons, and the joint life expectancy for married couples has been used for determining annual payments under PWs. The use of life annuities with guaranteed periods of payment has been permitted. These products have proved popular because they have addressed the bequest motive of pensioners.

The Chilean approach has implied compulsory annuitization at the level of the MPG—or the PBS after the 2008 reform—because monthly payments to holders of PWs are not allowed to fall below this level. When account balances are exhausted, the government assumes the payment obligation.

The conditions for lump-sum withdrawals and early retirement have been tightened over time. Before 2004, workers were allowed to retire early and to withdraw any excess balances in a lump sum, provided they could purchase a fixed real life annuity that was equal to 110 percent of the MPG and 50 percent of their average real earnings over the preceding 10 years. In 2004, these limits were raised to 150 percent and 70 percent, respectively, and months with no contributions were excluded from the calculation of the 10-year average.[22] Another rule change in 2004 allowed annuitizing workers to use a combination of a fixed real annuity at the MPG level and either a PW or a variable annuity.[23] The 2008 changes in the rules replaced the 150 percent MPG ratio with another ratio that is equal to 80 percent of the maximum private pension for which a pension solidarity supplement is provided.

Placing restrictions on lump-sum withdrawals is essential for countries that do not provide significant public benefits. The use of life annuities or life expectancy PWs prevents an early exhaustion of balances and poverty in old age. However, insisting on using fixed real annuities would not be advisable in the absence of an adequate supply of inflation-indexed financial instruments, not only from the government but also from the private sector. In addition, fixed real annuities may prove unduly expensive if real returns on inflation-protected bonds are low. Because fixed nominal annuities do not provide good protection against inflation, an attractive alternative would be escalating nominal annuities, rising at 3 or 5 percent per year.

Countries could also consider a combination of a minimum-level fixed real annuity (such as the MPG or PBS in Chile)[24] and a life expectancy PW. This approach would allow flexibility and participation in the higher returns of equity investments without imposing a heavy burden on the regulatory framework. In contrast, the offer of variable annuities, whether traditional profit-participating guarantee and bonus annuities or unit-linked annuities, would require a major strengthening of regulation and supervision and a very high level of transparency and integrity of annuity providers.

The offer of variable annuities would require adoption of clear and detailed rules on the initial calculation of annuity payments and their annual adjustment in light of net investment performance, reflecting investment returns on the underlying asset portfolios, the effect of longevity experience, and the evolution of operating costs. The rules would also need to specify the treatment of any minimum guaranteed benefits in the context of the prudential regulation of annuity providers and the reserves they will be required to maintain to support different types of retirement products. Variable annuities should not be considered until the insurance markets are well developed and the regulatory and supervisory frameworks become sufficiently robust and effective.

Countries where public pensions continue to play a significant part in the overall system could organize public provision in the form of either a universal pension financed from general revenues or a public pension from a contributory scheme in a traditional social security context. The public pension could equal between 25 and 30 percent of economywide average earnings for single pensioners and between 40 and 50 percent for married couples. In countries with equal pension rights for men and women, a universal or public contributory pension of between 25 and 30 percent of economywide average earnings per person, irrespective of marital status, could be adopted.

The public pension is usually linked to the growth of average earnings and thus provides both protection against inflation and participation in future income growth. The normal retirement age at which the public pension is payable is adjusted periodically on an ad hoc basis in most countries.

Normal retirement age could be linked to life expectancy at retirement, using a rule that would aim at maintaining a constant ratio between retirement life and active working life (*passivity ratio*). A passivity ratio of 0.5 would imply that for every one-year increase in life expectancy at a given normal retirement age, retirement age would increase by eight months. Adjustments in retirement age could take place on a triennial basis and could take into account reasonable estimates of expected improvements in longevity.

Many high-income countries have endogenized the retirement decision by applying appropriate actuarial decrements for early retirement and increments for late retirement, five years before or after the normal retirement age, or by operating a notional (or nonfinancial) defined contribution system where workers accumulate notional balances on their retirement accounts, which they use to purchase life annuities at retirement.

The government enjoys major advantages in offering indexed benefits to pensioners. It benefits from scale economies and is better able to handle both longevity and inflation risks. The public pension represents a floor of retirement income and ensures that old people are not unduly exposed to longevity, investment, and inflation risks.

To contain the cost of public pensions, some countries apply effective clawback provisions to people earning close to or significantly above average earnings.[25] Disability pensions and supplements are payable to workers who are unable to work or who have no other sources of income. Because public pensions represent a relatively low replacement rate of own earnings for workers earning close to or above average earnings, this approach leaves considerable scope for private provisions and supplementary types of retirement income.

Countries with large public benefits may adopt a more liberal approach to the regulation of payout options. The presence of public benefits payable for life mitigates workers' exposure to investment and longevity risks. Fewer restrictions need to be imposed on lump-sum withdrawals, and term annuities and PWs for fixed terms may also be permitted.

In Denmark and Sweden, a strong demand exists for term annuities of 5 and 10 years to supplement income during the first decade of retirement. The use of clawback provisions in Denmark implies that public benefits are lowered or even eliminated while pensioners receive income from term annuities, but the public benefits are restored once payments from term annuities end.

In countries with large public benefits, variable annuities may also be authorized without a requirement for a minimum fixed annuity from accumulated balances in individual accounts because this need is satisfied by the provision of life annuities from the public pillars. However, as already noted, the authorization of variable annuities should be conditional on the presence of robust regulation and effective supervision of insurance markets.

A key policy decision concerns the regulation of lump-sum withdrawals. Historically, universal benefits and social security pensions have been paid as life annuities, often linked to price or even wage inflation, but with no allowance for lump-sum distributions. This restriction has emanated from the basic objective of public pensions to provide income security in old age.

In contrast, DB occupational pension plans have allowed partial lump-sum commutations. These commutations have been motivated by the need to avoid excessive annuitization and provide for flexibility, liquidity, and bequests. They have been shaped by the limits allowed by tax rules on the exemption status of lump sums and have usually allowed lump-sum commutations of between 25 and 33 percent of the present value of future benefits.

In DC plans, government or plan restrictions on lump-sum withdrawals favor the use of life annuities or PWs. In Chile, lump sums are allowed only if a fixed real life annuity is purchased that achieves a specified targeted replacement rate. This rate equaled 50 percent of the average real earnings of retiring workers over the preceding 10 years but was raised to 70 percent in 2004.[26] This approach would be appropriate for all countries that do not operate universal or social security pensions.

Countries where public pensions from the zero and first pillars have a significant presence could adopt a targeted integrated replacement rate, permitting lump-sum withdrawals if the combined replacement rate from the zero, first, and second pillars exceeds a specified level. This level could vary between 50 and 70 percent of a worker's average real earnings over the preceding 10 years. Thus, if public benefits represent 30 percent of the reference earnings of a worker, the annuity from the second pillar would need to amount to between 20 and 40 percent, depending on the adopted target.

Countries that favor the development of voluntary savings may adopt somewhat lower targets. In fact, these integrated replacement rates may be seen as regulatory thresholds that will determine the level of excess balances that can be withdrawn as lump sums rather than desirable targets. Their main role is to ensure an adequate level of income over the whole of a person's retirement while avoiding excessive annuitization.

An alternative approach for such countries would be to mandate the offer of a minimum lump-sum option of between 25 and 33 percent of the value of accumulated balances, a rule that has been implemented in Switzerland and has aimed at lowering the risk of excessive annuitization. However, imposing no upper limits on lump-sum withdrawals, as is currently the case in Australia and Switzerland, is not consistent with the operation of a mandatory retirement saving pillar because it exposes retiring workers who opt for complete lump-sum withdrawals to the risk of early depletion of their accumulated savings and a significant decline in living standards in advanced old age.

Another policy decision concerns the treatment of annuitization risk. Two simple solutions that can be implemented, even in countries with less-developed insurance markets, are a gradual increase in the share of long-duration bonds in the investment portfolios of workers who are near retirement and a gradual purchase of deferred annuities a few years before and after retirement. In countries with more-sophisticated insurance markets, the use of adjustable and extendable annuities could be promoted.[27]

Annuitization risk can also be addressed by regulating the annuity conversion factor, as has been done in Switzerland. However, this approach raises many issues of sustainability, efficiency, and even fairness. It would not be recommended unless a model could be developed that would be able to achieve a smooth cyclical and secular adjustment[28] in the annuity conversion factor without political interference and without undermining the long-term solvency of annuity providers.

A further issue that policy makers need to address is the prevailing wide dispersion of annuity prices in decentralized, competitive markets. Fixing the annuity conversion factor across all providers avoids this problem but brings forth the difficulties and objections discussed in the preceding paragraph. Centralizing the offer of annuities in a monopoly provider also prevents this problem. Centralized provision enjoys some important advantages in terms of scale economies and risk pooling but also suffers from potential disadvantages in terms of operational inefficiency and exposure to political interference. In decentralized competitive markets, the main policy option is to take measures to improve the marketing of annuities. Creating a centralized electronic quotation system merits consideration because it lowers the search costs of retiring workers, minimizes the influence of brokers, and promotes greater transparency and competition.

A final policy issue concerns the use of different payout options over time. A particularly attractive concept is the use of deferred annuities that are purchased at the time of retirement and become payable 10, 15, or 20 years later in conjunction with the use of PWs, or term annuities, or even reliance on self-annuitization during the deferment period.[29] Of course, deferred annuities would need to be real annuities to protect old-age pensioners from the vagaries of inflation.

The rules could allow deferred annuities with refunds in case of death during the deferment period as well as annuities without any such refunds. Clearly, deferred annuities without refunds would be significantly cheaper and would allow a larger part of accumulated balances to be used as lump sums in a self-annuitization approach or for defining monthly payments under PWs and term annuities.

The combined use of self-annuitization and deferred annuities would alleviate the burden of financial management in advanced old age and would significantly reduce the risk of financial ruin that sole reliance on self-annuitization would entail. However, deferred annuities suffer from the greater difficulty in projecting long-term longevity trends and calculating their effects on the tail end of the age distribution. Moreover, because they should ideally take the form of deferred fixed real annuities, they need to have access to long-term inflation-linked instruments.

Financial Literacy and Default Options

The regulation of payout options entails various other aspects, such as the handling of longevity risks, the marketing of variable annuities, and the calculation of regular payments in PWs and of initial payments in variable annuities, but these topics are discussed under provider regulation in the next section because the rules would effectively constrain the policies of different providers rather than the choices available to retiring workers.

The policies set out previously imply offering constrained choice to retiring workers, mandating through one form or another a minimum use of annuitization and allowing limited choice from a menu of other instruments. To enable workers to make prudent and wise decisions, the authorities would need to compile a comprehensive database of retirement products, highlighting their main features, their cost, and their performance.

In most countries, the collection of data on annuities and other types of retirement products is very limited. Denmark and Sweden are notable for failing to collect any data on the distribution and performance of different types of retirement products, despite the preponderant use of variable annuities. A mitigating factor in both countries is that annuity contracts are based on collective labor agreements where representatives of employers and workers monitor the performance of annuity providers.

Chile is the exception because it has a very rich database of life annuities. However, information on the performance of PWs is very limited, while available data do not allow the calculation of replacement rates at retirement.[30]

In addition to compiling a comprehensive database, the authorities in different countries also need to undertake programs to expand financial literacy. Such programs should target both active and retired workers and should cover financial issues arising during both the accumulation and the payout phases of pension systems.

Finally, as emphasized previously, countries that decide to offer a constrained choice of retirement products to retiring workers need to specify the product that will act as the default option. A default option will enable retiring workers who lack the knowledge and sophistication necessary for assessing the different features of fairly complex financial products to choose a solution that enjoys government support and will protect them from the potentially abusive practices of brokers and selling agents. The considerable complexity of most retirement products implies a strong need for guidance and impartial advice. The default option will vary by country, depending on local conditions and social preferences.

Specification of the default option entails two main aspects. The first aspect involves the type of retirement product that will be used as the default. In some cases, this product will be a fixed real annuity, in others a guarantee and bonus variable annuity, and in others a PW. The second aspect concerns the identity of the provider. If a centralized provider is created, this provider would most likely be specified in the default option. In a decentralized competitive market, the default option would probably be based on a competitive auction that allocates new undecided retirees to the institution that levies the lowest operating costs or offers the highest payout benefits.

Regulation of Providers of Retirement Products

The regulation of providers of retirement products covers several issues. Foremost is the overall institutional organization of the market and the basic choice between a centralized single provider and a decentralized competitive structure. Other issues cover the regulation of marketing and pricing policies and the prudential regulation of providers in conjunction with the types of risk they assume.

This book does not address the readiness and sophistication of local financial and insurance markets to support the efficient offer of retirement products. Most developing and transitioning countries historically suffered from underdeveloped financial and insurance markets. However, over the past two decades, many countries in Asia, Eastern Europe, and Latin America have opened their markets to large multinational entities, which have in many cases acquired dominant positions in individual countries. Although the 2008 global financial crisis offers a sharp reminder that even large and sophisticated financial groups may suffer from lack of integrity and transparency and may engage in abusive and destructive practices, the fact remains that local financial and insurance markets cannot thrive if they remain isolated and do not benefit from the greater know-how and expertise of large multinational financial groups.

In addition, local markets require the creation and the promotion of a highly sophisticated and effective regulatory and supervisory framework. Again, recent experience has shown that even in the most advanced countries, regulation and supervision have been ineffective and have allowed individual institutions to take excessive risks and mistreat their clients. Nonetheless, local markets need to be integrated to the global regulatory system and to be able to adopt evolving sound practices in regulating and supervising the institutions operating in their midst.

The regulation of institutional structure. Centralized provision of life annuities—usually through a public entity, although it can in principle also be based on a highly regulated private entity—has several potential advantages. It allows a larger base of risk pooling, especially if annuitization is compulsory. It also benefits from scale economies and avoids the heavy marketing costs that decentralized providers incur. Because the achievement of lower operating costs is a critical attribute of pension systems that leads to better outcomes in the long run, this advantage significantly favors centralized provision, especially if centralized account administration and longevity insurance are combined with decentralized asset management.

The main disadvantages of centralized provision are the potentially weaker incentives for product innovation and operational efficiency that may result from compulsory participation and monopoly power. With public ownership or extensive public regulation, a high risk exists of extraneous interference in annuity pricing and asset management. Such interference may well result in transferring the investment and longevity risks back to the state. The key requirement is to adopt robust governance safeguards with high levels of transparency and public accountability.[31]

Centralized provision is quite common. The zero and first public pillars, where they exist, rely on centralized provision through a single public agency. Because they almost always involve the offer of inflation-indexed compulsory lifetime annuities, their products play a central part in the annuity markets of most countries.

Denmark and Sweden have gone one step further and have used centralized public agencies for the offer of supplementary lifetime annuities. These annuities operate alongside private providers that offer industry or employer schemes covered by collective labor agreements as well as personal pension plans. The presence of such lifetime annuities and the prevalence of collective labor agreements clearly have an important effect on the functioning of private annuity providers.

The Danish ATP (Arbejdsmarkedets Tillægspension, or Labor Market Supplementary Pension) fund operates a compulsory pension scheme with centralized asset management and offers variable guarantee and bonus annuities. Despite its public status, it has often taken the lead in promoting product innovation and adopting sophisticated asset management (Vittas 2008).

The Swedish Premiumpensionsmyndigheten (Premium Pension Authority, or PPM) is responsible for maintaining accounts and paying benefits as well as for handling the longevity risk of life annuities. For guarantee and bonus annuities, it also retains responsibility for centralized asset management and appoints internal and external asset managers for this purpose. But in the case of unit-linked annuities, asset management is decentralized.

This system, which is also used for the accumulation phase, allows participants to select investment funds from an approved list of asset managers. The PPM collects all individual asset mandates and transfers funds to the selected asset managers without revealing the names of their clients. Sweden authorizes 70 asset managers that operate 700 funds, offering a bewildering choice to retirees (Palmer 2008). In most countries, half a dozen asset managers, each with five or six funds, will be more than sufficient.

The Danish and Swedish experiences show that, despite their weaker incentives, public entities can take the lead in promoting product innovation or adopting innovative investment strategies. The Danish ATP fund has been a leader in the pricing of life annuities and the use of long-term interest rate swaps and other asset management techniques. In Sweden, the combination of centralized administration with decentralized asset management has been a public sector innovation, which the private sector has copied (Palmer 2008).

Countries that adopt a centralized structure could use a public entity to maintain accounts and pay benefits, as well as to handle the longevity risk of life annuities, but could organize asset management on a decentralized basis. This structure would be attractive in the case of unit-linked variable annuities, allowing participants to select investment funds from an approved list of asset managers. A competitive bidding process could be undertaken at specified time intervals to ensure that the most efficient institutions with the lowest operating fees were allowed to participate. The centralized institution would collect all individual asset mandates and transfer funds to the selected asset managers without revealing the names of clients.

Countries that favor a decentralized competitive market structure aim for greater competition, innovation, and efficiency. However, because of scale economies and high marketing costs, decentralized markets suffer from market consolidation, veering over time toward oligopolistic structures and the prevalence of a small number of providers. This development negates their innovation and efficiency advantages.

The case for a decentralized competitive structure is significantly weakened if strict restrictions apply to annuity products and their pricing. It is also weakened if insurance companies use common life tables, in which case competition is effectively limited to asset management and marketing campaigns. Thus, countries that adopt decentralized competitive structures need to monitor closely the behavior and performance of providers of retirement products to ensure that profit margins are reasonable and that the benefits of competition and innovation are not eroded by increasingly oligopolistic and wasteful practices.

Another possibility is to have decentralized account administration and decentralized asset management with centralized management of the longevity risk. This structure will address the problems posed by the non-diversifiable component of longevity risk. However, decentralized account administration will not provide any significant benefits and will suffer from wasteful marketing expenses and from a potential misuse of economies of scale by large insurance groups that have a poor record as asset managers. The centralization of both account administration and longevity insurance, combined with decentralized asset management, would seem a superior option.

Given the competitive inefficiencies of decentralized markets, especially in supplying variable annuities, and the advantages of allowing retiring workers a constrained choice from a broader menu of retirement products, an attractive approach to the organization of market structure may be to combine centralized and decentralized provision. A centralized provider, focusing on account administration and longevity insurance, in conjunction with decentralized asset management, could be used for variable annuities, while fixed real and nominal annuities could be offered through a decentralized competitive market.

The regulation of marketing and pricing policies. The regulation of marketing and pricing policies varies considerably between centralized and decentralized provision and between fixed and variable annuities. In general, regulation is much simpler in a centralized market structure. Elaborate controls are not needed on marketing campaigns, the creation of electronic quotation systems, and the application of conduct rules, such as a "know-your-customer" rule. Pricing policies need to reflect all relevant variables to ensure long-run sustainability and avoid unintended inter- and intragenerational transfers, but no concern exists about price dispersion and exposure to deceptive policies and heightened bankruptcy risk. The marketing of variable annuities is not faced with the perverse incentives that afflict decentralized markets.

In the case of fixed nominal or real life annuities, the centralized institution needs to respond to inquiries from retiring workers by providing appropriate quotations that take into account the choice of product and age cohort of applicants. To be able to do so effectively, the centralized institution needs to construct life tables by product and cohort and to apply the appropriate yield curves in calculating the initial annuity payments by type of product. The centralized institution must also set out a clear policy on the treatment of retiring workers with impaired health.

The main challenge for the centralized provider is the creation of a sophisticated delivery system where trained professionals have access to detailed data and can respond in a prompt and efficient manner to inquiries from retiring workers. To ensure a high quality of service, the provider may outsource this component of the centralized structure through competitive bidding to a small number of private operators, subject to clearly defined standards of accuracy and speed.

In the case of guarantee and bonus variable annuities, the centralized institution needs to set out clearly the calculation of initial payments, the offer of guaranteed benefits, and the determination of annual bonuses. It also needs to clarify its policies on the reversibility of annual bonuses. Using conservative assumptions with regard to the technical rate of interest and life tables will result in low initial payments that will give rise to significant transfers from older to younger cohorts unless the resulting large bonus reserve is partly funded with long-term debt. All these policy variables and objectives need to be spelled out in a transparent and effective way.

In the case of unit-linked annuities with decentralized asset management, the three main concerns are the selection of authorized asset managers, the organization of periodic switching among asset managers, and the handling of minimum guarantees. The management of longevity risk needs to be clarified in both types of variable annuities, including the treatment of retiring workers with impaired health.

The treatment of impaired lives poses a difficult managerial and regulatory challenge linked to the political difficulties of defining the admissible level of health impairment and the required documentation for establishing the health status of individual annuitants. In decentralized markets, greater room for experimentation exists, as is shown by recent developments in the U.K. annuity market, where some companies offer better prices to smokers relative to nonsmokers; other companies use postal codes as a factor in annuity pricing. The latter approach is based on the hypothesis that people who reside in the same neighborhood are likely to have similar backgrounds and similar life expectancies (Swiss Re 2008). Centralized providers in Denmark and Sweden have not so far created separate longevity pools on the basis of health status.[32]

The regulation of marketing and pricing policies presents a major challenge in decentralized competitive markets. The selling of life annuities, especially fixed nominal or real annuities, requires considerable marketing effort by insurance companies and deployment of brokers and agents to explain the relative advantages of life annuities over lump sums and PWs. Brokers tend to have strong incentives to influence the decision to annuitize and derive considerable benefits from channeling retiring workers to providers who offer the highest commissions and not necessarily the best prices and returns to annuitants.

The first requirement for effective regulation of marketing in a decentralized competitive market is compliance with basic conduct rules, such as the "know-your-customer" rule, and an adequate disclosure of the terms and conditions of different products. However, because fixed life annuity products are highly complex as well as irrevocable and nonportable, there is also a need for extensive training of agents and brokers. In addition to adequate training, brokers need to pass a certification test as well as the standard "fit and proper" test. Licensed brokers must be legally obligated to represent their clients, must generate their income from commissions on the sale of annuities, and must not be permitted to accept volume-related remuneration from insurers.

In the case of fixed annuities, adopting an electronic quotation system, such as the one introduced in Chile in 2004, merits serious consideration. It is a centralized service that compiles and validates individual data on retiring workers and solicits quotes from participating institutions. Such a system reduces the influence of brokers, lowers the search costs of retiring workers, enhances the quality of information available to them, and ensures broad access to competitively priced annuities.

The structure and level of commissions payable to brokers and agents need to be closely monitored and to be subject to caps, such as the 2.5 percent cap introduced in Chile in 2004, if they become too high and give rise to market distortions. In addition to being subject to an upper limit, commissions could be made payable over the whole duration of the annuity contract and not concentrated in the first few years. One way to achieve this structure is to prohibit upfront fees on retiring workers and allow only regular fees on monthly payments.

With regard to pricing policies, providers of fixed life annuities in decentralized competitive markets should be free to determine their own prices and adopt aggressive or passive marketing campaigns as they see fit. The supervisors need to monitor the pricing and marketing campaigns of individual providers to ensure that they do not adopt deceptive policies that could harm pensioners in the longer run. They also need to ensure that providers maintain adequate technical reserves calculated on a sound basis (this topic is addressed in the next section on the regulation of risk management).

The ineffectiveness of price competition is underscored by the wide dispersion in the prices of fixed nominal or real life annuities. The range of annuity quotations exceeds 20 percent in most markets, including Chile and the United Kingdom.[33]

Strict regulation of the prices of fixed life annuities is one way of addressing the issue of price dispersion, but it entails both benefits and costs, as the experience of Switzerland clearly indicates. Use of regulated annuity conversion factors for life annuities protects retiring workers of different cohorts from large fluctuations in market prices of both assets and annuities and also prevents an excessive dispersion of annuity prices across annuitants with similar characteristics. However, large income transfers across annuitants of different gender and marital status can be generated if price regulation is not carefully calibrated. In addition, the solvency of annuity providers can be jeopardized if regulated prices are not subject to flexible adjustment in line with changing market conditions, including changing interest rates and longevity experience.[34]

The marketing of variable payout annuities in a decentralized market raises even more complex issues. If providers are free to set initial payments and apply entry (front-load) and exit fees, a strong temptation will exist to adopt deceptive and irresponsible practices, offering annuitants high initial payments to attract their business but offering low bonuses in subsequent years to compensate providers for the elevated initial payments. If switching is not allowed, annuitants will be captive in providers that may produce worse results over the long term. Of course, poor bonus performance will reduce the attractiveness of such providers, but the high initial payments may still tempt retiring workers. Lack of comprehensive information on long-term performance may inhibit effective scrutiny of different providers. Hefty exit fees may also be used to discourage low-risk annuitants from switching when providers alter the risk profile of their business.

To protect retirees from such practices, which are not uncommon in retail financial markets, policy makers may be inclined to specify the calculation of initial payments. This approach may involve setting a low rate of interest for discounting future payments and using a common mortality table that may allow some improvements in longevity. Following this approach will entail low initial payments but will permit higher future bonuses if reserves are invested in higher-yielding assets.[35] Caps on commissions and other operating fees may also be applied to protect retiring workers.

When initial payments are subject to detailed regulations and are common for all providers, competition in the variable annuity market depends on the level and stability of prospective bonuses. The latter are a function of investment returns, operating costs, longevity experience, and the policy of profit distribution between annuitants and shareholders.

Retiring workers participating in variable annuities should be encouraged to select providers with high profit-participation rates, low operating costs, diversified investment portfolios, and a consistent record of sound performance. A focus on recent past performance, which selling agents often emphasize, is not sound practice because past returns are not good predictors of future performance.

Market regulators need to ensure that annuity providers follow transparent and consistent policies on the handling of operating costs and distribution of profits between shareholders and annuitants. The rules should discourage the use of transfer pricing whereby financial services obtained from affiliated companies are billed at artificially high prices. In addition, profit-distribution policies may be subject to minimum regulatory requirements. For instance, the profit-sharing rate may be set at 90 or even 95 percent of annual profits. Annuity providers are compelled to absorb any negative profits but are allowed to recoup their losses in subsequent years before determining profits available for distribution.

Regulating the profit-sharing rate introduces considerable rigidity in the system. A more flexible alternative is to allow annuity providers to determine their own profit-distribution policies but to require a high level of transparency. A central register should be created to compile comparative data on a consistent and informative basis on the investment performance and bonus policies of different providers.

Interestingly, neither Denmark nor Sweden has a central register that compiles performance data on a systematic basis. However, in both countries, the offer of variable annuities is based on broad collective labor agreements. Thus, representatives of workers and employers monitor the performance of providers and protect the interests of pensioners. In a system of non-employer-based individual accounts, a central register of performance data and an effective supervision of providers are indispensable.

Competition in the market for variable annuities where longevity risk is shared among annuitants may occasionally take a perverse form. To increase their market share and expand their business, annuity providers with a preponderance of low-risk clients may decide to offer attractive terms to new clients with higher-risk characteristics, effectively forcing low-risk annuitants—that is, individuals with short life expectancy—to share the higher longevity risk of high-risk annuitants and thus causing unfair transfers across different groups. Admittedly, such marketing campaigns may not be easy to design and implement. But a more likely occurrence is a friendly or hostile merger of two providers with different risk profiles. When mergers take place or marketing policies undergo drastic change, annuitants should be allowed to switch to another provider within a specified period and without incurring any exit fees.

An important aspect of pricing regulation is the legal requirement in many European countries to use unisex mortality tables. This requirement has potentially adverse effects on different providers and may distort marketing policies. A compensation mechanism is necessary to cope with the adverse effects of the compulsory use of unisex mortality tables. With such a mechanism, annuity providers are required to calculate their technical reserves on both gender-specific and unisex mortality tables. A government agency computes the factor that is needed to equate the total reserves under each calculation. Providers whose reserves are higher under gender-specific mortality tables than when calculated with unisex tables multiplied by the specified factor receive a compensating transfer through the government agency from providers with the opposite result (Vittas, Rudolph, and Pollner 2010).

The marketing and the pricing of PWs also raise important concerns. Because PWs do not generate high levels of upfront commission income, brokers and selling agents have little interest in promoting their use by retiring workers. For this reason, the marketing of life annuities and PWs has been highly asymmetrical in Chile (Rocha and Thorburn 2007). According to the 2008 changes in the pension law in Chile, brokers and selling agents are allowed to charge commissions for selling PWs. In other countries, such as the United Kingdom, hefty exit fees imposed by insurance companies have distorted the marketing of PWs, penalizing both retiring and retired workers who wanted to transfer their balances to a competing provider.

The pricing of PWs depends on the appropriate use of mortality tables and discount rates. In countries where PWs are used by low-income and low-balance people, the mortality table should reflect their lower life expectancy. The discount rate should be based on prospective long-term returns and should not be dominated by recent performance. These provisions are necessary to protect pensioners from an accelerated depletion of their balances and to create a level playing field with life annuities.

The regulation of risk management. The regulation of risk management addresses the level of technical reserves and risk capital that is required to support the specific risks undertaken by different providers of retirement products. It also covers the use of internal risk management and control systems and the application of stress tests for assessing the vulnerability of individual institutions to internal and external shocks.

The issues are conceptually the same for centralized and decentralized structures, although in competitive markets individual institutions may be tempted to adopt more risky policies. However, centralized single providers face different risks, such as the risk of complacency, persistence in misguided policies, and failure to take corrective action. Thus, despite the absence of competitive pressures for imprudent initiatives, the risk management policies of centralized entities need to be as closely monitored as those of competitive entities in a decentralized market. In fact, both the ATP fund in Denmark and the PPM in Sweden broadly follow the same regulatory and accounting rules as private insurance companies and pension funds in these countries and are supervised by the same national supervisory agencies.

The management of operational, counterparty, and liquidity risks presents the same challenges to all types of institutions, irrespective of the risk characteristics of the products they offer. Losses from operational risk may result from fraud or administrative failure, such as failure to comply with the requirement of legal segregation and external safe custody of assets, whereas losses from counterparty risk may arise from performance failure of a contractual counterparty. Installation of appropriate internal control systems helps lower losses from such risks. Control systems need to segregate duties and avoid conflicts of interest in assigning responsibilities.

The complexity of risk management and its regulation increase significantly with regard to underwriting risk, which covers investment, inflation, and longevity risks. Which risks a particular provider faces depends on the risk characteristics of the products offered. Institutions that do not assume any investment or longevity risk do not face underwriting risk. Such institutions, which include providers of PWs and unit-linked products without any guaranteed benefits, do not need to build any technical reserves. Their liabilities are equal to the value of their assets. Their capital requirements also are simple and straightforward. They are subject to a relatively small minimum initial capital and a capital adequacy requirement. The latter is related to the volume of assets under management and ranges between 1 and 2 percent of assets under management.

Two interesting questions arise with regard to the composition and use of the capital reserve of such providers. The first question concerns whether the capital reserve should be satisfied only with equity injections or whether subordinated long-term debt could also be used to attain the same objective of solvency and stability but at a lower effective cost. This issue is particularly relevant for providers that belong to large financial conglomerates. In practice, parent companies use long-term debt rather than group equity to finance their stakes in subsidiaries. Thus, authorizing and even requiring the use of subordinated debt for a significant proportion of the capital reserve is more consistent with prevailing practice.

The second question concerns use of the capital reserve. Imposing a rule that the capital reserve should be invested in the same assets as client funds ensures an alignment of interests between the providers and their clients. However, this argument does not hold if a substantial part of the capital reserve is financed with subordinated debt. In these cases, only the equity component of the capital reserve should be required to be invested in the same assets as client funds. The proceeds of subordinated debt should be invested in callable bonds of similar maturity.

The valuation of assets of providers of PWs and unit-linked products should be based on market values. This method is essential for a fair calculation of the value of benefits. The majority of assets are invested in equities and bonds traded on public markets. A small proportion may be placed in venture capital, infrastructure, and real estate, but such investments are ideally made through specialized investment funds. Their valuation is not at market prices but is based on model valuations provided by the managers of these funds or by independent appraisers. Model valuations are also used in the case of equities and bonds that are not actively traded.

Regulation of risk management of institutions that assume investment, inflation, and longevity risks is a much greater challenge. In countries with advanced financial and insurance markets, the first step is to require fair value accounting for the valuation of both assets and liabilities. Market values should be used as fair values for assets that are traded on active and liquid markets, but for less liquid assets, fair valuation could be obtained by applying acceptable valuation models.[36] All value changes—realized and unrealized—should ideally be shown in the profit and loss account.

Valuing liabilities is conceptually more difficult because there are no active markets for insurance and pension liabilities and, therefore, no readily observable market prices. By necessity, fair valuation is based on valuation models. The first step is to calculate future actuarial liabilities by applying appropriate survival probabilities that reflect reasonable estimates of future improvements in longevity. Actuarial liabilities are calculated by product and by cohort. Individual institutions may be allowed to use their own mortality tables, reflecting the demographic characteristics of their own clienteles. But they should be required to justify their choice, both with regard to their pricing decisions and with regard to their reserving policies. The present value of estimated actuarial liabilities is then calculated by applying market-based, maturity-dependent discount rates, obtained from a zero-coupon yield curve. Ideally, this curve should be based on AA-rated corporate bond and swap rates. The decomposition and maintenance of separate technical reserves by type and level of guaranteed benefits should also be required.

Asset and liability valuations should then be subject to stress tests that calculate the effect of significant changes in market prices on the financial position of individual institutions. Stress tests on insurance companies and pension funds are now applied in several countries, but the various stress tests are still at an early stage of development, are specified in static terms, do not reflect past experience, and are invariant to the state of financial markets. Ideally, stress tests should take into account the historical variance and covariance of asset returns and should account for the state of financial markets. The required solvency margin should be related to the size of the deviation of current prices from long-term trends. If individual institutions maintain reasonably matched positions between their assets and liabilities, the stress tests would have little effect on their equity positions or buffer funds. However, if they exhibit considerable deviation from full matching, the stress tests would indicate the size of the buffer fund that would be required to ensure solvency. The stress tests should also cover changes in future longevity and should assess the adequacy of the longevity risk fund.

The outlined approach could not be followed in countries where financial markets suffer from low volumes of trading, assets are illiquid, and institutions adopt buy-and-hold strategies. In these cases, the approach used by Chile has considerable appeal. Market rates of interest are used for calculating the technical reserves of liabilities that are matched by assets of similar duration, but lower prescribed discount rates are mandated for discounting unmatched liabilities. Coupled with higher capital reserve requirements for unmatched liabilities, this approach protects providers of fixed life annuities from adverse changes in interest rates.

Full matching of assets and liabilities minimizes exposure to investment and inflation risks but, as discussed in the earlier section on coping with provider risks, may prove overly expensive and even infeasible. It requires full access to long-duration inflation-indexed financial instruments for hedging the inflation risk of fixed real annuities. However, most countries do not have an adequate supply of such instruments. Various derivatives, including interest rate swaps and swaption contracts as well as interest rate futures and callable debt, may be used for managing investment and prepayment risks, but the use of such products and the counterparty risk they entail must be closely monitored.

The regulation of the management of longevity risk also faces major challenges. An essential requirement is to avoid the use of outdated mortality tables, which may be particularly detrimental in annuity pricing but may also cause problems for reserving policies. Developing countries tend to use outdated mortality tables because they lack comprehensive local data and rely extensively on mortality data from foreign countries. A serious effort must be made to build reliable and detailed data on longevity.

Reinsurance is an option for managing longevity risk, especially at the tail end of the age distribution. However, regulators need to remove any restrictions on the localization of insurance assets to encourage resort to global reinsurance markets. The use of reinsurance needs to be closely monitored to ensure that foreign reinsurers are respectable and creditworthy.

Use of longevity bonds and longevity derivatives could be encouraged when these instruments are well established in global markets. However, developing deep and reliable markets in these instruments is likely to take considerable time. In the meantime, providers of products with investment and longevity risks could adopt risk-sharing arrangements with annuitants. Risk sharing is widely used in Denmark and Sweden both for traditional participating guarantee and bonus annuities and for unit-linked annuities.

In the case of guarantee and bonus annuities, providers assume the investment and longevity risks up to the level of guaranteed benefits but share these risks among annuitants beyond that level. In the case of unit-linked annuities, the investment risk is assumed by annuitants reflecting the portfolio of the investment funds they select, but the longevity risk is shared among annuitants either on a cohort and product basis or across all annuitants of each type of product. Improvements in longevity as well as changes in investment returns are reflected in annual benefits.

Risk-sharing arrangements have many potential advantages but also introduce their own challenges. A high level of transparency and integrity on the part of annuity providers is required as well as transparent and robust rules to ensure consistent long-term fairness in the distribution of profits among shareholders and policyholders. Clearly, this issue is more important in the case of decentralized markets, where market discipline may be less powerful than is often assumed, but it is also relevant in the case of public monopolies, especially in ensuring fair treatment of all cohorts and avoidance of the use of surpluses for extraneous purposes.

The introduction of government guarantees for holders of retirement products should be considered. Such guarantees could be necessary in a system of mandatory saving for retirement purposes. They should cover both the accumulation and payout phases and should include life and term annuities as well as PWs. The government guarantees could emulate evolving practice in deposit insurance schemes, including upper limits on the amounts insured and a reasonable amount of coinsurance by pensioners to minimize the possible loss of market discipline at the point of purchase.

Guarantees should be financed by ex ante or ex post risk-based assessments, but some reliance on budgetary resources could also be contemplated. Adopting a speedy resolution mechanism with early interventions in providers facing financial difficulties and nearing insolvency would contribute to containing the costs of the guarantees. The potential cost of government guarantees should be estimated, and such estimates should be used to determine risk-based premiums on annuity providers.

Expanding the supply of financial instruments to promote efficient liability hedging by individual institutions should also be a policy priority. The imposition of inflation indexation in the absence of inflation-indexed instruments is not advisable because it may lead to the offer of poorly priced products with hefty risk premiums. But development of long-duration inflation-indexed instruments requires significant modernization of public debt management, focusing on the promotion of benchmark issues of inflation-linked bonds. It is also necessary to promote the issuance of inflation-linked corporate and mortgage bonds so that the offer of fixed real annuities does not rely entirely on public sector issues.

In addition, governments would need to promote the development of derivative markets, such as long-term interest rate swap and swaption contracts, to allow hedging of the investment risk of long-term liabilities. The use of longevity bonds and reinsurance markets would also be necessary to support the hedging of longevity risk. Developing longevity bonds and derivatives is likely to be a tall order for most countries because such products have yet to emerge even in the most advanced financial markets. Although long-term interest rate swaps and other derivative instruments are well established in global financial centers, their development in most emerging and low-income countries is still a long way off.

Summary and Main Policy Recommendations

This chapter covers a wide range of complex and challenging issues dealing with the development of sound markets for retirement products. It discusses the various risks faced by pensioners and the risk characteristics of alternative retirement products and also reviews the risks faced by providers of retirement products and the management and regulatory challenges of dealing with these risks. This section pulls together the main conclusions of the chapter, with particular focus on policies that can be adopted by developing and transitioning countries where financial and insurance markets are not well developed.

Basic Points

A first point that policy makers should bear in mind is that pensioners face several risks, and some of these risks pull in opposite directions. Examples are, on the one hand, longevity and bequest risks and, on the other, investment and liquidity risks. Purchasing life annuities protects against longevity but eliminates the possibility of bequests, whereas investing in long-term assets addresses the investment risk but exposes their holders to liquidity risk. A clear implication of these competing risks is that policy makers should target an adequate level of annuitization but should be wary of causing excessive annuitization.

A second point is that the various retirement products have their own risk characteristics and suffer from important shortcomings. Because of these shortcomings, policy makers should favor a combination of payout options, covering different products at a particular point in time as well as different payout options over time.

Menu of Retirement Products

Mandating complete reliance on fixed real (inflation-protected) annuities should be avoided for two reasons: fixed real annuities are costly in terms of low real returns,[37] and they require access to an ample supply of long-duration inflation-indexed bonds, which most countries lack.

However, requiring a minimum level of annuitization through fixed real annuities is essential. The public sector is best equipped to handle the offer of minimum-level fixed real annuities through a universal pension benefit (as in Australia, Denmark, and New Zealand, as well as Chile, since 2008, for the lower 60 percent of the income distribution of households); a social security pillar (as in most countries of the Organisation for

Economic Co-operation and Development); or a minimum pension guarantee for second-pillar benefits (as in Chile before 2008).

Fixed nominal annuities should not be mandated or even be encouraged because they fail to provide protection against inflation, especially for long-lived individuals. If use of fixed real or variable annuities is not feasible or advisable because of prevailing conditions in the local financial and insurance markets, then escalating nominal annuities represent an attractive alternative option.

Use of joint life annuities with guaranteed periods of payment deserves public policy support. These products address the bequest motive and the fear of capital loss in case of early death. They also help overcome the problems caused by impaired health and adverse selection. In addition, joint life annuities mitigate the distorting effects of the use of unisex life tables, which is compulsory in European Union countries.

Annuities with guaranteed periods of payment are very popular when they are offered, but they do not need to be mandated. However, the use of joint life annuities should ideally be imposed on both working spouses, and the reversion rate—that is, the pension of the surviving spouse—should not be lower than 60 percent of the original pension.[38]

Term annuities appeal to pensioners who wish to have higher incomes during the first years of their retirement life. They do not protect against longevity risk, but they may appeal to workers with impaired health. Term annuities may be included in product combinations once minimum levels of inflation-protected life annuitization are secured and provided the insurance market is reasonably well developed and effectively regulated.

PWs also do not provide full protection against longevity risk, but because of limits on annual withdrawals, they stretch balances over a longer period. PWs allow bequests but are exposed to investment and inflation risks. Unlike life and term annuities, they are portable and can be transferred to other financial institutions. Like term annuities, they have advantages for workers with impaired health and short life expectancies.

A combination of a minimum-level fixed real annuity (preferably but not exclusively provided through the public sector) and a life expectancy PW merits serious consideration in any country. This combination provides minimum security in old age while allowing participation in the higher returns of market investments. In contrast to variable annuities, it does not require a major strengthening of regulation and supervision.

Variable annuities—profit participating or unit linked, with or without minimum guaranteed benefits—have their own merits and attractions.

They appeal to pensioners who want to participate in the upside potential of investments in equities and real estate. But their offer requires a robust regulatory framework and a high level of transparency and integrity on the part of providers.

Variable annuities are exposed to investment risk, and complete reliance on them would not be advisable. Like term annuities and PWs, they may be included in product combinations once minimum levels of inflation-protected life annuitization are secured and the regulatory framework is sufficiently robust.

Reverse mortgages have many advantages for retiring workers who own and occupy their homes. However, like variable annuities, they require a robust regulatory framework to provide effective protection to pensioners from aggressive selling.

Deferred annuities (with or without refunds) are an attractive option in most countries. They are purchased at the time of retirement and are payable 10, 15, or 20 years later. Because they have greater exposure to the tail end of the age distribution, they are more difficult to price than immediate annuities. In countries with sophisticated insurance markets and reliable mortality data, they may be used in combination with term annuities, PWs, or even self-annuitization during the deferment period.

Countries that offer a constrained choice to retiring workers and do not mandate the use of a single retirement product for all should also specify the product that will be used as the default option. Having a default option helps workers who are unable or unwilling to make a decision on their own and protects them from abusive selling practices of brokers and selling agents of providers. The use of centralized electronic quotation systems and the offer of guidance and advice by regulatory agencies will also contribute to greater consumer protection.

Unlimited lump-sum distributions and the implied complete reliance on self-annuitization should be avoided, unless strong cultural factors favor them. Self-annuitization requires considerable financial savvy by retired workers and is very difficult to manage in advanced old age.

The level of permitted lump-sum withdrawals may be determined either as excess balances once the targeted level of annuitization is achieved or as an upper limit, normally between 25 and 33 percent, of accumulated balances.

Integrated Replacement Rates

The targeted level of annuitization reflects country preferences. A sensible approach is to have a public pension equal to between 25 and 30 percent of economywide average earnings for single pensioners (between 40 and 50 percent for married couples) and a targeted integrated replacement rate from the zero, first, and second pillars of between 50 and 70 percent of a worker's own average real earnings over the preceding 10 years.

These integrated replacement rates may also be seen as regulatory thresholds that will determine the level of excess balances that can be withdrawn as lump sums. Their main role is to ensure an adequate level of income over the whole of a person's retirement while avoiding excessive annuitization.

The public pension should ideally be linked to the growth of average earnings, thereby providing protection against inflation as well as participation in future income growth. The benefit from the second pillar may be a fixed real or an escalating nominal annuity, a variable annuity, or a program of PWs.

The normal retirement age at which the public pension is payable may be linked to life expectancy at retirement, on the basis of a rule that aims at maintaining a constant ratio between retirement life and active working life.

Annuitization risk—that is, the risk of low long-term interest rates and high annuity prices at the time of retirement—can be mitigated either by authorizing gradual purchases of annuities or by encouraging gradual portfolio shifts in favor of long-term bonds. In more-sophisticated markets, the development and use of adjustable and extendable annuities would also reduce exposure to annuitization risk.

Institutional Structure

Centralized provision of some services linked to retirement products, such as account administration, benefit payment, and risk pooling, has several potential advantages, including a larger base for risk pooling, economies of scale, and avoidance of heavy marketing costs. The disadvantages are potentially weaker incentives for operational efficiency and product innovation. Centralized provision of these services may be combined with decentralized asset management.

Countries that favor a decentralized competitive market structure need to closely monitor trends toward growing market consolidation. They need to ensure that profit margins are not excessive and that the benefits of greater competition and innovation are not eroded by increasingly oligopolistic and wasteful marketing practices.

Adopting a centralized electronic quotation system to lower search costs and improve the marketing of fixed nominal and real annuities as well as escalating annuities is a high priority. However, the marketing of guarantee and bonus or unit-linked variable annuities through a decentralized competitive market raises major regulatory and supervisory challenges. Offering variable annuities through a centralized provider but with decentralized asset management is preferable.

Regulation of Risk Management

The regulation of risk management needs to focus on the maintenance of adequate levels of technical reserves and risk capital. Institutions that offer PWs and unit-linked products without any guaranteed benefits do not present complex risk management issues.

However, for providers of products with guaranteed benefits, the regulatory framework needs to be more complex and robust. The use of fair value accounting and market-based maturity-dependent discount rates should be required, and the application of stress tests to assess the vulnerability of individual institutions to specified external shocks should be mandated.

Countries where financial markets are not sufficiently active and liquid should not rely on potentially misleading market valuations. The use of book values should be allowed, but unmatched liabilities of individual institutions should be subject to more-onerous technical and capital reserves.

Effective management of the longevity risk in fixed nominal and real annuities as well as in escalating annuities requires access to long-duration assets. For the more uncertain tail end of the age distribution, annuity providers should be encouraged to resort to global reinsurance. This approach will require removal of any asset localization requirements. Using longevity bonds and longevity derivatives could be encouraged when these instruments become well established in global markets.

The risk-sharing arrangements of some types of variable annuities whereby longevity risk is shared among annuitants offer several advantages. However, the offer of such annuities requires a high level of transparency and integrity and is best organized through a centralized structure along the lines previously discussed.

Government Guarantees

The introduction of government guarantee schemes covering all types of retirement products merits serious consideration. The government guarantees could emulate evolving practice in deposit insurance schemes, including upper limits on the amounts insured and a reasonable amount of coinsurance by pensioners to minimize the possible loss of market discipline at the point of purchase. The potential cost of government guarantees should be estimated, and such estimates should be used to determine risk-based premiums on annuity providers.

The high volatility of financial markets, which was recently underscored by the 2008 global crisis, highlights the need for a safety net to cover the accumulation phase at the point of retirement. The offer of a lifetime government guarantee that retirement savings will earn a specified minimum real rate of return deserves special study.

The conditions and other particulars of two options are worth considering: (a) a minimum zero real rate of return or (b) a specified fraction of the long-run rate of return of specified portfolios. In either case, asset allocation strategies during the accumulation phase will need to follow prescribed principles and patterns to discourage moral hazard and prevent gaming of the guarantees by retiring workers.

In addition, the authorities should compile a comprehensive database of retirement products and should undertake educational programs to expand financial literacy and improve understanding of the main features, cost, and performance of different retirement products.

Notes

1. Many authors have undertaken extensive research in this area; see Blake (1999); Brown, Mitchell, and Poterba (2001); Cardinale, Findlater, and Orszag (2002); Davis (2000); Fornero and Luciano (2004); Impavido, Thorburn, and Wadsworth (2003); James, Song, and Vittas (2001); Mitchell and others (2001); Palacios and Rofman (2001); and Valdés-Prieto (1998).

2. Hu and Scott (2007) address behavioral obstacles to the annuity market, drawing on recent advances in behavioral finance.

3. James and Vittas (2000) list 10 reasons for the underdevelopment of voluntary annuity markets. Adverse selection is one of them and far from the most important. More recently, Babbel and Merrill (2006) also underscore the multiplicity of factors that has held back the growth of annuity markets.

4. This section draws on chapter 3 of Rocha and Thorburn (2007).

5. The bequest motive becomes weaker as people reach advanced old age because children and even grandchildren have reached maturity and independence by that time. Liquidity risk is present throughout a person's life and relates to the inability to use in an emergency a person's annuitized wealth.

6. Chile is a notable exception in this respect, as will be discussed later.

7. An inflation rate of 3 percent per year would lower the real value of annuity payments by 26 percent over 10 years and by 45 percent over 20 years.

8. The pricing and marketing challenges of all types of annuities are discussed in greater detail in the section on financial literacy and default options.

9. In this study, the term *variable annuities* refers to payout products. It does not refer to variable annuities that are used during the accumulation stage but do not involve any annuitization. These products are extensively used in the United States, mainly for tax purposes, and are little more than mutual funds operated by insurance companies.

10. Impavido, Thorburn, and Wadsworth (2003) discuss the advantages of risk sharing between providers and annuitants in terms of lower capital requirements and lower charges.

11. Mean reversion implies that exposure to a prolonged decline in equity returns would be highest at the end of a prolonged period of high returns when accumulated balances would also be at their highest level. In contrast, accumulated balances would be at their lowest level at the end of a prolonged period of low returns, but mean reversion would then imply a low exposure to low future returns over a prolonged period. Most analysts who highlight the exposure of variable annuities to the risk of early erosion because of a prolonged market downturn assume a fixed amount of capital and do not allow for the possibility that accumulated capital would be higher at the end of a long period of high returns.

12. The concept of *delayed annuities* was recently introduced in the academic literature (Milevsky 2005; Scott, Watson, and Hu 2007; Webb, Gong, and Sun 2007). Although the potentially low cost of such annuities has been underscored, delayed annuities are no different from the traditional concept of deferred annuities. The cost advantage is substantially eroded if refunds are allowed in cases of early death, although such refunds may be necessary to enhance the attractiveness of such annuities.

13. Hedging the investment risk is less of a problem.

14. Adjustable annuities, resetting every three years, have been suggested by Blake and Hudson (2000).

15. Term annuities, along with life annuities from public schemes as well as from corporate plans, are popular in both Denmark and Sweden (Andersen and Skjodt 2007; Palmer 2008).

16. This discussion draws on the classification of PWs presented in Dus, Maurer, and Mitchell (2003).

17. The high exposure to the probability of ruin in advanced old age is discussed in Milevsky and Robinson (2000).

18. A progressive income tax scale created an additional wedge between gross and net replacement rates.

19. Reserving policies of insurance companies and pension funds are notoriously subjective. Profitable entities tend to use low discount rates to overstate their liabilities and overreserve to reduce their reported profits and pay lower taxes; entities facing financial difficulties tend to use high discount rates to understate their liabilities and underreserve to conceal their financial weakness. The same subjective approach may be applied with regard to longevity risk.

20. This section draws on chapters 3 and 4 of Rocha and Thorburn (2007).

21. Long-term interest rate swaps are playing an increasing part in hedging the long-term liabilities of insurance companies and pension funds. They tend to be over-the-counter customized instruments. Management of counterparty risk is a crucial aspect of the successful use of these instruments.

22. The tightening of retirement conditions and the increase in the targeted replacement rate have been justified by the need to counter the large rise in early retirement and the need to prevent a large future increase in spending on pension supplements. Other important factors have been the absence of a front-loaded public pension and the need to ensure adequate income in retirement.

23. The pension reform of 2008 effectively replaced the MPG with the PBS.

24. A minimum escalating nominal annuity could be used if inflation-indexed financial instruments were not in adequate supply.

25. Australia and Denmark apply clawback provisions on their universal pensions. In Australia, use is made of both an income and an asset test. The income test reduces pensions from the zero pillar at a rate of 40 percent of the excess over a threshold level that for single pensioners amounts to about 6 percent of the average wage and for couples amounts to about 11 percent. The Danish universal pension is subject to a clawback of 30 percent of the excess over a specified threshold level of income. The threshold is set by government decision and amounts to a relatively high level of about 75 percent of average earnings.

26. Depending on the rate of wage growth, the new requirement equals between 64 percent of the final wage with a 2 percent wage growth and 59 percent of the final wage with a 4 percent wage growth. Chile also has a requirement related indirectly to average wages, but this requirement is less demanding than the 70 percent rule.

27. The main features of these products are reviewed earlier in the chapter.

28. The adjustment should be cyclical to reflect fluctuations in interest rates over the business cycle and secular to reflect long-term improvements in longevity.

29. See Milevsky (2005) and Scott, Watson, and Hu (2007) for a discussion of the advantages of this approach, especially in the case of deferred annuities without refunds. The idea that retirement and annuitization should not be linked has been discussed in Milevsky and Young (2002) and Blake, Cairns, and Dowd (2008).

30. Blake, Cairns, and Dowd (2008) argue that policy makers should allow flexible retirement products that take into account risk aversion and bequest motives, especially in countries with large first pillars, although they also emphasize the need to provide better information to workers regarding the various trade-offs.

31. In recent years, several countries have made considerable progress in streamlining and strengthening the management and governance of their public pension funds. Vittas, Impavido, and O'Connor (2008) review the performance of four public pension funds under improved governance structures in four countries of the Organisation for Economic Co-operation and Development.

32. Multiple annuity pools created on the basis of state of health and expected longevity are exposed to the risk of political manipulation, and there may be pressure to expand the number of pools. Retaining one pool irrespective of health status is less problematic in a social security context, especially if universal health care is also provided, because redistribution losses by people of impaired health on the pension front will most likely be offset by redistribution benefits on the health care front. However, for mandatory capitalization pension systems that place a strong emphasis on the link between contributions and benefits, use of a single annuity pool is difficult to defend. Allowing a very small number of separate pools for large groups of people with clearly identifiable characteristics and expected outcomes could address this problem in a way that would contain pressures for an ever-expanding number of smaller pools. Nevertheless, incorporating various other factors, such as gender, race, occupation, socioeconomic status, neighborhood, and genetics, would raise highly sensitive political issues.

33. Annex 2 in Rocha and Vittas (2010) reviews the variation and dispersion of annuity prices in the United Kingdom using data obtained from the Web site of the U.K. Financial Services Authority. Rocha and Thorburn (2007) underscore the dispersion of annuity prices in Chile.

34. These two problems were experienced in Switzerland between 1985 and 2002. A fixed annuity conversion factor was imposed in 1985 on the decentralized market when the mandatory pillar was introduced. This factor was set at 7.2 percent, was the same for single and joint life annuities, and was kept constant for 17 years despite large fluctuations in interest rates and a secular increase in longevity. It caused significant transfers from single male to female pensioners and also put the finances of pension funds under considerable strain (Bütler and Ruesch 2007).

35. When this approach is followed, care must be taken to avoid specifying a similarly low rate of interest for the creation of technical reserves. Such a misguided approach will force annuity providers to maintain unnecessarily high levels of reserves and allow little room for investing in higher-yielding assets. For a discussion of this point in the context of payout policies in some transitioning European countries, see Vittas, Rudolph, and Pollner (2010).

36. The valuation of illiquid assets can become highly problematic, as has been highlighted by the recent experience of the market for subprime mortgage securities. A prudent institution would invest only a small proportion of its assets in such potentially illiquid and unstable markets.

37. The real return on inflation-protected securities tends to be low, mainly because in most countries only governments issue such securities (Chile is a notable exception). If long-term inflation-protected corporate and mortgage bonds were also available, the differential in real returns between fixed real and fixed nominal annuities would be smaller.

38. A reversion rate higher than 50 percent is advisable because of the presence of significant household economies of scale.

References

Andersen, Carsten, and Peter Skjodt. 2007. "Pension Institutions and Annuities in Denmark." Policy Research Working Paper 4437, World Bank, Washington, DC.

Antolín, Pablo. 2008. "Ageing and the Payout Phase of Pensions, Annuities, and Financial Markets." OECD Working Paper on Insurance and Private Pensions 29, Organisation for Economic Co-operation and Development, Paris.

Babbel, David F., and Craig B. Merrill. 2006. "Rational Decumulation." Wharton Financial Institutions Center Working Paper 06–14, Wharton School, University of Pennsylvania, Philadelphia.

Blake, David. 1999. "Annuity Markets: Problems and Solutions." *Geneva Papers on Risk and Insurance* 24 (3): 358–75.

Blake, David, Andrew Cairns, and Kevin Dowd. 2008. "Turning Pension Plans into Pension Planes: What Investment Strategy Designers of Defined Contribution Pension Plans Can Learn from Commercial Aircraft Designers." Discussion Paper PI-0806, Pensions Institute, London.

Blake, David, and Robert Hudson. 2000. *Improving Security and Flexibility in Retirement: Full Technical Report.* London: Retirement Income Working Party.

Brown, Jeffrey R., Olivia S. Mitchell, and James M. Poterba. 2001. "The Role of Real Annuities and Indexed Bonds in an Individual Accounts Retirement Program." In *The Role of Annuity Markets in Financing Retirement*, ed. Jeffrey R. Brown, Olivia S. Mitchell, James M. Poterba, and Mark J. Warshawsky, 107–52. Cambridge, MA: MIT Press.

Bütler, Monika, and Martin Ruesch. 2007. "Annuities in Switzerland." Policy Research Working Paper 4438, World Bank, Washington, DC.

Cardinale, Mirko, Alex Findlater, and Mike Orszag. 2002. "Paying Out Pensions: A Review of International Annuities Markets." Research Report 2002–RU07, Watson Wyatt, Arlington, VA.

Davis, E. Philip. 2000. "Issues in the Regulation of Annuities Markets." CeRP Working Paper 26/02, Center for Research on Pensions and Welfare Policies, Turin, Italy.

Dus, Ivica, Raimond Maurer, and Olivia S. Mitchell. 2003. "Betting on Death and Capital Markets in Retirement: A Shortfall Risk Analysis of Life Annuities versus Phased Withdrawal Plans." MRRC Working Paper 2003–063, Michigan Retirement Research Center, University of Michigan, Ann Arbor.

Fornero, Elsa, and Elisa Luciano, eds. 2004. *Developing an Annuity Market in Europe*. Cheltenham, U.K.: Edward Elgar.

Hu, Wei-Yin, and Jason Scott. 2007. "Behavioral Obstacles to the Annuity Market." Pension Research Council Working Paper 2007–10, Wharton School, University of Pennsylvania, Philadelphia.

Impavido, Gregorio, Craig W. Thorburn, and Mike Wadsworth. 2003. "A Conceptual Framework for Retirement Products: Risk Sharing Arrangements between Providers and Retirees." Policy Research Working Paper 3208, World Bank, Washington, DC.

James, Estelle, Xue Song, and Dimitri Vittas. 2001. "Annuity Markets around the World: Money's Worth to Annuitants and How Do Insurance Companies Cover It?" CeRP Working Paper 16/01, Center for Research on Pensions and Welfare Policies, Turin, Italy.

James, Estelle, and Dimitri Vittas. 2000. "The Decumulation (Payout) Phase of Defined Contribution (DC) Pillars: Policy Issues in the Provision of Annuities and Other Benefits." Policy Research Working Paper 2464, World Bank, Washington, DC.

Milevsky, Moshe A. 2005. "Real Longevity Insurance with a Deductible: Introduction to Advanced-Life Delayed Annuities (ALDA)." *North American Actuarial Journal* 9 (4): 109–22.

Milevsky, Moshe A., and Chris Robinson. 2000. "Self-Annuitization and Ruin in Retirement." *North American Actuarial Journal* 4 (4): 112–29.

Milevsky, Moshe A., and Virginia R. Young. 2002. "Optimal Asset Allocation and the Real Option to Delay Annuitization: It's Not Now-or-Never." Discussion Paper PI-0211, Pensions Institute, London.

Mitchell, Olivia S., James M. Poterba, Mark J. Warshawsky, and Jeffrey R. Brown. 2001. "New Evidence on the Money's Worth of Individual Annuities." In *The Role of Annuity Markets in Financing Retirement*, ed. Jeffrey R. Brown, Olivia S. Mitchell, James M. Poterba, and Mark J. Warshawsky, 71–106. Cambridge, MA: MIT Press.

Palacios, Robert, and Rafael Rofman. 2001. "Annuity Markets and Benefit Design in Multipillar Pension Schemes: Experience and Lessons of Four Latin American Countries." Pension Reform Primer Paper 107, World Bank, Washington, DC.

Palmer, Edward. 2008. "The Market for Retirement Products in Sweden." Policy Research Working Paper 4748, World Bank, Washington, DC.

Rocha, Roberto, and Craig Thorburn. 2007. *Developing Annuities Markets: The Experience of Chile.* Washington, DC: World Bank.

Rocha, Roberto, and Dimitri Vittas. 2010. "Designing the Payout Phase of Pension Systems: Policy Issues, Constraints, and Options." Policy Research Working Paper 5289, World Bank, Washington, DC.

Scott, Jason S., John G. Watson, and Wei-Yin Hu. 2007. "Efficient Annuitization: Optimal Strategies for Hedging Mortality Risk." Pension Research Council Working Paper 2007–09, Wharton School, University of Pennsylvania, Philadelphia.

Swiss Re. 2008. "Innovative Ways of Financing Retirement." Sigma Study 4, Swiss Re, Zurich, Switzerland.

Valdés-Prieto, Salvador. 1998. "Risks in Pensions and Annuities: Efficient Designs." Social Protection Discussion Paper 9804, World Bank, Washington, DC.

Vittas, Dimitri. 2008. "A Short Note on the ATP Fund of Denmark." Policy Research Working Paper 4505, World Bank, Washington, DC.

Vittas, Dimitri, Gregorio Impavido, and Ronan O'Connor. 2008. "Upgrading the Investment Policy Framework of Public Pension Funds." Policy Research Working Paper 4499, World Bank, Washington, DC.

Vittas, Dimitri, Heinz Rudolph, and John Pollner. 2010. "Designing the Payout Phase of Funded Pension Pillars in Central and Eastern European Countries." Policy Research Working Paper 5276, World Bank, Washington, DC.

Webb, Anthony, Guan Gong, and Wei Sun. 2007. "An Annuity People Might Actually Buy." Issue in Brief 7–10, Center for Retirement Research, Boston College, Chestnut Hill, MA.

CHAPTER 3

The Payout Phase of Pension Systems

A Comparison of Five Countries

This chapter provides a comparative summary of the payout phase in five countries: Australia, Chile, Denmark, Sweden, and Switzerland. All five countries have large pension systems with mandatory or quasi-mandatory retirement savings schemes that are mostly based on defined contribution (DC) plans. But they also exhibit important differences in the structure and role of different pillars, in the regulation of payout options, in the level of annuitization, in market structure, in capital regulations, and in risk management and use of risk-sharing arrangements. The different institutional and regulatory arrangements provide a rich set of experiences that may be useful and relevant for other countries that are reforming their pension systems.

The chapter is structured as follows. First the chapter provides an overview of the pension systems of the five countries, focusing on the relative role of different pillars and highlighting the target replacement rates in each country. Then the chapter examines the menu of available products and discusses the crucial role that product and marketing regulation plays in shaping the total market. It also summarizes information on the level of annuitization that prevails in each country. The chapter then focuses on the regulation of providers of retirement products, looking in turn at institutional arrangements, the prevalence of centralized or decentralized management, and the design of investment and capital regulations. It also briefly discusses risk management issues and the role of risk-sharing arrangements. The chapter concludes with a summary of policy lessons for other countries.

Overview of Pension Systems

This section provides an overview of pension systems, focusing on the systems of the five countries.

Overall Structure of Pension Systems

All five countries covered in this chapter have well-developed pension systems. As shown in table 3.1, they all have a multipillar structure combining public and private provision, including a mandatory or quasi-mandatory private pillar. All countries have a zero public pillar providing basic benefits, but the level of provision varies considerably. Only Sweden and Switzerland have contributory and earnings-related public schemes (first pillars). Denmark and Sweden have supplementary public schemes—the Labor Market Supplementary Pension (Arbejdsmarkedets Tillaegspension, or ATP) in Denmark and the Premium Pension Authority (Premiumpensionsmyndigheten, or PPM) in Sweden—that are mandatory and fully funded and operate alongside the private occupational funds. All five countries have voluntary third pillars for additional provision and for self-employed workers.

Table 3.2 describes in greater detail the overall structure of the five pension systems. More details on the benefits and costs of different pillars are offered below.

Structure and Cost of Public Pillars

There are large differences in the structure of the zero pillars among these five countries (table 3.3). Australia and Denmark offer universal pensions

Table 3.1   Structure of the National Pension Systems

Country	Pillar 0	Pillar 1	Pillar 2	Pillar 3
Australia	Yes	No	Yes	Yes
Chile	Yes	No	Yes	Yes
Denmark	Yes	No	Yes, plus supplementary scheme	Yes
Sweden	Yes	Yes	Yes, plus supplementary scheme	Yes
Switzerland	Yes	Yes	Yes	Yes

Sources: Andersen and Skjodt 2007; Brunner and Thorburn 2008; Bütler and Ruesch 2007; Palmer 2008; Rocha and Rudolph 2010; Rocha and Thorburn 2007; Vittas 2008; chapters 4 to 8 of this book.

Table 3.2 Overall Structure of the National Pension Systems

Country	Public unfunded pensions (pillars 0 and 1)	Mandatory or quasi-mandatory funded pensions (pillar 2)	Voluntary funded pensions (pillar 3)
Australia	Universal pension financed from general tax revenues and subject to clawback provisions	Occupational system, operating mostly DC plans, provided through corporate, industry, or retail funds	Voluntary plans for additional provision and for self-employed workers
Chile	Means-tested universal pension and declining supplement to low-income pensioners, financed from general tax revenues and a sovereign fund	Open pension funds operating DC plans and managed by independent pension fund administrators	Voluntary plans for additional provision and for self-employed workers, offered by pillar 2 pension funds and other financial institutions
Denmark	Two schemes that are subject to clawback provisions: • Universal pension financed from general tax revenues • Supplement to low-income pensioners	Two types of schemes: • Public schemes (mainly the ATP) operating DC plans • Occupational funds and insurance companies operating mostly DC plans, based on collective labor agreements	Voluntary plans for workers not covered by labor agreements and for additional provision, offered by pension funds, insurance companies, and banks
Sweden	Two schemes: • Contributory public scheme operating as notional defined contribution plan • Minimum pension guarantee for combined notional defined contribution and financial defined contribution benefits	Two schemes: • Public scheme (PPM) operating funded DC plan • Occupational funds operating mostly DC plans, based on collective labor agreements	Voluntary pension plans for workers not covered by labor agreements and for additional provision, offered by insurance companies and banks
Switzerland	Two schemes: • Contributory DB plan, subject to tight maximum and minimum limits, partly financed from general tax revenues • Means-tested supplement to low-income pensioners	Occupational funds and insurance companies operating mostly DC plans, but with absolute minimum guaranteed return and minimum annuity conversion factor	Voluntary pension plans for self-employed workers not covered by the mandatory pillar and for additional provision, offered by insurance companies and banks

Sources: Andersen and Skjodt 2007; Brunner and Thorburn 2008; Bütler and Ruesch 2007; Palmer 2008; Rocha and Rudolph 2010; Rocha and Thorburn 2007; Vittas 2008; chapters 4 to 8 of this book.

Table 3.3   Structure of Zero Pillars

Country	Type	Replacement rate	Clawback or top-up provisions
Australia	Universal	Single rate: 27.7% of average wage Couples: 41.7% of average wage	Income test: 50% clawback above low-income threshold Asset test: $A 1.5 clawback for each $A 1,000 of assets above threshold
Chile	Universal pension to impoverished old people	Basic pension (PBS): 17.0% of average wage Maximum pension with solidarity (PMAS): 57.0% of average wage	Top-up to pillar 2 pension Means-tested universal pension
Denmark	Universal pension Supplement to low-income pensioners	Combined: 35.0% of average wage	Universal pension: 30% clawback above high-income threshold Supplement: 30% clawback above low-income threshold
Sweden	Minimum pension guarantee for combined notional defined contribution and financial defined contribution benefits	About 30.0% of average wage	Top-up to notional defined contribution and financial defined contribution benefits
Switzerland	Minimum pension from pillar 1 Supplement for impoverished old pensioners	Combined: 24.0% of average wage	Means-tested supplement

Sources: Andersen and Skjodt 2007; Brunner and Thorburn 2008; Bütler and Ruesch 2007; Palmer 2008; Rocha and Rudolph 2010; Rocha and Thorburn 2007; Vittas 2008; chapters 4 to 8 of this book.

financed from general tax revenues. These pensions are subject to clawback provisions.[1] Denmark also pays a supplement to low-income pensioners. The level of the universal benefit is nearly 28 percent of the average wage in Australia for single pensioners and nearly 42 percent for couples. In Denmark, the combined universal pension and supplement amount to 35 percent of average earnings.

Chile closed down its old social security system to new workers when it implemented its pension reform in 1981. However, a new basic solidarity pension (*pensión básica solidaria,* or PBS) was introduced in 2008. The PBS is offered to pensioners who do not have adequate balances to purchase a life annuity above the PBS level. The PBS currently amounts to approximately 17 percent of the average wage. Low-balance workers are compelled to use phased withdrawals (PWs), and the government pays the PBS after their balances have been exhausted. To minimize the probability of triggering the PBS, the 2008 amendments to the pension law require that the calculation of PWs include a fair actuarial factor to account for this risk. The government also tops up any annuity payments that fall below the PBS level. In addition, the government provides pensioners in the lowest 60 percent of the income distribution a supplement that is equal to the PBS less 29.4 percent of the pension income of individual pensioners. The supplement is effectively eliminated when pension income is close to 60 percent of the average wage (the exact point of elimination depends on the level of the PBS relative to the average wage). This level is known as the maximum pension with solidarity support (*pensión máxima con aporte solidario*, or PMAS). The PMAS is gradually increasing and is expected to reach approximately US$600 in July 2011. The new universal pension effectively covers uninsured workers, who represent a significant proportion of all workers because of the continuing large relative importance of the informal labor market.

In Sweden, a minimum pension guarantee of about 30 percent of the average wage covers the combined benefits from the new notional defined contribution (NDC) and financial defined contribution schemes. In Switzerland, benefits from the first pillar are subject to a minimum level that is about 18 percent of the average wage. However, an additional means-tested supplement is paid from general tax revenues to pensioners with no other sources of income. This supplement is estimated at 6 percent of average earnings, bringing the level of the combined benefit to 24 percent of average earnings.

Only Sweden and Switzerland have a first pillar (table 3.4). The first pillar consists of contributory public schemes with earnings-related benefits.

Sweden implemented a radical reform of its pension system in the mid-1990s. A new public unfunded NDC scheme was introduced to replace the preexisting flat and earnings-related defined benefit (DB) pensions. The contribution rate for the NDC scheme is 16 percent of covered earnings. Out-of-employment periods are covered by government contributions; thus, most workers are likely to have full contribution records. The targeted replacement rate for people with average earnings and a normal retirement age amounts to 39 percent.

Table 3.4   Structure of First Pillars

Country	Type	Contribution rate (% of covered earnings)	Targeted replacement rate (%)
Australia	None	n.a.	n.a.
Chile	None	n.a.	n.a.
Denmark	None	n.a.	n.a.
Sweden	Notional defined contribution	16.0	39.0
Switzerland	Defined contribution	8.4	33.0

Sources: Andersen and Skjodt 2007; Brunner and Thorburn 2008; Bütler and Ruesch 2007; Palmer 2008; Rocha and Rudolph 2010; Rocha and Thorburn 2007; Vittas 2008; chapters 4 to 8 of this book.
Note: n.a. = not applicable.

In the NDC scheme, the retirement decision is left to individual workers (within certain limits), but the pension benefit is adjusted to take account of the remaining life expectancy on retirement. NDC balances earn notional interest at 1.6 percent in real terms, and NDC annuities are calculated with cohort life tables and a real rate of interest of 1.6 percent. The NDC annuities are indexed to prices but are adjusted for real wage increases above 1.6 percent. The NDC scheme is supported by five buffer funds that have been created since the introduction of the general supplementary pension scheme in 1960. The buffer funds, known as AP (*allmänna pension*) funds 1 to 4 and 6, have accumulated assets equivalent to 27 percent of gross domestic product (GDP).

Switzerland operates an earnings-related and unfunded first pillar. The contribution rate is 8.4 percent for workers in dependent employment, equally divided between employers and employees. Self-employed workers pay a slightly smaller contribution. The government covers by design 20 percent of old-age benefits and 50 percent of disability benefits. Pension benefits are set within a narrow range with very low dispersion. The maximum pension is double the minimum and amounts to about 36 percent of average earnings. The minimum and maximum benefits are set in Swiss francs by government decision, and their relation to average earnings may vary from year to year. The maximum benefit requires a full contribution history, but most people receive the maximum benefit because even housewives, students, and the unemployed are required to make contributions. The average benefit is close to 33 percent of the average wage.

The cost of public pensions from pillars 0 and 1 varies across the five countries, depending on the demographic structure of the population, the generosity of benefits, and the maturity of the system (figure 3.1).

Figure 3.1   Cost of Old-Age Benefits in Pillars 0 and 1

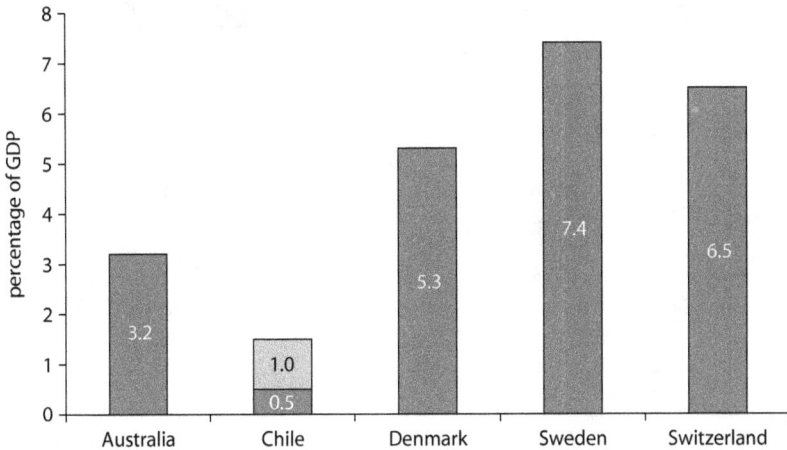

Sources: Andersen and Skjodt 2007; Brunner and Thorburn 2008; Bütler and Ruesch 2007; Budget Directorate 2009; Palmer 2008; Rocha and Rudolph 2010; Rocha and Thorburn 2007; Vittas 2008; chapters 4 to 8 of this book.
Note: The 1.0 percent figure in Chile is the expected annual long-term cost of the new solidarity pillar.

The highest level of cost among the five countries is found in Sweden, at over 7 percent of GDP, followed by Switzerland and Denmark. The high cost of these pensions clearly reflects the high level of public benefits, the universal coverage of the pension systems, and the age structure of the populations. The cost of public pensions is lower in Australia because the level of the age pension is much smaller and the population is significantly younger. The lowest level is found in Chile, mainly because the public benefit is much lower and the pension supplement is paid to low-income pensioners. The younger demographic structure is also a factor.

Structure of Private Pillars

All the countries have mandatory or quasi-mandatory second pillars based on DC schemes, but this pillar is organized differently across countries (table 3.5). In the cases of Denmark and Sweden, the second pillar includes a combination of public and occupational pension funds. In Denmark, the ATP involves centralized administration, asset management, and annuity provision, whereas in Sweden, the PPM has centralized administration and annuity provision but offers participants the option of decentralized asset management during both the accumulation and payout phases. Occupational funds in both countries are

Table 3.5   Structure of Second Pillars

Country	Institutional structure	Type of plan	Contribution rate
Australia	Occupational and open funds	Mostly DC	9%
Chile	Open funds	DC	10%
Denmark	Two schemes: • Public scheme (ATP) • Occupational funds	For both schemes, DC or hybrid	1% for public scheme and 11% for occupational funds
Sweden	Two schemes: • Public scheme (PPM) • Occupational funds	For both schemes, DC	2.5% for public scheme and 3.5–4.5% for occupational funds
Switzerland	Occupational funds operated by foundations and insurers	DC, with minimum investment return and annuity conversion factor	Age-related, 7–18% on coordinated earnings (8–9% on total earnings)

Sources: Andersen and Skjodt 2007; Brunner and Thorburn 2008; Bütler and Ruesch 2007; Palmer 2008; Rocha and Rudolph 2010; Rocha and Thorburn 2007; Vittas 2008; chapters 4 to 8 of this book.

covered by collective labor agreements. In Denmark, the DC schemes are mostly managed by multiemployer funds and life insurance companies; in Sweden, they are managed by multiemployer funds that follow the PPM model.

In the other three countries, the second pillar is operated only by private pension funds, but these funds are structured differently. The Chilean system is operated by open pension funds managed by dedicated pension fund managers, the Swiss system is based on occupational funds managed by single-employer or multiemployer foundations and insurance companies, and the Australian system combines single- or multiemployer occupational funds and retail funds.

Second pillars are now mostly (in Australia, Denmark, Sweden, and Switzerland) or entirely (in Chile) based on DC plans. In Australia, DB plans and especially hybrid funds, which combine elements of DB and DC plans, still have a significant presence. In Denmark, the ATP and some of the occupational funds offer deferred group annuities, which change their character to that of hybrid plans. In Switzerland, the mandatory component of pension plans is stipulated as minimum defined credits in notional retirement accounts. A minimum contribution rate and a minimum interest rate (MIR) are specified, as well as a minimum annuity conversion factor (ACF) on retirement. Both the MIR and ACF were held constant for 17 years after the creation of the mandatory system in 1985, but the MIR is now set annually in line with the level of market rates, and the ACF is set to decline gradually over the next few years until it reaches a more sustainable level.

Contribution rates vary within a rather narrow range. They are lowest in Sweden, where they equal a combined 6 to 7 percent, depending on the type of collective labor agreement (2.5 percent for the PPM and 3.5 to 4.5 percent for occupational plans). In Switzerland, the postulated minimum contribution rates, which vary by age, are calculated on so-called coordinated earnings, which range between 30 percent and 120 percent of average earnings. The average contribution rate, calculated on total earnings, amounted to between 8 percent and 9 percent in 2005.

In Australia, the contribution rate is a flat 9 percent, but the government makes a co-contribution for low-income workers. In 2007, a special one-off additional contribution was allowed for all participants up to $A 1 million (Australian dollars), which explains the very high level of annual contributions in that year.

In Chile, the contribution rate amounts to 10 percent, but Chilean workers also pay an average of 2.2 percent of salaries to cover the cost of group term life and disability insurance and the operating costs and profit margins of pension fund administrators (*administradoras de fondos de pensiónes*, or AFPs). In the other four countries, operating costs are either covered by employers or deducted from investment returns.

Contribution rates vary by collective labor agreement in Denmark. The Organisation for Economic Co-operation and Development's *Pensions at a Glance* study assumes an average contribution rate of nearly 12 percent of earnings, based on contribution rates of the ATP and the collective agreement with the largest coverage (OECD 2007). However, the average contribution rate in Denmark may be significantly lower, as will be discussed later.

The creation of second pillars has generated considerable flows of long-term savings into pension funds (figure 3.2). The level of annual contributions varies from 3.8 percent of GDP in Chile to 8.9 percent in Australia.[2] The higher level in Australia is explained by the near-universal coverage of the second pillar, the government co-contribution, and the fact that covered salaries represent a higher proportion of GDP than in Chile. In the case of Switzerland, annual contributions also cover contributions made for superobligatory benefits.

Denmark and Sweden report lower annual contribution flows relative to GDP, despite the near-universal coverage of their second pillars. In the case of Sweden, the lower flow is explained by the lower contribution rate to second-pillar schemes. However, including premiums paid on

Figure 3.2   Annual Contributions in Second Pillars

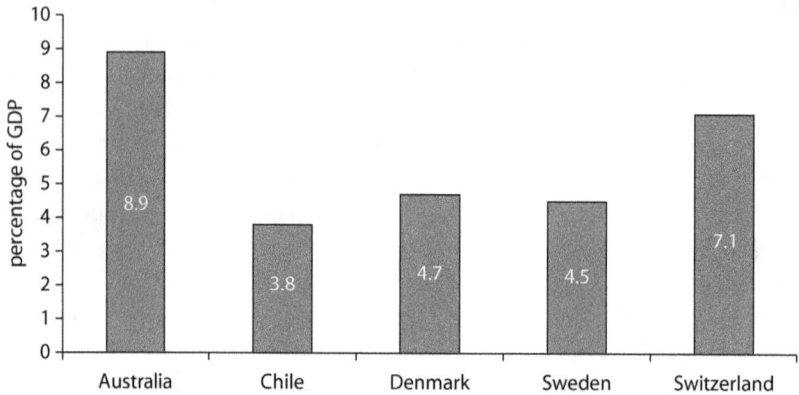

Sources: Andersen and Skjodt 2007; Brunner and Thorburn 2008; Bütler and Ruesch 2007; Palmer 2008; Rocha and Rudolph 2010; Rocha and Thorburn 2007; Vittas 2008; chapters 4 to 8 of this book.

voluntary insurance schemes (third-pillar plans), the total annual contributions amount to 6.7 percent of GDP. In the case of Denmark, the statistics imply that the average contribution rate is lower than the combined rate of 12 percent for the aforementioned ATP and occupational schemes. The combined rate is probably between 8.0 and 8.5 percent. In Denmark, workers contribute an additional 1.4 percent of GDP to personal pension plans.

All countries have third pillars that provide additional benefits and offer coverage to the self-employed and other workers who are not covered by the mandatory and quasi-mandatory second pillars. There are some differences in the organization of voluntary arrangements, but available information does not provide a detailed picture of the structure of third pillars. Voluntary schemes benefit from tax incentives that are particularly powerful in the case of high-income professionals and self-employed people. These individuals also benefit from greater investment freedom and a lighter regulatory burden.

The high level of annual contributions, combined with high investment returns and at least initially low levels of benefits, have resulted in a large accumulation of retirement assets. Available data do not allow a clear identification of assets that have been accumulated on behalf of active workers and assets that support the payout phase. In addition, the statistics on third-pillar assets are not comprehensively and separately identified in all countries.

Figure 3.3   Total Retirement Assets

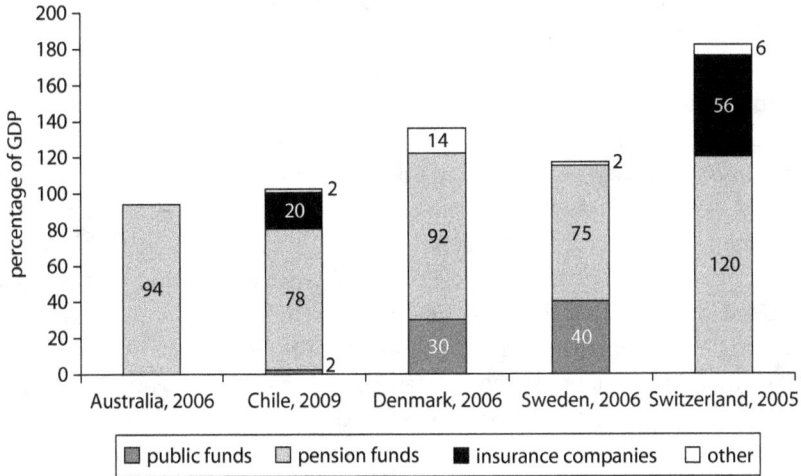

Sources: Andersen and Skjodt 2007; Brunner and Thorburn 2008; Bütler and Ruesch 2007; Palmer 2008; Rocha and Rudolph 2010; Rocha and Thorburn 2007; Vittas 2008; chapters 4 to 8 of this book.

Total assets in the second pillar range from 99 percent of GDP in Switzerland to 75 percent in Sweden (figure 3.3). Switzerland also reports high levels of third-pillar assets with insurance companies and banks, amounting to 23 percent of GDP. In Denmark and Sweden, third-pillar assets held with insurance companies are reported together with second-pillar assets. Those held with banks amounted to 18 percent of GDP in Denmark and 2 percent of GDP in Sweden.

Denmark and Sweden also report high levels of assets with public pension funds. In Denmark, these represent the accumulated assets of the ATP and a couple of smaller schemes. In Sweden, they include the buffer AP funds that support the benefits of the NDC scheme and the assets accumulated under the PPM scheme. In 2009, Sweden's PPM assets amounted to 12 percent of GDP. In Chile, in addition to pension fund assets, the recently created pension stabilization fund holds assets amounting to 2.3 percent of GDP. Insurers hold assets that amount to about 20 percent of GDP and back the provision of life annuities, and voluntary savings amount to approximately 2 percent of GDP. Australia established the Future Fund in 2006 to act as a demographic buffer fund for the universal old-age pension. Its assets amounted to 4.8 percent of GDP in 2009.

The total retirement assets in both public and private funds ranged from about 146 percent of GDP in Denmark (2008) to about 90 percent in Australia (2009).

Target Replacement Rates

Actual replacement rates (defined as the ratio of the initial benefit to the individual wage at retirement) depend on many factors, such as the generosity of public schemes, the period of contribution, the contribution rates to privately funded schemes, and actual net rates of return on these schemes relative to wage growth. Actual replacement rates also depend on how final balances in funded schemes are converted into streams of retirement income, such as annuities and PWs.

Comparing actual replacement rates across countries has proved difficult, as such a comparison requires detailed information on initial benefits from various pillars as well as on wages at retirement. However, it is possible to estimate target replacement rates by making some basic assumptions about key variables, such as the period of contribution, net rates of return, and the conversion of final second-pillar balances (figure 3.4).

The results are highly sensitive to the retained assumptions, especially the relation between the rate of growth of real wages and the real rate of net investment returns. This chapter specifies three scenarios. Scenario A (in figure 3.4) assumes no accumulation in the funded system. Scenarios B and C assume real net investment returns on the funded system of 3.5 percent per year and 5.0 percent per year, respectively, combined with a 2.0 percent growth of real wages. The calculations assume contributions over 40 years and a retirement life of 20 years. Use of a life annuity is assumed, and everything is indexed to prices.

The target replacement rates also reflect the interaction between the clawback provisions of the public pillars and the replacement rates achieved in the second pillar. In Australia, the replacement rate of the universal pension is set at 27.0 percent of the average wage for single pensioners. If the second pillar achieves a replacement rate of 34.0 percent, as would be the case if the investment return amounts to 3.5 percent (scenario B in figure 3.4), the age pension would be reduced to 14.0 percent of the average wage. But if the second pillar achieves a replacement rate of 54.0 percent, which would result from a 5.0 percent investment return (scenario C in figure 3.4), the public pension would be lowered further, to just 6.0 percent of the average wage.

These calculations imply a severe application of clawback provisions. However, at present, such provisions are not the case. Australia applies

Figure 3.4   Target Replacement Rates under Different Scenarios

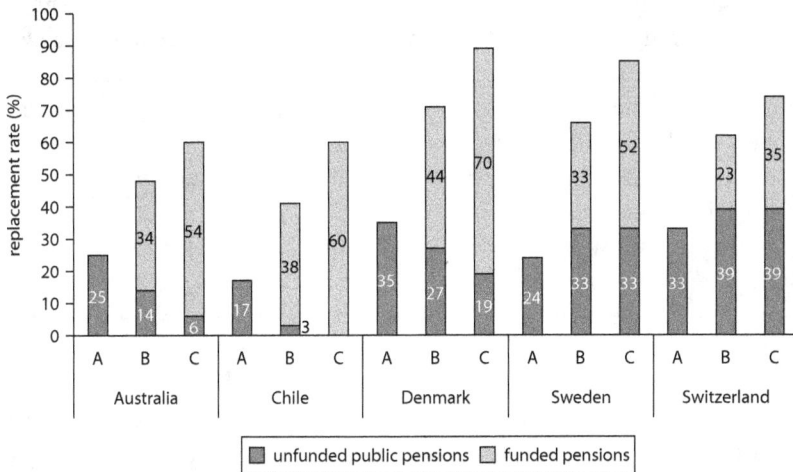

Sources: Andersen and Skjodt 2007; Brunner and Thorburn 2008; Bütler and Ruesch 2007; Palmer 2008; Rocha and Rudolph 2010; Rocha and Thorburn 2007; Vittas 2008; chapters 4 to 8 of this book.
Note: Scenario A = no retirement income from the second pillar; scenario B = 2 percent wage growth and 3.5 percent annual investment return in the accumulation phase; scenario C = 2 percent wage growth and 5 percent annual investment return in the accumulation phase. Calculations assume contributions over 40 years and retirement life of 20 years. Annuities are indexed to prices.

two tests for the clawbacks: (a) an income test that reduces the pension by 50 percent of the excess income above a low-income threshold of about 6 percent of the average wage (11 percent for couples) and (b) an asset test that used to deduct $A 3.0 on the biweekly pension for each $A 1,000 above a high threshold level of assets but since 2007, applies a clawback of only $A 1.5 per thousand.

The universal pension in Australia would be eliminated at a relatively low level of income (69 percent of the average wage for singles and 115 percent for couples) if the tests were strictly applied, but because of the limited use of lifetime income streams and the exemption of owner-occupied houses from the asset test, 53 percent of elderly Australians received the full universal pension in 2007. An additional 27 percent received a reduced age pension, and only 20 percent were not entitled to a public pension. However, in the longer run, when the mandatory system reaches maturity, a growing proportion of retirees likely will not receive the full age pension. Recipients of the full age pension are expected to decline sharply to 38 percent by 2050, and those receiving a reduced pension will grow to 40 percent.

In Denmark, the other country that has clawback provisions, the universal pension and supplement each amount to close to 18 percent of average earnings, yielding a combined benefit of 35 percent. The clawback rate for both benefits is 30 percent above a threshold income. This threshold is about 75 percent of average earnings for the universal pension, but only about 16 percent for the supplement.[3] The vast majority of Danish pensioners receive a universal pension, but a much smaller number receive a supplement.

Figure 3.4 shows that for a Danish worker with average earnings, a 3.5 percent investment return (scenario B in figure 3.4) and a contribution rate of 12 percent would produce a replacement rate of 44 percent from the second pillar. The combined public benefit would fall to 27 percent. If the investment return amounted to 5.0 percent (scenario C in figure 3.4), the replacement rate from the second pillar would equal 70 percent, and the public benefit would fall to 19 percent.[4]

Sweden and Switzerland do not apply clawback provisions to their main public benefits. As a result, the overall replacement rates are quite high, especially in the 5.0 percent investment return scenario. It should be noted, however, that the rules regarding the minimum interest rate and the minimum annuity conversion factor that are applied in the mandatory second pillar in Switzerland would result in a lower replacement rate of 36 percent in the second pillar, at least in the case of funds that do not provide supermandatory benefits.

In Chile, a new top-up benefit is paid to retired workers with low incomes and low balances. A worker with average earnings and a full contribution record would not qualify for the PBS but would receive a top-up benefit (pension solidarity supplement) of approximately 3 percent and 0 percent for portfolios with returns of 3.5 percent and 5.0 percent, respectively. Replacement rates from the second pillar would be 38.0 percent with a 3.5 percent investment return (scenario B in figure 3.4) and 60.0 percent with a 5.0 percent investment return (scenario C in figure 3.4).

Product Regulation and the Level of Annuitization

The regulation of retirement products and the terms and conditions attached to the use of alternative payout options play a major part in the choices that workers make when they retire. The offer of public pensions is another major regulatory factor that also affects the regulatory framework of payout options from the second pillar. This section discusses the differences in product regulation and reviews the prevailing level of annu-itization across the five countries.

Regulation of Payout Options

The five countries covered in this book have adopted different approaches to the regulation of payout options. Australia has the most lib-eral regime of the five countries, and Chile has the most restrictive. In Denmark and Sweden, the supplementary public schemes impose more restrictions than the private plans. Switzerland has a highly restrictive regime, although lump-sum payments are free from government restric-tions (table 3.6).

Australia imposes no restrictions on payout options from the second pillar. Lump sums, term annuities, allocated annuities (which are similar to the Chilean PWs but can be based either on fixed terms or on remain-ing life expectancy), and various types of life annuities are all permitted and left to the choice of individual retirees. The public age pension is a life annuity that is indexed to wages.

In Chile, the basic choice until 2004 was among lifetime PWs, fixed real (inflation-indexed) life annuities, and a combination of temporary lifetime PWs with deferred life annuities. Since 2004, retiring workers have been allowed to use a combination of a minimum pension fixed real annuity and either a PW or a variable annuity. The PBS is a life annuity that is indexed to prices.

Table 3.6   Regulation of Payout Options

Country	Free lump sums	Term annuities	Lifetime PWs	Fixed nominal annuities	Fixed real annuities	Guarantee and bonus annuities	Unit-linked annuities
Australia	Yes	Yes	Yes	Yes	Yes	Yes	Yes
Chile	No[a]	No	Yes	No	Yes	No	Yes
Denmark							
ATP	No	No	No	No	No	Yes	No
Other	No[a]	Yes	No	Yes	No	Yes	Yes
Sweden							
PPM	No	No	No	No	No	Yes	Yes
Other	No	Yes	No	Yes	No	Yes	Yes
Switzerland	Yes	No	No	Yes	No	No	No

Sources: Andersen and Skjodt 2007; Brunner and Thorburn 2008; Bütler and Ruesch 2007; Palmer 2008; Rocha and Rudolph 2010; Rocha and Thorburn 2007; Vittas 2008; chapters 4 to 8 of this book.
a. Restricted lump sums are permitted.

Lump sums are subject to tight restrictions. They are permitted for balances in excess of amounts required to provide specified pension benefits. Before 2004, the specified pension income was set at 50 percent of the retiree's average real earnings over the previous 10 years and 110 percent of the old minimum pension.[5] The 2004 amendments to the pension law raised these parameters to 70 percent and 150 percent, respectively, and also introduced a stricter definition of the average real wage, excluding periods of no contributions. The 2008 amendments to the pension law maintained the 70 percent of the real average wage requirement but replaced the minimum pension requirement with an 80 percent of the PMAS requirement.[6]

Workers meeting these conditions can opt for early retirement, but doing so does not preclude them from continuing to work. Even workers retiring at the normal age of retirement are allowed to continue to work. The rule is therefore more about withdrawal of AFP balances than a retirement provision. However, the potential release of excess balances and access to two incomes explains the prevalence of early retirement and the close association between annuitization and early retirement. The tightening of retirement conditions in 2004 reduced the proportion of early retirees as a share of total retirees from 41 percent to 37 percent between 2004 and 2007.

In Denmark, compulsory use of life annuities is imposed for the public ATP fund, except in the case of very small balances. The menu of payout options is richer in occupational pension plans and includes life annuities, term annuities, and lump sums. Available options depend on the terms of different collective labor agreements. Tax considerations play an important part in shaping individual choices. Public pensions are life annuities that are effectively indexed to wages.

In Sweden, the pattern of payouts is broadly similar to that in Denmark. The main difference is that, in addition to lump sums not being permitted in the public PPM scheme, they also are not permitted in the occupational pension schemes. The main choice in occupational plans is between life and term annuities. Public pensions from the NDC scheme are life annuities that are effectively indexed to wages.

In Switzerland, the basic choice is between lump sums and joint life annuities. The terms and conditions of pension plans are left to be determined by the plans' trustees in consultation with their sponsors. Term annuities and PWs, as well as deferred annuities, are not provided for in the government regulations of the mandatory pillar. Lump sums are not restricted by government regulations but are subject to plan restrictions.

Government rules mandate the offer of an option for a lump-sum com-mutation of at least 25 percent of balances. A three-year notice is required for the exercise of the lump-sum option. Public pensions in Switzerland are paid for life and are linked to the average of price and wage inflation.

Regulation of Life Annuities

In addition to regulating payout options, different countries also apply special rules to particular products. Of particular interest are the regula-tions and rules applied to the offer of life annuities (table 3.7).

The regulation of life annuities is most pervasive in Switzerland, at least as regards the minimum benefits of the mandatory pillar. Switzerland is the only one of the five countries that regulates the pricing of annuities.

Table 3.7   Types of Life Annuities

Country	Price regulation	Types and terms
Australia	None	Various but little demand
Chile	None	Prior to 2004: Fixed real annuities; joint life annuities for men; option for guaranteed annuities (very popular)
		Since 2004: Option of combination of a fixed real annuity (at least equal to PBS for normal age retirees and above 80% of PMAS and 70% of worker's real wage for early retirees) and either a PW or a variable annuity; joint life annuities for both spouses
Denmark		
ATP	Unisex life tables	Guarantee and bonus life annuities; longevity and investment risks shared with participants
Other	Unisex life tables	Guarantee and bonus or unit-linked life annuities; longevity and investment risks shared with participants
Sweden		
PPM	Unisex life tables	Guarantee and bonus or unit-linked life annuities; longevity and investment risks shared with participants
Other	Unisex life tables	Guarantee and bonus or unit-linked life annuities; longevity and investment risks shared with participants
Switzerland	Fully regulated (minimum annuity conversion factor)	Fixed joint life nominal annuities; possibility of bonus

Sources: Andersen and Skjodt 2007; Brunner and Thorburn 2008; Bütler and Ruesch 2007; Palmer 2008; Rocha and Rudolph 2010; Rocha and Thorburn 2007; Vittas 2008; chapters 4 to 8 of this book.

Annuities from the mandatory part of the occupational pillar must take the form of joint life annuities in Switzerland and are subject to a minimum conversion factor. The factor was set to equal 7.2 percent of accumulated balances for nearly the first two decades of the scheme, despite the intervening fall in interest rates and the continuing increase in longevity. The annuity conversion factor was lowered after the collapse of investment returns in the first few years of the new millennium and is scheduled to fall gradually to 6.8 percent by 2014. Stipulating a minimum annuity conversion factor aimed at protecting workers from annual fluctuations of investment returns and interest rates but keeping it unchanged for two decades has underscored the pitfalls of price regulation (Bütler and Ruesch 2007, 53).

The same annuity conversion factor is used for men and women, as well as married and single people. Women have a longer life expectancy and used to retire at a younger age. But the distortion of applying the same conversion factor to men and women is mitigated by the compulsory use of joint life annuities. In addition, the retirement age of women is gradually being raised to that of men. Applying the same uniform annuity conversion factor to single people—especially single men—imposes a heavy penalty on them. Nevertheless, available evidence shows that single men are as likely to use life annuities as are married men.[7]

Chile also applies extensive regulation to the use of life annuities. Until 2004, only fixed real life annuities (that is, annuities linked to inflation) and annuities denominated in a foreign currency (mainly the U.S. dollar) were permitted. Fixed nominal, escalating, and variable (bonus-based or unit-linked) annuities as well as term annuities were not allowed. However, in 2004, the government authorized the use of a combination of a fixed real annuity equal to the minimum pension guarantee (since 2008, the PBS) with either a variable annuity or a program of PWs. Early retirees can opt for a combination of alternatives when the fixed part of the annuity is at least higher than 150 percent of the PBS. The market for variable annuities has not developed yet.

The use of joint life annuities is compulsory for both spouses.[8] Life annuities with guaranteed periods are permitted and are widely used, implying the presence of a strong bequest motive. The guaranteed period ranges between 5 years and 25 years, with most annuitants opting for 10 years or 15 years. Deferred life annuities in conjunction with temporary PWs are permitted but are not widely used. Most deferred annuities go up to one year.

Insurance companies are required to maintain minimum mathematical reserves that are based on prescribed life tables and technical discount rates. Insurance companies are also subject to capital requirements for prudential purposes, but they are free to determine their own annuity prices. In fact, insurance companies change their annuity prices frequently and oscillate between aggressive and passive marketing campaigns.

In Denmark, the public ATP offers deferred group life annuities with guaranteed minimum benefits and annual bonuses that depend on investment performance and longevity experience (Vittas 2008). Guaranteed benefits used to be based on an interest rate of 4.5 percent, but this rate was lowered to 2.0 percent for all new contributions in 2002. A new scheme was introduced in 2008 that converts annual contributions to deferred annuities by using long-term market rates of interest and forward-looking life tables. This scheme applies to 80 percent of annual contributions. The remaining 20 percent is used, together with income from investment and hedging operations, to fund annual bonuses that depend on the overall investment performance and longevity experience of the fund.

The use of life annuities in occupational plans depends on the terms of different collective labor agreements. Some plans offer deferred group annuities with guaranteed annuity conversion factors and allow deductions for the payment of insurance premiums for term life and disability insurance but not for lump-sum withdrawals or term annuities. Other plans are more flexible and permit lump sums, term annuities, or life annuities, and the latter can be deferred or immediate. The choice of payout options must be indicated at the time of contribution and is influenced by the tax treatment of the different options, which has varied over time.

In occupational plans, life annuities can take the form of policies that offer either guaranteed benefits, which are supplemented with annual bonuses that reflect both investment returns and longevity experience, or unit-linked policies. The guaranteed rate in occupational plans used to be 4.5 percent but was lowered to 2.5 percent in 1994 and to 1.5 percent in 1999. Demand for unit-linked products has increased since the fall in guaranteed rates of return, but unit-linked premiums still represent a small fraction of total contributions. The collective labor agreements determine the calculation of initial payments and the distribution of profits between providers and policyholders, but the calculation of technical reserves for both guaranteed benefits and future bonuses is governed by the prudential rules established by the supervisory authority (see the discussion of capital and prudential regulations).

In Sweden, compulsory use of life annuities is required by the public PPM system. Workers have the right, but are not required, to select a joint life annuity. Two types of annuities are offered.

The first type is a profit-participating annuity with minimum guaranteed benefits and annual bonuses that depend on investment performance and also reflect the longevity experience of pensioners. In 2006, the guaranteed rate amounted to 2.75 percent. The total rate of return, including anticipated bonuses, was estimated at 6 percent. In 2007, however, the guaranteed rate was lowered to 0 percent, with the intention to increase the potential for a higher bonus and a higher total return by investing more aggressively in equities and other high-yielding assets.

The PPM uses highly conservative assumptions of future increases in longevity in calculating the guaranteed benefits. The assets backing these annuities are transferred from workers' individual accounts to the PPM, which is responsible for their management. The PPM has adopted a conservative portfolio that comprises 73 percent bonds and 27 percent equities.

The second type of life annuity is a unit-linked variable annuity, in which the investment risk is borne by individual retirees and the longevity risk is shared among the annuitant pool. Asset management is decentralized among authorized asset managers as during the accumulation phase. Most of the small number of PPM retirees have opted for the unit-linked product (Palmer 2008, 47–48).

Life annuities in occupational plans also take the form of either the traditional guarantee and bonus type or the unit-linked type. However, term annuities for 5 or 10 years are permitted and tend to predominate. The calculation of initial payments and the declaration of bonuses are governed by the collective labor agreements that cover the offer of these variable annuities. However, the maintenance of reserves for the guaranteed benefits and for future bonuses is subject to the prudential rules established by the supervisory authority.

Denmark and Sweden require the use of unisex life tables in determining annuity premiums and conversion factors, but annuity providers are otherwise free to set their own prices, subject to the terms and conditions stipulated in collective labor agreements.

All types of life annuities are available in Australia, which imposes no pricing and product restrictions on providers. However, very little use is made of life annuities.

Regulation of Term Annuities and Phased Withdrawals

Term annuities are not allowed in the compulsory pillars of Chile and Switzerland. The Swiss law does not provide for any type of term annuities (or PWs) from pension institutions. Recipients of lump sums can, in principle, purchase such products on the open market but are highly unlikely to do so because the terms of life annuities from the second pillar are more favorable than those products. In Chile, term annuities are not allowed, but lifetime PWs are provided for and even mandated in the case of retiring workers with low balances in their individual accounts (table 3.8).

Term annuities are permitted in Australia but are little used. Term annuities for up to 25 years are allowed in the occupational plans of Denmark and Sweden. These two countries do not have any detailed data on the pattern of payouts, but available evidence from other sources suggests that the use of term annuities of between 5 and 10 years is widespread in occupational pension plans.

In both Denmark and Sweden, term annuities take two forms: guarantee and bonus annuities and unit-linked annuities. In either case, monthly payments are determined on the basis of the term of the annuity and a stipulated interest rate. Then, monthly payments are adjusted once a year to reflect the performance of the fund in which the reserves are invested. The capital is exhausted at the end of the agreed-to term.

Phased withdrawals are a form of term annuities. PWs differ from term annuities in that they can have either a fixed term or a variable term, and

Table 3.8   Types of Term Annuities and Phased Withdrawals

Country	Types and terms
Australia	Term annuities for 5 to 25 years
	Allocated annuities (lifetime phased withdrawals)
Chile	Lifetime phased withdrawals
Denmark	
ATP	Not allowed
Other	Term annuities, mainly for 5 to 10 years
Sweden	
PPM	Not allowed
Other	Term annuities, mainly for 5 to 10 years
Switzerland	Not allowed in the mandatory pillar

Sources: Andersen and Skjodt 2007; Brunner and Thorburn 2008; Bütler and Ruesch 2007; Palmer 2008; Rocha and Rudolph 2010; Rocha and Thorburn 2007; Vittas 2008; chapters 4 to 8 of this book.

withdrawals can vary on the basis of a specified withdrawal rule. PWs may follow the fixed benefit rule or the fixed-percentage benefit rule. The latter is widely used by retirees who adopt self-annuitization plans. However, the most important type is the lifetime or life expectancy PW, in which the withdrawal fraction is set each year equal to the inverse of the remaining life expectancy of the account holder or the remaining joint life expectancy of the account holder and spouse, if a joint benefit is specified.

Use of lifetime PWs is compulsory in Chile for retirees with low account balances—that is, balances that cannot purchase an annuity that is at least equal to the PBS (prior to 2008, the minimum pension guarantee). In those cases, the monthly withdrawal equals the PBS, and when the account balance is exhausted, the government steps in and takes responsibility for continuing payments for the remaining life of beneficiaries. The 2008 amendments to the pension law require the creation of reserves in individual accounts that cover a much higher-than-average life expectancy. The reserves will lower the probability of triggering the PBS and limit the exposure of the government. This change is likely to reduce the relative attractiveness of PWs compared with annuities.

The authorities prescribe rate of return and the life tables that pension companies must use in calculating the annual benefits of PWs. This requirement is linked to the need to prevent abuse of the public pension, because use of an overly generous rate of return and inappropriate life tables in calculating the annual benefit from PWs could accelerate the depletion of account balances and expose the government to larger PBS payments.

Phased withdrawals are known as *allocated annuities* in Australia. They are either life expectancy PWs similar to those used in Chile or fixed-term PWs. The latter often are set equal to life expectancy at retirement. Use of allocated annuities has experienced significant growth. Allocated annuities are fundamentally investment products that are placed in a wide array of instruments, ranging from capital-guaranteed products to market-linked funds. Their balances fluctuate with changes in investment performance. They provide considerable flexibility and access to funds but offer no protection against longevity risk.

Although the choice of payout options has not been restricted in Australia, allocated annuities have been subject to specified rules and restrictions. Until 2007, allocated annuities were subject to both a minimum and a maximum annuity conversion factor. For a 65-year-old beneficiary, the minimum annuity conversion factor was 6.37 percent in 1998, and the maximum was 12.35 percent.[9] The minimum and maximum limits decreased as people grew older. The maximum payment per year aimed at ensuring that the account balance would not be exhausted before the recipient reached age 80, and the minimum payment was the account balance divided by life expectancy at that age.

The imposition of a minimum limit aimed to limit the use of tax-advantaged savings by wealthy retirees and was similar in spirit to the minimum distributions imposed on individual retirement accounts in the United States. However, the imposition of a maximum limit on the annuity conversion factor was not very meaningful in the context of permitting free withdrawals of accumulated balances in the form of lump sums. Changes in the regulations that were implemented in 2007 removed the maximum limit and lowered the minimum limit. The new minimum limit for a 65-year-old beneficiary is 5 percent.

Regulation of Marketing

With the notable exception of Chile and, to a lesser extent, Denmark, life insurance companies have not undertaken aggressive campaigns in marketing annuities (table 3.9). This lack of marketing effort is clearly related

Table 3.9   Marketing Regulation

Country	Types and terms
Australia	Occupational plans are not active providers of annuities. Marketing of annuities is subject to ordinary conduct rules.
Chile	Licensing requirements are in place for pension advisers. Caps are set on their commissions. An electronic quotation system is used.
Denmark	
ATP	No marketing is involved.
Other	Annuities are provided through occupational plans. Marketing focuses on enhancement of brand names, competition for mandates, and declaration of bonuses.
Sweden	
PPM	No marketing is involved other than creation of brand names by decentralized asset managers.
Other	Annuities are provided through occupational plans. Marketing focuses on enhancement of brand names, competition for mandates, and declaration of bonuses.
Switzerland	Annuities are provided through occupational plans. Little marketing is involved in view of federal regulation of products and prices.

Sources: Andersen and Skjodt 2007; Brunner and Thorburn 2008; Bütler and Ruesch 2007; Palmer 2008; Rocha and Rudolph 2010; Rocha and Thorburn 2007; Vittas 2008; chapters 4 to 8 of this book.

to the weak demand for voluntary life annuities in most countries, which is primarily explained by the presence of social security and company pensions. In most countries, life insurance companies focus their marketing activities on promoting life insurance and investment products, including the offer of retirement savings facilities.

Because of the limited marketing effort, regulation of marketing annuities and other options during the payout phase has lagged regulation of saving products in the accumulation phase in all countries except Chile.

In Australia, marketing and selling of annuity products are subject to the same conduct rules, such as the "know your customer" rule and adequate disclosure of the terms and conditions of different products. There is no requirement to offer a minimum number of annuity options or to disclose the level of commissions received from different companies.

In Denmark and Sweden, little individual choice exists in the selection of annuity provider, which is often determined in the collective labor agreement that sets the terms and conditions of different pension plans. Marketing activity is targeted at the trustees of different plans, who may decide to transfer the whole plan to another provider. Life insurance companies and other pension institutions compete by attracting attention to their investment performance record, their bonus distribution policies, and the allocation of profits between shareholders and policyholders.

Marketing activity per se is subject to little regulation, other than observance of typical conduct rules, which are more relevant for the offer of payout options in personal pension plans. Insurance companies and pension funds are free to set their own prices, but under European Union law, they are required to use unisex life tables in calculating annuity prices. Perhaps because the offer of most variable annuities is governed by collective labor agreements, in which representatives of employers and workers monitor the performance of providers and protect the interests of workers, neither Denmark nor Sweden has thus far created a central register with a systematic compilation of performance data on different providers. The complexity of collective labor agreements, which cover many types of benefits, has also impeded the development of a central database. A central register of performance data would be indispensable in a system of non-employer-based individual accounts.

In Switzerland, the scope for marketing is even more limited because the pricing of annuities in the obligatory part of the second pillar is subject to federal regulation. The same annuity conversion factor is used for both men and women, although women live longer and retire earlier than men,[10] and for both joint and single life annuities, even though joint life annuities have a much higher probability of continuing to make payments for a longer period. General conduct rules apply in the case of voluntary personal pension plans.

Chile is the exception among the five countries, probably because of the central role played by open-market annuities in the provision of retirement income after the closing down of the social security system to new entrants and the granting of recognition bonds to workers who joined the private pension pillar. However, the marketing of the two main payout options, PWs and life annuities, is highly asymmetrical and one-sided. The AFPs focus on the very profitable accumulation phase of the pension business and adopt a passive marketing stance on PWs. The commission income that pension companies can generate from offering PWs is a modest fee of about 1 percent of benefit payments, whereas the fees during the accumulation phase, excluding premiums for term life and disability insurance, still amount to close to 15 percent of contribution amounts.

In contrast, life insurance companies engage in very active marketing of annuities, using employees and company agents as well as independent brokers. They have strong incentives to market annuities, which represent the core of their business. Pension advisers play an important part, not only in the choice of the annuity option but also in the decision to retire early.[11] During the 1990s, when commissions paid to brokers reached very high levels of 5 to 6 percent of the value of the annuity contract, brokers reportedly offered kickbacks to their clients, effectively increasing the amount of funds that early retirees could withdraw as lump sums.

Chile extensively regulates marketing activity in the annuity market. Pension advisers have to pass a certification test administered by the supervisory agency as well as a basic "fit and proper" test. Most applicants take a 120-hour course on annuities. Licensed pension advisers are legally obligated to represent their clients and generate their income from commissions on the sale of annuities. They are not permitted to accept volume-related remuneration from insurers. However, they are not required to disclose the level of commissions they receive from different insurers. Pension advisers do not have a self-regulatory body that may sanction or enforce a code of good practices on its associates.[12]

Regulators were concerned during the 1990s about the bias in favor of early retirement, the dispersion of annuity prices, the high level of commissions, and the spread of illegal marketing practices, such as the cash rebates. New rules were adopted in the 2004 and 2008 revisions of the pension system: the conditions for early retirement were tightened, a cap of 2 percent was imposed on annuity commissions, banks were allowed to participate in the distribution of annuities, the menu of retirement products was expanded by allowing use of PWs or variable annuities in combination with fixed real annuities for higher-income individuals, and a new electronic quotation system was introduced.

The electronic quotation system, the Pension Consultations and Offers System (Sistema de Consultas y Ofertas de Montos de Pensión, or SCOMP), has attracted particular interest because it represents an attempt to reduce the influence of brokers in the selection of annuities. The aim is to enhance the quality of information available to consumers as well as to enable direct access to a full range of annuity quotations. Quotations are solicited from SCOMP-participating institutions, and SCOMP validates the personal data of the workers concerned. SCOMP receives quotations from insurers and also calculates the PW and sends this information to the applicants. Workers can select one of the offers made within 15 days or seek another offer outside SCOMP, but only from an insurer who made an offer under SCOMP. The offer made outside SCOMP must be better than the first offer. In addition to the quotation system itself, a list of all potential retirees, including those reaching normal retirement age and those eligible for early retirement, is prepared and circulated to all SCOMP institutions (brokers, insurance companies, and AFPs). This openness further reduces the influence of individual brokers. However, workers who object to the circulation of their personal data can have their names removed from this list.

Level of Annuitization

Ascertaining with a reasonable degree of precision the level of annuitization in different countries is difficult because adequately detailed data are not available. In principle, researchers would like to know the proportion of people who opt for lump sums, the proportion who buy life annuities, and the proportion who use PWs. In practice, however, people may use a combination of payout options, withdrawing part of their balances in lump sums and using the remainder for life annuities or PWs. In those cases, the allocation of balances to each payout option could be weighted, but the information that would be required for making these computations is not available. An alternative approach is to use the proportion of the total accumulated balances of retiring workers that is allocated to each option, but this information is not published in any of the five countries.

Figure 3.5 estimates the level of annuitization in different countries. The figure is based on 100 percent annuitization with universal coverage

Figure 3.5   Level of Life Annuitization

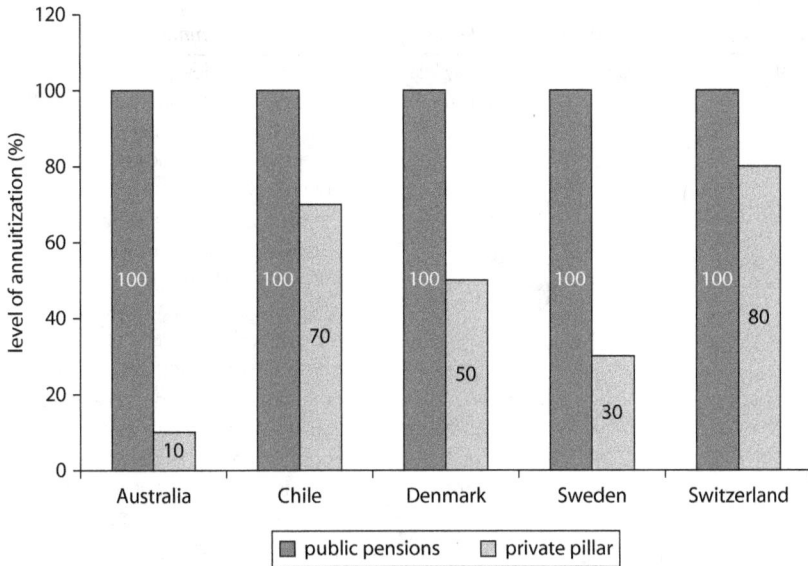

Sources: Andersen and Skjodt 2007; Brunner and Thorburn 2008; Bütler and Ruesch 2007; Palmer 2008; Rocha and Rudolph 2010; Rocha and Thorburn 2007; Vittas 2008; chapters 4 to 8 of this book.

from the public pillars, including, in the case of Denmark and Sweden, the supplementary public ATP and PPM schemes, and in the case of Chile, the PBS. The level of public benefits is between 30 percent and 40 percent of average earnings in Denmark, Sweden, and Switzerland. In Australia, it is lower because only half of pensioners receive the full age pension, and in Chile it is about 17 percent for recipients of the PBS.

Despite the imposition of mandatory or quasi-mandatory participation in funded second pillars, the level of annuitization of accumulated savings in the second pillar varies considerably across the five countries (table 3.10). This variation mostly reflects differences in the menu of permitted payout options, and the menu itself reflects the level of benefits from the public pillars (which take the form of pensions for life and are thus equivalent to full annuitization). In addition to the menu of permitted payouts, the level of annuitization also reflects other factors, such as risk aversion, clawback provisions, tax incentives, and the terms and conditions of annuities.

The estimated level of annuitization from the second pillar is highest in Switzerland, at 80 percent, followed by Chile at 70 percent. It is very

Table 3.10   Level of Annuitization in the Second Pillar

Country	Level of annuitization	Percentage of balances	Comments
Australia	Very low	Probably less than 10%	Lump sums are allowed without restrictions and account for 48% of all payouts from superannuation funds. Retirees also favor allocated and term annuities over life annuities.
Chile	High	About 70%	Lump sums are restricted. The share of annuitants in total retirees exceeds 60% overall and exceeds 70% excluding disability and survivor pensioners. PW holders account for most of the remaining 30%.
Denmark	High	100% for the ATP; 50% for occupational schemes	For the ATP, annuitization is mandatory, except for very low balances. For occupational schemes, annuitization depends on the terms of collective labor agreements. The average level of annuitization is relatively high and is based on choices made during the contribution period: 50% of contributions are allocated to life annuities, 35% to term annuities, and 15% to lump sums.
Sweden	High for PPM; low for occupational schemes	100% for PPM; probably less than 30% for occupational schemes	For PPM, annuitization is mandatory. For occupational schemes, annuitization depends on the terms of collective labor agreements. Lump sums are not permitted in occupational plans, but extensive use is made of term annuities for 5 or 10 years.
Switzerland	High	80% for occupational schemes	Lump sums are allowed, but joint life annuities are favored by the terms and conditions of annuities.

Sources: Andersen and Skjodt 2007; Brunner and Thorburn 2008; Bütler and Ruesch 2007; Palmer 2008; Rocha and Rudolph 2010; Rocha and Thorburn 2007; Vittas 2008; chapters 4 to 8 of this book.

low in Australia, at less than 10 percent. It is probably 50 percent in Denmark and less than 30 percent in Sweden.

In Chile, there are data on the number of retirees who opt for life annuities or PWs and estimates of the proportion of accumulated balances that are converted into life annuities. In 2007, about 62 percent of pensioners selected life annuities, including deferred annuities. However, excluding disability and survivor pensioners, who are covered by group disability and term life insurance and who have no choice in the matter, the share of retirees who selected annuitization rises to 71 percent. No data are published on the size of accumulated balances that are used for PWs, and thus no published data reflect the share of accumulated balances that are annuitized. However, this proportion is also likely to be close to 70 percent.

Most annuities are joint life annuities, reflecting the regulation that forces married males to take this type of annuity. The share of annuities with guaranteed periods is large, and most of these annuities are guaranteed for periods of 10 to 15 years and even longer. The strong demand for guaranteed annuities reveals a preference for bequests.

A very strong association exists between annuitization and early retirement in Chile. Of early retirees, 90 percent buy annuities and only 10 percent use PWs. In contrast, 65 percent of normal age retirees use PWs, and only 35 percent purchase annuities. Of all annuitants, 60 percent are early retirees, and only 15 percent are normal age retirees (the remainder are retirees with disabilities and survivors). If retirees with disabilities and survivors are excluded, the share of early retirees in the stock of annuities increases to 80 percent.

Several factors explain the high level of annuitization and its relation to early retirement. First, restrictions on lump sums have increased the demand for all retirement products, including life annuities. Second, the demand for life annuities has been stimulated by the absence of a front-ended public pillar benefit, while the back-ended minimum pension guarantee has provided a low level of protection to middle- and high-income retirees. Third, the marketing of retirement products has been highly asymmetrical. AFPs have focused on the accumulation phase of the pension business and have not actively marketed PWs. In contrast, life insurance companies have depended on the annuity business and have marketed their products aggressively. Until 2008, insurance brokers were allowed to obtain their income only from commissions on annuity premiums and not from the selling of PWs. They targeted their marketing efforts primarily to higher-income workers, frequently inducing these workers to retire early and annuitize.

In Switzerland, no official statistics exist on the level of annuitization in the second pillar. Published data show the level of annual benefits, divided between annuity payments and capital (lump-sum) payments, but do not report the proportion of accumulated capital of newly retired workers (both under the mandatory and supermandatory parts of the system) that is withdrawn as a lump sum and the part that is converted into a life annuity. The published data also do not report the number of new retirees who convert all their accumulated capital into an annuity, those who withdraw the total capital, and those who withdraw a fraction of the available capital and convert the rest.

Lump-sum payments have fluctuated over the years by between 15 percent and 20 percent of all benefit payments. This fluctuation would imply that the level of annuitization is between 80 percent and 85 percent. The same broad level of annuitization also would be obtained if the size of accumulated balances of retiring workers were estimated on the basis of the change in annual pension payments and the inverse of the regulated annuity conversion factor were applied.[13] This calculation shows that lump-sum payments represent between 20 percent and 25 percent of the total value of balances of retiring workers. On the basis of these calculations, one could reasonably assume that the level of annuitization in the second pillar amounts to 80 percent.

This assumption would be a high level of annuitization, coming on top of the full annuitization of first-pillar benefits. The high level is attributed to the way pension plans are structured. Although no government restrictions exist on lump-sum payments, the rules of most pension funds, which are determined jointly by employer and worker representatives, appear to favor annuitization.[14] The existing strong link between the accumulation and decumulation phases of the second pillar, in which both are with the same sponsor with almost no exceptions, has reinforced the preference for life annuities.

In some plans, individuals are allowed to cash out their old-age savings and could, in principle, purchase another annuity contract on the open market. In practice, almost no one does so, mainly because occupational pension plans offer two advantages over open-market annuities. First, they are not affected by adverse selection problems. Second—and far more important—the regulated annuity conversion factor has been much higher than what could be obtained in the open market.[15]

In Denmark, ATP balances must be converted into life annuities, except for very small account balances, which are paid out as lump sums. The level of annuitization in occupational pension plans depends on the rules specified in different collective labor agreements. Detailed data on payouts are not available, but the level of planned annuitization can be gauged from choices made at the time of contribution. These data are required for tax purposes. Available data indicate that 50 percent of contributions were allocated to life annuities in 2004, down from 60 percent in 2000. Use of lump sums fell from 30 percent to 15 percent, and demand for term annuities rose from 10 percent to 35 percent. Additional immediate or deferred annuitization is possible at retirement, but no information on this option is available (Andersen and Skjodt 2007, 4–21).

In Sweden, use of life annuities is compulsory for the public PPM scheme. Lump sums are not permitted in occupational plans, but extensive use is made of term annuities for 5 or 10 years. As in Denmark, no data are available on payouts, but Palmer (2008, 22) calculates that replacement rates for workers over 75 years old fall drastically to 58 percent of income at age 65, compared with 74 percent for retirees between ages 65 and 74. Though other factors may explain part of this decline, Palmer infers that the decline is mainly the result of the extensive use of term annuities from occupational pension plans. Use of life annuities is likely to be low, although no detailed data are available.

The level of annuitization is low in Australia, but obtaining reliable estimates of the actual use of lifetime income streams is very difficult. Readily available data show that lump sums have been declining steadily in recent years as a proportion of total benefits, and pension payments have correspondingly increased. From a level of nearly 20 percent in 2002, pension payments rose to 52 percent of total benefit payments in 2009.

Large differences exist in the composition of benefit payments across different types of pension funds. Pension payments accounted for 69 percent of total benefits in public pension funds in 2007, but they represented 30 percent in retail funds and had even smaller shares in corporate and industry funds.

The large majority of pension payments involve term and allocated income streams that are not paid for life. Allocated and term annuities have been far more popular than life annuities and have accounted for more than 80 percent of all balances invested in regular income streams. Assets backing life annuities represent less than 2 percent of the total assets of life insurers and correspond to less than 0.5 percent of GDP.

The preference for lump sums has been reinforced by the clawback provisions of the age pension. The age pension is subject to both income and asset tests. However, for a number of years in the 1970s and 1980s, the asset test had been suspended, encouraging retirees to opt for lump sums and avoid regular income streams. Even after its reintroduction, the asset test was significantly less onerous than was the income test. The preference for lump sums also reflects a strong inclination for greater control and flexibility in financial management and for reliance on self-annuitization.

In summary, the main factors that have affected the level of annuitization have been restrictions on lump-sum payments and other payout options, the presence and rules of public schemes, the intensity of marketing, and the prevailing mentality.

Restrictions can be legal restrictions imposed by the government or plan restrictions applied by the sponsors and trustees of occupational plans. The presence and rules of public schemes play an important part, as shown by the experience of the zero and first pillars everywhere and by the experience of the ATP in Denmark and the PPM in Sweden. The absence of a public pillar pension for middle- and high-income workers in Chile is a notable factor. An important third factor is the intensity of marketing activity, which has been underscored by the role of insurance brokers in Chile. Finally, culture and tradition also play their part, as is highlighted by the prevailing pension mentality in Switzerland, which contrasts sharply with the lump-sum mentality in Australia.

In the case of Chile, the more restrictive menu is justified, given the key role of the second pillar. Inflation-indexed life annuities protect against investment, inflation, and longevity risks, and joint life annuities for married couples extend longevity insurance to spouses. The more liberal rules for occupational schemes in Denmark and Sweden also seem justified, given the high level of annuitization in the zero and first pillars and in the public schemes in the second pillars of the two countries. Use of short-term annuities allows higher payouts in the first years of retirement. This approach responds to public demand, especially in countries that have well-developed national health systems.

The very high level of annuitization in Switzerland is partly explained by restrictions on lump-sum payments in plan rules that may have led to overannuitization. The recent government regulation that introduced an obligation that pension plans offer an option of a minimum 25 percent lump-sum payment is probably a response to public demand and an attempt to correct the emphasis on annuitization.

The Australian case is more intriguing. The rapid growth of the second pillar would call for some restrictions on lump-sum withdrawals and for a greater promotion of annuitization. There is an inherent contradiction in mandating workers to save for retirement during their working lives but allowing unrestricted access to lump sums in retirement. However, the historical application of clawback provisions for the universal pension has encouraged the emergence of a so-called lump-sum mentality, whereas the public has shown a strong preference for flexibility and financial control over retirement wealth.

The Value of Annuities and Money's Worth Ratios

Money's worth ratios (MWRs) measure the value of an annuity to its purchaser at the time the annuity is bought. The MWR is defined as the ratio of the expected value of benefits payable under the contract to the paid premium. A cohort life table and an interest rate yield curve are required to calculate the present value of promised benefits.

MWRs are calculated by using two life tables, one covering the general population and the other covering the population of annuitants. Two interest rate yield curves are used, one based on risk-free interest rates on government bonds and the other based on interest rates on corporate bonds. In most countries, calculations are based on annuity quotes, as data on sold annuities are not readily available. Chile is a major exception because it has a very rich database on sold annuities.

The calculation based on the population of annuitants and corporate bond rates reflects the expected longevity experience of annuitants and the risk of insurance insolvency faced by them, especially when insurance companies invest primarily in corporate bonds. However, country comparisons are often focused on calculations based on the general population and government bond rates because the underlying data are more reliable. Moreover, in countries where the corporate bond market is underdeveloped and insurers invest primarily in government bonds, use of the risk-free rate would be more appropriate. Use of the risk-free rate would also be appropriate when governments guarantee annuity payments, at least up to the level of the government-guaranteed benefits.

An MWR that is close to unity, perhaps around 0.97, would indicate an efficient and competitive annuity market that offers fair prices to annuitants. This MWR would allow for a 3 percent load factor to cover commissions paid to brokers and other expenses as well as risk premiums and profit margins. In most countries where such calculations have been made, MWRs based on the annuitant population and government bond (risk-free) rates have been higher or close to this level. But MWRs based on corporate bond rates have been significantly below this level. This situation has reflected higher load factors because of higher expenses and higher risk premiums resulting from greater uncertainty about future longevity and asset-liability mismatching.

In the country studies commissioned for this project, MWRs were calculated for only two countries, Chile and Switzerland, and in the latter case, only for annuities from the mandatory component of the second pillar. In Australia, the very small size of the annuity market did not warrant a detailed calculation of MWRs, and in Denmark and Sweden, the calculation was impeded by the lack of data on ex ante and ex post bonus payments. Without detailed data on bonus payments, the calculation of MWRs, based only on minimum guaranteed benefits, would have been meaningless.

The calculated MWRs are very high in both Chile and Switzerland. Joint life indexed annuities in Chile had an MWR of 1.078 in March 2004, when discounted by the government bond yield curve and based on cohort annuitant tables. However, the MWR fell to 0.892 when corporate bond rates were used (Rocha and Thorburn 2007, 172).

In Switzerland, the MWR for joint life nominal annuities of the second pillar amounted to 1.152 in 2004, when discounted by the government bond yield curve. The very high MWR reflects the use of a fixed annuity conversion factor of 7.2 percent at a time of very low interest rates. In 2000, when interest rates were much higher, the MWR stood at 1.025 (the five-year bond rate equaled 3.80 percent in 2000 against 2.36 percent in 2004).

The MWRs in Chile and Switzerland compare favorably with those prevailing in other countries, indicating that they may not be sustainable in the longer run (table 3.11). Switzerland has already decided to gradually lower the uniform annuity conversion factor in its second pillar, and in Chile, use of improved mortality data and greater appreciation of the long-term risks of annuities may contribute to a lowering of MWRs.

Table 3.11   Money's Worth Ratios for Joint Life Annuities as Calculated Using Cohort Annuitant Tables

Country	Government bond rates	Corporate bond rates
Indexed		
Chile, 2004	1.078	0.892
United Kingdom, 2002	0.880	—
Nominal		
Switzerland, 2004	1.152	—
United Kingdom 1999	0.987	0.873
United States, 2000	0.929	0.841
Canada, 1999	0.980	0.868

Source: Bütler and Ruesch 2007; Rocha and Thorburn 2007.
Note: — = not available.

Provider Regulation

The regulation of providers of retirement products covers both the providers of annuities (which are usually life insurance companies) and the providers of PWs (which are usually the pension institutions that handle the accumulation accounts). The regulatory framework includes the institutional structure of the market, the regulation of investments, and solvency regulations. The solvency regulations relate to the valuation of assets, the measurement of liabilities, and the application of risk-based capital rules. Investment and capital regulations aim to ensure the solvency of annuity providers and play a crucial part in protecting the interests of policyholders. This section also discusses country approaches to risk management and risk sharing.

Institutional Structure

Most countries have adopted a competitive decentralized institutional structure in which multiple pension institutions and life insurance companies compete in providing retirement products, subject to the product regulations and restrictions on payout options discussed in the preceding section. In Chile, only institutions specializing in life insurance and pension fund administration are authorized to offer retirement products. These institutions are set up as profit-seeking institutions. In the other four countries, participating institutions also include not-for-profit mutual groups, such as industry funds in Australia, multiemployer pension funds in Denmark and Sweden, and pension foundations in Switzerland (table 3.12).

Sweden and, to a lesser extent, Denmark have also created a centralized structure for a significant component of their retirement systems. Sweden established a centralized structure for the funded component of its public pillar. Centralized administration lowers operating costs because of scale economies and avoidance of high marketing costs, and the centralized offer of life annuities benefits from use of a larger customer base and thus more efficient risk pooling. The centralized institution, the PPM, is a state institution.

During the accumulation phase, the PPM offers centralized administration, and asset management is decentralized among a large number of approved asset managers that offer an even larger number of investment funds. Individual participants select the asset managers and investment funds. The PPM collects all individual mandates and transfers funds to the asset managers without revealing the names of their clients.

Table 3.12   Institutional Structure

Country	Types and terms
Australia	Decentralized competitive structure
	High operating costs and fees in retail funds
	Weak marketing of life annuities
Chile	Competitive but highly concentrated structure in accumulation phase and phased withdrawals
	High operating fees and profit margins
	Competitive decentralized structure for life annuities
	Price competition and high money's worth ratios
Denmark	
ATP	Centralized administration and asset management during both accumulation and payout phase
Other	Decentralized structure
	Competition for plan mandates among multiemployer funds and life insurance companies
	Accumulation and payout phase by the same institution, subject to pension plan rules
Sweden	
PPM	Centralized administration but decentralized asset management during accumulation phase
	Centralized administration, longevity risk pooling, and asset management for traditional annuities
	Centralized administration and longevity risk pooling but decentralized asset management for unit-linked annuities
Other	Four large multiemployer schemes with similar structure to PPM
Switzerland	Decentralized and fragmented structure among foundations and insurance companies
	Accumulation and payout phase by same institution governed by pension plan rules
	Pervasive product and price regulations

Sources: Andersen and Skjodt 2007; Brunner and Thorburn 2008; Bütler and Ruesch 2007; Palmer 2008; Rocha and Rudolph 2010; Rocha and Thorburn 2007; Vittas 2008; chapters 4 to 8 of this book.

During the payout phase, retiring workers are compelled to use the life annuities offered by the PPM on a centralized basis. Two types of life annuities are provided: (a) profit-participating annuities with minimum guaranteed benefits and annual bonuses and (b) unit-linked annuities. The first are managed centrally by the PPM, which assumes the investment risk of guaranteed benefits but declares annual bonuses on the basis of investment performance and longevity experience. For unit-linked annuities, a pattern similar to that of the accumulation phase is used: centralized administration, including centralized longevity risk pooling by the

PPM, and decentralized asset management, based on decisions of individual annuitants. Retirees bear the investment and longevity risk, the latter through risk pooling with other annuitants.

The institutional structure of the four main occupational funds (for salaried employees, blue-collar workers, local government employees, and civil servants) follows a pattern similar to the PPM's. A central agency in each plan collects contributions and organizes benefits, and decentralized asset managers are chosen by workers who opt for unit-linked annuities. The main difference is that occupational plan benefits are for the most part provided in the form of 5- or 10-year term annuities.

Denmark follows a mixed approach. In the case of the ATP (the supplementary public fund), account administration, risk pooling, and asset management are all centralized. However, in occupational and personal pension plans, a high degree of decentralization occurs. In occupational pension plans, much depends on the rules of collective labor agreements. Insurance companies and multiemployer pension funds compete for winning occupational mandates. Individual workers have limited choice. Most insurance companies are profit-seeking commercial entities, but multiemployer pension funds and some insurance companies are organized as mutual not-for-profit institutions. In Denmark and Sweden, the determination of annual bonuses and the distribution of net investment returns between policyholders and shareholders are important issues.

Switzerland has a highly decentralized structure and its system suffers from a high degree of fragmentation, reflecting the presence of a large number of pension funds. However, the extensive product and price regulation of the payout phase limits the scope for competition and excessive spending on marketing campaigns, while pension plan rules restrict the choice of individual workers, during both the accumulation and the payout phases. The only workers in the mandatory pillar who have individual choice are those who decide to commute to a lump sum all or a substantial part of their pension balances.

Australia probably has the most decentralized structure, with large numbers of insurance companies and superannuation funds competing in a market that is not constrained by pervasive product and price controls. Some of the institutions are single-employer or multiemployer funds that operate as not-for-profit entities, and a significant number are set up as master trusts, owned and operated by profit-seeking financial groups. Retail funds have high operating costs and fees, which result in significantly lower net investment returns. The apparent preference of retiring workers for lump sums limits the potential for aggressive marketing campaigns in the selling of life annuities. Pension institutions focus on promoting allocated annuities, which are effectively investment products. Use of life annuities declined in recent years from very low levels, even though the share of lump sums in total benefit payments also experienced a fall. Term and allocated annuities have experienced significant increases.

Chile has a system that is based on a competitive decentralized structure. AFPs and life insurance companies are established as profit-seeking commercial undertakings. Strong competition exists among a small number of AFPs in the accumulation market and among a larger number of insurance companies in the annuity market. The competitive environment has resulted in large marketing costs, mostly taking the form of high commissions paid to agents and brokers. However, a growing consolidation of the two markets (which is much more pronounced among pension administrators), the threat of regulation, and the adoption of informal agreements among competing institutions in the two main segments of the market have resulted in a major containment of marketing costs. AFPs operate with high operating fees and high profit margins. Life insurance companies engage in greater price competition, which has resulted in thinner margins and high MWRs.

As a mechanism to induce price competition in the accumulation phase, a recent change in the regulation requires all new entrants to the pension system to be allocated, for a period of two years, to the pension fund that levies the lowest fee. A public auction conducted by the pensions' supervisor is used to identify the AFP that would manage the contributions of the new entrants to the system. The winner has to offer the same fee to the rest of its affiliates. The first auction took place in February 2010, and the winner offered a fee that was 24 percent lower than the weighted average fee of the industry. Interestingly, the winner was a new AFP that did not face the high marginal cost that lowering operating fees to existing affiliates would have implied.

Capital and Prudential Regulations

Financial institutions used to be subject to highly restrictive investment regulations in most countries. Ostensibly the regulations had a prudential objective, but in practice it was often mixed with fiscal and macroeconomic objectives. In general, investment regulations have not been binding and have been significantly liberalized over time. Investment regulations have a greater effect on annuity providers because of the paramount need to avoid asset and liability mismatching. However, this issue has increasingly been tackled by capital and prudential regulations.

The capital and prudential regulation of providers of retirement products depends on the type of products they offer and the risks they assume (table 3.13). Such regulations have a greater effect on fixed nominal or real annuities if providers assume the investment and longevity risks. They are less onerous for products that transfer the risk to pensioners.

In the case of PWs, in which pensioners assume both the investment and longevity risks, capital regulation is relatively simple, as is clearly shown by the experience of the Chilean AFPs, which are not allowed to offer annuities and can provide only PWs. In contrast, the capital

Table 3.13   Capital and Prudential Regulations

Country	Main regulations by type of institution
Australia	*Superannuation funds*
	No capital buffer requirement
	Actuarial funding and solvency certificate
	Own life tables and discount rates subject to review
	Licensing of trustees
	Life insurance companies
	Solvency margins on wind-up basis
	Capital adequacy margins on a going-concern basis
	Own life tables and discount rates subject to review
	Close monitoring of free assets and target surplus
Chile	*Pension fund administrators*
	Capital adequacy requirement (*encaje*)
	Market valuation of assets
	Life insurance companies
	Capital adequacy requirement
	"Held to maturity" valuations
	Prescribed life tables
	Calce rule discount rates and capital backing for mismatched asset-liability maturity bands
Denmark	
ATP	Broadly similar to occupational funds
Other	*Life insurance companies and pension funds*
	Solvency I capital requirement
	Fair value accounting
	Decomposition of technical provisions
	Use of market-based maturity-dependent discount rates
	Own life tables subject to review
	Application of static stress testing

(continued next page)

Table 3.13 (continued)

Country	Main regulations by type of institution
Sweden	
PPM	Broadly similar to occupational funds
Other	*Life insurance companies and pension funds*
	Solvency I capital requirement
	Fair value accounting
	Own life tables subject to review
	Own discount rates subject to ceiling
	Application of static stress testing
Switzerland	*Pension funds*
	Combination of book and market valuations
	Own life tables and discount rates subject to review
	Temporary underfunding permitted
	Expert certificate requirement
	Life insurance companies
	Solvency I capital requirement
	No underfunding allowed
	Own life tables and discount rates subject to review
	Combination of book and market valuations
	Application of static stress testing

Sources: Andersen and Skjodt 2007; Brunner and Thorburn 2008; Bütler and Ruesch 2007; Palmer 2008; Rocha and Rudolph 2010; Rocha and Thorburn 2007; Vittas 2008; chapters 4 to 8 of this book.

regulation of annuity providers is much more complex. It depends on the particular features of the types of annuities that are offered (fixed or variable, nominal or real, with or without guaranteed periods, with or without deferment periods) and on the types of risk-sharing arrangements that are used. According to the 2008 amendments to the pension law, AFPs need to build reserves to account for the probability that individuals may trigger the minimum return guarantee. The formula for calculating PWs includes a fair actuarial factor, which translates into reserve accumulation.

Chile is the first country in the world that has mandated for the second pillar the use of retirement products with regular income streams over the expected life of beneficiaries (in the form of life annuities or lifetime PWs). As a result, Chile has introduced a rigorous regulatory regime on providers of retirement products to minimize the bankruptcy risk faced by pensioners. It has also introduced state guarantees to protect pensioners against provider insolvency as well as aberrant behavior.

The capital regulation of pension companies includes a stipulated minimum capital that rises with the number of beneficiaries but is generally low and does not act as a barrier to entry. For an AFP with 10,000 members or more, the minimum capital amounts to UF 20,000 or about US$840,000.[16] A more stringent capital requirement is the obligatory reserve (*encaje*) of 1 percent of the value of assets under management. The *encaje* was initially set equal to 5 percent of assets, but this percentage was found to be excessive and was quickly lowered to the current level. The *encaje* is similar to the capital requirement imposed on insurance companies for their unit-linked business.

The *encaje* is required to be invested in units of the same funds to ensure an alignment of interests between the pension companies and their members. It is designed to support the minimum relative rate of return guarantee that AFPs are required to observe. The guarantee initially specified that the average real rate of return of any company could not be lower than 50 percent of the average of all AFPs over the preceding 12 months. The period of calculation was later extended to 36 months and was then applied to each of the five funds that AFPs were required to offer. The spread below the average was differentiated by type of fund, being higher for the more volatile A and B funds. The *encaje* and the minimum relative rate of return guarantee are intended to protect workers from aberrant managers. They were effective in forcing AFPs to stay close to the average of the industry. The minimum relative rate of return guarantee has never been called.

AFPs do not suffer from any mismatching between their assets and liabilities because the value of liabilities is, by definition, equal to the value of assets. The only other capital regulation concerns the valuation of assets, which is required to be mark-to-market values. Because most assets have to be invested in instruments that are traded on public markets, asset valuation is straightforward. The only major deviation from this practice concerns placements in bank deposits. However, these placements are usually short-term, and thus the use of book rather than market values for them does not create any large discrepancies.

The capital regulation of life insurance companies is far more complex. Because annuity business dominates the balance sheets of life insurers, the valuation of assets and liabilities and the regulation of any mismatches between them play a critical part in determining the capital adequacy of life insurers. Chile introduced the *calce* reserve rule to regulate the asset-liability mismatches. The rule imposes higher technical reserves and capital requirements for companies that suffer from unmatched liabilities.[17]

The *calce* reserve rule was adopted because insurance companies were not required to use mark-to-market asset valuation, partly because they followed a buy-and-hold strategy and held debt instruments to maturity.

Insurance regulators are now taking steps to introduce risk-based supervision that will focus on market valuation of assets and use of market rates of interest for valuing liabilities.

In addition to the *calce* reserve rule, insurance companies were required to operate with a leverage of not higher than 15, which implied a required equity ratio of 6.7 percent. The leverage limit was raised to 20, lowering the required equity ratio to 5.0 percent. In addition, an asset sufficiency test has been introduced. This test requires a detailed calculation of future asset cash flows, allowing for credit and prepayment risks, and of the reinvestment rate that would be needed to equalize asset and liability flows.

The last element in the annuity regulation of insurance companies concerns the offer of a government guarantee to annuitants in cases of insurer insolvency. The guarantee covers 100 percent of payments up to the PBS level and 75 percent of any annuity payments above the PBS level, up to UF 45 per month (approximately US$1,900). The cost of the guarantee is not prefunded but is covered from general tax revenues. However, the authorities have in place a speedy resolution mechanism that allows early interventions in companies that face financial difficulties.

Denmark completely revamped the solvency monitoring of life insurance companies and pension funds over the past decade or so. This reform covered the use of fair value accounting for both assets and liabilities and introduced stress testing. The change has been gradual. Market values are used as fair values for assets that are traded on active and liquid markets, but for less liquid assets, fair valuation is obtained by applying sophisticated and acceptable valuation models.

The valuation of liabilities faces more difficult conceptual issues because Denmark has no active market for insurance and pension liabilities and, therefore, no readily observable market prices. By necessity, fair valuation is based on valuation models. A fair valuation model must overcome two major obstacles: (a) the difficulty of determining the nominal value of insurance and pension liabilities in a market that is dominated by with-profits policies that are subject to minimum guaranteed benefits and (b) the perennial question of the appropriate rate of discount for calculating the present value of these liabilities.

The valuation model that Denmark adopted involves the decomposition of technical provisions by level of guaranteed benefits and the use of a market-determined zero-coupon yield curve, published by the central bank on a daily basis.[18] Pension institutions are free to set their own life tables but may be asked to provide justification for the tables used.

However, all pension institutions are required to use the same maturity-dependent discount rates, which are given by the market-determined zero-coupon yield curve.

Investment rules were relaxed in 2001, with a significant increase in the limit for investments in risky assets. However, this relaxation was accompanied by the introduction of the so-called traffic light system. This system of stress testing is divided into two scenarios, yellow and red, and measures the ability of individual pension institutions to cope with adverse changes in market conditions, such as changes in interest rates and substantial declines in equity prices. However, the stress tests are still at an early stage of development. They are specified in static terms, do not reflect past experience, and are the same irrespective of the state of financial markets.

Currently, the required capital of pension institutions follows the European Union Solvency I approach, which does not take into account the riskiness of assets. When the institution bears the investment risk, capital must be no less than 4.0 percent of technical provisions plus 0.3 percent of the risk sum for life insurance and pension business. The capital requirement is reduced to 1.0 percent when the institution does not bear the investment risk, as, for example, in unit-linked products that are offered without any guarantees. Denmark (in line with other European Union countries) will introduce risk-based capital requirements when the Solvency II approach is finalized.

In Sweden, insurance companies and pension funds are subject to prescribed rules on the investment of assets backing their technical reserves for guaranteed benefits, but they are free from quantitative restrictions for all other assets.[19] Risk-based supervision has followed a broadly similar approach to that used in Denmark but with a time lag. The traffic light system was introduced in 2006, and the use of a market-determined discount rate based on government bond and swap rates was mandated in 2007. However, the stress tests follow different specifications from those used in Denmark, and insurance companies and pension funds are not yet required to use a market-based yield curve published by the central bank. Insurance companies and pension funds use the same cohort life tables that are prepared by the insurance federation. Although the specifications of the stress tests differ from those used in Denmark, they share the same shortcomings: they are specified in static terms, do not reflect past experience, and are the same irrespective of the state of financial markets.

In Switzerland, life insurance companies are subject to strict prudential rules and are not allowed to have any underfunding in their pension operations. Following the imposition of new standards of transparency in 2004, life insurance companies are required to create a separate security fund for liabilities related to the pension funds they manage, and the assets of their pension business must be segregated from other assets. Moreover, their pension business must be reported in a separate annual report, and strict rules apply to the distribution of investment profits. According to these rules, insurance companies must allocate at least 90 percent of the net investment income to the accounts of insured individuals. Insurance companies have been using cohort life tables elaborated by the insurance association since 2000.

Insurance regulation in Switzerland is gradually moving in the direction of a Solvency II approach. In addition to imposing risk-based solvency requirements, this approach will also mandate the use of market-based maturity-dependent discount rates and will require a fair valuation of both assets and liabilities. Use of the traffic light system to assess the vulnerability of individual companies to specified financial shocks will also be included.

In contrast, the solvency regulation of pension funds remains imprecise. Pension funds are required to employ certified pension experts to attest that they are able to meet their financial obligations. The prudential rules do not mandate the use of fair values for assets. In addition, pension funds are free to use their own mortality tables and discount rates for estimating the present value of liabilities. Autonomous pension funds are allowed to have a temporary underfunding, whereas public sector pension funds that benefit from a cantonal guarantee have been allowed to operate with significant actuarial shortfalls on the grounds that the cantonal authorities would stand behind the pension funds and guarantee their liabilities.

The prudential supervision of autonomous pension funds is fragmented among several cantonal authorities and is characterized as passive and largely ineffective. Pension funds tend to understate their funding shortfalls and are usually required to correct their reported funding gaps but without any specified deadlines. As a result, funding gaps can persist for several years. The prudential regulation and supervision of pension funds is currently under intensive review.

In Australia, there are significant differences between the capital regulation of pension funds and the capital regulation of life insurance companies. On the one hand, superannuation funds are not required to maintain capital buffers. Instead, a superannuation fund that offers a defined benefit is required to have an actuary sign a funding and solvency certificate indicating that the fund is solvent and likely to remain so for a period of up to five years. On the other hand, the Life Insurance Act requires life companies to maintain both solvency and capital adequacy margins. Capital required to satisfy solvency requirements is determined on the basis that each statutory fund has sufficient assets to fund existing liabilities in the event of a wind-up of that fund. Capital adequacy rules require sufficient assets to fund existing liabilities on a going-concern basis. Capital adequacy requirements are generally higher than solvency requirements and act as an early warning trigger against the breach of solvency levels.

Though not explicitly risk based, the approach seeks to take into account risk factors and the likely volatility of assets and liabilities through the use of conservative prudential buffers. Most life insurers hold assets in excess of the capital adequacy requirements, and many have a policy of monitoring these excess or "free" assets against what is known as a *target surplus*. No regulatory requirements apply to the target surplus, and the methodologies and rationale behind the development of a target surplus by life insurers vary widely. However, the Australian Prudential Regulatory Authority is increasingly focused on the target surplus policies and practices of insurance companies, which it uses in its own risk rating of insurers and in determinations of the resources it devotes to their supervision.

Risk Management

The risks faced by annuity providers can be classified into five major categories: underwriting risks, market risks, credit and other asset risks, operational risks, and liquidity risks (Rocha and Thorburn 2007, 44–46, 60–70). The handling of these risks depends on the sophistication of internal management systems and the complexity of operations and instruments.

In the five countries covered in this book, insurance companies and pension funds have, over time, considerably improved their risk management capabilities, although their success in dealing with these risks has been influenced by many factors that are not related to risk management per se. For instance, corporate sponsors of pension schemes in Australia, as in most Anglo-American countries, have converted their pension schemes to a DC basis, benefiting from the contribution holidays they were able to take as well as from the release of some of the funding surplus that had been built into the schemes. The investment risk has been transferred to workers, although pension funds and insurance companies retain some investment risk in connection with their capital-guaranteed products. Because life annuities are little developed in Australia, retired workers bear the longevity risk.

Life insurance companies and superannuation funds are required to have in place risk management strategies and to develop risk mitigation and control policies. Segregating duties and avoiding conflicts of interest in assigning responsibilities are underscored as important components of internal control systems. But the preponderance of investment-linked assets and the underdevelopment of life annuities have implied a limited exposure to investment and longevity risks. As a result, except for DB and hybrid superannuation funds and investment products with guaranteed benefits, little interest has emerged in promoting the use of hedging instruments, such as long-term interest rate swaps, longevity bonds, or longevity derivatives.

Switzerland is at the other extreme of the spectrum. Use of a uniform annuity conversion factor protects retiring workers from fluctuations in interest rates at the time of retirement and from the dispersion of annuity prices among competing providers. Investment and longevity risks are borne by providers, which are exposed to large risks when regulated prices deviate significantly from market levels and large shortfalls emerge.

However, changes in the uniform annuity conversion factor in the face of changing demographics and investment returns cause long-term risks to be shared among successive generations of retirees, while investment risk is lowered by more frequent changes in the minimum interest rate in line with changes in market returns. Inflation risk is borne by pensioners, although pension funds are expected to make adjustments to pension payments to cover inflation, provided that their financial situation permits such adjustments.

Insurance companies and the large pension funds in Switzerland have adopted increasingly sophisticated asset and liability management strategies. In the 1990s, the larger institutions considerably expanded their investments in domestic and foreign equities. The high returns relative to the minimum guaranteed interest rate allowed greater leeway to pension funds to assume higher risks and also to take contribution holidays or increase benefits. Smaller funds applied more conservative investment policies.

Asset and liability management policies in Switzerland became more conservative when financial returns declined in the new millennium. Greater emphasis is now placed on ensuring that the pension funds are able to meet their long-term obligations. The larger institutions undertake detailed measurement of risks and calculate the impact on their financial position of adverse changes in interest rates, foreign exchange, equity prices, private equity, and real estate values. Use of hedging facilities also has increased, including interest rate derivatives and swap contracts.

Because pension funds have little scope in setting the terms of the annuity contracts in the mandatory part of the system, they have not adopted an active management of longevity risk. Almost all pension funds use the mortality tables provided by the Swiss Federal Insurance Fund (FIF), with possible adjustments based on past experience, especially for pension funds with a high degree of homogeneity among their annuitants (for example, construction workers, teachers, or bank employees). In 2000, insurance companies introduced cohort life tables for pricing their annuities on the open market, but in the mandatory pillar most institutions augment their actuarial liabilities by 0.4 to 0.5 percent every year until the new FIF mortality rates become available (that is, every 10 years). So far, no attempt has been made to use longevity bonds or derivatives to hedge longevity risk.

In Sweden, life insurance companies and pension funds engage in asset and liability matching that is dictated by the prevalence of 5- to 10-year term annuities. Because retired workers assume both the investment and the longevity risks, providers are essentially concerned with managing the risks arising from the offer of minimum guaranteed benefits. Providers invest in domestic and international equities and real estate to enhance returns and bonuses but maintain an adequate cushion of bond holdings to cover their guaranteed benefits.

The PPM, for which use of life annuities is compulsory, has a longer horizon. It adopts a highly conservative estimation of future trends in longevity. In addition, the recent lowering of the guaranteed benefits from an interest rate of 2.75 percent to 0 percent has simplified its risk management task.

In Denmark, pension institutions had expanded their equity investments in the 1990s but were hit by the dramatic fall in interest rates and large declines in equity prices between 2001 and 2003. They reacted by reducing their equity portfolios (in large part because of the fall of equity prices); by selling short-duration bonds and buying long-duration ones, especially foreign bonds; and by engaging in extensive hedging operations, mostly through the use of long-term interest rate swaps in the more liquid euro market.

Investment and risk management policies in Denmark reflect the terms and conditions of collective labor agreements. Some of them provide for risk sharing among both active and retired workers. The statutory ATP fund operates a scheme with deferred group annuities in which guaranteed benefits are specified for each year's contributions and periodic bonus payments aim to maintain the real value of benefits and reflect longevity experience and investment performance. The ATP fund is hedging all its pension liabilities in the euro interest rate swap market and is using excess investment returns from its active investment management to finance longevity reserves and periodic bonuses. It has also expanded its investments in foreign bonds. Some multiemployer pension funds and life insurance companies follow similar policies, but others make less extensive use of long-term swap contracts. However, all pension institutions have adapted their guaranteed benefits to the new reality of lower nominal interest rates and have adjusted their investment portfolios to the demands of the traffic light system and regular stress testing.

Finally, in Chile, life insurance companies are required to offer indexed annuities and cover the inflation risk by investing predominantly in inflation-indexed securities. Life insurance companies have expanded their investments in higher-yielding corporate and mortgage bonds, which are also indexed to inflation. This move has allowed them to offer better terms on their annuity products and thus raise the money's worth ratios. However, insurance companies assume the longevity risk as well as extensive reinvestment risk in view of the significant mismatching in the duration of assets and liabilities. Very little use is made of reinsurance arrangements and risk-hedging instruments. Despite several attempts, the market has not succeeded in issuing a longevity bond in Chile. A government guarantee protects pensioners from the risk of insolvency of individual insurance companies.

Risk-Sharing Arrangements

Risk-based capital requirements force annuity providers to apply conservative assumptions on their investment and longevity risks. However, this approach is not immune from problems. Excessive conservatism may lead to overly expensive products and higher-than-anticipated profits, creating pressures for the sharing of excess profits with annuitants and for price regulation. To avoid these problems, annuity providers use risk-sharing arrangements, whereby annuitants share in the investment and longevity risks.

Risk-sharing arrangements are not formally used in the mandatory pillar of Switzerland. However, as already noted, the recent change in the uniform annuity conversion factor has effectively introduced an intergenerational risk-sharing arrangement.

In Australia, the use of risk-sharing arrangements is limited to allocated annuities with capital guarantees. Risk-sharing arrangements were authorized in principle in Chile in 2004 with the introduction of variable annuities in conjunction with the purchase of PBS fixed real annuities. During the accumulation phase, workers will continue to bear the investment risk, within the limits set by the relative rate of return guarantees that are applied to the different types of permitted funds, but in the payout phase, the risks will be shared among annuitants using these products. However, despite its authorization in 2004, the variable annuity market has yet to be developed in Chile.

Risk-sharing arrangements are widely used in Sweden and Denmark. Pension institutions assume the investment and longevity risks up to the level of guaranteed benefits; pensioners share these risks for bonus payments. Inflation risk is covered by the payment of bonuses, which aims foremost to maintain the real value of benefits. In Sweden, a basic objective of public policy is to prevent intergenerational transfers; thus, active workers bear the investment risk during the accumulation phase but do not share in the investment and longevity risks of pensioners.

However, in Denmark, the ATP and some occupational pension schemes offer deferred group annuities whereby the investment and longevity risks of profit-participating policies are shared among both active and retired workers. In contrast, in unit-linked annuities, the use of which has been growing in both Denmark and Sweden, individual pensioners bear the investment risk, and only the longevity risk is shared among annuitants.

Lessons for Other Countries

Policy makers in countries that have reformed or are planning to reform their pension systems face several questions regarding the organization of the payout phase of the new systems. The first question concerns the feasibility of creating a sound market for lifetime retirement products. The second concerns the role that restrictions on payout options can play in promoting an adequate level of annuitization. Other questions address the regulation of pricing and marketing policies, the institutional structure of markets, the creation of a robust regulatory framework, and the development of appropriate hedging instruments for managing the main risks of retirement products. The experience of markets for retirement products in the five countries reviewed in this chapter suggests several lessons for other countries.[20]

The Feasibility of Sound Market Development

The experience of Chile confirms the feasibility of developing a sound market for retirement products from a very low initial base. When Chile implemented its 1981 pension reform, the market for retirement products did not exist. Twenty-nine years later, Chile has a well-developed and rapidly growing market for PWs and life annuities.

The Chilean approach entailed restrictions on lump-sum distributions. These restrictions were justified by the absence of an adequate public pension for middle- and high-income workers. Chile also mandated the use of fixed inflation-indexed annuities or lifetime PWs to protect pensioners from inflation risk. Requiring the use of joint life annuities, initially for married males and more recently for married couples, provided protection to surviving spouses, and allowing the use of guaranteed life annuities for 10 or 15 years addressed the bequest motive. As the market matured, the rules were adapted and allowed the use of combinations of minimum fixed real annuities with either PWs or variable annuities.

Chile created a rigorous regulatory regime for providers of retirement products to minimize the bankruptcy risk faced by pensioners. It also promoted the offer of inflation-indexed products and financial instruments to support the efficient operation of providers of retirement products and introduced state guarantees to protect pensioners against provider insolvency as well as aberrant behavior.

The market for lifetime retirement products is not well developed in Australia. This situation is not attributed to any major supply constraints but largely reflects the presence of a modest means-tested universal age pension, the strong preference of Australians for lump-sum withdrawals and term annuities, and their effective reliance on self-annuitization. The absence of any restrictions on lump sums and term annuities has been a contributing factor.

Denmark and Switzerland provide large annuitized benefits to most retiring workers from their public and occupational pillars, and in Sweden, the two components of the public pillar offer large benefits, also in the form of life annuities. All three countries have adopted policies that promote the offer of lifetime retirement products on a sound financial basis. Sweden, in particular, has adopted many changes to the structure of its public pension system and to the regulation of insurance business, and those changes have transformed the landscape for the retirement products market. However, as in Denmark and Switzerland, the market continues to be dominated by lifetime products from the public and occupational pillars. The demand for life annuities in the open market continues to be limited in all three countries.

Regulation of Payout Options

The degree of annuitization observed in different countries is largely explained by regulatory or plan restrictions on payout options. If a high degree of annuitization is a policy objective, the menu of retirement products and payout options must be regulated accordingly. However, avoiding overannuitization is important and implies taking into account other conditions prevailing in different countries, in particular the presence and relative importance of public pensions from pillars 0 and 1. The optimal policy on payout options is bound to be country specific.

The Chilean approach to product regulation is appropriate for countries that expect the new second pillar to play a major role in retirement provision and social protection. The restrictions on lump sums increase the potential demand for all retirement products, including life annuities. A PW formula that is based on life expectancy prevents a very premature exhaustion of funds.[21] The imposition of fixed annuities indexed to inflation and joint annuities for married couples helps to prevent an early exhaustion of funds and poverty in old age. The introduction of new products, such as variable and adjustable annuities, should require a minimum fixed annuity component that provides a minimum level of investment and longevity insurance. This protection is very important in countries where the public social security system is either closed down or reduced to a subsistence level.

Countries with larger zero or first public pillars could adopt a more liberal approach to the regulation of payout options because, in these cases, the exposure of retiring workers to investment and longevity risk is more limited. Fewer restrictions could be imposed on lump-sum withdrawals, although very liberal rules for lump sums can significantly hinder the development of the market for retirement products, especially the market for life annuities.

The appropriate policies in this area will vary significantly from country to country. In some cases, it may be appropriate to continue restricting lump sums but to adopt a more liberal approach to the design of retirement products. For example, the regulation of PWs and term annuities may be more liberal, thereby allowing designs that enable a faster withdrawal of funds. Term annuities play an important part in Denmark and Sweden and have a rapidly growing presence in Australia. Likewise, variable and adjustable annuities may be introduced without the obligation of a minimum fixed annuity component.

Regulation of Pricing and Marketing Policies

The experience of Switzerland indicates that pervasive regulation of products and prices entails both benefits and costs. Use of a minimum annuity conversion factor for joint life annuities avoids an excessive dispersion of annuity prices across annuitants with similar characteristics and also protects retiring workers of different cohorts from large fluctuations in market prices of both assets and annuities. A high level of price dispersion and exposure to annuitization risk are present in countries that do not regulate prices.

However, rigid price regulation may generate large income transfers across annuitants of different gender and marital status and may even jeopardize the solvency of annuity providers if it is not subject to flexible adjustment to market prices. The Swiss authorities are still grappling with the problem of defining a pricing formula that will protect annuitants from price dispersion and annuitization risk while being flexible enough to avoid unintended intra- and intergenerational transfers and to cope well with changing financial market conditions.

The regulation of pricing policies for variable annuities is confronted with some difficult challenges. In Denmark and Sweden, where these products are widespread, pricing issues such as the calculation of initial payments and profit-sharing rules are governed by collective labor agreements. As a result, they require less government regulation. But in systems that are based on non-employer-based individual accounts, pricing policies need to be subject to government regulation and oversight. The calculation of initial payments may need to be regulated to prevent deceptive offers. And a central register of performance data of different providers, emphasizing operating fees, profit-sharing rules, and consistency of investment policies rather than just past investment returns, should be created to enhance the transparency of the system.[22]

The regulation of the marketing of retirement products, especially life annuities, is another area of major policy interest in countries with open annuity markets. Adopting an electronic quotation system, such as the one introduced in Chile in 2004, should receive ample consideration. This system would be a centralized service that would compile and validate individual data on retiring workers and would solicit quotes from participating institutions. Such a system would reduce the influence of brokers, lower search costs for retiring workers, enhance the quality of information available to them, and ensure broad access to competitively priced annuities.

A necessary requirement of an effective regulation of marketing would be compliance with basic conduct rules, such as the "know your customer" rule, and an adequate disclosure of the terms and conditions of different products. Because annuity products are highly complex as well as irreversible and nontransferable, extensive training of agents and brokers would also be needed. Licensing and training of brokers and financial advisers involved in the marketing of annuities would be essential for promoting good business conduct and for preventing potential abuse of less-informed consumers.

In addition to adequate training, brokers would need to pass a certification test as well as the standard "fit and proper" test. Licensed brokers must be legally obligated to represent their clients, must generate their income from commissions on the sale of annuities, and must not be permitted to accept volume-related remuneration from insurers. Because supervision of brokers and pension advisers can be costly and time consuming, support in enforcing codes of good practices from self-regulatory organizations is welcome. Some countries have felt the need to introduce harsher regulations, such as the imposition of regulated caps on broker commissions in Chile or the complete prohibition of the involvement of brokers in Colombia.

The Institutional Structure of Markets

Another policy issue concerns the institutional structure of the market for retirement products. The main choice is between centralized provision through a single provider and provision through a decentralized competitive market. Centralized provision is usually channeled through a public entity, although it could also, in principle, be based on a highly regulated private entity. The zero and first public pillars, where they exist, rely on centralized provision through a public agency. As these pillars almost always involve the offer of inflation-indexed compulsory lifetime annuities, their products play a central part in the annuity markets of most countries. Denmark and Sweden, among the countries covered in this book, also use public agencies for the centralized offer of supplementary lifetime annuities.

Centralized provision has several potential advantages. It allows for a larger base of risk pooling, especially if annuitization is compulsory. It also benefits from scale economies and avoids the heavy marketing costs that decentralized providers incur. The main disadvantages are the potentially weaker incentives for product innovation and operational efficiency that may result from compulsory participation and monopoly market positions.[23] With public ownership or extensive public regulation, there is also a high risk of extraneous interference in annuity pricing and asset management. Such interference may well result in transferring the investment and longevity risks back to the state.

However, because of scale economies, decentralized markets veer over time toward oligopolistic structures that negate their innovation and efficiency advantages. Recent progress in several countries in adopting robust governance safeguards and high levels of transparency for their public pension funds strengthens the case for the centralized provision of lifetime annuities, meeting at least some of the retirement needs of pensioners.[24]

Creation of Robust and Effective Prudential Regulation and Supervision

Another major challenge concerns the creation of a robust and effective prudential regulatory and supervisory framework for the providers of retirement products. The framework should involve risk-based supervision rather than a checklist of rule compliance. It should also rely on risk-based solvency rules that specify solvency capital requirements on the basis of the asset and liability risks borne by providers.

Providers of retirement products should be able to price their products freely and use mortality tables that are most appropriate for their own clientele. Any regulated parameters should be kept up to date by frequent validation and revision and should use market-based criteria to minimize persistent biases in pricing and selection. Providers of retirement products should be allowed to offer all types of retirement products, avoiding the market segmentation that has been prevalent in Chile. However, the institutions involved should be required to maintain separate accounting data for different products, distinguishing clearly between products with and without guaranteed benefits and avoiding cross-subsidization among different products.

Strict regulation of risk management should also be introduced, requiring providers of retirement products to maintain adequate levels of technical reserves and risk capital and regularly apply rigorous stress tests to their various products, depending on the allocation of investment and longevity risks. Clear rules should apply to the valuation of assets and liabilities and to the capital buffers that would be needed to cover the financial impact of asset and liability mismatches. These issues are challenging even in countries with the most developed markets. Regulatory practices would need to evolve and adapt to the emerging lessons from the growing global experience in the management of the many and varied risks facing the markets for retirement products.

Finally, intervention and bankruptcy rules should be modernized to prevent an early depletion of provider assets in a bankruptcy scenario. An effective resolution mechanism will prevent a significant reduction in the residual value of assets left to honor annuity and PW payments as well as prevent an increase in the cost of any government guarantees. In a system of mandatory savings, pensioners may deserve preferential treatment over other claimants on the assets of providers of retirement products.

The introduction of government guarantees for holders of retirement products, life annuities, or PWs may well be necessary in a system of mandatory saving for retirement purposes. Such guarantees should cover both the accumulation and payout phases. They should emulate evolving practice in deposit insurance schemes, including a reasonable amount of coinsurance by pensioners (to minimize the possible loss of market discipline at the point of purchase), funding by ex ante or ex post risk-based assessments, and also some reliance on budgetary resources.

Promotion of Efficient Risk Management

Regulation of payout options and retirement products needs to include the supply of financial instruments and hedging tools that would enable the providers of retirement products to adopt efficient risk management techniques. Imposing inflation indexation in the absence of inflation-indexed instruments may lead to the offer of poorly priced products with hefty risk premiums. Countries that consider mandating the use of inflation-linked annuities should make a serious effort to expand the supply of inflation-indexed financial instruments from both the public and the private sectors or should consider using alternative types of annuities, such as escalating annuities. Escalating nominal annuities, where regular monthly payments are adjusted once a year at a predetermined rate of between 2 percent and 5 percent, would be a more suitable product for countries with underdeveloped financial and insurance markets.

Development of sound annuity and PW markets necessitates the adoption of a clear and ambitious capital market agenda for the payout phase. For the government, development of long-duration inflation-indexed instruments implies a significant modernization of public debt management, focusing on promotion of liquid benchmark issues and adoption of reliable issuance programs. For the private sector, sound development implies adoption of rules that eliminate any obstacles to the issuance of long-dated inflation-linked instruments.

In addition, governments need to promote the development of derivative markets, such as long-term interest rate swap and swaption contracts, to allow the hedging of the investment risk of long-term liabilities. They should also promote the use of longevity bonds and reinsurance markets to support the hedging of longevity risk. Developing longevity bonds and derivatives is likely to be a tall order for most countries because such products have yet to emerge, even in the most advanced financial markets.

An alternative approach would be to rely on extensive risk-sharing arrangements, similar to those widely practiced in Denmark and Sweden. These arrangements offer an attractive option in addressing the highly complex longevity and investment risks in markets with an inadequate supply of long-term instruments.

However, risk-sharing arrangements introduce their own challenges. They presuppose a high level of transparency and integrity of annuity providers, adoption of effective pricing rules (involving the use of cohort mortality tables to minimize subsequent adjustments in annual bonuses), and rules that prevent transfers of income across different cohorts.

Transparent and robust rules also are needed to ensure consistent long-term fairness in the distribution of profits between shareholders and policyholders. Such rules are clearly more important in the case of oligopolistic decentralized markets, where market discipline may be less powerful than is often assumed, but they are also relevant in the case of public monopolies, especially in ensuring fair treatment of all cohorts and preventing the use of surpluses for extraneous purposes.

Conclusion

Clearly, the lessons learned from the experience of the five countries reviewed in this chapter are manifold and challenging. The development of retirement products is a new challenge that emerges from the changing landscape in most countries, the result of increasing longevity, globalized competition, and market fluidity. Complete reliance on traditional social security systems and defined benefit company pensions is no longer feasible anywhere in the world. As the development of robust systems of retirement savings, both during the accumulation and the payout phases, attracts increasing attention in most countries, it is hoped that the review of lessons contained in this chapter will help policy makers in many developing countries better formulate their policy options and address more effectively the difficult challenges ahead.

Notes

1. The clawback provisions are discussed later in this chapter.

2. In Australia, annual contributions reached 15 percent of GDP in 2007 as a result of the special additional contribution allowed in that year.

3. These threshold levels applied in 2003 (OECD 2007). The levels may vary from year to year because the thresholds are set in absolute terms and not in relation to average earnings.

4. The replacement rates for Denmark are significantly higher than those of the other countries. This difference is another indication that the assumed average contribution rate of 11 percent to occupational pension funds may be too high.

5. The basic solidarity pension has replaced the minimum pension.

6. This 80 percent requirement of the maximum pension with solidarity support becomes effective in 2012.

7. This finding is probably explained by two factors: single men have a weaker bequest motive, and annuity conversion factors in the open market are likely to be significantly lower (Bütler and Ruesch 2007, 19, 49).

8. Until 2008, only married men were required to use joint life annuities.

9. In the relevant tables, the minimum pension factor was expressed as a divisor and equaled 15.7 for the minimum benefit and 8.1 for the maximum benefit (Knox 2000, 25).

10. As already noted, the normal retirement age of women is gradually being raised to that of men, but women continue to have a longer life expectancy than men.

11. In 2008, brokers were replaced by pension advisers. Stricter certification requirements have been imposed.

12. The Colegio de Corredores de Seguros de Chile (Insurance Brokers Association of Chile) does not operate as a self-regulatory organization.

13. This rough calculation overlooks two offsetting factors: (a) any increase in payments because of inflation adjustment in pensions and (b) the termination of pension payments to deceased pensioners.

14. However, many pension funds, especially those of small companies, allow the entire capital to be withdrawn on retirement.

15. One can argue that the high regulated annuity conversion factor has compensated workers for the lower-than-market returns that have been earned during the accumulation phase, at least during the first 20 years of the operation of the second pillar.

16. The UF (*unidad de fomento*) is a unit of account that is indexed to consumer prices and is widely used in the valuation of contracts and tax parameters. The UF was approximately equal to US$42 in December 2009.

17. For a detailed exposition of this complicated rule, see Rocha and Thorburn (2007, 118-30).

18. During the 2008 global financial crisis, the regulators allowed pension institutions to use the mortgage bond interest rates for valuing liabilities. The dispensation was granted for one year and was later extended. It was prompted by the large impact of the crisis on the mortgage bond market. The intention was to prevent an even bigger collapse of the market and to allow pension institutions to remain technically solvent. It was a form of regulatory forbearance but was seen as a pragmatic response to the exceptional impact of the global crisis. The dispensation will be removed when normal market conditions are restored. The market capitalization of the Danish mortgage bond market is higher than the government bond market.

19. A 25 percent limit is placed on equity investments for the technical reserves of guaranteed benefits. The corresponding limit for the PPM is set at 30 percent.

20. These questions, as they affect the design of the payout phase in Central and Eastern European countries, have been addressed in Vittas, Rudolph, and Pollner (2010).

21. This requirement was recently extended to a well-above-average life expectancy, limiting the exposure of government funds to this risk.

22. If the authorities choose to specify a low technical interest rate, say 0 percent or 1 percent, for the calculation of initial payments to provide greater scope for future bonuses, they should avoid the trap of applying the same technical rate for the calculation of technical reserves. The latter should require the use of market-based maturity-dependent discount rates to ensure a proper valuation of reserves and allow room for investments in equities and other real assets.

23. Despite their weaker incentives, public entities have often taken the lead in product innovations. A good example is offered by the Danish ATP fund, which has been a leader in both product innovation and sophisticated asset management.

24. Vittas, Impavido, and O'Connor (2008) review the recent experience of four public pension funds in some Organisation for Economic Co-operation and Development countries.

References

Andersen, Carsten, and Peter Skjodt. 2007. "Pension Institutions and Annuities in Denmark." Policy Research Working Paper 4437, World Bank, Washington, DC.

Brunner, Gregory Gordon, and Craig Thorburn. 2008. "The Market for Retirement Products in Australia." Policy Research Working Paper 4749, World Bank, Washington, DC.

Bütler, Monika, and Martin Ruesch. 2007. "Annuities in Switzerland." Policy Research Working Paper 4438, World Bank, Washington, DC.

Budget Directorate. 2009. "Informe de Finanzas Públicas: Proyecto de Ley de Presupuestos del Sector Público para el Año 2010." Budget Directorate, Ministry of Finance of Chile, Santiago.

Knox, David. 2000. "The Australia Annuity Market." Policy Research Working Paper 2495, World Bank, Washington, DC.

OECD (Organisation for Economic Co-operation and Development). 2007. *Pensions at a Glance*. Paris: OECD.

Palmer, Edward. 2008. "The Market for Retirement Products in Sweden." Policy Research Working Paper 4748, World Bank, Washington, DC.

Rocha, Roberto, and Heinz Rudolph. 2010. "A Summary and Update of Developing Annuities Markets: The Experience of Chile." Policy Research Working Paper 5325, World Bank, Washington, DC.

Rocha, Roberto, and Craig Thorburn. 2007. *Developing Annuities Markets: The Experience of Chile*. Washington, DC: World Bank.

Vittas, Dimitri. 2008. "A Short Note on the ATP Fund of Denmark." Policy Research Working Paper 4505, World Bank, Washington, DC.

Vittas, Dimitri, Gregorio Impavido, and Ronan O'Connor. 2008. "Upgrading the Investment Policy Framework of Public Pension Funds." Policy Research Working Paper 4499, World Bank, Washington, DC.

Vittas, Dimitri, Heinz Rudolph, and John Pollner. 2010. "Designing the Payout Phase of Funded Pension Pillars in Eastern European Countries." Policy Research Working Paper 5276, World Bank, Washington, DC.

CHAPTER 4

Australia

Mandating Retirement Savings without Lifetime Annuitization

This chapter examines the structure of the Australian market for retirement products and looks at the effect of government policies on the demand for different products. In the context of the development of global annuity markets, it seeks to show why the market for life annuities in Australia is so poorly developed and how recent policy changes are likely to make life annuities even less attractive.

The Australian experience with annuities is best approached by first examining the contextual arrangements because they have a strong direct influence on actual practice. These contextual arrangements include (a) a long-standing and relatively generous public pillar offering a noncontributory universal pension to all aged residents (the age pension) but subject to large clawback provisions, (b) a mandatory occupational pillar with a strong defined contribution (DC) orientation, and (c) pervasive taxation and social security regulations that influence consumer and market participant behavior.

This chapter is a summary, prepared by the editors, of the paper by Gregory Brunner and Craig Thorburn titled "The Market for Retirement Products in Australia" (Brunner and Thorburn 2008). Antony Randle updated the paper.

The promotion of the mandatory second pillar has been motivated by a desire to ensure that Australians have a better income in retirement than they could expect from the government-provided age pension. The pillar is also designed to boost national saving and reduce the rate of growth of government pension outlays.

The management of the second pillar is left to the private sector and supported by a comprehensive prudential regulatory and supervisory framework, which is based on a formal risk-based model. This framework provides both a risk rating for pension providers and life insurance companies and a matrix of supervisory response. Pension and annuity providers who offer guaranteed income streams are subject to capital requirements to ensure that their commitments can be honored.

An important characteristic of the Australian market is that apart from mandating lifetime saving for retirement through occupational plans, the authorities do not impose any restrictions on investment choices or on payout options. Both active and retired workers are allowed great flexibility and personal choice regarding how they invest their retirement assets. A range of mild tax incentives is provided to encourage retirees to invest in income stream products. However, much greater reliance is placed on common sense and prudent management by individuals rather than on any form of restrictions on payout options to ensure that accumulated assets are used primarily by individuals to support themselves in their retirement.

The structure of the chapter is as follows. The next section reviews the overall structure and state of development of the pension system and highlights the role played by different pillars and players. The following section then reviews the menu and degree of use of available retirement products and discusses factors that influence the choice of retirement products. That section also looks at targeted replacement rates and the interaction of second-pillar retirement benefits, the clawback provisions of the universal pension, and various tax incentives. The section also discusses the use of risk-sharing arrangements in the Australian market and assesses the overall level of annuitization. The penultimate section focuses on the institutional structure of the Australian pension and annuity market and on the prudential regulation and supervision of superannuation funds and insurance companies. It reviews the prevailing philosophy on solvency monitoring and highlights the increasing emphasis on efficient risk management and risk-based supervision. The last section offers some concluding remarks.

The Australian Pension System

The Australian pension system includes a public pension, for which most aged residents are eligible, supplemented by a mandatory occupational scheme.

Public Pensions

For a considerable time, the Australian retirement system consisted of a public pillar universal pension paid to all aged residents (known as the *age pension*). Established in 1908, the age pension provided a flat-rate pension through the federal government on a pay-as-you-go basis. In 2006, the Future Fund was established to act as a demographic buffer fund to meet part of the unfunded liabilities of the age pension system. The Future Fund had accumulated assets amounting to 4.8 percent of gross domestic product (GDP) in June 2009.

The majority of Australians looked to the age pension as their main source of retirement income. For a long period, the pension was subject to an income- and asset-based means test, but progressively into the 1970s, the means testing was made more liberal until it focused on income only and not on assets. Because many older Australians could arrange their financial affairs such that they had considerable assets but generated limited income for means-testing purposes, an asset-based test was reintroduced in 1985. Currently, both asset and income tests apply. The rate of pension payment is calculated under both tests, and the test that results in the lower rate is used.

The government enacted laws in 1997 to set the level of the age pension at 25 percent of an average wage measure, so the pension was indexed to wages as a matter of course. Rates were indexed twice a year in March and September, to the greater of the consumer price index (CPI) or male total average weekly earnings (MTAWE). The single rate was benchmarked to 25 percent of MTAWE, and the combined rate for married couples was set so that the single rate was 60 percent of the combined rate. Thus, the combined rate amounted to 41.7 percent of MTAWE, and the pension of the second spouse was equal to two-thirds the rate of the first spouse.

The government made changes to these arrangements in 2009 under the banner of "Secure and Sustainable Pensions." The changes focused principally on the inadequacy of the single pension. The single pension is now benchmarked at 27.7 percent of MTAWE. This change has brought the single rate to 66.7 percent of the combined rate. The basis of the semiannual indexation was also changed. Pensions are now indexed to the Pensioner and Beneficiary Living Cost Index, which is calculated by the Australian Bureau of Statistics. This change was predicated on the view that the new index was more indicative of pensioner expenditures than was the CPI. Pensions are now increased by the higher of the new index or the CPI and cannot be lower than the effective benchmark. The age at which people qualify for an age pension is to be increased from the present 65 years. Beginning in 2017, it will increase at a rate of six months every two years and reach 67 years in 2023. The pension is subject to income tax.

The income test permits a full pension for those with limited income. In March 2007, a single pensioner could retain the full pension and earn an additional 128 Australian dollars ($A) biweekly, an amount that corresponded to 6 percent of the average wage.[1] This amount was increased to $A 142 biweekly under the 2009 reforms. As the pensioner's income increased, the pension was reduced by 40 cents for each additional dollar of other income. The rate of reduction has now been increased to 50 cents for each additional dollar of other income. The age pension was eliminated when income reached $A 1,554 biweekly, or approximately 66 percent of average earnings. However, the threshold levels for couples who are entitled to the combined rate were respectively set at higher levels of approximately 11 percent and 102 percent of average earnings. Table 4.1 presents a summary of the thresholds adopted in the 2009 reforms.

The asset test applies against asset holdings instead of income receipts. A peculiarity of the asset test is that the principal home of pensioners is

Table 4.1   Income Test Details, March 2010

	Income level	
Family situation	For full payment (biweekly)	For part payment (biweekly)
Universal pension (single rate)	$A 644.20, or 27.7% of average wage	n.a.
Universal pension (combined rate)	$A 971.20, or 41.7% of average wage	n.a.
Single	Up to $A 142, or 6.1% of average wage	Up to $A 1,554.20, or 66.4% of average wage
Couple (combined)	Up to $A 248, or 10.8% of average wage	Up to $A 2,362.00, or 101.5% of average wage

Source: Australian Department of Human Services, Centrelink Web site, http://www.centrelink.gov.au.
Note: n.a. = not applicable. The average biweekly wage is $A 2,326.

exempt from the test,[2] while the clawback provision used to be low at $A 3 per $A 1,000 of assets above threshold but was reduced further to $A 1.5 per thousand in September 2007. Because of the exemption of owner-occupied homes, the asset test reduces the pension according to separate schedules for homeowners and for nonhomeowners, reflecting the benefit that a person gains from owning rather than renting. Following the change in the rules in 2007, the level of assets for the complete elimination of the age pension is a very high multiple of average wage incomes. For couples entitled to the combined rate, the upper threshold is higher than 15 times the average wage income for homeowners and 17 times the average wage income for nonhomeowners (table 4.2).

Despite the application of a rather low threshold for the income test, the vast majority of Australians of pensionable age receive the full or partial age pension. An estimated 53 percent of pensioners received the full age pension in 2009, and another 30 percent received a reduced age pension, whereas only 20 percent were not entitled to any age pension. Even in 2050, when the superannuation pillar will have reached maturity, the proportion of old persons who are officially projected to be entitled to a full or partial age pension will fall only slightly to 79 percent (see figure 4.1). However, recipients of the full pension will decline sharply to 30 percent, while those receiving a reduced age pension will grow to 49 percent, leaving the proportion of people with no age

Table 4.2   Asset Test Details, March 2010

Family situation	Asset level	
	For full payment[a]	For part payment
Homeowners		
Single rate	$A 178,000, or 2.95 times average annual wage	$A 645,500, or 10.66 times average annual wage
Combined rate (couples)	$A 252,500, or 4.17 times average annual wage	$A 957,500, or 15.83 times average annual wage
Nonhomeowners		
Single rate	$A 307,000, or 5.07 times average annual wage	$A 774,500, or 12.79 times average annual wage
Combined rate (couples)	$A 381,500, or 6.31 times average annual wage	$A 1,086,500, or 17.95 times average annual wage

Source: Australian Department of Human Services, Centrelink Web site, http://www.centrelink.gov.au.
Note: n.a. = not applicable. The average annual wage is $A 60,542.
a. Before September 20, 2007, assets over these amounts reduced the rate of pension payable by $A 3.00 every two weeks for each $A 1,000. After that date, assets exceeding the thresholds reduce the pension by $A 1.50 every two weeks. The $A 1.50 clawback for the assets test was not changed in the 2009 reforms.

Figure 4.1   Projections of Superannuation Assets and Age Pension Coverage

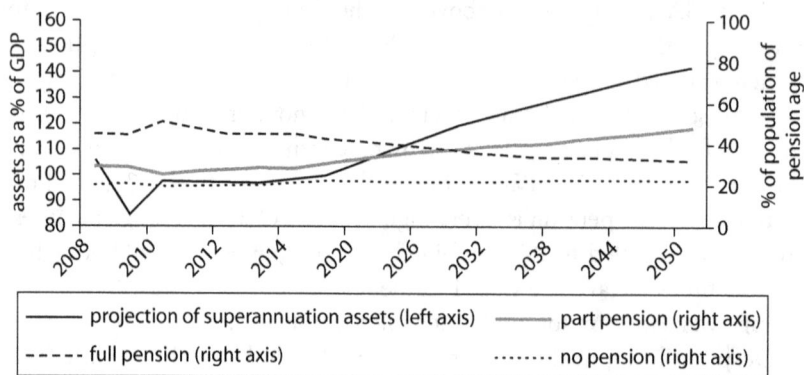

Source: Treasury 2010, 146.

pension virtually unchanged at 21 percent (Treasury 2010, 146). This small effect on the total number of recipients is explained by the relatively high level of the upper threshold of the asset test and the unwillingness of pensioners to purchase retirement products with regular income streams.

The age pension continues to be funded on a pay-as-you-go basis. The current expenditures are approximately 2.7 percent of GDP; however, expenditures are expected to rise as the population ages. Short- and long-run projections of pension costs have been made allowing for the demographic transition and the growth of superannuation assets. These estimates, shown in table 4.3, suggest an increase of about 1 percentage point of GDP by 2039/40 and a slight increase in the following decade.

Under the Charter of Budget Honesty Act 1998, the government is required to prepare a periodic intergenerational report to assess the long-term sustainability of government policies over a 40-year period, including the financial implications of demographic change. Some of the conclusions of the 2002/03, 2007, and 2010 intergenerational reports lie at the heart of the government approach to retirement incomes (Treasury 2002, 2007, 2010). These reports conclude that although important fiscal challenges will arise from the aging population because of spending pressures in areas such as health, age pensions, and age care, "population ageing is not a crisis" (Brunner and Thorburn 2008, xxxviii), in part because it is a gradual phenomenon with scope to take some corrective

Table 4.3   Projected Pension Cost

Year	Cost (as a % of GDP)
2009/10	2.7
2014/15	2.7
2019/20	2.8
2029/30	3.3
2039/40	3.7
2049/50	3.9

Source: Treasury 2010.

measures. The rise in age pension costs will also be mitigated by the growth of the private superannuation pillar and the greater effect of claw-back provisions. In addition, the government created a new fund in 2006, known as the Future Fund, with the task of accumulating sufficient financial assets to cover its unfunded pension liability by 2020.[3]

Occupational Schemes and the Superannuation Guarantee

Although the history of occupational superannuation schemes in Australia dates to before federation, not until the middle of the 20th century did such schemes become a more common feature of employment arrangements. Larger employers tended to be the main providers of occupational schemes for their staff. Most often, these schemes offered defined benefits (DBs) with limited portability when members changed employer and had relatively poor vesting of benefits in the event of early departure. Consequently, they strongly favored long-term career employees with a single firm. Benefits on withdrawal and on retirement tended to be provided as a lump sum because the tax basis was favorable.

Benefits in the form of a pension were provided by a limited number of private sector employers, most usually life insurance companies and banks, and by schemes for public sector employees at both the federal and the state levels and for various government authorities. The public sector schemes were operated on an unfunded, pay-as-you-go basis.

Given the relatively small number of schemes that provided pension benefits, integration with the means-tested universal pension was not common. A culture built up (the "lump-sum mentality") that encouraged the expectation that a retirement benefit from an occupational scheme taken as a lump sum was to be used for early retirement consumption or to be invested to maintain the entitlement to the public age pension. Although all Australians who were employed were able to access schemes operated by life insurance companies, which were particularly directed at the self-employed and employees who were not covered by an employer-sponsored scheme, overall coverage was about 30 percent under the second pillar (Bateman and Piggott 1997) for most of the 20th century until steps were taken to secure the second pillar in the 1980s.

In the mid-1980s, as part of a national agreement on wage policy, a productivity award superannuation component was allocated to be made as a contribution to a superannuation scheme. This initiative represented the seed of further changes that had a dramatic effect on the superannuation landscape.

In 1992, the federal government created the superannuation guarantee (SG) system. Under this system, employers pay a contribution for all employees to an approved superannuation scheme.[4] The rate of contribution was initially set at 3 percent but was raised gradually until it reached 9 percent in 2002.[5] The mandatory nature of the second pillar resulted in a major expansion of coverage, which reached approximately 95 percent of workers by 1995.[6]

The vast expansion in coverage and the gradual increase in the contribution rate brought about a huge rise in annual contribution flows (table 4.4). Contributions equaled nearly 7 percent of GDP in 2002. In 2007, contributors were allowed to make a one-off additional posttax contribution of an amount of up to $A 1 million, which explains the large increase in that year to 15 percent of GDP. In 2009, total contributions amounted to 9 percent of GDP. With the addition of investment income and when the young age of the new pillar is taken into consideration (which implies relatively low levels of benefits and withdrawals that amounted to less than 5 percent of GDP in 2009), the overall result was a massive increase in the level of superannuation assets, which reached 110 percent of GDP in June 2007, up from 68 percent in 2002 and 49 percent in 1995. However, this level fell to 85 percent of GDP in 2009 following the negative investment returns that resulted from the global financial crisis.

Table 4.4   Annual Contributions and Total Assets of Superannuation Funds

Year to June or end-June	2002	2005	2007	2009
GDP ($A billion)	759.0	933.7	1,083.8	1,260.0
Contributions ($A billion)	51.6	68.9	165.1	112.1
Contributions (% of GDP)	6.8	7.4	15.2	8.9
Total assets ($A billion)	518.1	756.5	1,187.0	1,073.3
Total assets (% of GDP)	68.3	81.0	109.5	85.2

Sources: APRA, Annual Superannuation Bulletin, various years.

In addition to the increase in annual contributions and total assets, the SG set in motion several other changes. First, a large increase has occurred in the number of schemes operating on a DC basis. Although DB structures can be maintained, various factors, including stricter regulatory and compliance requirements, changes in employment patterns, and growing competitive pressures, have resulted in the progressive closing of DB schemes and their replacement, at least for new employees, with DC schemes. Of funds with more than four members in June 2009, some 46 percent were accumulation, or DC, funds, and another 47 percent were funds offering a combination of accumulation and defined benefits. Only 7 percent were pure DB funds, compared with 22 percent 12 years earlier. Although the importance of DB funds has declined sharply in the past decade, the reported assets of DB funds understate the present value of their future payment obligations because some large public sector schemes are not fully funded.

Second, a parallel increase has occurred in the relevance of multiemployer schemes. Originally, under the productivity award, employers with employees covered by such an award found themselves contributing to an industry scheme as well as, if they had one in place, an occupational scheme. Over time, using administrative efficiency as the main argument, employers have tended to close their occupational schemes and transfer their employees to master trusts and other types of funds. This process was substantially hastened by the introduction of comprehensive licensing requirements for pension funds in 2004. The maintenance of a single-sponsor occupational scheme has become less relevant as companies have opted to outsource arrangements or have seen the number of members in such schemes fall to uneconomic levels.

Third, small schemes with fewer than five members, known as *self-managed superannuation funds*, have become popular. Originally, small enterprises and family businesses established schemes to provide for their SG obligations. These schemes soon became an attractive source of financing for business operations or for other purposes. Regulations were introduced to limit related investments, and money belonging to the fund can no longer be used for personal or business purposes. To ensure adequate control by fund members, all members must be trustees of the fund unless the fund employs a professional trustee supervised by the Australian Prudential Regulation Authority (APRA). Attracted by the greater control they can exercise over the invested funds and the potential for lower charges, individuals with high net worth have been encouraged to establish schemes, particularly after taking a benefit from another scheme. On June 30, 2009, there were 415,000 self-managed superannuation funds, and the number of small funds is growing at approximately 2,500 a month.

Other efforts have been made to increase the coverage of superannuation. In 1997, a spouse contribution initiative was launched, enabling schemes to offer members the option to establish a separate member account for their spouse and make additional contributions. Most recently, the government has introduced and enhanced a co-contribution where the government makes a matching payment when members make contributions to their scheme.[7]

All classes of funds (other than small funds) have been consolidating for some time. (See table 4.5 for types of schemes.) Corporate funds have declined particularly rapidly in both number and share of industry assets (see table 4.6) as costs of administration have increased and the introduction of near-universal employer superannuation has eroded any competitive benefits from offering in-house superannuation. Public sector funds have also experienced large declines. In contrast, industry funds and especially retail and small funds have registered large increases in market shares.[8]

The consolidation trend was given substantial new impetus by the recent introduction of more stringent prudential regulations, including rules related to fund governance and risk management, and the requirement that the trustees of all APRA-regulated funds be licensed and the funds registered by the middle of 2006. The licensing and registration criteria are rigorous and require trustees to demonstrate that they are fit and proper and have adequate resources and robust risk management systems in place to mitigate the risks of operating a superannuation fund. As a result, the number of funds, excluding small funds and pooled trusts, were reduced to 463 at the end of June 2009, almost one-twelfth of their number 15 years earlier.

The number of accounts continued to expand even after the attainment of near-universal coverage in 1995. Superannuation funds reported 33 million accounts in 2009, which is close to an average of 3 accounts per worker. This figure signifies a trend to multiple account holding and may also imply a large number of inactive accounts. Retail funds have more than half of all outstanding accounts, followed by industry funds. The large presence of retail funds raises concerns about the operating efficiency of the second pillar because retail funds are notoriously more expensive than other types of funds, suffer from a much wider dispersion of investment returns and operating fees, and report significantly lower investment returns.[9]

Table 4.5   Types of Schemes

Type	Description
Corporate schemes	These schemes are sponsored by a single employer or established for a corporate group. The employer and employees each appoint half the members of the trustee board. Most schemes are DC. Some DB schemes remain but are mostly closed to new members.
Retail schemes	These schemes are publicly offered on a group or individual basis by financial institutions with an administration company and a trustee company, usually subsidiaries of the financial group. They are used for personal superannuation by the self-employed and by employers not wishing to establish their own superannuation scheme. In some cases, a master trust structure is adopted where the trust arrangement allows a single trustee operating under an umbrella trust deed to administer and manage the superannuation schemes of a number of unrelated employers or individuals. Now they are mostly offered on a DC basis, but historically some schemes invested in life insurance policies with benefits derived from the terms of the underlying insurance contract.
Industry schemes	These multiemployer superannuation schemes usually cover a specific industry or range of industries and will accept contributions from any employers in those industries. Most commenced in the mid-1980s and were set up on a pure DC basis, with supplementary insurance coverage based on mortality expectations and paid for by a premium deduction that was based on the insurance policy taken out by the scheme.
Public sector schemes	These schemes are provided for employees of the federal, state, or municipal governments. A separate scheme is operated for the military and often, in the case of the states, for emergency services personnel. More recently, a separate scheme also exists for universities (collectively) and municipalities. Many DB schemes were closed to new members and moved to partial, and then full, DC-based operations.
Small, excluded, and self-managed schemes	These small schemes have fewer than five members, and all the individual members are also on the board of trustees. These schemes are operated fundamentally on a DC basis, although they could have a hybrid basis (so be DB under the law). Members who do not wish to operate the fund can appoint an APRA-regulated corporate trustee. More than 320,000 small funds exist; most are regulated by the Australian Taxation Office, with APRA having responsibility for 6,700.
Approved deposit fund	This type of scheme is recognized in the law and is designed to accept benefits from other funds and accumulate them until eventual retirement. These schemes often operate as retail schemes, but they can be established in any category.

Source: Authors' compilation.
Note: APRA = Australian Prudential Regulation Authority.

Table 4.6   Superannuation Fund Assets by Type of Fund

Type of fund	Share of total assets (%)			
	1995	2000	2006	2009
Corporate	21.4	13.8	5.7	5.0
Industry	4.4	10.1	16.6	17.9
Public sector	22.7	21.1	16.7	14.3
Retail (including retirement savings accounts and eligible rollover funds)	22.7	27.5	32.7	28.5
Small funds	8.7	15.5	23.5	31.0
Balance of statutory funds	20.1	12.0	4.8	3.3
Total	100.0	100.0	100.0	100.00
Total ($A billion)	229	484	918	1,073
Total (% of GDP)	49	74	92	85

Source: APRA 2008.

Life Insurance Companies

The Australian life insurance industry represents a significant, though declining, part of the financial services sector. At the end of June 2009, total industry assets were $A 213 billion, or 17 percent of GDP. In 2007, superannuation business represented about 90 percent of total life insurance office assets. However, the life insurance industry accounted for 20 percent of superannuation assets, down from 41 percent in 1997.[10]

Currently, 32 life insurance companies operate in Australia, down from 50 in 2000. Major industry participants include the large wealth management groups such as independent, bank-owned, and foreign institutions. Major banks have acquired a strategic stake in the industry: they now account for over 50 percent of industry assets. Wealth management companies typically have a range of legal entities to provide for the management of wealth. Despite the large number of players, the industry is quite concentrated. The top three life insurance groups accounted for 63 percent of total industry assets and 75 percent of new business premiums in 2006. The top 10 life insurance groups represented 93 percent of total assets.

The major products offered by the life insurance industry are pure risk, annuities, and investment products. Of the two broad types of life insurance products, regular (or annual) premium and single premium, single premium business now accounts for 80 percent of life insurance premiums, of which 97 percent relates to superannuation business. The vast majority of premiums are directed to investment accounts, of which investment-linked accounts predominate.

Table 4.7   Superannuation Assets of Life Insurance Companies

Assets	Year to end of June					
	2002	2003	2004	2005	2006	2007
Total assets ($A billion)	188.4	186.5	196.9	211.4	231.7	256.6
Total assets (% of GDP)	24.8	23.0	22.9	22.6	23.1	23.7
Superannuation assets (% of total assets)	86	86	87	88	89	90
Investment-linked assets (% of domestic assets)	64.2	64.0	66.6	68.4	71.2	73.9
Non-investment-linked assets (% of domestic assets)	35.8	36.0	33.4	31.6	28.8	26.1
Assets backing lifetime annuities (% of total superannuation assets)	2.4	2.8	2.6	2.5	2.1	1.7
Assets backing term annuities (% of total superannuation assets)	3.3	4.3	3.6	3.9	3.2	2.8
Assets backing allocated annuities (% of total superannuation assets)	13.5	12.7	12.3	12.2	12.4	13.7
Investment accounts (% of total superannuation assets)	14.1	13.8	12.6	11.0	9.6	8.4
Investment-linked assets (% of total superannuation assets)	66.7	66.4	69.0	70.4	72.7	73.4
Total superannuation assets (%)	100.0	100.0	100.0	100.0	100.0	100.0
Total superannuation assets ($A billion)	137.4	136.6	144.4	160.9	178.5	201.0
Total superannuation assets (% of GDP)	18.1	16.9	16.8	17.2	17.8	18.5
Life annuities (% of GDP)	0.50	0.54	0.49	0.49	0.42	0.37

Source: APRA, Life Office Market Reports, various years.

Annuities form only a small component of life insurance business. Annuity business attracts about one-sixth of total premiums. The business has shown some volatility in recent years, usually in response to changes in government incentives under its retirement income policy. However, allocated annuities, mostly related to superannuation, dominate total annuity business. Since 2005, lifetime annuity business has almost completely disappeared.[11] Life annuities accounted for less than 2 percent of all superannuation assets held with life insurance companies in 2007 and corresponded to 0.37 percent of GDP (table 4.7).[12]

Menu of Retirement Products

At the benefits stage, Australians are not limited by any regulation of the products they can choose to meet their retirement income needs. Benefits from private pension accumulation may be paid as a lump sum, a temporary income stream, or a lifetime income stream (pension or annuity).[13] Australians are free to mix these products in various combinations to meet their retirement income needs.

Some of these products are defined in government legislation and provide for a range of tax benefits. Although use of income streams is not mandatory, the government has created a range of incentives to encourage people to take up these products. The overall policy objective has been to facilitate capital drawdown over the whole of retirement life. Concessions have been targeted to ensure an adequate replacement rate and overall equity. According to Stanhope (2004), the exemption rules to the age pension asset test are the main incentive rules affecting retiree choice of retirement income products. By investing in assets that receive the exemption, many individuals, particularly those with assets between $A 180,000 and $A 650,000 (for singles), gain much greater access to the age pension.

Capital Lump Sums

Lump-sum payments from superannuation funds are permitted without any restrictions. Australia follows the pattern of several other Anglo-American countries in encouraging, through tax incentives or even compulsion, saving for retirement during the accumulation phase but imposing no restrictions on lump-sum withdrawals in the payout phase. Such countries include Canada, New Zealand, South Africa, and the United States. Hong Kong, China, also has such rules. In contrast, most countries in Latin America and Europe (both Western and Eastern Europe) impose restrictions on lump-sum payments.

During the 1990s, lump-sum payments accounted for 80 percent of all benefit payments. Among industry funds, the near totality of benefits were paid out as lump sums, while among retail funds lump-sum payments represented over 90 percent of total benefits. Among corporate funds, lump sums accounted for 87 percent of all benefits, while the corresponding proportion in public pension funds was 54 percent. Thus, the so-called lump-sum mentality was widespread and even affected public pension funds that offered pension benefits for life. During the first decade of the new millennium, the share of lump-sum payments has steadily declined in favor of pension payments.

However, as will be discussed later, available data suggest that most pension payments take the form of allocated pensions or annuities, which do not provide protection against longevity risk.

Income Streams

Income stream products come in many different forms. The closest to lump-sum payments are fixed-term income streams, followed by life expectancy income streams and allocated income streams. Lifetime income streams are at the other end of the spectrum but have a weak presence outside public pension funds.

Fixed-term income streams. A fixed-term income stream is payable for a set time, which can be for any period from 1 year to about 25 years. A term income stream may allow the purchaser to receive back, at the expiration of the contract, a percentage of the original capital, which is known as the *residual capital value*. Many of the short-term products specify an income of interest only and a residual value of 100 percent of capital. Survey data suggest sales with terms greater than 5 years account for over 90 percent of the total.

Fixed-term income streams are inflexible when it comes to accessing invested capital on an ongoing basis. Although most fixed-term income streams are commutable (that is, accessible) to some extent, penalties may be involved for early cashing of benefits. Thus, except in very limited circumstances, not planning to access the capital at any time prior to the end of the term is preferable. If the purchaser dies within the fixed period, the payments can continue to a beneficiary or to the person's estate, or a lump sum may be payable. Fixed-term income streams that are offered at a fixed rate of interest provide protection against investment risk but do not protect from longevity risk.

Life expectancy income streams. The life expectancy income streams are a special type of fixed-term income stream. They are guaranteed (usually by the provider of the income stream) to be payable for a time period broadly equivalent to the life expectancy of the primary beneficiary at the time of purchase. When a life expectancy income stream is purchased, a person can choose the term over which it is payable, subject to certain limits. The term, however, will be fixed from commencement. For example, if a person's average life expectancy is over 17.7 years (at age 65 for men), the minimum term of the investment must be at least 18 years. The maximum term of the product must be equal to the period from the commencement day of the income stream until a person reaches age 100. Therefore a fixed term of 35 years is permitted. Payments may also take into account the life expectancy of a spouse. Reversionary benefits can be paid to a spouse or dependent.

Allocated income streams. Allocated income streams are the most popular method by which superannuation fund members take income streams, representing more than 80 percent of all money invested in income streams. They are investment accounts within a relevant fund or financial provider. Investment and longevity risks are borne solely by the purchaser. The investment account balance increases as investment earnings are added and decreases as regular income payments are made. Most allocated income streams offer a range of investment choices.

Regulations require that payments occur at least annually. They used to be subject to minimum and maximum amounts to ensure that a mixture of income and capital was drawn down over a period of time approximating a person's life expectancy (these regulations are updated each July), but the maximum limit was removed in 2007. The variance between the minimum and maximum limits was quite large, and people choosing the maximum could face sharply declining income as they aged. In 1998, the minimum annuity conversion factor for a 65-year-old male beneficiary was 6.37 percent, while the maximum equaled 12.35 percent.[14] The maximum and minimum limits decreased as people grew older. The maximum payment per year aimed to ensure that the account balance would not be exhausted before the person reached age 80, whereas the minimum payment was the account balance divided by life expectancy at that age. The imposition of a maximum limit on the annuity conversion factor was not very meaningful in the context of permitting free withdrawals of accumulated balances in the form of lump sums. Changes in the regulations that were implemented in 2007 removed the maximum limit and set lower minimum limits. The new minimum limit for a 65-year-old beneficiary is 5 percent.

Survey data indicate a tendency of pensioners to take lower pensions, reflecting a desire to preserve capital. This view about conservatism is supported by data that indicate that the vast majority of pensioners seek little or no increases in the annual pension they are drawing, preferring instead to preserve capital and experience declines in the real value of their pensions.

Allocated income streams provide considerable flexibility. Holders typically have access to the funds in their investment accounts, and they are able to withdraw all or part at any time, but with possible tax implications. The fact that earnings on the underlying assets of allocated products are tax-free probably contributes to their popularity.

Market-linked income streams. Market-linked income streams are a variation of allocated income streams. They are account-based products offered by superannuation funds or annuity providers. They are sometimes referred to as *term allocated pensions* or *growth pensions*. They were introduced in September 2004 and have not proved very popular.

A market-linked income stream must have income payments made for a fixed term. The fixed term is determined broadly by reference to a person's life expectancy at the commencement of the income stream. A person can choose a term anywhere between certain minimum and maximum terms. The minimum term must be equal to a person's life expectancy in full years. For a man 65 years of age, the life expectancy is 17.7 years; hence, an 18-year term would be relevant. The maximum term is equal to the period from the commencement day of the income stream until the primary beneficiary reaches age 100. Each year, the account balance is divided by a factor applicable to the remaining term. To allow some flexibility in the payments from a market-linked product, a person can select an income stream that is within 10 percent of either side of the calculated figure.

Unlike allocated income streams, market-linked income streams are considerably less flexible when it comes to accessing the capital investment. Generally, most market-linked income streams are noncommutable, unless they are being converted to purchase another complying income stream or in circumstances of extreme financial hardship. The investment choices available for market-linked pensions are virtually the same as are available for allocated income streams. After the death of the account holder, a reversionary benefit can continue to be paid to a spouse or other dependent, or the balance of the account can be paid to a person's beneficiary as a lump sum.

Lifetime income streams. Lifetime income streams are guaranteed to be payable for the whole of the primary beneficiary's life. As previously discussed, Australians have not been keen on purchasing lifetime annuities, and DB pensions that are paid for life have been in long-term decline.

This type of income stream is designed to provide a person with income for life regardless of the person's age. In some cases, income payments may be made for the lifetime of another person, usually a spouse, which is commonly referred to as a *reversionary income stream*. Because the payment is for life, it is often structured to increase annually with movements in inflation or some other set rate of increase.

Some form of income protection can be obtained by selecting what is generally referred to as a *guarantee period* with the lifetime pension or annuity. Should the main beneficiaries die within the guarantee period, income payments may continue to another beneficiary until the end of the guarantee period. The most common guarantee period selected has been 10 years. If the income stream is reversionary, a guarantee period can be selected that is the longer of the beneficiary's life expectancy or the spouse's life expectancy, but not greater than 20 years. Lifetime income streams are the only products that provide protection against longevity risk, and if they are issued with a fixed rate of interest, they also protect against investment risk. However, unless they are linked to the price index, they do not protect against inflation risk.

Table 4.8 summarizes the different types of income stream products and shows how their features vary.

In addition to the range of income stream products, Australians have access to some other specific retirement savings products and to a general range of other investment options.

A retirement savings account (RSA) is an account offered by banks, building societies, credit unions, life insurance companies, and prescribed financial institutions (RSA providers). It is used for retirement savings

Table 4.8   Comparison of Different Types of Income Stream Products

Features	Fixed-term income streams	Life expectancy income streams	Allocated income streams	Market-linked income streams	Lifetime income streams
Account based	No	No	Yes	Yes	No
Annual income payment guaranteed	Yes	Yes	No	No	Yes
Investment choice	No	No	Yes	Yes	No
Fixed term	Yes	Yes	No	Yes	No
Access to capital	Yes	No	Yes	No	No
Recipient can vary annual income received	No	No	Yes	No	No
Residual capital value allowed	Yes	No	n.a.	No	No
Income tested	Yes	Yes	Yes	Yes	Yes
Death benefits payable	Yes	Yes	Yes	Yes	Possibly[a]

Source: FaCSIA 2007.

Note: n.a. = not applicable.

a. Death benefits are payable only when a guarantee period exists and all beneficiaries die within the guarantee period.

and is similar to a superannuation fund. RSAs are capital guaranteed, and providers try to ensure that fees and charges are kept at low levels. An RSA account is subject to the same taxation and superannuation rules as a superannuation fund account; for example, it must be preserved until a condition of release has been met. However, because it is a low-risk account, it offers low returns and is considered suitable for small balances and for people with broken and infrequent work patterns. The balance of an RSA can be transferred to another RSA or superannuation provider on request.

The Pension Loans Scheme is available to part-rate pensioners and some self-funded retirees who own real estate in Australia. Under this scheme, a person who is of pensionable age, or the partner of someone who is, may be able to obtain a loan that will increase their biweekly pension payment up to the maximum pension rate. Repayments can be made at any time, or the debt, including the accrued interest, can be left to be recovered from the person's estate. The loan is secured against the value of any real estate the person owns.[15]

Tax Incentives and Clawback Provisions

The treatment for tax and clawback purposes of the income arising from various investments, including income stream products, has had an important influence on how Australians of pensionable age arrange their financial affairs. By making a particular product more or less attractive relative to other products, the authorities aimed to influence the demand for different products. However, although superannuation is a tax-effective investment vehicle, it has suffered from frequent changes in both tax and clawback rules. These changes have increased the complexity of saving and investment decisions, including the decision to purchase regular income streams, and have diluted the effect of specific measures.

At some point, pensioners found retaining investments in low-interest-bearing accounts relatively attractive because it allowed them to maintain their right to the age pension. This problem was addressed in several different ways, including by basing the assessment of some investments on a deemed income level rather than on the actual level. These policies also aimed at preventing the perverse behavior of seeking lower returns on assets simply to receive a higher age pension and encouraged pensioners to invest at market rates of interest.

Before a major reform of the tax and clawback rules in July 2007, the prevailing rules favored pension and annuity payments. These payments were included in the assessable income of pensioners and were subject to taxation at the relevant marginal rates of tax, but if they were paid from a taxed fund to a taxpayer 55 years of age or older, they generally attracted a tax rebate of 15 percent. This favorable tax treatment was expected to have a major effect in encouraging use of these products. However, that expectation was never fulfilled, probably because superannuation balances were small and still building and because people reaching retirement tended to take lump sums.

Pension and annuity payments that were paid for life or life expectancy and had no residual value were also exempt from both the income and the asset tests. Allocated, market-linked, and fixed-term income streams, which are not paid for life, were not exempt from the asset test, but the component of regular payments that represented a return of capital was exempt from the income test. The exempt amounts were, however, reduced in 2004 (table 4.9).

Before July 2007, so-called reasonable benefit limits were applied on the amount of benefits that individuals could receive at a reduced tax rate. These limits were higher—almost double—for the capital value of income streams than for lump-sum payments.[16] To qualify for the higher limit of income streams, the pensions or annuities had to be payable for life or life expectancy, at least annually, and with no residual capital value. Allocated income streams did not meet these qualifying criteria because they had flexible payment amounts and terms. For people who took a mixture of lump-sum and pension payments, at least half of all benefits had to be taken as benefits subject to the complying standards (that is, payable for life) to be eligible for the reasonable benefit limit.

Major changes to the treatment of superannuation for people over 60 who have superannuation benefits taken from a taxed fund became effective on July 1, 2007. The changes sought to provide greater incentives to save for superannuation by simplifying the arrangements for the

Table 4.9   Income and Asset Test Comparison

Feature	Market-linked income streams	Allocated income streams	Lifetime income streams	Life expectancy income streams
Asset test concession				
Before September 20, 2004	n.a.	0%	100%	100%
From September 20, 2004	50%	0%	50%	50%
Income tested	Yes	Yes	Yes	Yes

Source: FaCSIA 2007.
Note: n.a. = not applicable.

taxation of benefits and reducing the amount of tax levied from benefits paid. The main changes were as follows:

- All lump-sum benefits paid from a taxed source (such as a superannuation fund) and all pensions from a taxed source became tax-free. Taxed funds cover about 90 percent of Australian employees and are typically private sector accumulation funds.
- Reasonable benefit limits were abolished.
- A person who receives a lump sum or a pension payment from a taxed source was no longer required to file a tax return.
- In addition, the complicated system of age-based limitations on tax-advantaged contributions was removed and replaced with a fully deductible annual limit of $A 50,000 irrespective of age. The amount that can be contributed at reduced tax rates is limited to control the use of tax benefits by individuals with high net worth. Contributions for the self-employed became fully deductible, and the opportunity to participate in the government co-contribution arrangement was made available to the self-employed.
- The current tax on contributions and investment earnings of superannuation funds of 15 percent remained in force.

Treatment of the capital value of income streams also changed significantly for the asset test of the age pension. Every complying income stream product bought on or after the implementation date (September 20, 2007, for this proposal) became fully subject to the asset test. Previously, if an income stream product met certain requirements, it was either 50 or 100 percent exempt from the asset test, depending on when it had been bought. The new rule meant that the value of assets that would be subject to the asset test would experience a significant increase.

However, to compensate the growing number of retirees for the impact of the new rule, the government lowered the clawback rate at which the age pension is reduced under the asset test from $A 3.00 to $A 1.50 biweekly for every $A 1,000 in assets above the lower threshold. The reduction in the clawback rate of the asset test is designed to increase incentives to save and to boost the retirement incomes of pensioners whose rate of payment is determined by the asset test. It will also increase the number of people who are eligible for a part pension. The $A 1.50 clawback rate was not changed in the 2009 reforms.

The removal of tax on funded lump sums paid to people over age 60 and changes to the treatment of income streams for the age pension have eroded some of the tax and clawback advantages that were previously conferred on annuities and complying pensions and have reduced the earlier bias in favor of income streams. These changes could lead to an increase in the proportion of benefits taken as lump sums and allocated income streams and create a higher risk that retirees could outlive their savings. However, earnings on assets supporting these pensions remain tax exempt, providing a modest incentive for people to draw income streams on retirement.

Targeted Replacement Rates

When it was introduced in 1908, the age pension was designed to ensure that an individual would live in modest comfort. This aim still remains; however, as early as the mid-1970s, reform proposals began to emerge that sought to shift the emphasis for retirement income policy away from poverty alleviation toward income maintenance through compulsory superannuation. This shift toward greater financial independence has been given further impetus because of the projected fiscal costs of the aging population. A number of government initiatives have sought to encourage independence through deferral of age pension take-up and higher superannuation contributions.

Replacement rates depend on the interaction among tax rules, clawback provisions, actuarial projections on longevity, and assumptions about length of working life and net investment returns. The Organisation for Economic Co-operation and Development's study *Pensions at a Glance* estimated for 2003 that on the assumption of a 3.5 percent net investment return and a 2 percent wage growth rate, the gross replacement rate for a person with average earnings from both the reduced age pension and a life annuity obtained from superannuation balances would amount to 43 percent, whereas the net replacement rate would be higher at 56 percent (OECD 2007, 101). As a result of the means test, the replacement rate for a pensioner earning half the average income before retirement was estimated at 71 percent on a gross basis and 84 percent on a net basis. For a pensioner earning twice the average before retirement, the estimate was 29 percent gross and 41 percent net. Applying a 5 percent net investment return would raise the gross replacement rate for the average earner to 54 percent and the net replacement rate to 70 percent.

The government has not set an explicit replacement rate target for Australia's retirement income system. However, the former Senate Select Committee on Superannuation (2003) noted a strong consensus among superannuation industry representatives that an adequate retirement income was between 60 and 65 percent of preretirement gross income.

Analysis undertaken by the Treasury's Retirement and Income Modelling (RIM) Unit indicates that current policy based on the basic age pension and mandatory and voluntary private savings will deliver substantially higher replacement rates in Australia over the longer term. The RIM Unit calculates replacement rates on the basis of a comparison of potential net expenditure before and after retirement (Rothman 2007). The calculation includes income from the age pension, all private pension payments, and all investments, as well as drawdowns from capital less any tax payments. As shown in figure 4.2, the RIM Unit projects that average replacement rates rise from about 50 percent in 2005 to about 85 percent in 2050 and to higher levels for people from higher income deciles. The higher levels reflect contributions above the SG level and additional private savings made by higher-income groups.

Level of Annuitization
The level of annuitization is low in Australia, but reliable estimates of the actual use of lifetime income streams are very difficult to obtain. Readily available data show that lump-sum payments have been declining steadily

Figure 4.2   Potential Aggregate Replacement Ratios for Selected Deciles

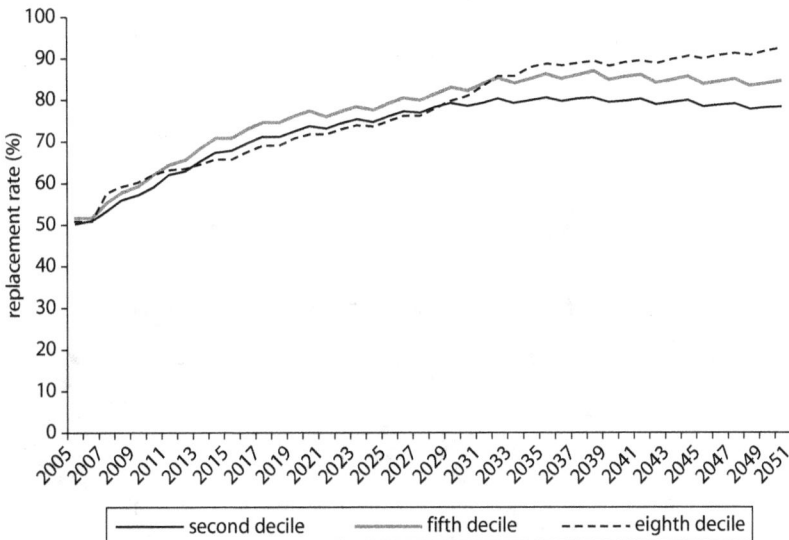

Source: Rothman 2007.

in recent years as a proportion of total benefits. From a level of nearly 80 percent in 2002, lump-sum payments have fallen to approximately 56 percent of total benefit payments in 2009 (table 4.10).

The rise of pension payments, which cover all types of income streams, including lifetime payments as well as allocated and life expectancy pensions, was given greater impetus following legislative changes in 1998,[17] which made offering pensions more attractive for a wider range of superannuation funds. The decline in the proportion of benefits taken as a lump sum has also been associated with the rapid growth of superannuation balances.

Large differences exist in the composition of benefit payments across different types of pension funds (table 4.11). Pension payments accounted for over 40 percent of total benefits in public pension funds in the late 1990s. Their share increased steadily over time and reached 66 percent in 2009. A large part of these pensions is believed to involve payments for life, but no reliable information is available on this score.

In the late 1990s, industry funds paid virtually no pensions, but pension payments have grown in recent years and now represent 12 percent of total benefit payments. For retail funds, pension payments have grown from 8 percent of total payments in the late 1990s to 30 percent in 2007. Outside the public pension funds, the large majority of pension

Table 4.10   Composition of Benefit Payments

Payment	2002	2005	2009
Lump sums (% of total)	79.1	67.7	56.4
Pensions (% of total)	20.9	32.3	43.6
Total (%)	100.0	100.0	100.0
Total ($A billion)	32.5	32.5	61.9
Total (% of GDP)	4.3	3.6	4.9

Source: APRA 2007, 2010.

Table 4.11   Proportion of Pension Payments by Type of Fund
percent

Type of fund	2002	2005	2009
Public pension	41.5	66.0	65.7
Retail	15.0	21.0	36.4
Corporate	14.7	30.0	33.9
Industry	5.6	11.5	19.1
Other	3.7	5.1	68.4

Source: APRA 2007, 2010.

payments involve allocated pensions and other income streams that are not paid for life.

Until the late 1990s, the average balance in private superannuation was relatively small. Fewer than 10 percent of lump sums exceeded $A 200,000. People receiving a small lump sum were likely to use it for debt repayment or home improvements and for general living expenses. However, data on intended disbursement of lump sums indicate that large lump sums were used to a greater extent for investment in financial assets.

Despite attempts in the past to encourage Australians to take up annuity-type products, people still have a strong bequest motive and are very averse to products with little or no residual value and no possibility of capital withdrawal. Allocated pensions accord with retirees' stated preference for products that offer tax advantages, the possibility of a residual sum, control of the portfolio supporting the pension, and flexibility regarding the timing and size of a pension. Since 2000, sales of allocated pension products have grown dramatically, whereas the market for life annuities has stagnated.

Australians have shown considerable interest in reverse mortgages and other types of home-equity release products, which allow homeowners to access the equity in their home without having to sell and move from the home. In a reverse mortgage, the house is used as security for a loan, which is provided as a lump sum, as a regular stream of monthly payments, or as a combination of both. The owner retains title to the house but grants the provider a mortgage to secure repayment of principal and interest under the loan. The outstanding balance of the loan grows over time as the interest is capitalized (rather than repaid). The loan and interest on it are paid back when the house is sold; when the borrower permanently moves away (for example, moving into long-term care); or upon death. Equity-release products are generally available to consumers 55 years of age and older who own their own homes free of any debt or who have only a small mortgage outstanding. The amount available to be borrowed is usually restricted to between 20 and 40 percent of the total property value.

The market for equity-release products in Australia is developing rapidly. According to recent market information, reverse mortgages grew from $A 459 million at the end of 2004 to $A 2.48 billion at the end of 2008. The average age of borrowers is 74, although younger borrowers are the fastest-growing group. Although lump sums continue to dominate, accounting for 97 percent of all outstanding loans, regular drawdowns are increasing and represented 3 percent of new loans in 2008, indicating that more people are using the product to supplement their pensions (SEQUAL 2009). This growth of reverse mortgages has the potential to further affect attitudes toward annuities by giving many retirees access to additional income streams without purchasing an annuity product.

Reverse mortgages have not been without their problems in the United Kingdom and the United States, which have seen cases of misselling and evictions. In Australia, the product is subject to a range of existing consumer regulations. In addition, some reverse mortgage providers have established an industry association, Senior Australians Equity Release Association of Lenders (SEQUAL), which has a code of conduct and compels its members to belong to an approved external dispute resolution scheme.

Money's Worth Ratios

One factor, which has a bearing on the popularity of lifetime annuities, is the value that they provide to their purchaser as measured by the money's worth ratios. Knox (2000) found that the majority of money's worth ratios for Australian annuities were in the range of 85 to 95 percent of the purchase price. He also observed that the results in Australia, even though the market was poorly developed, were consistent with major international markets and that the money's worth ratios compared favorably with recent research for the U.K. and U.S. markets. However, in more recent research, Ganegoda (2007) reported that when compared with previous calculations for Australian annuities, the money's worth of Australian annuities had apparently dropped significantly, reflecting high loadings such as administrative costs and profit margins. Allocated annuities receive the same tax and income test treatment as life annuities. Despite the higher risks retained by their holders, many retirees perceive allocated annuities as having considerable advantages over life annuities, mainly because of their greater flexibility.

Marketing Rules

The Australian superannuation industry is highly decentralized, with a large number of superannuation funds and a plethora of competing fund managers. Although the number of institutions has declined significantly in recent years as a result of an ongoing consolidation process, more than 450 still existed in June 2009.

Despite the decentralized nature of the system and the high complexity of income stream and equity-release products, however, no special marketing rules have been imposed on the sale of these products. Industrywide codes of conduct and "know your customer" rules affect the operations of superannuation funds, insurance companies, and providers of reverse mortgages, but no specific requirements promote transparent and competitive quotations.

The lack of clear and robust marketing rules may inhibit the development of the annuity business because the products are highly complex and a widespread perception exists that annuity products do not represent good value for money. The authorities wisely advise retirees to avoid investing all their capital in lifetime income streams because they lack flexibility and do not allow accessibility to capital. However, this sound advice needs to be accompanied by assurances that the marketing of annuities is well regulated and that retirees will receive proper advice and competitive quotations.

Risk-Sharing Arrangements

The limited use of fixed or variable lifetime income streams implies that retirees bear most of the financial risks of retirement, ranging from investment and inflation risks to credit and operational risks and longevity risk. Except for the age pension, which they receive from the government for life and which is effectively linked to wage inflation, Australian retirees engage in self-annuitization.

Until the introduction of compulsory superannuation and the growing realization that to live comfortably in retirement additional savings will be necessary, people had a strong incentive to manage their financial affairs with a view to maximizing their access to the age pension. Retirees could "double dip" by taking their lump sum, spending it as they wished, and then applying to receive the age pension. The ability to retire early financed by their accumulated superannuation balances until they became eligible for the age pension was facilitated by the law, which allowed retirement at age 55.[18]

Despite these incentives, however, no compelling evidence indicates deliberate rapid rundown of accumulated balances. Some survey evidence (Kalisch 1992) showed little dissipation of lump sums on such things as overseas trips and other forms of consumption; just over 85 percent of lump sums were directed toward financial, property, or business investments. Recent cohort studies also indicate that although age pensioners are, on average, drawing down their wealth in retirement, this drawdown is apparently at a very slow pace. If this pattern persists, it would allow pensioners to maintain significant assets through many years of retirement. It may indicate that pensioners are managing their wealth effectively and are drawing on their assets in a way that has regard to their expectations of a long life.

Regulation and Supervision

This section describes the institutional structure of the Australian pension and annuity market and looks at the prudential regulation and supervision of superannuation funds and insurance companies.

Institutional Structure

The institutional structure of the superannuation industry is highly decentralized, with a large number of competing institutions. Despite an ongoing consolidation process, the industry has more than 450 institutions, with more than 150 retail funds. Since July 1, 2005, most employees can choose which superannuation fund they wish to join, although many employment awards still nominate an industry or corporate fund as the default option. Public offer funds, which include not only retail funds but also a growing number of industry funds, some corporate funds, and even two public sector funds, compete aggressively to attract participants. Unlike the situation in many other countries, the market in Australia is not constrained by pervasive product and price controls, but it suffers from considerable dispersion in investment returns and operating fees, with retail funds reporting on a consistent basis by far the lowest net investment returns.

Members of public pension, industry, and large corporate funds generally benefit from economies of scale and from the absence of heavy marketing costs and agent commissions. Participants in retail funds, who usually do not have access to any of the privileged funds, suffer not only from high marketing costs but also from high profit margins that their fund managers apply to assets under management.

The sharp decline in sales of life annuities in recent years has resulted in a reduction in the number of life annuity providers; only four companies provided regular quotes on life annuities in 2007, compared with 11 in 1998 (Ganegoda 2007). Most insurance companies and superannuation funds compete actively in the offer of allocated annuities, which are investment products and do not provide to their holders any insurance against the risk of outliving their savings.

APRA is the main supervisory authority, responsible for the prudential regulation of institutions involved in deposit taking, insurance, and superannuation. Another supervisory authority, the Australian Securities and Investments Commission, is responsible for market integrity, consumer protection, and corporate financial behavior and covers market conduct issues. APRA has adopted a similar regulatory approach to both life insurance and superannuation. The main differences arise in relation to solvency requirements and reflect the different legislative bases under which the industries are regulated.

Solvency Regulation
Solvency regulation differs for pension funds and life insurance companies.

Pension funds. Solvency regulation draws a clear distinction between DB schemes, on the one hand, and accumulation or DC schemes, on the other. DB schemes are clearly defined in the law, and all other schemes are considered as DC. The effect of the law is to restrict the more straightforward rules applying to DC schemes to those schemes that do not carry material levels of risk that would normally be associated with a DB scheme. Hybrid schemes, which cover both DC and DB elements, are classified for solvency regulation purposes as DB schemes.

DB schemes are interpreted to include schemes that provide a defined conversion factor for a pension benefit or some other form of predetermined benefit. DC schemes are permitted to provide defined benefits for death or invalidity during the accumulation phase without risking their DC status. A DC scheme can be capital guaranteed (that is, guaranteed not to credit members with a negative earning rate). Finally, a DC scheme can provide member protection, meaning that it may guarantee that the earnings will not be less than the expenses charged (that is, the accumulated value of the member account will not be eroded because the income is less than the expense charges), and this protection may be provided for a subset of the members if desired.

DC schemes. The solvency rules for DC schemes require them to be technically solvent by having net realizable assets greater than or equal to the minimum guaranteed benefits of members. Minimum guaranteed benefits include the accumulated value of all contributions (with interest and less expense charges). Trustees of the schemes assess their technical solvency.

Reserves in a DC scheme may arise from the following sources:

- Specific contributions from the sponsor
- Investment returns in excess of those credited to the various accumulating balances
- The difference between the charges made on member accounts and the actual cost of the services (for example, rebates received on insurance arrangements)
- The unvested benefits of members who withdraw early
- Other sources.

These reserves may be used, among other purposes, to support (a) a smoothing of crediting rates over time, (b) an element of mismatch in the investment strategy, (c) the provision of a guarantee on account balances when they are not invested fully in assets of a capital-guaranteed nature, or (d) payments for the cost of member protection. They may even be used to facilitate the retention of some of the death and disability risk rather than to insure it in full. Deferring costs is prohibited, so expense charges cannot be reduced in the current period in the expectation that they will be recovered at a later date (that is, smoothing of expenses is not permitted).

All funds are expected to have a crediting rate policy, an insurance risk policy, or an investment policy such that the level of risk actually retained is manageable. Developing these policies, in case some risk is retained, is expected to include sophisticated risk analysis, and because most schemes have only small reserves, trustees generally seek to avoid rather than retain and manage risks. Aside from the fiduciary liability of the trustees, retention and management of risk requires a far more extensive and detailed policy than a policy that simply does not retain the risk at all.

If a scheme is determined to be solvent at the beginning of the accounting and reporting year, the trustees may increase the benefits (usually by determining the addition of investment earnings), but they are not permitted to increase the amounts to such an extent that the scheme would become insolvent at the end of the year. In other words, the trustees may not increase benefits by more than the scheme can afford. This rule obliges trustees to consider the actual solvency position before adding to benefits.

If the scheme is technically insolvent, benefits can still be added in certain circumstances. First, a scheme must obtain the report of an actuary, and that report should propose an arrangement whereby the scheme would be expected to become solvent again within not more than five years. If this recovery is not possible, then the scheme must be wound up. Second, any addition must be made only after the actuary has approved it; it must be in compliance with the arrangement to restore the scheme to solvency. During a period of insolvency, any payment from the scheme is banned except with the approval of the actuary. Such an arrangement also has to have the approval of the supervisory authority.

DB schemes. For DB schemes, solvency is measured by the minimum benefit index (MBI), which is given by the ratio of net realizable assets over funded minimum benefits for current contributory members. This calculation sets aside the assets and liabilities for current beneficiaries (and thus former members) of the scheme. The financial position of DB schemes must be certified by the actuary or auditor, who is required to report to the supervisor and the scheme trustees if the financial position of a scheme is likely to become unsatisfactory.

All DB schemes must have an actuarial investigation at least every three years. Actuarial projections for long-term investment returns and wage growth, as well as mortality tables, are key assumptions in this process. The actuary also recommends the rate at which employer contributions should be made for the next three years. A DB scheme must also have a funding and solvency certificate from the scheme actuary.

A DB scheme with an MBI of less than 1.0 is considered technically insolvent. This finding triggers the requirement for a program to resolve the situation or, failing that, for the fund to be wound up. Schemes in this state must also have a new funding and solvency certificate prepared and then renewed at least annually during the resolution stage. These special funding and solvency certificates specify contributions required with the aim to restore solvency over a period not exceeding five years. The funding and solvency certificate also should consider adverse situations in which the certificate may cease to become valid, such as the progressive aging of active members and the effect of layoffs.

To strengthen the robustness of DB schemes, additional requirements were introduced in the late 1990s in relation to the vested benefits index (VBI) and the accrued benefits index (ABI) that go beyond the MBI requirements. An annual actuarial investigation would be required if these actuarial ratios were not above unity. The MBI captures only those benefits under the SG. The VBI represents the total amount that a fund would be required to pay if all members were to leave the fund voluntarily on the valuation dates, together with the value of all pensions. The ABI provides an indication of progress toward funding members' accrued retirement and other benefits. These benefits represent the present value of expected future benefits arising with respect to membership of the fund up to the valuation date. The VBI indicates whether the fund is in an unsatisfactory financial position as defined in the regulations, but APRA also expects that the ABI should be greater than unity. The actuarial standards also make clear that actuaries should set funding rates that keep a fund's VBI above 1.0. For all superannuation funds that reported VBI data in June 2008 (APRA 2008), 91 percent of non–public sector funds reported a VBI of at least 100 percent, and 56 percent of public sector funds reported a VBI of at least 100 percent. Of the public sector funds that reported VBI data in June 2008, 28 percent reported a VBI of less than 70 percent.

Life insurance companies. The legal framework establishes a two-tier regulatory regime for life insurance companies: the first tier is solvency, and the second tier is capital adequacy. Profits are reported on the basis of policy liabilities, which are the sum of best-estimate liabilities and future profit margins.

Three separate but related valuations are carried out. The methodology is similar, but the assumptions are different in each case and some additional provisions are applied. The first is the *best-estimate valuation*, which uses realistic assumptions to value future liabilities and profit margins. The second is the *solvency valuation*, which is largely based on a runoff assessment and uses more conservative assumptions. The third is the *capital adequacy valuation*, which is based on a going-concern assessment and uses less conservative assumptions than the solvency valuation because it is based on a continuing rather than closing-down scenario. However, the need to provide for business growth plans can make it more onerous that the solvency valuation. Moreover, the capital adequacy requirement cannot be less than the solvency requirement; thus, in practice, the two valuations are quite similar for mature stable cases, but capital adequacy is more onerous for rapidly growing businesses.

Life insurance companies are required to establish and operate a series of statutory funds and to attribute each policy to a particular fund. Although the legal structure is that each fund is part of the company accounts and is not a separate legal entity, some constraints and protections separate the funds from other assets and liabilities of the insurer.

Companies may—and often do—establish separate funds for particular business lines. Establishing a separate statutory fund for annuity business has been popular. This practice has considerable administrative advantages and facilitates the management of asset liability risks, but an additional reason for its popularity could be the favorable taxation result that may emerge because the investment earnings on free capital in the annuity statutory fund are subject to a lower tax rate.

The solvency regulation is not explicitly risk based in the sense that set risk factors are used in calculating the value of assets, liabilities, and sums insured. However, it does seek to take into account risk factors and the likely volatility of assets and liabilities through the use of conservative prudential buffers. These buffers attempt to put a value on the impact of economic shocks, such as a significant fall in equity prices, sudden changes in interest rates or other adverse events, and to ensure that adequate reserves are held so the impact of these events is mitigated.

Most life insurers hold assets in excess of the capital adequacy requirements, and many have a policy of monitoring these excess or "free" assets against what is known as a *target surplus*. The target surplus has been described by the Institute of Actuaries of Australia (2006) as "an amount of buffer capital, additional to regulatory requirements that a life insurance company chooses to hold given its risk tolerance levels, to allow for adverse performance." No regulatory requirements exist in relation to the target surplus, and APRA has observed that the methodologies and rationale behind the development of target surplus by life insurers vary widely. Nevertheless, APRA has signaled its increasing focus on the target surplus policies and practices of insurance companies. APRA is interested in seeing that the life insurer (plus its board) has developed a target surplus philosophy, that it has considered the desired level of probability of failure, and that steps are in place to deal with the situation when the target surplus level is under pressure. APRA expects the appointed actuary of a company to comment on whether a target surplus philosophy has been developed, how the present capital position measures up against the target, and what action steps (if any) are planned.

APRA notes that "the level of free assets that an insurer holds above its regulatory requirements is a matter for the insurer itself. However, the way an insurer manages and develops its target surplus, and the level of this surplus, bears on APRA's own risk rating of the insurer and, hence, on the level of resources which APRA devotes to its supervision" (APRA 2004, 5). This focus on the target surplus also moves APRA toward the Solvency II capital model being developed in Europe. The Solvency II model draws on the Basel II approach to banking and has three components: solvency capital, minimum capital, and supervisory review.

Risk-Based Supervision

APRA has adopted a risk-based supervisory approach for both insurance and superannuation. Two supervisory tools, the Probability and Impact Rating System (PAIRS) and the Supervisory Oversight and Response System (SOARS), are designed to ensure that APRA supervisors assess risks rigorously and consistently and that any supervisory interventions are both targeted and timely. PAIRS seeks to calculate an overall risk of failure for supervised entities. It assesses the likelihood that an institution will fail to honor its financial promises to beneficiaries (depositors, policyholders, and superannuation fund members). SOARS provides a framework of supervisory stances that can be adopted depending on the level of risk in each institution.

There are four supervisory stances indicating the intensity of APRA's involvement. *Normal* means that no special action is taken beyond regular supervision activities. Institutions in *Oversight* have some aspect of their risk position or operations—such as minor but persistent weaknesses in the control framework or insufficient capital—that requires more-extensive examination by APRA. *Mandated Improvement* institutions are operating outside APRA's acceptable bounds for prudent risk management. These institutions must have acceptable plans to correct the deficiencies, and they are likely to be subject to more-intense supervisory attention. Institutions in *Restructure* are no longer viable in their current form and need some combination of new management, new ownership or new capital, or a new business arrangement.

The main differences between insurance and superannuation supervision were that until July 1, 2004, only the trustees of for-profit retail funds open to members of the public rather than to employees of a particular employer were required to meet entry threshold tests of capital and capacity and to go through a licensing process. However, in July 2004, a new licensing system commenced for all trustees of prudentially regulated funds. All trustees must now be licensed by APRA, and all superannuation funds with a licensed trustee must be registered. The universal licensing regime brings superannuation funds into line with all other regulated financial institutions and permits APRA to identify—and to bar—problematic trustees before they have accepted any investments.

Risk Management

Life insurance companies are required to have in place a risk management framework and a written risk management strategy. This strategy should identify and quantify risks through the use of risk-mapping techniques and appropriate risk indicators. Life insurance companies should also develop risk mitigation and control policies. Segregation of duties and avoidance of conflicts of interest in assigning responsibilities are underscored as important components of internal control systems. By deterring the concealment of inappropriate actions, such policies facilitate early detection of errors and prevent the magnification of financial losses.

The risk management strategy must deal with all major types of risks facing life insurance companies. Particular emphasis is placed on the management of life insurance and reinsurance risks and on the management of asset and liability mismatch risk. Life insurers are required to have clear policies on product design, pricing, underwriting, claims management, and reinsurance. The importance of relying on expert actuarial advice and monitoring compliance with established policies is emphasized.

On asset and liability mismatch risk, insurers are expected to assess the risk tolerance of different stakeholders and to adopt policies that quantify, monitor, and control exposure to mismatch risk. They are also required to have clear asset management policies regarding the use of internal and external managers and the selection and performance criteria of external managers. Because of the preponderance of investment-linked assets, the exposure of life insurers to mismatch risk is limited to the types and level of guarantees offered in their investment-linked products.

Superannuation funds are also required to have risk management strategies in place. In addition to management of investment risk, particular emphasis is placed on outsourcing of risk because many funds rely extensively on third-party service providers. Like insurance companies, superannuation funds have a preponderance of investment-linked accounts in which the investment risk is borne by participating workers. But DB and hybrid funds, in which the investment risk is borne by the funds, are required to quantify, monitor, and control their exposure to asset liability mismatch risk.

The limited use of lifetime pensions and annuities implies limited exposure of life insurers and superannuation funds to longevity risk. As a result, they have shown little interest in promoting the development of hedging instruments, such as longevity bonds or longevity derivatives.

Concluding Remarks

Observers have often puzzled over why the annuity market, especially the market for lifetime annuities, is not more developed in Australia. Australians are living longer and face uncertainty regarding the level of their retirement income. The two main reasons for the limited use of lifetime annuities appear to be (a) that people can rely on the age pension if they have to and (b) that they have a great desire for flexibility in investment options, which is not available if they purchase a lifetime annuity.

In the past 20 years, a dramatic change has taken place in the attitudes of Australians toward saving for retirement. Most now feel that if they are to have a comfortable standard of living in retirement, they will need to supplement the government-provided age pension. Australians have built up substantial balances in the private pension system, mainly as a result of the compulsory SG requirements, but increasingly through additional private savings. These balances continue to be taken as lump sums at retirement, but evidence suggests that withdrawn balances are invested prudently in a range of retirement income products. The greatest motivation is to ensure that the funds will last people through retirement and something will be left when they die to leave to their beneficiaries. The funds are not being exhausted rapidly, and people do not appear to fear that they will outlive their savings.

The buildup of retirement savings will to some extent cushion the effect of an aging population. Forecasts in the government's intergenerational report (Treasury 2007) indicate that fiscal pressures will build from about 2020 onward, not only because of age pensions, but also because of higher spending on health care. The sense is that no "aging crisis" exists, although some changes will have to be made in the level of benefits, taxation, or private contributions to superannuation in the longer run. The government seems more than comfortable to leave the investment of retirement income savings to individuals. Most people seem to be investing their funds wisely, and the rundown of accumulated assets is occurring only slowly. Some concerns have been expressed that the current system may lead people to undertake excessive consumption in their early years of retirement and may thus have to rely on the age pension in later life, but with changing attitudes toward the need to secure their retirement, the opposite may in fact be true. People may be too conservative in their spending and spend too little rather than too much. This pattern reduces individual welfare, but it does reduce recourse to the age pension.

Australians do not appear to have any significant concerns about longevity risk, and hence demand for products, such as lifetime annuities, that provide a hedge against this risk is small. Many Australians expect that they will have sufficient resources to ensure that they have a comfortable retirement, and those who do not can always rely on the age pension.

Finally, for many Australians, their home provides an additional buffer, particularly given a growing understanding of equity-release products.

Over several years, the authorities have taken a number of initiatives aimed at reducing incentives for early retirement. These initiatives include the standardization of the retirement age for men and women by phasing in a higher age for women, the increase in compulsory preservation age for occupational superannuation from 55 to 60, and the introduction of a deferred pension bonus plan. The government appears satisfied that it has its parametric settings broadly correct.

Notes

1. On July 22, 2010, $A 1 was approximately US$0.89.

2. The exemption of the principal home is attributed to the strong attachment to home ownership and the associated financial security it involves in the Australian culture. Australia exhibits a high level of home ownership; as a result, the influence of the treatment of the principal private residence is particularly important in retirement plans and is politically material in considering policy options. In 2001, overall home ownership was 70 percent, a relatively high rate by global standards (Brunner and Thorburn 2008).

3. As of May 2007, this liability stood at about $A 103 billion, and it is expected to grow to about $A 148 billion by 2020. By March 2010, accumulated assets of the Future Fund were $A 58 billion.

4. Limited exceptions are provided for the SG contribution obligation that relate to employees with very low wages, part-time employees under 18 years of age, and employees 70 years of age and older.

5. The timetable for the employer contribution rates was as follows: in 1992, 3 percent for employers with payrolls less than $A 1 million and 5 percent for those with higher payrolls; in 1996 to 1998, 6 percent; in 1998 to 2000, 7 percent; in 2000 to 2002, 8 percent; in 2002 to 2003 and thereafter, 9 percent. In legal effect, the SG does not oblige payment into a scheme. However, if no such payment is made, then a higher rate (the same contribution plus a loading fee to cover an interest and an administration element) must be made through the taxation system to the Australian Tax Office. Employees for whom such a payment has been made are entitled to claim the normal SG contribution from the Australian Tax Office and to transfer it to a scheme of their choice. As a result, employers have a strong incentive to make the payments directly to approved schemes rather than through the Australian Tax Office.

6. The remaining gaps in coverage are explained by exemptions for some low-paid workers and itinerant workers, as well as the continuing lower coverage in the self-employed sector.

7. The government's co-contribution was introduced in July 2003 and matched dollar for dollar member contributions up to a limit of $A 1,000. The measure was available in full for incomes up to $A 27,500 when it was introduced and subject to a linear phaseout up to a maximum level of $A 40,000 in taxable income. In 2004, the government increased the matching to $A 1.50 for every $A 1.00 up to a limit of $A 1,500. The benefit thresholds were also adjusted to $A 28,000 and $A 58,000 respectively, providing a gentler phaseout. Eligible members automatically receive this payment in their member account in the superannuation scheme when their tax return is processed. The government again adjusted the co-contribution rate for the fiscal year that commenced on July 1, 2009. The co-contribution rate for the period to June 30, 2012, will be $A 1.00 for every dollar contributed, to a maximum of $A 1,000. The co-contribution will be reduced by 3.333 cents for every dollar earned over $A 31,920 and will be reduced to zero for incomes over $A 61,919. The co-contribution rate will be $A 1.25 per dollar contributed in the following two years with a deduction of 4.167 cents per dollar over the minimum and will revert to $A 1.50 with a reduction of 5.000 cents commencing July 1, 2014.

8. The balance of statutory funds of life insurance companies is the difference between superannuation assets reported by life insurers and the assets that superannuation funds report as held with insurance companies. This balance mainly covers assets backing various types of annuities and capital funds.

9. For the 10-year period ending in June 2006, retail funds reported an average investment return of 5.3 percent against 8.0 percent for public sector funds, 7.8 percent for corporate funds, and 6.7 percent for industry funds (APRA 2007, 51). Recent publications have focused on the rate of return as a performance measure. For the year ended June 30, 2009, the rates of return were as follows: public sector 12.3 percent, industry and retail funds 11.7 percent, and corporate funds 10 percent.

10. APRA changed the basis of reporting, so these figures cannot be consistently updated.

11. In 2007, only 4 companies were providing regular quotes on life annuities, compared with 11 in 1998 (Ganegoda 2007).

12. Changes in data reporting do not allow updating of this information.

13. A distinction is drawn in Australia between pensions and annuities. Pensions are offered by superannuation funds, and annuities are offered by life insurance companies. Pension income streams can be created only with balances that are within a superannuation fund and certain types of lump-sum payments made to an employee on termination of employment; in contrast, annuity income streams can accept any type of savings, including deposits directly from a bank account. Pensions and annuities are otherwise identical

products, offering regular (fixed or variable) income streams, either for life or for specified terms.

14. In the relevant tables, the minimum pension factor is expressed as a divisor and equals 15.7 for the minimum and 8.1 for the maximum benefit (Knox 2000, 25).

15. The Pension Loans Scheme has had limited acceptance among retirees.

16. In 2005/06, the reasonable benefit limits amounted to nearly $A 650,000 for lump-sum payments and $A 1.3 million for the capital value of qualifying income streams.

17. In 1998, the government extended the income streams qualifying as complying pensions and annuities to include noncommutable income streams that pay a guaranteed income for a person's life expectancy.

18. The age is now 60 for people who commenced working after 1995.

References

APRA (Australian Prudential Regulation Authority). 2004. "Life Insurance: Industry Overview." *APRA Insight* (Quarter 2): 2–7. http://www.apra.gov .au/Insight/upload/APRA-Insight-2nd-Quarter-2004.pdf.

———. 2007. "Celebrating 10 Years of Superannuation Data Collection: 1996–2006." *APRA Insight* (Special ed.): 1–68. http://www.apra.gov .au/Insight/APRA-Insight-Issue-2-2007.cfm.

———. 2008. "Statistics Annual Superannuation Bulletin." APRA, Sydney, Australia, June.

———. 2010. "Statistics Annual Superannuation Bulletin." APRA, Sydney Australia, February. http://www.apra.gov.au/Statistics/upload/June-2008- revised-Annual-Superannuation-Bulletin-PDF.pdf.

Bateman, Hazel J., and John Piggott. 1997. "Private Pensions in OECD Countries: Australia." OECD Labour Market and Social Policy Occasional Paper 23, Organisation for Economic Co-operation and Development, Paris.

Brunner, Gregory Gordon, and Craig Thorburn. 2008. "The Market for Retirement Products in Australia." Policy Research Working Paper 4749, World Bank, Washington, DC.

FaCSIA (Department of Families, Community Services, and Indigenous Affairs). 2007. "Retirement Income Streams." FaCSIA, Canberra. http://www.fahcsia .gov.au/sa/seniors/pubs/Documents/retirement_income_streams/retirement_in come_streams.pdf.

Ganegoda, Amandha. 2007. "Explaining the Demand for Life Annuities in the Australian Market." CPS Discussion Paper 05/2007, Centre for Pensions and Superannuation, University of New South Wales, Sydney, Australia.

Institute of Actuaries of Australia. 2006. "Life Financial Reporting Tax and Legislation Sub Committee Discussion Note: Target Surplus." Institute of Actuaries of Australia, Sydney, Australia, April. http://www.actuaries.asn.au.

Kalisch, David W. 1992. "Interaction between Age Pension and Superannuation." In *Economic and Social Consequences of Australia's Ageing Population: Preparing for the 21st Century*, ed. Economic Planning Advisory Council, 74–96. Canberra: Australian Government Public Service.

Knox, David. 2000. "The Australia Annuity Market." Policy Research Working Paper 2495, World Bank, Washington, DC.

OECD (Organisation for Economic Co-operation and Development). 2007. *Pensions at a Glance*. Paris: OECD.

Rothman, George P. 2007. "The Adequacy of Australian Retirement Incomes: New Estimates Incorporating the Better Super Reforms." Paper presented to the 15th Colloquium of Superannuation Researchers, University of Sydney, Australia, July 19–20.

Senate Select Committee on Superannuation. 2003. *Planning for Retirement*. Canberra: Commonwealth of Australia.

SEQUAL (Senior Australians Equity Release Association of Lenders). 2009. "Australia's Reverse Mortgage Market Reaches $2.5 Billion." Media release issued by SEQUAL and Deloitte Touche Tohmatsu, Sydney, Australia, May 1.

Stanhope, Bill. 2004. "A Risk-Free Return Is a Risk-Free Return: The Insurance Predilection in Public Policy for Retirement Income Streams." *Australian Economic Review* 37 (2): 205–14.

Treasury. 2002. *Intergenerational Report 2002–03*. Canberra: Commonwealth of Australia. http://www.budget.gov.au/2002-03/bp5/html/01_BP5Prelim.html.

———. 2007. *Intergenerational Report 2007*. Canberra: Commonwealth of Australia. http://www.treasury.gov.au/igr/.

———. 2010. *2010 Intergenerational Report: Australia to 2050: Future Challenges*. Canberra: Commonwealth of Australia. http://www.treasury.gov.au/igr/igr2010/report/pdf/IGR_2010.pdf.

CHAPTER 5

Switzerland

Rigid Regulation and the Challenge of Sustainability

Switzerland's pension system has a three-pillar structure. A relatively small pay-as-you-go (PAYG) public pillar is complemented by a fully funded occupational pillar. Although the latter was mandated only 25 years ago, employer-based pensions have a long history, which is still reflected in the institutional fragmentation of the second pillar. Tax-favored savings, primarily targeting the self-employed, constitute the third pillar.

This chapter focuses on the rate of annuitization in the second pillar and the value of second-pillar annuities. Switzerland has a high level of annuitization by international standards (approximately 80 percent), and the money's worth ratios of annuities are very high (with the exception of annuities of single men). Replacement rates for workers with full careers are equally high.

Occupational pension plans are tightly regulated, especially with regard to the mandated minimum benefits. A minimum interest rate (MIR) for mandatory savings and a minimum annuity conversion factor (ACF), at which the accumulated retirement balances are transformed

---

This chapter is a summary and update, prepared by the editors, of the paper by Monika Bütler and Martin Ruesch titled "Annuities in Switzerland" (Bütler and Ruesch 2007).

into annuity streams, introduce elements of defined benefit (DB) plans into notional defined contribution schemes. However, pension funds have considerable leeway in setting their own conditions and benefits, provided that the board of trustees on which employers and employees have equal representation approves. Because of this freedom, the level and types of benefits offered vary considerably. Supervision of the second pillar is impeded by its high institutional fragmentation and by the lack of adequate transparency regarding the investment performance and financial soundness of individual institutions.

The strict regulation of minimum contribution rates, MIRs, and minimum ACFs has aimed at achieving targeted replacement rates while protecting individual workers from the vicissitudes of financial markets. However, a significant fall in the level of financial market returns and a significant increase in longevity have raised questions about the sustainability of the level of the regulated variables. In fact, the authorities have taken steps to lower both the MIR and the minimum ACF. But the regulations have also overlooked distortions and redistribution among different groups of workers. Addressing these distortions would require a more fundamental restructuring of the second pillar.

The structure of this chapter is as follows. The next section offers a brief overview of the Swiss pension system. Then, in the following section, the chapter reviews the main retirement products and reports on the level of annuitization, targeted replacement rates, money's worth ratios, and risk-sharing characteristics. Next the chapter analyzes the main regulatory provisions, focusing on investment and prudential rules and the financial soundness of pension funds. The last section offers some concluding remarks.

Overview of the Swiss Pension System

This section describes the components of the Swiss pension system.

The Public Pillar

The public pillar was introduced in 1948 to provide a basic subsistence level of income to all retired residents in Switzerland, with a full contribution period of 45 years for men and 44 years for women. The public pillar has no specified target replacement rate, but the average replacement rate with respect to preretirement income is approximately 35 percent. It is much higher for low-income individuals with a full contribution period and very low for high-income people. Although a link exists between contributions and benefits for low-income workers, dispersion of benefits is limited because the maximum pension is equal to twice the minimum pension. The vast majority of workers with full contribution periods are entitled to the maximum benefit.

The first pillar operates on PAYG principles. It has a small trust fund that covers less than one year's benefits. It is financed with a payroll tax of 8.4 percent on all labor income of employed workers, with no ceiling, and split equally between employers and employees. Self-employed workers pay 7.8 percent on their declared income. Nonworking individuals, including students, are required to contribute a specified minimum amount that allows them to be insured for a full contribution period. By law, 20 percent of total old-age expenditures are financed out of general federal government revenues. However, an earmarked fraction of the value added tax on consumption is also used to cover the deficit of the pillar. Contribution rates have remained unchanged since the mid-1970s.

For a long time, the public pillar was viewed as stable, efficient (at reducing poverty in old age), and cheap (because of very low administration costs). But like most PAYG systems in Europe, the Swiss first pillar is plagued by unfavorable demographics resulting from increases in longevity and low fertility rates, which have led to a strong rise in the old-age dependency ratio. If the current levels of contributions and benefits are left unchanged, the present value of future contributions falls short of the present value of future claims by about a third. There are virtually no reserves to cushion the anticipated aging population.

Revisions of the first pillar in 2000 have led to a number of important structural changes. First, individual benefits have replaced family and household benefits. Second, individuals with responsibility for children up to age 16 or other dependents are now entitled to child care credits. Third, contributions during marriage, including child care credits, are split between the spouses. This change led to a substantial improvement for divorced women but reduced the entitlements of couples with a nonworking spouse and no children. Fourth, the legal retirement age for women has been raised stepwise from 62 years to 64 years, and most probably, it will be raised to 65.

Pensioners can claim supplementary, means-tested benefits to cover their living costs if their total income is too low. In principle, these supplementary benefits are equivalent to the difference between an individual's or couple's income and the expenditures deemed necessary. The latter include actual rent (or mortgage payments), so-called basic needs (a fixed sum per person), and actual health expenditures. Not all individuals who qualify for supplementary benefits claim them, because they are still associated with a certain social stigma, especially in rural regions. The take-up rate is approximately 50 percent. The combination of a relatively flat benefit structure and supplementary benefits has led to a low poverty rate among the elderly in Switzerland, although gaps remain for low-income earners.

Occupational Pension Plans

The Swiss second pillar, organized as an occupational pension system, has a long history but did not become mandatory until 1985. A sizable fraction of the working force was already covered before 1985. Coverage expanded from 60 percent in 1984 to 90 percent in 1987 but has since stabilized at about 80 percent. Coverage is mildly overstated because of double-counting of some individuals. The coverage of women is lower than that of men because many women engage in part-time jobs and earn less than the stipulated minimum threshold level.

The main goal of the second pillar is to supplement first-pillar benefits and maintain preretirement living standards. The target replacement rate, including benefits from the first pillar, differs between companies, but it is usually in the range of 50 to 70 percent of preretirement labor income (before taxes and social security contributions). Most pension funds specify their target replacement rate as a fraction of insured earnings. Apart from retirement income, the second pillar also provides disability benefits and survivor benefits during the accumulation period.

The mandatory part of the second pillar is applied on so-called coordinated earnings of workers, which range between a minimum threshold level and a maximum level. These levels are set by regulation. The minimum threshold level is currently close to 30 percent of average earnings; the maximum level equals three times the maximum pension benefit from the public pillar, or about 110 to 120 percent of average earnings.

Employers are legally required to create pension plans that cover the coordinated earnings of their employees, but they are free to offer insurance for income below or above these threshold levels. Most employers provide insurance for income above the maximum level, but very few cover income below the threshold level.

Contributions to the mandatory part (and in most cases also to the supermandatory part) are a certain percentage of coordinated (insured) earnings. By law, the employer has to pay at least half, but on average, the fraction paid by employers is approximately 60 percent.

The law also mandates minimum contribution rates by age. They range from 7 percent at age 25 to 18 percent for age 55 and older (table 5.1). However, as long as average contribution rates are in line with the legally stipulated rates, pension funds are free to deviate from the specified pattern. Many providers use uniform contribution rates for all ages, thus compensating for lower rates for older workers with higher rates for younger workers.

Contributions, which are also called *old-age credits*, are credited to notional retirement accounts and accumulate notional interest. The Swiss Federal Council determines the minimum rate of interest. It equaled 4 percent per year for 17 years (from 1985 to the end of 2002), but because of the fall in capital market returns, the rate was lowered in 2003 to 3.25 percent. The Federal Council has since reset the minimum rate of interest. It was lowered to just 2 percent in 2009 (table 5.2).

When occupational pension plans first became mandatory, most schemes were operated as DB plans. At that time, the accumulated pension capital was not fully portable. However, changes in regulations mandated the full portability of retirement savings and caused a conversion

Table 5.1   Mandatory Minimum Contribution Rates by Age

Age (years)	Contribution rates (%)
25–34	7
35–44	10
45–54	15
55–65	18

Source: Data provided by Federal Bureau of Statistics.

Table 5.2   Evolution of the Minimum Interest Rate, 1985–2010

Year	MIR (%)
1985–2002	4.00
2003	3.25
2004	2.25
2005	2.50
2006	2.50
2007	2.50
2008	2.75
2009	2.00
2010	2.00

Source: Data provided by Federal Bureau of Statistics.

of schemes, so that now over 85 percent operate as defined contribution (DC) plans.

The accumulated capital is now fully portable when the insured individual changes employer (with minor deductions, especially for short employment spells). By law, an employee changing firms gets the accumulated total contributions accrued at the MIR. The law is silent as to how accumulated reserves have to be distributed. In practice, the low minimum rate implies that job changers receive less than their fair share during the high return periods. This feature was considered an important obstacle to mobility in the Swiss labor market in the 1990s, when market returns were much higher than the MIR.

Asset Accumulation and Investment Performance

Pension funds can be set up under different organizational forms. They can be established as public or private foundations or cooperatives, and they can be single- or multiemployer funds. The funds are managed by boards of trustees on which employers and employees have equal representation. Funds must be registered when they cover the mandatory part of the system. In 2008, Switzerland had more than 2,400 registered pension funds with mandatory benefits for their 3.65 million members. The funds had nearly 1 million beneficiaries. An additional 5,000 accounting and administrative entities, with no members, offered various supermandatory benefits, but such funds are not required to be registered, and no statistics have been compiled on them since 2003. The number of both types of funds has been in steady decline over the years, but institutional fragmentation is still high.

An important classification concerns the degree of risk coverage. Autonomous institutions assume all relevant risks, but most institutions contract out some or all of the risks to insurance companies. In 2008, 26 percent of members were covered by pension funds that were completely managed by insurance companies. However, those institutions accounted for only 1 percent of total assets. Large autonomous funds covered 47 percent of members and accounted for 75 percent of assets (table 5.3).

The second pillar is fragmented, but it is also highly uneven. In 2008, the 91 largest pension funds that reported assets of 3 billion Swiss francs (Sw F) or more had 56 percent of all members and accounted for 65 percent of all assets. At the other end of the spectrum, 1,880 funds (77 percent of all funds) had less than Sw F 100 million in assets and accounted for 13 percent of members and 9 percent of assets.

Table 5.3 Risk Coverage of Pension Funds

Type of fund	Number of funds	Members (million)	Beneficiaries (million)	Assets (Sw F billion)	Funds (% of total)	Members (% of total)	Beneficiaries (% of total)	Assets (% of total)
Autonomous	458	1.720	0.64	401.19	18.8	47.1	68.8	74.5
Autonomous (with reinsurance)	514	0.430	0.08	68.82	21.1	11.8	8.6	12.8
Semiautonomous	1,173	0.560	0.07	61.22	48.2	15.3	7.5	11.4
Fully insured	256	0.940	0.14	6.88	10.5	25.8	15.1	1.3
Savings associations	34	0.003	0.00	0.41	1.4	0.1	0.0	0.1
Total	2,435	3.650	0.93	538.52	100.0	100.0	100.0	100.0

Source: Data provided by Federal Bureau of Statistics.

These funds had on average about 250 members. However, most of these funds are fully or partially insured, which lowers their risk exposure.

Total regular contributions collected by all Swiss pension funds amounted to 6.6 percent of gross domestic product (GDP) in 2008. Of the contributions, employers made 59 percent, a proportion that has been a declining trend over the years (table 5.4). Both employers and employees make additional contributions that are increasingly linked to the weak financial situation of pension funds.

In 2008, accumulated balances on the notional old-age credit accounts amounted to Sw F 165 billion and represented 31 percent of both GDP and the total assets of pension funds. These balances represent the contributions and MIR that must be credited to the retirement accounts under the mandatory system. Because the system was introduced in 1985 and applies only to the so-called coordinated earnings of members (that is, between about 30 percent and 120 percent of average earnings of all Swiss workers), not surprisingly, they account for a fraction of total pension fund assets. Old-age credit balances grew by almost 5.6 percent per year since 2000, when they amounted to Sw F 106 billion, or 26 percent of that year's GDP.

The total assets of pension funds increased from 64 percent of GDP in 1987 to 118 percent in 2000 but then fell back to 99 percent of GDP in 2008 (table 5.5). Because the system is approaching maturity, two major factors in the evolution of assets are the performance and volatility of financial markets. This relationship is reflected in the fluctuating share of equity holdings in total assets. Investment policies became more aggressive in the 1990s, and the share of equities rose from 19 percent in 1996 to 33 percent in 2000. The share of equity holdings in total assets subsequently fell to 21 percent in 2008, but it is likely to rebound in subsequent years.

Foreign assets accounted for 26 percent of total assets in 2008. Investments in alternative asset classes (included with other assets in

Table 5.4   Regular Contributions to Pension Funds, 1996–2008

Indicator	1996	2000	2005	2008
Employees (Sw F billion)	9.05	10.29	13.00	14.83
Employers (Sw F billion)	15.66	15.55	19.09	21.17
Total (Sw F billion)	24.71	25.84	32.09	36.00
Employers (%)	63.40	60.20	59.50	58.80
GDP (Sw F billion)	376.67	422.06	463.80	541.83
Contributions (as a % of GDP)	6.60	6.10	6.90	6.60

Source: Data provided by Federal Bureau of Statistics.

Table 5.5   Asset Composition, 1996–2008

Type of asset	1996	2000	2005	2008
Share (%)				
Liquid assets	9.6	7.4	8.5	8.7
Claims on sponsors	12.8	6.3	2.8	1.9
Bonds	31.4	31.4	37.5	40.8
Mortgages	7.7	5.1	3.1	3.1
Shares	19.2	33.0	28.1	21.2
Real estate	15.8	12.6	14.1	16.6
Other assets	3.5	4.2	5.1	6.9
Total assets	100.0	100.0	100.0	100.0
Total (Sw F billion)	344.51	486.99	542.63	538.52
Total (% of GDP)	93.1	118.1	117.0	99.4
Foreign assets (% of total)	—	—	28.7	25.8
Direct investments (% of total)	88.9	84.7	70.9	63.2
Indirect investments (% of total)	11.1	15.3	29.1	36.8

Source: Data provided by Federal Bureau of Statistics.
Note: — = not available.

table 5.5) have grown over time but still accounted for a small share of total assets in comparison with the asset allocation patterns of Anglo-American pension funds. A growing and more visible trend in investment policy has been the increase in indirect investments, which accounted for 37 percent of total assets in 2008. Indirect investments represent collective investments made through contracts with insurance companies and banks.

Claims on sponsoring employers have declined over time. In 2008, they accounted for just 2 percent of total assets. However, this positive development was overshadowed by the large financial shortfall of pension funds, which totaled Sw F 56 billion in 2008. The structure of liabilities shows that, from a position of 10 percent surplus in 2000, the pension funds in aggregate reported a shortfall of an equal size in 2008 (table 5.6).

This deterioration affected both private and public sector funds, although the situation was much more serious in the latter, in which the shortfall represented 19 percent of technical provisions. Public pension funds had one-third of technical provisions in 2008, but they accounted for two-thirds of the aggregate shortfall. Pension funds have considerable leeway in the rate of discount they use for valuing their pension liabilities, and the reported data may understate the level of the funding shortfall.

The investment performance of pension funds has exceeded the MIR specified in the rules because market returns on equities and bonds, in

Table 5.6   Liability Structure, 1996–2008

Indicator	Percent			
	1996	2000	2005	2008
Funding surplus	5.5	10.4	−1.6	−10.5
Employer reserve	1.9	1.8	0.9	1.2
Fluctuation reserve	—	—	7.8	1.6
Technical provisions	89.5	84.6	90.6	105.5
Other liabilities	3.1	3.2	2.3	2.2
Total	100.0	100.0	100.0	100.0
Funding ratio (surplus to provisions)	6.2	12.3	−1.7	−9.9

Source: Data provided by Federal Bureau of Statistics.
Note: — = not available.

Figure 5.1   Market Interest Rates and the Minimum Interest Rate, 1990–2010

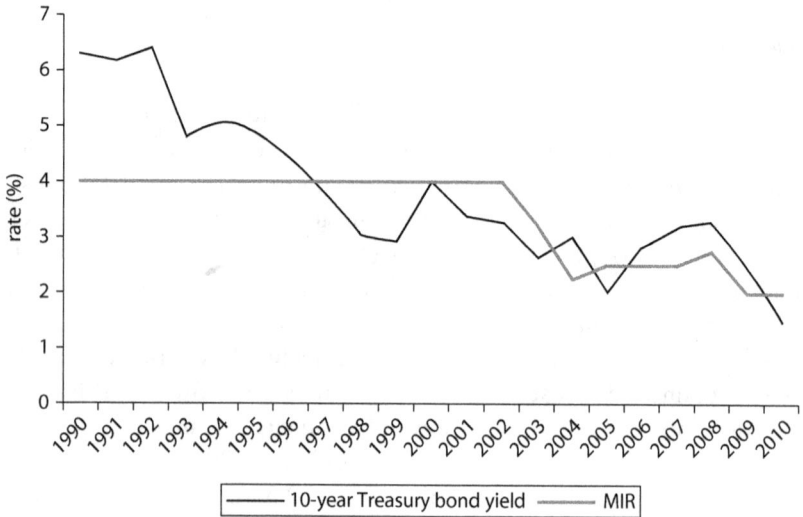

— 10-year Treasury bond yield — — MIR

Sources: Bütler and Ruesch 2007; data provided by Swiss National Bank.

which pension funds invested the vast majority of their assets, exceeded the MIR. In addition the MIR has been close to the yield on 10-year zero-coupon government bonds for most of the period (figure 5.1).

The cumulative returns between 1987 and 2004 of the average actual portfolio of pension funds exceeded the cumulative returns based on the MIR by 42 percent, or an average of 2.07 percent per year. The total returns of a simulated portfolio based on an asset allocation of 30 percent Swiss equities, 20 percent foreign equities, and 50 percent bonds would have been higher by 84 percent, or an average of 3.66 percent per year. An all-Swiss equities portfolio would have produced total excess returns of 179 percent, or an average of 6.23 percent per year (table 5.7).

However, the MIR does not necessarily represent the effectively credited return on old-age balances. Some pension funds credited a higher rate of interest. Nevertheless, most pension funds used the MIR to calculate the returns on the old-age capital and used excess returns to accumulate reserves, finance early retirement programs and inflation indexing, or take contribution holidays.

During the four years between 2005 and 2008, the investment performance of the pension funds has reflected the fluctuations in financial returns in global markets. Reasonable returns were recorded between 2005 and 2007, but large losses were suffered in 2008, causing total assets to fall significantly (table 5.8). The cumulative compound return over the four-year period amounted to just 1.9 percent, which corresponds to less than 0.5 percent per year. This return exceeds the MIR over this period.

Because pension funds are employer based and do not have to incur high marketing costs, their operating costs are relatively low by international standards, though still higher than those of the first pillar. Costs are

Table 5.7   Ratio of Investment Portfolio Returns to the Minimum Interest Rate, 1987–2004

Indicator	Returns-to-MIR ratio	Annual excess return (%)
MIR	100	n.a.
Bond index performance (Pictet)	121	1.12
Empirical portfolio	142	2.07
Simulated portfolio	184	3.66
Swiss equities (MSCI index, Switzerland)	279	6.23

Source: Bütler and Ruesch 2007.
Note: n.a. = not applicable.

Table 5.8   Net Investment Income, 2005–08

Indicator	2005	2006	2007	2008
Net investment income (Sw F billion)	53.78	34.26	14.17	−77.72
Total assets (Sw F billion)	542.63	583.27	605.46	538.52
Net investment income (as a % of total assets)	9.9	5.9	2.3	−14.4

Source: Data provided by Federal Bureau of Statistics.

comparable to those of occupational pension funds in most other high-income countries. Administration costs amounted to 2.3 percent of total contributions in 2008, and asset management expenses absorbed a similar amount (table 5.9). Total costs amounted to 0.31 percent (31 basis points) of total assets.

Personal Pension Plans

The third pillar in the Swiss pension system comprises voluntary additional savings directed at filling potential gaps in the provision of old-age income, primarily for the self-employed (who are not covered by the second pillar) and for people with contribution gaps (for example, foreign workers and those with career breaks). Contributions up to specified limits are fully tax deductible and are known as conditional savings, or pillar 3a. Unconditional individual savings are classified as pillar 3b.

Insurance companies, as well as most banks and other financial intermediaries, provide third-pillar accounts. The rate of annuitization in the third pillar is very low. This low rate is not surprising given the predominance of life annuities in the first and second pillars. Individuals with a higher demand for a life annuity are much more likely to explore the option to increase the tax-favored contributions to the more generous second pillar.

The mathematical reserves held by life insurance companies for individual life policies and individual annuities amounted to Sw F 93 billion in 2008, corresponding to 17 percent of GDP (table 5.10). About one-third of these reserves related to conditional savings (pillar 3a savings) that enjoyed tax benefits, and the remaining two-thirds related to unconditional accounts. The market is highly concentrated, with 75 percent accounted for by the top five companies. Conditional third-pillar savings

Table 5.9   Operating Costs, 1996–2008

Type of cost	1996	2000	2005	2008
Costs (as a % of contributions)				
Administration	3.0	4.1	2.2	2.3
Asset management	4.1	3.9	2.5	2.3
Total costs	7.1	8.0	4.7	4.6
Costs (as a % of total assets)				
Administration	0.22	0.22	0.13	0.16
Asset management	0.29	0.21	0.15	0.15
Total costs	0.51	0.42	0.28	0.31

Source: Data provided by Federal Bureau of Statistics.

Table 5.10   Third-Pillar Assets, 1996–2008

Type of institution	1996	2000	2005	2008
Insurance companies (as a % of GDP)	15.9	20.2	18.8	17.1
Banks (as a % of GDP)	4.7	3.9	5.7	5.7
Total (as a % of GDP)	20.6	24.1	24.5	22.8
Total (Sw F billion)	77.70	101.50	113.43	123.37

Sources: Data provided by Federal Bureau of Statistics and Swiss National Bank.

with banks amounted to Sw F 31 billion in 2008. The groups of large commercial banks and cantonal banks each control about one-third of the market. Total assets in the third pillar represent 23 percent of GDP.

Retirement Products and Money's Worth Ratios

Upon retirement, the accumulated capital in the second pillar can be withdrawn either as a monthly lifelong annuity or as a capital lump sum. The annuity is always a lifelong income stream computed from the fraction of accumulated pension capital that is not withdrawn as a lump sum. No other forms of annuitization are in the mandatory pillar, such as phased withdrawals, term annuities, or variable annuities.

Annuity payments are strictly proportional to the accumulated retirement assets (retirement credits plus accrued interest). Until the end of 2004, the legal ACF, which applies to the mandatory part of the second pillar, was fixed at 7.2 percent for all workers retiring at the statutory age, regardless of marital status or gender. This factor was computed using a discount rate of 4 percent (corresponding to the underlying technical interest rate, not to the legal MIR) and period mortality tables that were approximately correct for men at that time but not for women (mainly because of the lower statutory retirement age for women).

Because of the increase in longevity in the intervening years, the authorities decided to lower the ACF, starting from 2005. The ACF is being reduced gradually until it reaches 6.8 percent in 2014 (table 5.11). The intention is for the ACF to continue to be the same for all retirees, irrespective of marital status or gender. However, a transitory wedge between the rate for men and women was introduced as a political compromise to compensate women for the increase in their retirement age.

In November 2005, the Federal Council announced its intention to further reduce the ACF to 6.4 percent by 2016. A law to that effect was adopted by the Swiss parliament in late 2008. However, in a referendum

Table 5.11   Legal Annuity Conversion Factors, 2000–14

Year	Women Birth year	Women Retirement age	Women ACF (%)	Men ACF (%)
2000	1938	62	7.20	7.20
2001	1939	62	7.20	7.20
2002	1940	62	7.20	7.20
2003	1941	62	7.20	7.20
2004	1942	62	7.20	7.20
2005	n.a.	(64)	(7.20)	7.15
2006	1943	63 (64)	7.15	7.10
2007	1943	64	7.20	7.10
2008	1944	64	7.10	7.05
2009	1945	64	7.00	7.05
2010	1946	64	6.95	7.00
2011	1947	64	6.90	6.95
2012	1948	64	6.85	6.90
2013	1949	64	6.80	6.85
2014	1950	64	6.80	6.80

Source: Data provided by Federal Bureau of Statistics.
Note: ACF = annuity conversion factor; n.a. = not applicable. Retirement ages are for women; the numbers in parentheses correspond to the legal, but not effective, retirement age (women turning 64 in the years 2005 and 2006 would have retired before).

held in March 2010, the Swiss public rejected this proposal by a large majority (73 percent voted against the proposal, with turnout a relatively high 45 percent). The matter has now gone back to the drawing board. The public is critical of banks and insurance companies, which they blame for poor performance, excessive risk taking, and excessive compensation. A debate is ongoing regarding necessary rules for profit sharing when financial markets perform well.

Pension funds are free to apply any conversion factor to the supermandatory part of retirement savings. Nonetheless, very few companies used this option until a few years ago. But growing financial constraints forced many employers to change their approach. In 2005, the large insurance companies that provide insurance predominantly for many small and medium companies reduced the conversion factor for nonmandatory retirement capital, in quite a dramatic way, to between 5.4 percent and 5.8 percent. The fact that virtually all companies came up with an identical number to the third digit after the decimal point (5.835) for the reduced male conversion factor caused considerable protest. Although insurance companies use identical mortality tables, the coincidence did not suggest a high degree of competition.

A pension fund can apply a lower rate than the legal ACF under certain conditions. For this purpose, it has to use the resources freed up as a consequence of a lower conversion rate to improve the benefits for the covered individuals. The law does not put restrictions on how these means should be distributed. In practice, many pension funds make use of this option, though no data exist on the importance of this alternative measure. Most funds finance early retirement programs and inflation indexing. A deviation from the (too high) legal ACF has several advantages. It allows the fund to tailor the benefits to the needs of the beneficiaries and gives more flexibility and financial leeway to the fund. However, there is also a risk that the additional benefits will be distributed unequally among different subgroups of potential beneficiaries.

In principle, benefits are fixed nominal annuities, but the law states that pension providers have to adjust current old-age benefits to inflation within the scope of their financial capacity. Because of the financial strain on most funds, current benefits are no longer fully indexed to inflation. This method is different from that applied in the 1980s and 1990s, when benefits not only were indexed to inflation but also were sometimes even indexed to the growth rate of wages. These more generous benefits could be financed because the MIR that had to be granted on old-age credits was considerably below market returns. Given the current situation of low inflation, the nonindexation of benefits has not caused a significant fall in the real value of pensions.

The law mandates the use of joint life annuities and the same ACF, irrespective of gender, family status, or income. If they are under age 18 (under age 25 if still dependent), children of retired people get an additional pension of 20 percent of the main claimant's benefit. When a retired individual dies, the spouse receives a benefit amounting to 60 percent of the previous pension and any dependent children receive a benefit of 20 percent each. Until 2005, surviving husbands of deceased female retirees did not get a widower's pension. The recent change to this law was not disputed mainly because of its low cost.

Depending on the pension fund, a fraction of the accumulated capital can be withdrawn as a lump sum. To mitigate adverse selection effects attributable to short-run deterioration of an individual's health status, pension funds can require the capital option to be requested up to three years prior to retirement. Until 2004, pension funds were not required to allow this capital option, but from 2005, they have been required to allow retirees to withdraw at least 25 percent of the old-age capital (in the mandatory part) as a lump sum. No legal restrictions pertain to how much can be cashed out. The decision regarding what fraction, if any, of the accumulated capital must be annuitized is left to the individual pension fund. Many pension funds, especially those set up by smaller employers, have allowed much higher lump-sum withdrawals.

The option to withdraw a fraction (or all) of the accumulated capital as a lump sum entails in general two potential problems. The first is the risk that individuals might outlive their savings. This possibility would be an issue for the public pillar because individuals can claim means-tested supplementary public benefits in case of insufficient retirement income. The second is the risk of adverse selection, because individuals with impaired health and short life expectancy are more likely to opt for a capital lump sum, thus leaving the funds with the annuity obligations of the long-lived.

In reality, no evidence shows that pension funds have suffered from adverse selection. Differences in money's worth ratios (MWRs) across different subgroups of the population suggest that single men would be expected to opt for the lump sum much more often than married men because of their higher-than-average mortality rates and the absence of survivor benefits. But as reported in Bütler and Teppa (2005), this imbalance has not happened in practice. Single men have been as likely to choose the annuity as married men, although in many cases they get a worse deal from an annuity than do married men.

Several explanations can be advanced for this finding. The absence of family ties may be a factor. Single men may attach greater value to the longevity insurance provided by the annuity; in contrast, married men may place greater value on the bequest motive and thus opt for partial lump sums to a greater extent than single men. The fact that annuities from the mandatory pillar are offered at highly advantageous terms compared with free market annuities may also explain the relatively limited use of lump sums by all participants.

For women, the picture is a bit different—although adverse selection effects are also much smaller as a result of the smaller differences in survival rates between single and married women. Married women are more likely to opt for the capital option, presumably because they are the second earner in the family and they already benefit from a high degree of annuitization stemming from the primary earner.

Data collected by Bütler and Teppa (2005) show that small account balances are much more likely to be withdrawn as a lump sum. For very high balances, the fraction that is cashed out is higher, reflecting the presence of bequest motives, better investment opportunities, and a preferential tax treatment.

Benefits and Level of Annuitization

No official statistics describe the level of annuitization. Available data do not report the proportion of accumulated capital of newly retired workers (both under the mandatory and supermandatory parts of the system) that is withdrawn as a lump sum and the part that is converted into an annuity. They also do not report the number of new retirees who convert all their accumulated capital into an annuity, those who withdraw the total capital, and those who withdraw a fraction of the available capital and convert the rest.

Published data show the level of annual benefits, divided between annuity payments and lump-sum payments. In 2008, annuity payments amounted to 4.2 percent of GDP, and lump-sum payments were 1.1 percent of GDP (table 5.12). Total benefits have been steadily increasing in relation to GDP, reflecting the growing maturity of the system. Both the number of beneficiaries and the level of the average benefit have been on a rising trend. Lump-sum payments have absorbed about 20 percent of total benefits, implying a level of annuitization of 80 percent.

The same broad level of annuitization is obtained if the size of accumulated balances of retiring workers is estimated on the basis of the change in annual pension payments and by applying to the payments the inverse of the regulated ACF. This rough calculation would overlook two offsetting elements: (a) any increase attributable to inflation adjustment in pensions being paid and (b) the termination of pension payments to deceased pensioners. On the basis of this calculation, lump-sum payments

Table 5.12   Structure of Benefits, 1996–2008

Indicator	1996	2000	2005	2008
Type of payment (Sw F billion)				
Annuity payments	12.53	16.33	20.76	22.63
Lump-sum payments	2.84	3.91	4.59	5.75
Total	15.37	20.24	25.35	28.38
Share of total (%)				
Annuity payments	81.5	80.7	81.9	79.7
Lump-sum payments	18.5	19.3	18.1	20.3
Total	100.0	100.0	100.0	100.0
Share of GDP (%)				
Annuity payments	3.3	3.9	4.5	4.2
Lump-sum payments	0.8	0.9	1.0	1.1
Total	4.1	4.8	5.5	5.3

Source: Data provided by Federal Bureau of Statistics.

would represent between 20 percent and 25 percent of the total value of balances of retiring workers, implying a level of annuitization between 75 percent and 80 percent. One could thus reasonably assume that the level of annuitization in the second pillar amounts to 80 percent.

The high level of annuitization is attributed to the way pension plans are structured. Although no restrictions apply to lump-sum payments, the rules of most pension funds, which are determined jointly by employer and worker representatives, appear to favor annuitization. The existing strong link between the accumulation and decumulation (payout) phases of the second pillar, in which both are with the same sponsor with almost no exceptions, has probably reinforced the preference for life annuities.

Although, in some plans, individuals are allowed to cash out their old-age savings and could, in principle, purchase another annuity contract on the open market, virtually nobody does so. Occupational pension plans offer two advantages over market annuity products. First, they are hardly plagued by adverse selection problems. Second, and far more important, the regulated ACF has been substantially higher than the factor available on the open market. The high regulated ACF has effectively compensated workers for the lower-than-market returns that have been credited to their accounts over the accumulation phase, at least during the first 20 years of operation of the second pillar. As discussed in the preceding section, the appropriate level of the ACF is currently the object of intense political debate.

Replacement Rates

As mentioned previously, no target replacement rates exist for the first pillar. The motivation for introducing a compulsory occupational system was to ensure a replacement rate of approximately 60 percent relative to the preretirement income for lower- and middle-income people. The minimum contribution rates in the second pillar are in line with this goal. Together with the income from the first pillar and the fact that no social security deductions are given on pension benefits, replacement rates are generally high even for high-income groups (table 5.13 and figure 5.2). Because federal and cantonal taxes in Switzerland are progressive, and because of the availability of additional pension benefits for young children, the effective net replacement rate can exceed 100 percent in some cases.

The effective replacement rates can be lower as a result of interruptions in the working career, low-income spells, and unemployment. Nevertheless, an uninterrupted working history is still the rule in Switzerland (thanks to a low unemployment rate), notably for high-income male individuals.

Table 5.13 Replacement Rates

| | Gross income before retirement | | | | | | | | |
| | Sw F 50,000 | | | Sw F 100,000 | | | Sw F 200,000 | | |
Indicator	Single	Married + adult children	Married + 2 minor children	Single	Married + adult children	Married + 2 minor children	Single	Married + adult children	Married + 2 minor children
Net income before retirement (Sw F)	41,000	42,000	44,000	73,000	77,000	80,000	135,000	143,000	147,000
Income after retirement									
First pillar (Sw F)	20,000	30,000	36,000	25,000	38,000	46,000	25,000	38,000	46,000
Second pillar (Sw F)	12,000	12,000	17,000	37,000	37,000	52,000	87,000	87,000	122,000
Net income from both pillars after taxes (Sw F)	30,000	40,000	52,000	55,000	68,000	89,000	92,000	106,000	139,000
Replacement rates									
Gross (%)	0.65	0.85	1.07	0.63	0.75	0.98	0.56	0.63	0.84
Net (%)	0.75	0.95	1.18	0.75	0.88	1.11	0.71	0.78	0.98

Source: Bütler and Ruesch 2007.

Note: The computations are based on the following (very realistic) assumptions: For "married + adult children," the wife does not have any second-pillar income but qualifies for the same first-pillar pension as the main breadwinner (mainly through child care credits and part-time income). For "married + 2 minor children," it is assumed that the wife is too young to claim her own benefits. The pension fund replaces 50 percent of coordinated income (income − 25,300) with no upper income limit. Children's benefits are 40 percent (first pillar) and 20 percent (second pillar) of the main claimant's benefits each. The tax base is the city of Zürich.

Figure 5.2   Replacement Rates as a Function of Income: First and Second Pillar

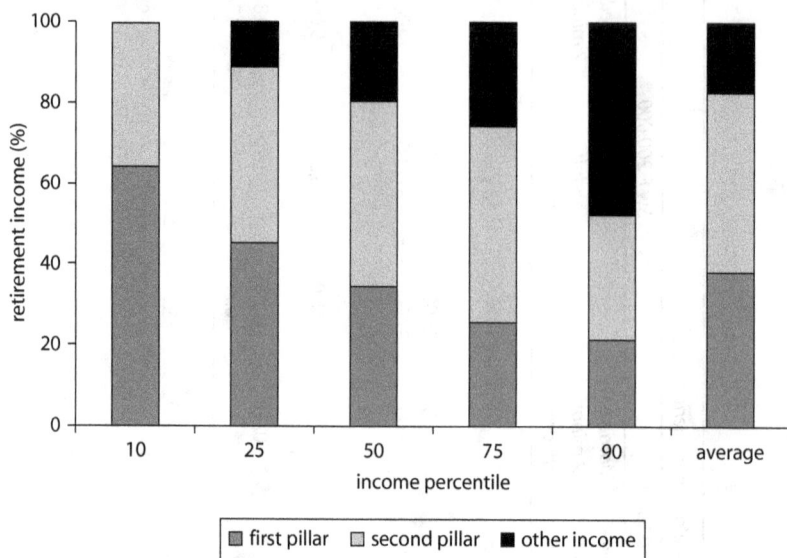

Source: Bütler and Ruesch 2007.
Note: Only individuals between ages 65 and 70 in 2002 are considered. The average monthly incomes are Sw F 2,947 (10 percent level), Sw F 5,155 (25 percent level), Sw F 7,521 (50 percent level), Sw F 9,962 (75 percent level), and Sw F 13,263 (90 percent level), with an overall average of Sw F 5,765.

Money's Worth Ratios

Bütler and Ruesch (2007) computed MWRs for the minimum ACF of 7.2 percent that was set by regulation in the mandatory part of the system until 2004. The same rate applied to all retirees, regardless of gender and marital status. The calculations were based on mortality tables for the whole population of men and women, without allowing for the higher mortality rates of single men. Three different sets of interest rates were used: (a) the nominal yield curve published by the Swiss National Bank, (b) the interest rate on five-year Swiss government bonds, and (c) a fixed rate of 3.5 percent. Nominal interest rates were used because annuities were specified in fixed nominal amounts.

The results of the calculations were reported for retirees in the second pillar between 2000 and 2005 (table 5.14). The reported ratios differed substantially from year to year when the nominal yield curve was used to discount future benefits. The most striking feature, however, was the high level of MWRs. For joint life annuities, the MWRs ranged from 1.03 in 2000 to as much as 1.30 in 2005, using the nominal yield curve

Table 5.14   Money's Worth Ratios for Second-Pillar Retirees, 2000–05

Year	Annuitant	Swiss National Bank yield curve	5-year bond Rate (%)	MWR	Fixed 3.5%
2000	Female, single	1.069	3.80	1.117	1.155
	Male, single	0.890		0.917	0.943
	Male, married	1.025		1.068	1.103
2001	Female, single	1.134	3.13	1.211	1.160
	Male, single	0.937		0.981	0.947
	Male, married	1.086		1.154	1.108
2002	Female, single	1.151	2.73	1.275	1.165
	Male, single	0.953		1.023	0.951
	Male, married	1.102		1.212	1.112
2003	Female, single	1.242	1.61	1.475	1.170
	Male, single	1.020		1.152	0.955
	Male, married	1.187		1.393	1.116
2004	Female, single	1.206	2.36	1.346	1.175
	Male, single	0.991		1.071	0.959
	Male, married	1.152		1.276	1.120
2005[a]	Male, single	1.099	1.42	1.186	0.963
	Male, married	1.302		1.440	1.124
2005[b]	Female, single				
	(62 years old), 5.454%	1.039	1.42	1.076	0.893
	Male, single, 5.835%	0.891		0.961	0.780
	Male, married, 5.835%	1.055		1.167	0.911

Source: Bütler and Ruesch 2007.
Note: MWR calculations are from pooled gender survival tables as a function of the underlying risk-free rate profile since 2000. For all computations, the common conversion factor is 7.2 percent, the female retirement age is 62, and the age difference of married spouses at retirement is 3.7 years.
a. In 2005, no females retired at the statutory retirement age.
b. These rows depict the MWRs using the lowest quoted conversion rates to be applied on the nonmandatory capital stock. The computations are based on a constant nominal interest rate of 3.5 percent. Joint annuities are for males only. Mortality rates are updated by improvement rates from the Swiss Federal Statistical Office.

for discounting purposes. Even for single men, the MWRs ranged between 0.89 in 2000 and 1.10 in 2005.

The uniform conversion factor also led to dramatically different outcomes for different subgroups of the population. In particular, female retirees fared substantially better because of the lower statutory retirement age. But a much more striking result was the large difference between single and married men. With the uniform conversion factor, single men received a much lower payoff because they were effectively forced to purchase a joint life annuity when they had no spouse to protect.

The reported ratios underestimated the true magnitude of the advantage for married men for two reasons: First, the computations ignored mortality differences between married and single men. Second, in some cases, minor children (or children still in school) of retiring men claimed additional postretirement survivor benefits.

Given these numbers, one might at first sight be surprised that single men did not take the capital option more often. Data from a number of Swiss pension funds show that most single men did not take that option. Bütler and Teppa (2005) argue that a lack of alternative longevity insurance by the family and an absence of a bequest motive have led single men to choose the annuity. In addition, the MWR obtainable from the free market would have amounted to 0.89 in 2005, which would have been substantially lower than the ratio of 1.10 obtainable through the mandatory pillar. It is notable that insurance companies also used the same annuity conversion rate for single and married men in the nonmandatory part of the system.

Because MWRs in the Swiss second pillar are very high, considerable pressure is exerted by pension funds and insurance companies to lower the conversion factor even for the mandatory part of the second pillar. Many autonomous funds have indeed already started to use lower conversion factors. The reported MWRs can thus be seen as upper bounds. As the computations show, the new conversion factors used by the insurance companies for the capital exceeding the mandatory level bring the numbers more closely to values computed with the nominal yield curve.

However, certain caveats apply in these computations. The reported MWRs correspond to the official picture as stated in the law. But under certain circumstances, the conversion factor requirement can be relaxed when the pension fund uses the newly available resources to increase the benefits of its retirees. Some pension funds also compute the level of pension payments on the basis of conversion factors that are more in line with reality, financing the gaps between the official and internal factors with additional levies on employees and the employer.

As the MWRs demonstrate, uniform conversion factors redistribute resources on a remarkable scale. In relative terms, the main losers from this redistribution are single men, and the main beneficiaries are married men with a younger spouse and young children late in life. Because the latter group is more affluent on average, the implied shift in resources is probably not socially desirable. As a result of the increase in the female retirement age, women have lost their advantage in the scheme.

However, a stable conversion factor has its merits. Large swings in benefits, caused by fluctuations in the market interest rate, can be avoided. This stability not only increases intergenerational equity but also limits the spillover effects to the first pillar (via means-tested benefits). But to keep the system financially stable, the conversion factor needs to account for increases in longevity and changes in medium- and long-term market conditions. Insurance companies, which are crucial to a well-functioning system, are now starting to lose interest in participating in the annuity market, given that the obligations within the mandatory part are currently more difficult to meet.

Future reforms of the second pillar should aim at linking the conversion factor to demographic parameters and medium- to long-term market conditions. Such reforms would contribute to the financial stability of the system and help shield it from political pressure. Discussions also must consider whether a uniform conversion factor (and the implied redistribution) should be maintained. Contrary to conventional wisdom, women would not lose from such a change. But the occupational scheme would become more flexible and better equipped to handle changes in living patterns and labor market participation.

The calculation of MWRs showed that, on the basis of the zero-coupon yield curve, even the conversion factors used by insurance companies outside the mandatory part of the second pillar veered on the high side for 2005. Abstracting from administrative expenses and using the risk-free rates implied by the zero-coupon yield curve on government bonds, one could justify using a conversion factor of 5.53 percent for married men and a conversion factor of 5.25 percent for single women. However, this approach would imply significant fluctuations from year to year in ACFs and would expose retiring workers to considerable annuitization risk. Using a long-term rate to determine the ACF would avoid this risk but would create other problems, such as an unintended intergenerational redistribution or potential financial stability issues for annuity providers. An alternative that would mitigate these problems would be to allow use of installment annuities. This approach would involve using part of accumulated capital to purchase an immediate annuity and part to purchase deferred annuities. Such an approach could also be combined with the purchase of variable annuities and use of lump-sum payments.

Risk-Sharing Characteristics

Unlike Denmark and Sweden, Switzerland does not use annuity products with formal risk-sharing arrangements, such as profit-participating annuities with minimum guaranteed benefits and annual bonuses that depend on investment performance and longevity experience. As discussed in the respective country chapters, in these "guarantee and bonus" policies, the investment and longevity risks are assumed by annuity providers up to the level of the guaranteed benefits but are shared among annuitants in the declaration of annual bonuses.

The Swiss pension system entails a less direct but equally extensive arrangement for risk sharing that has both intra- and intergenerational elements. In Denmark and Sweden, intergenerational transfers are in principle not allowed, and the prudential and conduct regulations have sought to ensure that such transfers do not take place. In Switzerland, the stipulated minimum contribution rates, MIR, and minimum ACF aim to protect individual workers from investment, annuitization, and longevity risks. However, as recent experience has shown, when financial market returns fall or life expectancy increases, the minimum rates are adjusted, albeit with some delay, to ensure the financial viability of the mandatory part of the second pillar.

Over the first 20 years of the mandatory system, the MIR was substantially below market returns. The level of accumulated capital was lower by as much as 40 percent, compared with what it would have reached on the basis of the market returns obtained by pension funds through their asset allocation policies. But workers were compensated by a generous ACF that exceeded its equilibrium rate by about 20 percent. Although no formal link exists between the accumulation and decumulation phases, most workers who annuitize all or a significant part of their accumulated retirement capital in practice obtain an annuity from their main pension fund. This investment is encouraged by the fact that the minimum ACF in the mandatory pillar is much higher than the conversion factor that could be obtained on the open market.

Individual workers and pensioners face the risk of insolvency of their own pension institution. This risk is effectively limited to cases of fraud and gross negligence in asset management. Funding gaps in individual pension funds are usually identified before they become critical, and although corrective action is often slow, insolvency is usually avoided. In addition, the rights of individual workers and pensioners are protected by the creation of the Guarantee Fund (discussed further later).

Faced with growing funding shortfalls, pension funds have resorted to various measures that involve a certain element of risk sharing. First, inflation adjustments have not been effected. Even though inflation has been very low, it has been positive and has implied a slight decline in the real value of pension benefits. Second, pension funds have assessed extraordinary contributions on both employers and employees, and the possibility of applying such contributions on pensioners is also contemplated. These contributions would effectively reduce the nominal level of benefits.

Regulation and Supervision

The mandatory part of the second pillar is tightly regulated. The law and implementing regulations, including decisions of the Federal Council, set the minimum terms and conditions regarding the level of insured earnings, the contribution rates, the MIR, and the minimum ACF. Organization and management of pension funds is also tightly regulated, with clear rules on equal representation and institutional independence of pension funds from their sponsoring employers.

However, the rules allow considerable flexibility and leeway to pension funds that offer supermandatory benefits. This flexibility creates considerable variation in the actual terms and conditions, and the large number of funds impedes effective supervision. Adequate transparency of pension funds, especially with regard to investment performance and financial soundness, is lacking.

This section discusses some aspects of the regulatory and supervisory framework. Use of the MIR and minimum ACF, as well as the problems created by the lack of flexibility in their setting, has already been covered in preceding sections. This section focuses on investment rules and on the prudential regulation of pension funds.

Investment Rules

Pension fund investments are subject to quantitative restrictions with regard to both issuers and asset classes. These limits are not very restrictive and are rarely binding in practice. Rules also apply to the use of collective investments and derivatives and, especially, to investment in securities issued by the sponsor of the plan. Except for the latter rule, the quantitative restrictions were recently simplified by grouping assets in very broad classes.

No requirements apply to the use of market values for the valuation of assets. Fixed income instruments are valued at the lower of market or face value, and variable income assets, including equities and real estate, are valued either at market value or at cost, if it is lower than market value. Valuation rules apply to all funds, regardless of their organizational form.

Prudential Regulation

The prudential regulation of pension funds has been imprecise until recently. Pension funds have been required to employ certified pension experts to attest that they are able to meet their financial obligations. The prudential rules do not mandate the use of fair values for assets. In addition, pension funds are free to use their own mortality tables and discount rates to estimate the present value of liabilities.

The technical discount rate has not been regulated by law. Most pension funds applied a technical discount rate of 4 percent that was equal to the MIR, but some used higher discount rates. Bütler and Ruesch (2007) show that several pension funds used discount rates ranging between 3.0 percent and 3.5 percent in 2004/05, but some financially weak pension funds continued to apply discount rates in excess of 4.0 percent when the MIR was set at 2.25 to 2.50 percent.

Autonomous pension funds are allowed to be temporarily underfunded. Public sector pension funds that benefit from a cantonal guarantee have been allowed to operate with significant actuarial shortfalls on the grounds that the cantonal authorities would stand behind the pension funds and guarantee their liabilities.

In contrast, life insurance companies are subject to stricter prudential rules and are not allowed to have any underfunding in their pension operations. They are subject to more complex and comprehensive capital rules. The capital regulations of life insurance companies comprise general rules, which are legally binding for all life insurance companies, and specific rules for those companies that manage pension funds. In addition to minimum capital requirements and premium- and risk-based capital adequacy (solvency) requirements, insurance companies must place in a security fund all reserves representing liabilities to policyholders. The supervisory authorities verify the adequacy of the security fund on a regular basis, and any shortfall must be covered within one month. If the insurance company goes bankrupt, the insured workers and retirees have a privileged claim on the value of the security fund.

In April 2004, new standards of transparency were imposed on life insurance companies to bring them in line with the rules that applied to autonomous and semiautonomous pension funds. Life insurance companies are required to create a separate security fund for their liabilities related to the pension funds they manage. The assets of their pension business must be segregated from other assets, and their pension business must be reported in a separate annual report. In addition, strict rules apply to the distribution of investment profits. According to these rules, insurance companies must allocate at least 90 percent of the net investment income to the accounts of insured individuals. Another important new feature is the asset segregation rule, which requests the separation of assets belonging to the pension funds from other assets.

Insurance regulation is gradually moving in the direction of a Solvency II approach that would require risk-based solvency requirements, mandate the use of market-based maturity-dependent discount rates, and require the fair valuation of both assets and liabilities.

Insurance supervision is carried out by the new Financial Markets Authority, which absorbed the Federal Office of Private Insurance and is better developed and more effective than pension fund supervision. Supervision of pension funds is fragmented among several cantonal authorities and is characterized as passive and largely ineffective. Supervision of occupational pension institutions is overseen by the Swiss Federal Council. Pension institutions without national or international importance are supervised by cantonal supervisory authorities. The Federal Office for Social Insurance (Office Fédéral des Assurances Sociales, or OFAS) supervises the cantonal supervisory authorities as well as pension providers with national or international importance. Moreover, the OFAS is also in charge of the Suppletory Institution and, more important, the Guarantee Fund. It is worth noting that the different layers and the large segmentation of the supervisory authority potentially reduce the quality and transparency of supervision.

Pension funds are not penalized, even in the presence of severe problems such as large underfunding. They are invited to correct the funding gap but without setting any deadlines. Certain problems, such as recovering from a funding gap, can therefore take several years. Consequently, no penalties are imposed for duration gaps in asset and liability management. Sanctions concern only violations against the obligation to disclose information, the disclosure of false information, the avoidance of control, and the misuse of contributions. The fines for such violations are very modest, ranging between Sw F 10,000 and Sw F 30,000.

Financial Soundness of Pension Funds

Extensive discussions have taken place regarding the financial soundness of pension funds because of the decline in financial market returns and the continuing increase in longevity. Pension funds are required to submit annual reports on their financial situation, which must be approved by certified experts. The supervisory authorities review the reports, and if a shortfall is identified, the pension funds must take action to strengthen their financial situation.

Pension funds have considerable leeway in selecting their discount rates, which need to be approved as appropriate by their certified experts. Discount rates vary considerably. Public pension funds use higher discount rates than do private ones; financially weak pension funds also tend to use higher discount rates to understate their underfunding.

According to a report prepared by the OFAS (2009), 47 percent of all pension funds, excluding those that were fully insured, suffered from a funding shortfall in 2008. Among public pension funds enjoying a public guarantee, 91 percent, or a total of 60 pension funds, showed a funding shortfall; of those, 42 had a funding ratio of less than 90 percent. The report did not indicate the number of funds with significantly lower funding ratios, but the average shortfall for these 42 funds amounted to 35 percent. In addition, the report did not elaborate on the technical rates used by pension funds in calculating the present value of their pension liabilities, other than noting that they varied across institutions and averaged 4.0 percent for DB plans and 3.6 percent for DC plans.

Faced with a funding shortfall, many pension funds took action to remedy the situation. Measures included additional contributions from employers and employees as well as pensioners, cutbacks in benefits, and reductions in the interest rate credited on accumulated old-age credit balances. A few small private pension funds have failed, and the Guarantee Fund (as discussed below) has been forced to intervene and cover their pension liabilities; however, the amounts involved have so far been small.

Risk Management

Although Switzerland has extensive rules on the design and operation of pension plans, it has relatively few provisions on how the pension funds should deal with risk. In particular, asset and liability management, as well as management of longevity risk, is left to the discretion of the pension funds. Because of the high fragmentation of the second pillar, the variation of strategies is broad.

Insurance companies and the large pension funds have adopted increasingly sophisticated asset and liability management strategies. In the 1990s, the larger institutions expanded considerably their investments in domestic and foreign equities. The high returns relative to the minimum guaranteed interest rate allowed greater leeway to pension funds to assume higher risks and also to take contribution holidays or increase benefits. Smaller funds applied more conservative investment policies.

Asset and liability management policies became more conservative when financial returns declined in the new millennium. Greater emphasis is now placed on ensuring that pension funds are able to meet their long-term obligations. The larger institutions undertake detailed measurement of risks and calculate the impact on their financial position of adverse changes in interest rates, foreign exchange, equity prices, private equity, and real estate values. There is also increasing use of hedging facilities, including interest rate derivatives and swap contracts. Stress tests are based on historical simulations, with both assets and liabilities valued at market prices or fair values. However, pension funds are not yet required by law to value all their assets and liabilities at market values. They are also not yet required to use a market-based yield curve for valuing their liabilities.

Because pension funds have little scope in setting the terms of the annuity contracts in the mandatory part of the system, they have not adopted an active management of longevity risk. Almost all pension funds use the mortality tables provided by the Federal Insurance Fund, with possible adjustments based on past experience, especially for pension funds with a high degree of homogeneity among their annuitants (for example, construction workers, teachers, or bank employees). In 2000, insurance companies introduced cohort life tables for pricing their annuities on the open market, but in the mandatory pillar, most institutions augment their actuarial liabilities by 0.4 to 0.5 percent every year until the new Federal Insurance Fund mortality rates become available (every 10 years). So far, no attempt has been made to use longevity bonds or derivatives to hedge longevity risk.

The financial difficulties experienced at the turn of the new millennium have induced the authorities to tighten significantly the regulation and supervision of insurance companies. There is a gradual move toward a Solvency II approach with risk-based solvency requirements, mandated use of market-based maturity-dependent discount rates, and fair valuation of both assets and liabilities. Progress on improving the risk management of pension funds is lagging, mainly because of the high fragmentation of the sector and the presence of many public funds with weak financial positions. However, all these issues are currently under intensive review.

The Suppletory Institution and the Guarantee Fund

The Suppletory Institution covers individuals seeking insurance on a voluntary basis—in particular, self-employed individuals, as well as employees whose employer is not affiliated with an occupational pension provider despite the legal provisions. It also fulfills the task of insuring the recipients of unemployment compensation against the risk of death or disability. The Suppletory Institution is considered a pension fund. It is financed by all parties concerned, like any other pension fund, with the exception of some special costs that are covered by the Guarantee Fund.

The most important task of the Guarantee Fund is to act as a reinsurance institution for the beneficiaries of insolvent pension providers that are in the process of liquidation by the regulators. It covers workers during the accumulation phase as well as pensioners with annuities up to 150 percent of the corresponding value of the mandatory part. A worker whose pension fund goes bankrupt receives the capital accumulated by contributions on the coordinated salary plus up to an additional 50 percent if he or she has contributed to a supermandatory part. A pensioner receives the annuity corresponding to the mandatory part plus, again, up to 50 percent more in case of supermandatory benefits.

The Guarantee Fund also subsidizes pension funds with an unfavorable age structure (an important issue at the onset of the mandatory occupational system) and reimburses the Suppletory Institution for its special expenditures.

The Guarantee Fund is financed on a PAYG basis and does not primarily accumulate reserves. In the past, its reserves have always been less than one-tenth of the total accumulated retirement assets in Switzerland and were even negative at times. The contribution rate is 0.1 percent of the coordinated earnings at present. The PAYG financing has a major downside. To cover its obligations in bad times, the fund might have to increase the contribution rate when the individual funds face greater difficulties financing their primary obligations. If the Guarantee Fund faces a liquidity problem itself, the government can grant a conditional loan.

Concluding Remarks

Switzerland has had a long experience with a fully funded pension system. The 1985 law that mandated occupational pension coverage for all workers above a certain income merely institutionalized what had already been common practice in medium and large firms. Not surprisingly, the current structure still reflects the long history of the system and the preferences of workers and employers, with all its advantages and disadvantages. Occupational pension plans have always played—and still do play—an important role in attracting and keeping skilled and motivated workers. Annuity schemes are thus considered to be primarily a part of the labor market but not part of the financial market.

Economic, demographic, and socioeconomic changes during the past decades have uncovered a number of shortcomings of the Swiss system. Its structure is tailored to the needs of single-earner families under relatively stable (market) conditions. Fixed minimum interest rates and benefit conversion factors do not go along well with the large increase in life expectancy and the fall in market returns during the past decades. However, high divorce rates and a sizable increase in the labor market participation of women have changed the desired structure of the second pillar. All these changes have led to several modifications of the law, including a greater flexibility for pension funds to set the parameters of their scheme.

The second pillar is well integrated with the PAYG first pillar with respect to the coverage of labor income. However, in the payout phase, the law does not require a minimum amount of annuitization (together with the first pillar) to prevent the elderly from outliving their savings. Beneficiaries have the right to withdraw at least 25 percent of their accumulated assets as a lump sum, even if the resulting total pension benefits fall short of the subsistence level. Although the level of annuitization is estimated at about 80 percent, very large differences exist across pension funds, with many of them almost exclusively cashing out the old-age balances.

Approximately 80 percent of the population above age 24 is covered directly by the second pillar. The accumulated assets in the occupational pension system amount to approximately 100 percent of GDP, and annual contributions amount to approximately 7 percent. Given the large size of the second pillar and the high effective replacement rates in old age, it is not surprising that there is little scope for a voluntary annuity market in the strict sense of the term. Open-market annuities make up less than 1 percent of pensions. They come in many different forms (most containing a minimum capital payment in case of death) and insure a highly nonrepresentative part of the population. As a consequence, it is not possible to compute any meaningful estimates of MWRs on the open market.

A main feature of the system is a seemingly rigid legislation, coupled with the possibility for autonomous pension funds to deviate from the specified requirements under certain conditions. This approach has at least two important consequences. First, the rules are usually stricter for insurance companies, notably concerning the required funding ratio. This stringency can be justified on the grounds that it is more difficult for the insured workers to monitor an insurance company than a pension fund directly organized by the employer (and managed by a board composed of employer, employee, and retiree representatives). But having stricter rules also makes it more difficult for insurance companies to compete with the autonomous pension funds. Second, it is very difficult to get a good picture of what is really relevant in practice. The system has literally hundreds of different schemes, with large differences with respect to the funds' structure of old-age credits (including the degree of the super-mandatory part), their practice and conditions of annuitization at various ages, their asset and liability management, and their risk strategy (mirrored in the organization structure).

The main regulatory issues concern the MIR during the accumulation period and, even more important, the ACF at which the accumulated assets have to be translated into a lifelong annuity. A major problem is that the requirements are not rule based and thus are not automatically adjusted to changing market conditions and increases in longevity. As a consequence, the rules are susceptible to political pressure and result in a too sluggish response to a changing environment, leading to potential financial problems for the pension providers.

The rationale for minimum standards in the Swiss system is a strong emphasis on the stability of pension benefits across different cohorts. As a consequence of the conversion factor philosophy, the annuity rate (annuitization) risk is basically nonexistent. This lack of annuitization would not be a problem per se if the legal requirements were based on prudent estimates of long-run market conditions and mortality rates that would lead to MWRs that were in line with the financial sustainability of the system. Current political initiatives seem to go in the direction of maintaining the popular stability aspect of the system (basically protecting pensioners from the annuitization risk) but also taking into account the projected increases in longevity and the fall in the long-run market interest rate.

The computation of MWRs in the occupational pension scheme is complicated by a number of specificities of the Swiss system. First, pension funds can deviate from the legal conversion factor under certain conditions. The reported MWRs thus constitute an upper bound for the annuities' values. Second, integrating the existing forms of inflation indexing is difficult. Almost all funds use conditional indexing in the spirit of "if the financial situation of the pension fund allows it." Moreover, as Switzerland uses no inflation-indexed bonds, the discounting is somewhat tricky. Third, the discounting itself constitutes a major problem. By using the nominal yield curve, one ignores the fact that higher returns can be achieved at relatively low costs (in terms of additional risks) because of the still substantial interest rate differential with respect to other countries. Again, the reported MWRs are possibly too high. The values computed by the customary technical interest rate (which should reflect long-run market returns and is applied in most pension funds) are also open to critique.

Despite the high conversion factors, more than 90 percent of pension funds report funding ratios above 100 percent. However, the reported funding ratios may result from an understatement of pension liabilities because of the use of high technical discount rates in calculating their present value. Since the crisis in the early 2000s, the financial situation has improved in most funds. One reason for this finding might be that the MWRs computed with the nominal yield curve overestimate the true MWRs, as argued previously. Many pension providers claim that the realized return on the assets had been well over the MIR, thereby allowing for the financing of "excess benefits" and an accumulation of reserves. Nonetheless, one cannot easily generalize this result because of the high variance in the realized returns across pension providers.

Pension funds under public law that enjoy an explicit warranty from the cantonal or federal authority are in a much more delicate financial situation, with many of them well below a sufficient funding level. This susceptibility demonstrates that incentives matter a lot more than investment regulations, which are the same for all legal forms of pension funds.

Transparency has been an important policy issue in the Swiss occupational pension scheme—a problem exacerbated by the extensive fragmentation of the system. The new transparency requirements make it much easier for insured individuals to assess the performance and standing of their pension provider. The requirements also facilitate the supervision of the system, although the large differences between the providers still complicate a standardized assessment of the pension funds. Some internal mechanisms (notably the structure of governance of the pension funds) also seem to have compensated for the lack of transparency and insufficient supervision in the past.

Drawing conclusions for other countries is not easy. The history of old-age provision and the structure of the labor market are very important for the successful implementation of any system. Nonetheless, two big risks can be identified in setting up an annuity scheme and should be borne in mind. The first is an explicit guarantee of the state that seems to lead to excessive risk taking and to generous benefits. If the second pillar is large enough, as in the Swiss case, this risk taking constitutes a big threat for public finances. The second—and equally important—risk stems from inadequate regulation of the scheme. If the rules are not adjusted to market conditions and demographic changes in some standardized way, they will become, at least in the medium run, a punching ball of politics and may thus threaten the viability of the pension funds and the equitable treatment of different generations.

References

Bütler, Monika, and Martin Ruesch. 2007. "Annuities in Switzerland." Policy Research Working Paper 4438, World Bank, Washington, DC.

Bütler, Monika, and Federica Teppa. 2005. "Should You Take a Lump-Sum or Annuitize? Results from Swiss Pension Funds." CEPR Discussion Paper 5316, Centre for Economic and Policy Research, London.

OFAS (Office Fédéral des Assurances Sociales). 2009. "Rapport de l'Office Fédéral des Assurances Sociales sur la Situation Financière des Institutions de Prévoyance et des Assureurs-Vie." OFAS, Bern.

CHAPTER 6

Sweden

Promoting Personal Responsibility with a Strong Public Commitment

This chapter reviews the current status of the annuity market in Sweden and analyzes where it is headed. In Sweden, as in other high-income countries, voluntary demand for annuities has been held back by the offer of comprehensive public and occupational pensions. However, recent changes in the design and structure of both public and occupational schemes suggest a large increase in the future in the demand for private annuities.

By converting to a defined contribution (DC) setting, the recent reform of public pension provision signaled a limit to the public commitment. Nevertheless, the public schemes will continue to play a dominant role in the Swedish system for the average wage earner. Contributions for the mandated public pillar are 18.5 percent of earnings up to a ceiling of about US$60,000, divided between notional defined contribution (NDC) accounts (16 percent) and financial defined contribution (FDC) accounts (2.5 percent). Contributions to occupational plans, which are moving rapidly in the direction of FDCs, are 3.5 to 4.5 percent of earnings. The benefits that workers will receive from the two components of the public

---

This chapter is a summary and update, prepared by the editors, of the paper by Edward Palmer on "The Market for Retirement Products in Sweden" (Palmer 2008).

pillar will take the form of life annuities, the value of which will depend on individual account values and cohort life expectancy at retirement. Most benefits provided under occupational schemes will take a similar form; hence, workers now bear a considerable share of the longevity risk.

To date, occupational pension plans, as well as private individual insurance, have been dominated by profit-participating policies that provide a minimum guaranteed return and distribute additional bonuses depending on investment and longevity performance. Unit-linked products have gained importance since the mid-1990s and are expected to continue to do so. Finally, changes in the regulation and supervision of insurance companies and pension funds are likely to stimulate innovation, which will enhance the attractiveness of annuities as well as impart greater confidence in the soundness of annuity providers.

The structure of the chapter is as follows. The next section discusses the overall structure and recent changes in public and occupational pensions and reports expected replacement rates from the combination of new schemes. That section is followed by a brief review of the development of the demand for private annuities. A summary of the changing landscape for insurance providers and insurance products is then provided, followed by a detailed discussion and analysis of prudential regulation and risk management issues. The last section offers some conclusions.

Public and Occupational Pensions

Beginning with the initial reform legislation in 1994, Sweden transformed its earnings-related public pension commitment from a defined benefit (DB) scheme to a DC scheme with a combined NDC and FDC and a guaranteed defined benefit for people with no benefit or a low benefit.[1] The two public DC schemes are autonomous from the public budget, whereas the guarantee is financed with general taxes. This move was accompanied by similar changes in the major occupational schemes from DB to FDC, beginning in 1996, with the large occupational scheme for blue-collar workers negotiated by the Swedish Employers' Association (Svenska Arbetsgivareföreningen, or SAF) and the Swedish Trade Union (Landsorganisationen, or LO) (see the SAF-LO agreement shown later in table 6.2).

Public Pensions: The New NDC Scheme

The NDC scheme[2] is based on career life individual accounts that are credited with contributions made by individuals—and employers on their behalf—before retirement, during the accumulation phase. The NDC rate is 16 percent of earnings. In the Swedish version of the NDC, account balances are credited with a rate of return that is based on the growth in the covered per capita wage. Individuals can claim an annuity from age 61. No maximum or so-called full-benefit pension age applies. Workers can continue to contribute and augment their pension accounts throughout their lives. NDC and FDC annuities can be claimed at the same or different times for the whole accumulated amount or for part of the account balance. At the same time, individual workers may choose to exit from the labor force or to continue to work and make additional contributions. As in any pay-as-you-go scheme, in the NDC scheme contributions from active workers are used to pay pension benefits to current pensioners.[3]

In addition to earnings, benefits from other forms of social insurance compensating for periods with income loss give rise to contributions to NDC and FDC accounts. The most important of these are benefits for unemployment, sickness, disability, and compensated parental leave. Also, noncontributory credits are given for military service, for higher education, and to parents (one at a time) for up to four years after the birth of a child. These credits are financed from the central government budget, with annual transfers into the NDC and FDC schemes.[4] The amounts of these contributions are also posted to individual accounts, and the money is transferred to the NDC fund. In the FDC scheme, money is transferred to individual financial accounts. In the national budget, the costs for these transfers are viewed as part of the overall costs of unemployment, sickness, disability, and other schemes.

The NDC benefit is a yearly payment until death that is determined by dividing the amount in the individual's NDC account at the chosen time of retirement with an annuity divisor, which is determined by cohort life expectancy at the time of retirement and a real rate of return of 1.6 percent. Benefits are price indexed and adjusted further for deviations (positive and negative) in the real rate of growth of the average covered wage from the 1.6 percent real rate of growth assumed in the calculation of the annuity.

The NDC eliminates the annuity risk for the insurer until retirement, and the annuity divisor makes the pension system (almost) robust with regard to changes in longevity. The efficiency of the annuity divisor in reducing the longevity risk depends on how the life expectancy factor is handled in practice. In Sweden, estimates of life expectancy are based on cross-sectional data available at the time that benefits are calculated and do not take into account likely future changes in cohort longevity, which, of course, a true financial scheme is compelled to do. As a result, given continued upward revisions, longevity is underestimated in the Swedish annuity divisor. In an NDC scheme, liabilities cannot exceed assets, just as in funded schemes. In the Swedish NDC framework, an automatic balancing mechanism (ABM) is used to attain this equivalence, which will also cover any deficiency in the calculation of longevity. When necessary (when liabilities are greater than assets),[5] the Swedish ABM adjusts account values of workers and benefits of pensioners with an index that is based on the deviation of liabilities from assets. The Swedish ABM also adjusts upward, but only to a level equivalent to the path of the per capita wage index—that is, the level of indexation that would have occurred without the ABM intervention. NDC pensions were lowered in 2009 and 2010 when the ratio of the value of NDC assets over the value of liabilities fell below unity.

The NDC scheme increases personal responsibility in the decision to retire or to continue working. It eliminates the politically sensitive concept of the normal retirement age and establishes a more direct link between working contributions and retirement benefits. The ABM shields the scheme from the effect of the secular increase in longevity.

Public Pensions: The New FDC Scheme

In line with the 1994 legislation, implementation of the FDC scheme started in 1995 with the first payments of contributions. The FDC rate is 2.5 percent of earnings for participants born in 1954 and later but progressively lower for participants born between 1938 and 1953. The FDC scheme is managed by a separate government agency, the Premium Pension Authority (Premiumpensionsmyndigheten, or PPM), which was set up for this purpose. The PPM is the clearinghouse for fund transactions and the monopoly annuity provider. It maintains individual accounts, collects and makes available (daily) information on participating funds, and provides other information services to participants. The PPM was merged in 2010 into a new Swedish Pensions Agency that was created to administer all public pensions. It now operates as a department of the Swedish Pensions Agency.

The Swedish Tax Agency collects contributions to the financial account scheme, together with all other social insurance contributions (including NDCs) and with taxes in general. New contributions are transferred to individual accounts annually, after income tax reconciliation, on average about 18 months after they have been paid. During the interim, they are held in an account at the National Debt Office, where they earn a bond rate of return.

The PPM acts as a broker between participants and the participating private funds. Fund shares purchased with new payments of contributions, fund choices by new entrants, and requests for fund switches are all grouped together and executed jointly on each transaction day by the staff of the PPM. The transactions are registered on individual accounts kept by the PPM. A fund manager's client is the PPM, not the individual participant.

All fund managers licensed to operate in Sweden and fulfilling the requirements stipulated in the European Union (EU) directive on undertakings for collective investments in transferable securities (85/611/EEC, including modifications) are allowed to participate in the PPM system. Fund managers are required to follow the rules and regulations set out by the Swedish Financial Supervisory Agency, which supervises the funds. Fund providers must sign an agreement with the PPM, which includes agreeing to provide information upon request, not to charge withdrawal fees, to compute and report electronically and on a daily basis fund share values to the PPM, and to provide a periodic report of administration charges.

A company registered to do business in the PPM system can offer one or more funds. In December 2009, 88 domestic and foreign companies offered 777 funds in the PPM system. A publicly managed default fund exists for people who make no choice. Throughout the short life of the system, it has held the assets of about a third of the system's participants, but a smaller percentage of total assets because, on average, choosers have higher account balances. Switching is allowed on a daily basis, although switching transactions take about three business days. In 2009, about 15 percent of participants performed one or more switches, with an average of five switches per year per switching person. The number of switches has risen steadily from 1.2 million in 2005 to 2.6 million in 2007 and 4.5 million in 2009. Nearly all switches (99.8 percent) were performed in 2009 using the PPM's Web site.

The agreement that fund managers conclude with the PPM also involves accepting a system of maximum fee charges. A fund can levy its normal administrative fee minus a discount that depends on the balance of PPM assets held. Because of economies of scale in large holdings of PPM assets, the size of the allowable administration fee decreases with the scale of PPM assets managed by all funds in a registered company. Before April 2007, the allowable fees were based on individual funds' holdings of PPM balances. In 2009, total costs for the scheme amounted to 26 basis points, according to the PPM annual report.

Participants in the PPM-administered FDC scheme increased from 4.4 million in 2000, the first year of operation, to nearly 6.2 million in 2009 (table 6.1). At maturity, the number will be around 9 million, given present net immigration patterns. Note that individuals retain their balances even after emigrating from the country. In 2009, 664,000 pensioners were in the PPM plan, about a quarter of all pensioners.

The PPM is the sole provider of annuity products for the public FDC scheme. These products are specified in law. Participants can choose between single and joint life annuities, which can take the form of variable annuities, either traditional with-profits annuities or unit-linked annuities. To date, about 90 percent of PPM pensioners have chosen an individual annuity and about 10 percent a joint life annuity. Most pensioners (85 percent) have selected unit-linked annuities. Lump-sum payments or withdrawals over periods shorter than a life are not permitted. A preretirement survivor benefit can also be contracted.

If they choose a traditional variable annuity, participants turn over their fund balances at retirement to the PPM, which currently enlists the investment services of a publicly managed fund for its bond portfolio and, beginning in 2007, four private funds for managing its equity portfolio. A unit-linked annuity leaves the account balance in the individual's

Table 6.1   PPM Scheme: Participants, Pensioners, and Total Assets

Year	Participants (million)	Pensioners (million)	Total assets purchase value (SKr billion)	Total assets market value (SKr billion)	Total assets market value (% of GDP)
2000	4.42	—	55.8	52.1	2.3
2001	4.89	—	74.2	65.0	2.8
2002	5.08	—	94.2	59.3	2.5
2003	5.22	0.08	115.6	93.9	3.8
2004	5.35	0.16	138.0	124.8	4.9
2005	5.46	0.25	161.6	192.4	7.2
2006	5.69	0.34	211.2[a]	267.4	9.4
2007	5.84	0.45	248.8	308.3	10.0
2008	6.00	0.56	278.4	230.6	7.2
2009	6.17	0.66	308.9	340.2	10.9

Source: Data provided by PPM.

Note: — = not available.

a. In 2006, the timing of the transfer of yearly contribution payments from the Treasury to the PPM changed from January to the preceding December, which led to payments of two years' contributions during that year—one in January and one in December.

chosen private fund. In both cases, annuity payments are recalculated at the beginning of each calendar year by taking into account the investment performance and longevity experience for each pool of annuitants. Participants can transfer account balances to their spouses, but to date only a few thousand participants have done so. Annual pension amounts are still very small because of the very short coverage time and the gradual transition rules.

The annual flow of new funds into the system has been just about 1 percent of gross domestic product (GDP). The market values of the overall portfolio fell considerably below its purchase value with the dot-com equity crash in 2001 and 2002 and did not fully recover until 2005 (see table 6.1). They fell again below book value in 2008, reflecting the high losses suffered in the global financial crisis, but recovered in 2009. At year's end 2009, total assets equaled 340 billion Swedish kronor (SKr), equivalent to about 10.9 percent of GDP. The average nominal rate of return from 1995 through 2009 was 3.2 percent (with an inflation rate of around 2.0 percent). In 2009, in addition to the funds that were posted on individual accounts, the PPM also held SKr 27.6 billion that represented the contributions made during 2009 and invested with the National Debt Office.

When the first opportunity to select investment funds was given in 2000,[6] about two-thirds of those eligible made active choices. The remaining one-third of accounts were placed in the default fund, which is managed by a public institution, the Seventh AP Fund, which was set up specifically for that purpose.[7] Since then, over 90 percent of new entrants have *not* made an active choice and have been placed in the default fund. This fact has drawn considerable attention both in Sweden and internationally. On closer reflection, however, this behavior is not so surprising. Many new entrants are in their teens and early 20s. They are often students, and not infrequently, they have intermittent earnings well into their 20s. These days, Swedes reach a normal level of labor market participation between the ages of 25 and 27. Another large group of new entrants are immigrants entering the Swedish labor market for the first time. To date, the default fund has outperformed the average of all privately managed funds in the PPM scheme, which for many must provide an incentive to stay. The real test will be to see to what extent these new participants opt out of the default fund over time.

Public Pensions: The Minimum Pension Guarantee

The pension guarantee is a defined benefit that can be claimed from age 65. It is means tested against the individual's combined NDC and FDC benefits. It is price indexed and financed with revenues from the central government budget. Parliament has discretion to increase the pension guarantee's real level, but it has never done so to date. Roughly, the amount of the guarantee is approximately 30 percent of the average wage. Figure 6.1 provides an overview of the public guarantee benefit.

Occupational Pension Schemes

Occupational pension benefits in Sweden date to 1770 when the Riksdag (the parliament of Sweden) granted civil servants the right to retire at age 70 with the salary they had prior to retirement. Regulated private pension insurance plans were created during the first half of the 20th century. Since 1974, Sweden has had four major occupational pension benefit schemes. They are based on collective labor agreements and together cover about 90 percent of all employees. The occupational plans provide a two-tier supplement to public system benefits. First, they offer a top-up for covered earnings under the (nominal wage–indexed) ceiling in the public system (SKr 360,000 or US$60,000, using an exchange rate of SKr 6 per US$1), and second, they provide a benefit for earnings above the ceiling. Table 6.2 presents an overview of the number of employees covered by each collective agreement.

Figure 6.1   The Guaranteed Pension and Its Relation to the Combined NDC-FDC Pension, 2007

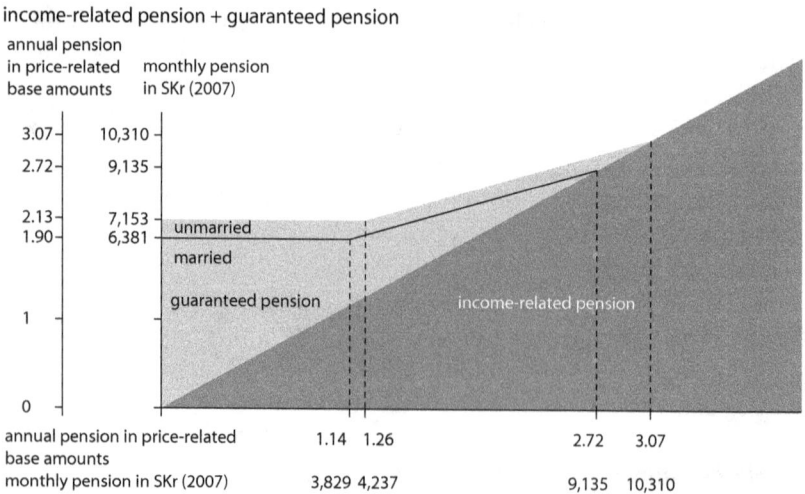

Source: Swedish Social Insurance Agency 2008.
Note: FDC = financial defined contribution; NDC = notional defined contribution.

Table 6.2   Major Groups Covered by Contractual Benefits in Sweden, 2005

Occupational plan	Number of covered employees	Percentage of employees
Private white-collar employees, ITP-ITPK[a]	700,000	16.4
Employees covered by the SAF-LO agreement	1,831,000	43.0
Civil servants and other national government employees, KAP-KL	256,000	6.0
Municipal and county council employees	853,000	20.0
Insurance and bank employees, architects, journalists	130,000	3.0
All covered employees	3,770,000	88.4

Source: Palmer 2008.
a. Figures are for 2004.

The four major occupational schemes cover the following groups of employees. The SAF-LO agreement, which encompasses over 40 percent of all employees, covers workers in agriculture, mining, lumbering, industry, trade, transport, and communications. The second-largest agreement, KAP-KL (KollektivAvtalad Pension–Kommuner och Landsting, or Collective Pension–Municipalities and Regions), covers employees working with health care services, services for the elderly and people with disabilities, other social services, and education, as well as police officers and fire fighters. All of these groups are employed by the local governments or county councils. The agreement for the third-largest group is known as ITP-ITPK (Industrins och handelns tilläggspension–Individuellt styrd komplettering till ITP, or Industry and Commerce Supplementary Pension–Individually Controlled Supplement to the ITP). It covers most privately employed white-collar workers but excludes people working in banking, insurance, journalism, and architecture. The latter groups have their own separate supplementary plans. The fourth-largest scheme covers civil servants and other national government employees. Among the latter are university employees and people working in social security, employment, and judiciary services.

Before 1994, the landmark year for the reform of the public pension system, occupational plans were all DB plans. The plan covering white-collar workers (ITP) was a *financial* defined benefit plan (that is, it was prefunded). Plans for workers covered by the SAF-LO agreement were funded at the time of retirement, whereas the plans for public sector workers were pay as you go. Beginning with the SAF-LO plan in 1995, all four major plans have been transformed to FDC for coverage below the ceiling in the public scheme, with the ITP plan being the last to move in 2007.[8] Private sector plans have also converted to FDC for coverage for earnings above the ceiling, with transition rules (in the case of employees covered by ITP, the first cohort covered is the cohort born in 1979), but public sector plans remain largely DB for earnings above the ceiling. Contribution rates range from 3.5 percent to 4.5 percent, with a scheduled increase to 4.5 percent for SAF-LO, the only major plan still under 4.5 percent.

Replacement Rates after the Reforms of the 1990s

A consequence of the reform of the public pension system and the accompanying reforms of the occupational schemes is that all earnings below the ceiling for the public scheme are covered by DC plans. The typical employee is covered by three DC plans: first, the public NDC plan with a contribution rate of 16 percent; second, the public FDC plan administered by the PPM, with a contribution rate of 2.5 percent; and third, a contractual plan, with a contribution rate of 3.5 to 4.5 percent.

Table 6.3 presents calculations of income replacement rates for a person born in 1975 who enters the labor force at 22 years of age and works all years up to retirement at one of the ages specified in the table. Pension amounts are calculated using unisex life expectancy (a requirement of a

Table 6.3   Individual Benefits as a Fraction of Final Earnings

Age	NDC contribution rate of 16%	PPM (2.5%) + occupational scheme (3.5%)			Total NDC, PPM, and occupational scheme		
		2% return	5% return	8% return	2% return	5% return	8% return
61	0.32	0.12	0.23	0.47	0.44	0.55	0.79
62	0.33	0.13	0.25	0.52	0.46	0.58	0.85
63	0.35	0.14	0.27	0.57	0.49	0.62	0.92
64	0.37	0.15	0.29	0.63	0.52	0.66	1.00
65	0.39	0.15	0.31	0.69	0.54	0.70	1.11
66	0.42	0.16	0.33	0.76	0.58	0.75	1.18
67	0.44	0.17	0.36	0.83	0.61	0.80	1.27
68	0.47	0.18	0.39	0.92	0.65	0.86	1.39
69	0.50	0.19	0.42	1.01	0.69	0.92	1.51
70	0.53	0.20	0.45	1.12	0.73	0.98	1.65

Source: Palmer 2002.

Note: Calculated for a person entering the labor force at 22 years of age who works every year until retiring at the age indicated in the table. Earnings grow at a rate of 2 percent per year. Indexation in the NDC scheme is also 2 percent per year. Unisex life expectancy for a person born in 1975 is used to calculate annuity values. The NDC annuity is based on life expectancy and an assumed real rate of annuity growth of 1.6 percent during the annuity period. The calculations do not include a possible increment deriving from the capital of nonsurvivors.

European Court of Justice ruling for both public and occupational schemes). Inheritance gains (account balances of participants who die before reaching the age of 61 that are distributed to surviving participants in the insurance pool) are not included in these calculations, which means that benefits are slightly underestimated. Calculations have been performed assuming that the occupational scheme pays a contribution rate of 3.5 percent.

Of course, the replacement rate depends on the rate of return and age of retirement. The results suggest that the replacement rate would be sufficient even if the worker were to work fewer years than the number (from age 22) assumed in the calculations. In contrast, the transition to DC for all major schemes means that persons with short earning careers (20 to 25 years or fewer) will not receive much more than the public guarantee benefit and will need to save more on their own to achieve an earnings replacement rate well over the guaranteed level of about 30 percent.

The Demand for Retirement Products

This section examines the evolution of the demand for retirement products in Sweden. The point of departure is a survey of the landscape surrounding the determinants of the demand for private insurance over the past quarter century. The survey identifies and discusses a number of institutional changes that have paved the way for future growth in the magnitude and diversity of privately provided retirement products. The section then discusses the factors that affect the demand for private insurance and finally discusses the role played by various retirement products in the overall income of present pensioners.

The Changing Landscape Surrounding Private Insurance

In 2009, 24 percent of the total financial assets of households were in private individual insurance (table 6.4). This calculation excludes the reserves held in collective insurance and pension schemes as well as holdings of unlisted equities and owner-occupied housing equity. In 1980, private insurance constituted only 9 percent of the total assets of households, even though for at least the two decades prior to the mid-1980s private insurance provided the best after-tax return among all forms of personal saving in Sweden (Palmer 1985). In 1980, only about 4 percent of persons 18 to 64 years of age used a tax deduction for payments of private insurance premiums, but this figure rose to 40 percent in 2004

Table 6.4   Financial Portfolio of Households, Year-End 1980, 2005, and 2009

	1980		2005		2009	
Financial asset	SKr billion	Percentage of total	SKr billion	Percentage of total	SKr billion	Percentage of total
Individual insurance	34	9.3	567	26.1	756	23.6
Listed equities	36	9.8	565	22.4	597	18.7
Mutual funds	—	—	484	19.2	398	12.4
Bonds	182	49.6	107	4.2	170	5.3
Bank deposits	43	11.7	619	24.6	1,047	32.7
Currency	28	7.6	87	3.5	80	2.5
Other	44	12.0	2	0.1	153	4.8
Total financial assets	367	100.0	2,521	100.0	3,201	100.0
GDP (SKr billion)	548		2,769		3,113	
Share of GDP (%)		67.0		91.0		102.8

Sources: For 1980 and 2005 data, Palmer 1985, 2008; for 2009 data, Statistics Sweden.
Note: — = not available.

(Johannisson 2003). In other words, the demand for private insurance has increased substantially since 1980.

A number of factors explain this strong growth in the private insurance market. The first were structural changes in the financial market in the 1980s. Well into the 1980s, the Swedish financial system was constrained by a comprehensive array of quantitative restrictions on bank and insurance company portfolios, such as lending ceilings on banks and portfolio composition requirements for all financial institutions. These restrictions favored investments in bonds at the expense of equities, while interest rates were regulated by the central bank rather than determined by market forces (Gottfries, Persson, and Palmer 1989). A general wave of financial liberalization in Europe in the 1980s spread to Sweden, and after the mid-1980s, most financial market restrictions had been lifted. The process of financial deregulation had been concluded by 1990.

With financial deregulation, the Swedish stock market began to grow and develop as a major source of risk capital. This growth was accompanied by strong performance and high rates of return on equities, stimulating public interest in the equity market. These developments had two effects. The first was that the interest of savers was now focused on the stock market with its high returns rather than on the insurance market with its more conservative investment policies and illiquid savings. The second was that a blossoming stock market and the growth in the number of investment funds prepared the ground for the introduction of unit-linked insurance in Sweden, which was to develop rapidly into a popular saving vehicle after the mid-1990s.

A second influence on the growth in the private insurance market was a first step in the reform of the public pension system. Reform began with a cross-party political agreement to abolish the publicly provided widow's benefit from 1990, beginning with the cohort of women born in 1945. Before the announcement of this change in 1988, the proportion of persons between 20 and 64 years of age who claimed a tax deduction for insurance premiums was increasing slowly. In the early 1980s, almost twice as many men as women used a deduction. Following the removal of survivor benefits, the number of persons using a tax deduction doubled from 1987 to 1990. Since 1991, more women than men have used a deduction to purchase voluntary private insurance, which is a logical consequence of the abolition of the widow's benefit.

The growth in the proportion of the population contracting private insurance continued to be strong through the turn of the century despite a reduction in the ceiling on the yearly premium that could be deducted for tax purposes from a little over US$11,250 to US$5,625 in 1995 (using an exchange rate of SKr 6 per US$1). The present ceiling is not absolute; smaller deductions can be claimed up to a higher absolute ceiling. The average size of a deduction was US$1,570 in 1990 (Johannisson 2003). With the decrease in the ceiling and the increase in demand from women with generally lower earnings, the average size of the deduction decreased to US$1,000 in 2003. Women claim more deductions than do men in all but the highest income class (earnings of SKr 1 million, or about US$167,000 per year).

A third major structural change was a substantial reform of the tax system, implemented in 1991. With this reform, all forms of saving were given the same income tax status. This change improved the relative price of saving in financial instruments compared to borrowing for current consumption or for housing investments. Individual saving had reached a postwar low at the end of the 1980s, and a major focus of policy in the initial years of the 1990s was to attempt to reverse the downward trend.

In 1993, a fourth major change, already alluded to, occurred when legislation enabling unit-linked insurance went into effect. Whereas traditional life insurance still followed conservative insurance principles, unit-linked insurance allowed the individual to make his or her own investment choices during the accumulation phase, including choices from among equity funds. Since 1993, an increasing share of growth in the assets of life insurance companies has come through unit-linked contracts.

A fifth legislative change influencing the development of private insurance was the introduction of individual retirement saving accounts in 1994. New saving in an individual retirement saving account is tax deductible under the same (gross) rule as premiums paid for private insurance. As with private insurance, accounts must be held at least up to age 55, and withdrawals must be made over a period of at least five years. Banks and investment funds provide the account services, and the saver can usually choose among a number of alternative funds. Individual retirement saving accounts are not a perfect substitute for insurance because they do not cover the risk of longevity, but they are more liquid than traditional insurance with life annuities. Hence, they have become an attractive saving tool that competes with insurance policies.

A sixth major structural change was the reform of the public pension system, already discussed, which had three important repercussions for the development of the private insurance market. First, the introduction of DC principles in the public schemes clearly limited the scope of the public commitment and, in doing so, focused interest on individual responsibility for providing for retirement. Second, one of the components of the reform was the mandatory financial account scheme itself, which would provide an injection of new money into the market, with the entire working-age population as participants. Third, as was discussed previously, the reform of the public system led to conversion of a large segment of the quasi-mandatory occupational pension schemes from DB to FDC account plans and to future prefunding of (at the time) unfunded commitments.

Finally, new legislation was implemented from May 1, 2008, making it possible to switch providers within the European Union for all new contracts and for existing contracts that do not prohibit such a switch. Further liberalization is expected to follow, enabling freedom of movement even for contracts existing prior to May 2008 that explicitly prohibit switching. The increase in freedom to move between providers can be expected to increase competition for customers through provision of better insurance products with lower administration fees. This change should also help spur the development of a more robust domestic annuity market.

Current Demand for Private Annuities

The current demand for annuities has been shaped by the availability of retirement income from public and occupational pension schemes and by an opinion that prevailed into the 1990s that this coverage was sufficient for the average worker. Data for 2004 show that the income of Swedes 65 years and older is on average 65 percent that of workers 55 to 64 years old (table 6.5). Remarkably, this ratio has remained unchanged for more than a decade. The relative income of persons over 75 experienced a small improvement from 56 to 58 percent, whereas that of people 65 to 74 years of age remained constant at 74 percent. Of note is that the income of people older than 75 is 22 percent lower than those 65 to 74 years of age.

Some of the difference between older and younger pensioners reflects the fact that until 2001 public benefits were only price indexed. As retirees grew older, the value of their priced-indexed benefits relative to the average older worker's earnings fell as real earnings increased.[9] From 2001, pensions granted under both the old and the new rules have a positive real growth increment. When real covered wages grow by more than 1.6 percent, the difference gives rise to real indexation of benefits equal to the difference between 1.6 percent and the actual rate of growth of the per capita (covered) wage—in addition to normal price indexation. This increment still falls short of full wage indexation, however.

For persons over 65, earnings and entrepreneurial income constitute about 6 percent of income, capital income 12 percent, pensions 78 percent, and housing allowances (for low-income pensioners) about 4 percent of total income. Earnings and entrepreneurial income constitute about 15 percent of total income for persons 65 to 69 years of age, with a steeply declining profile thereafter. As people age, the importance of earnings decreases and, by definition, the relative importance of pensions and capital income increases. Palmer (2008) examines the data for Sweden, which also show that 71 percent of the total pension income of persons 65 and older comes from public pensions, 23 percent from

Table 6.5   Relative Income of Elderly People

Age (years)	Percentage of income of people ages 55–64	
	1991	*2004*
65–74	74	74
75+	56	58
65+	65	65

Source: Palmer 2008.
Note: Income is measured as equivalent disposable income.

occupational pensions, and 6 percent from voluntary private individual insurance.

The data also suggest that the different sources of benefits fulfill different needs. A first group of pensioners, 6 percent of all beneficiaries in 2004, were under the minimum age (61) to claim a public benefit. Their benefits consisted of an occupational pension, a private individual pension, or (in surprisingly few cases) both. In many cases, employees obtain occupational benefits as a form of severance pay, which by no means precludes taking a new job, and some do so. Private benefits can be claimed from age 55 and are withdrawn over a period of *at least* five years. They, too, can be combined with continued earnings from work.

The next cohort is the age group 61 to 64. For this group, the data show that occupational benefits are the main benefit. The reason is straightforward: occupational benefits are used to support early retirement from the labor force, both for those few occupations where early retirement is specified in the employment contract (for example, firefighters) and for those people who voluntarily decide to leave the labor force in their early 60s without drawing on their public benefit.

Sometimes early exit is not entirely voluntary but instead the result of an agreement initiated by the employer, with the aim of downsizing staff, usually involving some form of financial remuneration for some of the income loss associated with early exit. When workers instead voluntarily opt to use their occupational benefits to leave the labor force before the age of 65, their occupational supplement to the public benefit is reduced after age 65 to compensate for this early retirement benefit. The worker will have "saved" on the actuarial reduction in the public benefit. This example demonstrates the close integration in the use of occupational and public pensions in Sweden.

Finally, the data also suggest that a tendency may exist to claim occupational benefits from age 65 for the required minimum five-year period, where this is permitted, because the statistics show that amounts fall substantially from age 70. The meaning of age 65 is changing, however, because of the reform of the public pension system. From the mid-1970s until 2001, the de facto mandatory pension age was 65, as a part of the centrally negotiated labor agreements governing occupational benefits. The age was raised across the board to 67 in 2001, with the passage of right-to-work legislation to age 67. Hence, before 2001, both public and occupational benefits were normally claimed at age 65.

In 2004, private individual benefits provided a substantial supplement to yearly income primarily for persons under 75 years of age. First, they were important for persons retiring before age 65. Second, persons 65 to 69 years of age constituted the largest group holding a private pension. This fact could be due to one of two factors. The first would be an increase in the demand for private insurance among younger cohorts of retirees already in the 1970s and 1980s. The second would be a tendency for individuals to take advantage of the possibility of claiming benefits according to the five-year minimum rule to supplement income in the initial stage of retirement. The data also show that private life annuities have not been an important form of longevity insurance for the older cohorts of retirees.

Finally, the relative insignificance of annuities among present older cohorts reflects saving decisions made well over a quarter century ago. Evidence from other sources indicates that at least into the mid-1980s Swedes viewed their mandated public saving as sufficient longevity protection. A series of studies undertaken about two decades after the 1960 introduction of the universal mandated earnings-related DB scheme (the *allmän tilläggspension,* or general supplementary pension) in Sweden all indicated that individual private saving was lower than it otherwise would have been had the scheme not been introduced (Berg 1983; Markowski and Palmer 1979; Palmer 1981). Together the studies suggested that the decline may have been about 4 percent of disposable income per year between 1960 and 1980.[10]

The Future Demand for Private Annuities

The data for Sweden suggest that claimants have chosen to use private insurance as an income supplement in younger pension years—up to age 75—rather than as a life annuity. One can reasonably expect that the demand for retirement products to help finance consumption in the early years of retirement will continue to be significant. In fact, such demand should be strengthened by the entrance of DC schemes to the public system, with an actuarial deduction that discourages early retirement through a reduced public benefit. With the significant changes in the structural landscape discussed previously and, moreover, following the large-scale transition to the DC world from the mid-1990s, undoubtedly the demand for annuities will change significantly in coming years.

The scale of future demand can be illustrated by the volume of premiums presently flowing into the market and the present level of assets in the companies managing insurance and the PPM. This information is summarized in table 6.6. In 2009, premium payments to life insurance companies, which for the most part are linked to occupational

Table 6.6   Premiums and Assets of Life Insurance Companies and Pension Funds

	2005		2009	
Company or fund	SKr billion	Percentage of GDP	SKr billion	Percentage of GDP
Premiums				
Life insurance companies	142	5.1	177	5.7
PPM	24	0.9	30	1.0
Total premiums	166	6.0	207	6.7
Assets				
Life insurance companies	1,904	68.8	2,238	71.9
Self-administered company funds	105	3.8	86	2.8
PPM	240	8.7	373	12.0
AP buffer funds	769	27.8	827	26.6
Total	3,018	109.1	3,524	113.3

Source: Data provided by Statistics Sweden.

and individual pension plans, amounted to SKr 177 billion, or 5.7 percent of GDP. Including the premiums paid to the PPM raises the total to 6.7 percent of GDP.

The total assets accumulated by life insurance companies amounted to SKr 2,238 billion, or 72 percent of GDP. The PPM assets (which include the contributions transferred by employers but still held with the National Debt Office rather than posted to individual accounts) amounted to SKr 373 billion, or 12 percent of GDP. About 3 percent of GDP is held by self-administered occupational pension funds, and the five AP buffer funds hold 27 percent of GDP. The total contractual savings corresponded to 113 percent of GDP, although not all of these assets will be available to support the future growth of the annuity market.

Insurance Providers and Insurance Products

Sweden has two categories of providers of annuity products: private insurance companies, which provide annuity products for group occupational and individual accumulation schemes, and the PPM, which is the monopoly provider of annuity products for the financial pillar of the mandatory pension system. The tax law restricts the types of products that insurance companies can provide. This section surveys the suppliers of retirement insurance products and presents and discusses their products.

Overview of Providers of Private Insurance Products

At present, 44 life insurance companies operate in Sweden. Despite this relatively large number of companies, the bulk of business is concentrated in only seven companies. These seven major companies account for 95 percent of individual premium payments and hold 97 percent of the total assets of life insurance companies. The same seven companies are the major providers of both individual voluntary insurance and occupational group schemes. Of the seven companies, three are owned by three of the largest banks in Sweden.[11]

Two other companies have a limited area of activity. One, Alecta, offers collective insurance but does not sell individual voluntary insurance. The other, FPG, reinsures the pension liabilities of companies that operate a book reserve system and retain the premium payments of employees covered under the ITP. In addition, a public agency (Statens Pensionsverk) administers and invests a large portion of the financial resources accumulated for civil servants and other national government employees.

The premium payments for occupational and individual voluntary insurance constitute 95 percent of total premiums for all life insurance products in Sweden. The remaining business of private life insurance companies consists of health and accident insurance. Health is largely covered by the public sector in Sweden. Accident insurance is the largest of these two remaining segments of the life insurance business.

The Mandatory FDC Scheme and the Market

Individual choices in the mandatory FDC scheme administered by the PPM have favored Sweden's seven largest private insurance providers. Together, these seven companies held 43 percent of total PPM assets at the end of September 2007 (table 6.7). The default fund (the Seventh AP Fund) held an additional 29 percent. Thus, the seven major companies and the public default fund managed about three-quarters of all PPM assets.

The largest company in the market for PPM assets was Swedbank Robur Försäkring, owned by Swedbank, with a 14 percent market share. Robur was one of the first companies to provide investment funds in the private market in Sweden, beginning in 1967, and was able to benefit from its early lead in this market. The second-, third-, and fourth-largest companies were SPP (part of which is now a subsidiary of Handelsbanken), AMF, and Folksam, all of which were historically major players in the market for occupational pension schemes. Undoubtedly, this status gave them an initial advantage in attracting PPM clients.

Table 6.7   PPM Assets Held by the Seven Largest Private Insurance Companies and the Seventh AP Fund, 2007

Company or fund	Share of total PPM assets (%)	Share of GDP (%)
Seventh AP Fund	29	2.7
Seven major private insurance companies		
Swedbank Robur Försäkring	14	1.3
Handelsbanken and SPP	9	0.9
AMF	9	0.9
Folksam	5	0.5
Länsförsäkringar	3	0.3
Skandinaviska Enskilda Banken	2	0.2
Skandia	1	0.1
Total	43	4.2
Seventh AP Fund and the seven major private companies	72	6.9
Total PPM assets	100	9.6

Source: Palmer 2008.
Note: Data are from September 28.

The top four private providers managed 29 of the largest 50 funds, ranked in terms of asset values. The next three major providers managed an additional 6 of the top 50 funds, which means that 35 of the largest 50 funds were managed by Sweden's seven largest private insurance providers. The second- and third-largest funds in the system, AMF Pension Aktiefond Sverige and AMF Pension Aktiefond Världen (Swedish and world market index funds, respectively), held 6 percent of all PPM assets.

In 2009, the 10 largest funds, including the default fund, accounted for 44 percent of total PPM assets, while the share of the top 20 funds equaled 54 percent of total assets. The Premium Savings Fund, which is the default fund managed by the Seventh AP Fund, accounted for 26 percent of total assets. Of the 20 largest funds, 16 belonged to the groups listed in table 6.7.

In 2009, 53 percent of all PPM assets were invested in funds holding only equities. Only 6 percent were invested in funds holding only interest-bearing investments. About 85 percent of the portfolio of the default fund and a large percentage of the portfolios of the balanced and life-cycle (generation) funds were also invested in equities. As a result, almost 90 percent of all PPM assets were invested in equities at the end of 2009. This asset allocation pattern has been prevalent since the creation of the PPM.

At first glance, the percentage of PPM assets held in equities seems high. However, the heavy preference for equities is less surprising when one considers the career-age profile of PPM participants. Although people born in 1938 and later are covered in the mandatory financial scheme, the accounts of the older cohorts are very small. According to the transition rule for replacing the old system, mandatory contributions to the FDC scheme are 4/20th of the FDC rate for persons born in 1938, rise by 1/20th for each subsequent year of birth, and reach the full contribution rate for persons born in 1954. With a contribution rate of 2.5 percent for the FDC scheme and with not much of a full career left to contribute before retirement, the relevance of this system for the overall pension of older participants is minimal. Hence, older cohorts not surprisingly tended to "take a gamble" and invest heavily in equities. In contrast, for younger cohorts covered by the PPM scheme, who were born in the 1960s and later, having a large percentage of their portfolios invested in equities is, in fact, wise.

Retirement Products

The Swedish market offers two classes of insurance products: traditional insurance and unit-linked insurance (called *fund insurance* in Sweden). Traditional insurance is an umbrella term for a number of retirement products and covers lump-sum payments (*kapitalförsäkring*), phased withdrawals (*temporary annuities* in the Swedish terminology), and life annuities.

Before discussing the features and role of different retirement products, one should note that, by law, retirement products cannot be claimed before age 55. This low age limit has been set for over half a century and has not changed despite the rise in longevity of 60-year-olds by six or seven years over this period. The age limit applies in principle to both individual voluntary insurance and occupational pension schemes, although the latter can set a higher minimum age.

In principle, possible retirement at 55 is not in harmony with the present goal of policy makers to encourage postponement to beyond the age of 65. However, powerful interests favor maintaining this low age, represented by both employee and employer confederations, which see possible advantages in being able to offer a pension at a younger age than the minimum retirement age of 61 in the mandatory public system. Implicitly, by maintaining the low minimum age of 55 for claiming retirement products, policy makers enable early exit from the labor market financed through private individual saving.

In addition to individual voluntary insurance and the quasi-obligatory collective occupational schemes, the employer and the employee can agree on arrangements other than the standard retirement arrangements. Employer payments for insurance in this connection are tax deductible, whereas benefits when claimed are taxed as normal income. This option allows employers to create tailored individual agreements for selected employees as an extra incentive in employment contracts as well as to negotiate compensation for severance not available in the standard collective agreements. Individual agreements falling under the second category can compensate for a combination of lost earnings or lost pension rights in the standard schemes resulting from earlier retirement. A study of Swedish data by Eklöf and Hallberg (2006) estimates that the probability of employees exiting the labor force early would fall by 14 to 25 percent, depending on the year examined, if the possibility of employers giving a "golden handshake" of this kind were to be eliminated.

Lump sums. Three main types of lump sums are available only for individual voluntary insurance. The first is a lump-sum benefit that becomes available when the policyholder reaches an age specified in the policy. Premium payments are tax deductible up to a specified ceiling, and the benefit is taxed together with other income sources.

The second type is a lump-sum benefit that becomes available to the heirs of the policyholder, when death occurs during an age interval of x to y and where, in principle, x and y are determined by the terms of the contract. This insurance form has been attractive to persons whose purpose was to avoid creating a gift or inheritance tax for their heirs, where by law the heirs can be the policyholder's spouse, legal cohabitant, or children. As of 2005, Sweden no longer had a gift or inheritance tax, making this form of saving less attractive.

The third type became available January 1, 2005, following the abolition of gift and inheritance taxes. This type enables the holder to place an unlimited sum of money into an account, which can be claimed during a period of five years from the age of 55. Normally, claimants would be the policyholder's spouse, legal cohabitant, or children, and the aim of the policyholder would be to avoid paying the wealth tax during his or her lifetime, while leaving the sum to these legal heirs upon death. Shortly after the introduction of this benefit form, the wealth tax was abolished, however, so interest in this product in its otherwise limited segment has probably waned significantly.

Phased withdrawals and annuities. Annuities can be contracted for a fixed or lifelong payout period. A fixed-period benefit (temporary or term annuity) must be paid out during at least five years. Normal forms of this benefit are payments during a period of 5 or 10 years. Life annuities are available as single or joint life annuities, also covering the spouse or legal cohabitant. Individual insurance policies are often set as a combination of (a) life insurance before the age of 55, when they serve to provide preretirement survivor benefits, and (b) a joint life annuity after retirement, when they provide retirement income and postretirement survivor benefits. Single and joint life annuities are available through individual contracts as well as through individual choices in the occupational and PPM schemes. Historically, these products have been a part of a DB package. With the transition to DC, they are retirement products that individual financial accounts can finance.

No product data are available in Sweden because insurance companies are not required to report their product distribution. On the basis of data on income sources for different age groups, one can infer that the vast majority of occupational and individual insurance benefits take the form of phased withdrawals over fixed periods of 5 or 10 years. The typical payout window, already discussed, is between the ages of 55 and 75.

Traditional term or life annuity products offer a guaranteed benefit and a bonus. The guaranteed rate of return, which varies between companies, is currently between 2 and 5 percent per year (with a rate of inflation of 1 to 2 percent). For many years, it was 3 percent for all companies. The amount of the bonus is determined by the performance of the insurance provider's investment portfolio. The bonus is distributed to participants during both the accumulation and the decumulation phases. Hence, a company's clients can benefit from successful investment performance. Both the guarantee and the bonus are used for marketing purposes to attract customers.

Unit-linked products. With unit-linked insurance, the participant invests individual account balances in market funds during the accumulation phase. On retirement, account balances can be converted into one of the insurance products already described or can be left in the individual's account, allowing the individual to determine the investment profile of his or her own account. The coming year's benefit is recalculated on the basis of the remaining funds in the participant's account at the end of each year. Here it is also typical to offer a choice between a monthly payment and a single payment for the whole year. If the insured selects a monthly payment, the remainder of the annual payment is invested by the insurance provider, which also shares this return with the customer. In practice, the customer chooses a rate of return for payments for the year (for example, up to 5.5 percent given present alternatives). If the actual rate of return falls short of this amount, the difference is deducted from the account holder's balance before calculating the payment for the next year.

Management of Risks and Supervision

This section analyzes prudential regulation and risk management issues with regard to life insurance.

Portfolio Regulations for Life Insurance Companies

Companies providing life and pension insurance must follow regulations regarding the portfolio composition of the technical reserves that cover guaranteed insurance commitments (that is, liabilities taking the company's guaranteed rate of return into consideration). For these reserves, companies are allowed to have up to 25 percent of their assets in equities, an additional 25 percent in real estate, 10 percent in lending with security other than real estate, and a maximum of 3 percent in cash. The remainder of the portfolio is to be held in bonds, with a possible maximum of 100 percent. Companies are free to invest all assets in excess of these technical reserves free of any quantitative restrictions if they follow prudent investment policy.

Liquidation of a company presents a special problem, however, and according to EU legislation, the home country is responsible for determining the procedure to be applied in these cases. According to Swedish rules, in the case of liquidation, participants have the right to all technical reserves—corresponding at least to their premium payments—and the right to other reserves after deduction of other debts, for example, unpaid wages and salaries of employees. The European Union has established a minimum solvency requirement for life insurance companies, which from 2002 is €3 million.

Finally, even the legislation regarding investment funds is important in the context of unit-linked products. Unit-linked insurance couples individuals to investment funds, which are either owned by the insurance company, in which case the individual is contracted, or owned by other fund managers, whose funds are open to choice within the contract. For an investment fund to operate in Sweden, it must adhere to EU rules and regulations, but no additional rules apply. The specific requirements of the PPM for funds to join the system have already been described.

Portfolio Composition of Life Insurance Companies

At the end of the 1990s, before the collapse of equity prices in 2000 to 2002, the proportion of assets held in equities for all insurance companies together was about 50 percent. In 2002, the share of equities fell to 37 percent, still higher than the 25 percent limit imposed on the assets backing technical reserves. By 2006, Swedish companies' equity share in total assets had returned to 50 percent. Equity holdings fell to 43 percent in 2008 but rebounded to 53 percent in 2009.

Looking at the aggregate portfolio in a different light, one finds that the ratio of less risky assets (short-term paper, deposits, and bonds) to riskier assets (equities, loans, and real estate) amounted to 1.26 in the financial "crisis" year of 2002 but decreased to 0.91 by the end of 2006. The ratio rose again to 1.12 in 2008 but declined to 0.76 in 2009. In general, holdings of equities, with a steadily growing allocation in foreign equities, dominate bonds in insurance company portfolios, except in periods of crisis, when a retrenchment occurs to equity investments.

Within the framework of traditional insurance, Swedish companies compete on the basis of guarantees and bonuses, with the latter being a profit-sharing mechanism when assets significantly exceed liabilities. Prudent practice dictates that the surplus should be large enough to prevent a fall below unity in the asset-to-liability ratio, given a normal corridor of variance associated with the equity content in the portfolio.

In the crisis year 2002, the asset-to-liability ratio was below unity for all major companies and significantly so for many smaller companies. As a result, companies were forced in the immediately ensuing period to reduce bonus commitments already promised. This extraordinary measure was unpopular with clients. By the close of 2005, the ratios of many, though not all, companies were comfortably above unity. Ratios leveled out thereafter through 2007, indicating that they had reached what companies considered to be desirable levels (Palmer 2008).

The financial picture for occupational insurance in 2002 resembled that of individual voluntary insurance. With the exception of one company, long-term pension liabilities were greater than the market value of assets. Recovery began in 2003, and by 2004 solvency ratios were once again above unity. They continued to climb, and in 2007 they were significantly over unity, completing the adjustment back to normality. During the 2008 global financial crisis, insurance companies and pension funds experienced large significant declines in their solvency ratios, but most entities remained well above the level of unity.

Risk Management and Risk-Sharing Arrangements

Because a large proportion of Swedish insurance portfolios is in equities, volatility of asset values is higher than it would be with a larger share of interest-bearing assets. Clearly a bond portfolio would reduce the investment risk. Historically, Swedish government bonds have had a return of about 3 percent, compared with a return of 8 percent for equities listed on the Swedish Stock Exchange (Frennberg and Hansson 1995). Hence, the historical data indicate that having a large equity component in insurance portfolios is to the advantage of plan participants.

The Swedish law regulating investments of insurance companies is designed to be cautious for the basic commitments of the plan—the guaranteed benefit—but to leave freedom for investments for the remainder of assets. In this framework, the insurance provider bears the risk for meeting the guaranteed level, and the individual bears the risk for returns above that level.

The conversion from DB to DC now taking place shifts the risk entirely onto the individual during the accumulation phase. The period during which the provider is exposed to risk is the much shorter annuity period. From that point, providers of DB and DC insurance face the same risk. The Swedish guarantee and bonus system does not alter this fact in any way. What it does do is provide a framework for dealing with risk. Namely, the guarantee is a commitment to be fulfilled, while the provider and participant share the remaining investments and mortality risk through the bonus.

Within the DC framework, participants can continue to hold their accounts in funds of their choice. This option is available in all three insurance categories in Sweden: private individual voluntary, private occupational, and public PPM insurance. The outcome of the participant's investment strategy determines the amount left on account at the end of each period, and each current year payment is determined by this account balance and the value of the divisor, which is determined by a life table. This approach frees the insurance company of a negative risk.

In the case of phased withdrawals over 5 or 10 years, which are popular insurance product choices in Sweden, the insurer is freed from all risk. The individual participant takes on the investment risk, while the longevity factor is known. Unused account balances for those who die before the expiration of the contract are distributed as a contracted survivor benefit. With these product forms, insurance companies bear neither investment nor longevity risk.

In mutually owned (not-for-profit) occupational schemes, the employer ostensibly bears the risk during the annuity period in either the DB or DC case (where the annuity is tantamount to a defined benefit). The employer takes on the role of the owner of the insurance company. In the capacity of owner, employers are obliged to transfer capital to a plan in financial difficulty. The employer's financial obligation is only ostensible, however, because a need to provide additional capital at the expense of profits can be passed on to concurrent workers in the form of lower future wage increases.

In general, practically all Swedish insurance companies use the same life tables, which are known to be conservative. To the extent that providers use the same life tables more or less to the letter, investment portfolios constitute the remaining means for competition. Until 2008, life tables used by Swedish insurers were based on cohort projections made in 1985 and last revised in 1990. They became progressively outdated, especially for older pensioners.

In the traditional insurance framework, where an annuity is calculated from some age x, the insurer can hedge against the longevity risk by using conservative life expectancy estimates. In this case, de facto, the insured bears the longevity risk. This scenario suggests that, if beneficiaries were aware of the differences in the risk assumed by the insurer, all other things equal, they would choose the company offering the best annuity, which is tantamount to the company willing to take on a larger share of the risk instead of passing it on to the insured.

The risk assumed by providers of insurance can differ depending on whether the insurance is individual voluntary or occupational insurance. In occupational group insurance, employers bear the risk, which in theory could lead to a situation in which the administrator takes a greater investment risk. The data examined in Palmer (2008) suggest that such can be the case, which would explain why the average ratio of assets to pension liabilities is considerably higher for occupational plans than for individual plans.

A way to manage the investment risk would be to match a birth cohort's annuity pool to a financial instrument with about the same duration as the cohort's life expectancy at retirement, or perhaps longer, for example, until most in the cohort have passed away. If the financing of a retired birth cohort's pooled annuity is matched by an asset with a period of duration (roughly) commensurate to the longevity of the cohort, then the investment risk is minimized. With present retirement patterns and longevity, this method would require the regular issuance of bonds with a duration of approximately 20 years or more. The government is the logical issuer of such bonds. Whether it is in the interest of the country's taxpayers to issue such bonds is an important issue. An alternative vehicle with a similar purpose, but not yet well established in Sweden, is the mortality bond.

The expected length of retirement of Swedish cohorts born in the 1950s to the 1970s is 18 to 20 years at age 65. Moreover, the average length of a commitment for insurance companies is slightly longer—22 years (FSA 2004)—because the average retirement age of a covered participant is under 65. The bonds with the longest duration issued in Sweden since the mid-1990s are two separate issues of 16 to 17 years in 1997 and 2004 for SKr 40 billion and SKr 64 billion, respectively. These bonds are not typical in the Swedish market, however.

Since the mid-1990s, Swedish government bond issues are typically for 10 years in amounts of about SKr 40 billion. In March 2008, the Swedish government's entire debt was SKr 1,075 billion (about 35 percent of GDP) of which about SKr 500 billion was financed with Swedish government bonds. Private insurance companies administering the individual voluntary and occupational schemes hold roughly 60 percent of the total stock of government bonds. Clearly, a strong link exists between the government and insurers.

The 10-year government bond rate, shown in figure 6.2, fell to a low approaching 3 percent in mid-2005. Thereafter, it increased to over 4 percent in 2006. Given that most insurance providers in Sweden discount liabilities with a rate of 3 percent, examination of figure 6.2 shows that for a short period in 2005, the market rate for 10-year bonds came close to falling below the rate used for discounting liabilities—and did so for the few companies using a rate of 3.5 percent.

The money-weighted duration of the present stock of government bonds is only five and one-half years. The turnover time for treasury bills is about a year. A calculation of the weighted duration of both bonds and bills suggests that the government rolls over its debt completely about every four years. This turnover time is considerably under what would satisfy the insurer who wants to match cohort annuities for life expectancies of close to 20 years with a single market asset. In contrast, the frequent issuance of 10-year bonds certainly helps insurers manage their investment risk, because this duration corresponds to the average money-weighted payout time of annuities.

Figure 6.2   Ten-Year Government Bond Rate, Monthly Values, January 1987–March 2008

Source: Data provided by Swedish National Debt Office.

In 2006 to 2007, for example, the money-weighted coupon rate of the present stock of bonds was 5 percent, which is sufficient to cover the most ambitious guaranteed rate of return offered by Swedish providers of individual voluntary insurance. In addition, with an average rate of inflation of 1.5 percent per year over the entire period since the central bank converted from a fixed to a floating exchange rate in 1992,[12] the *real* coupon rate of return is about 3.5 percent. A normal return of 5 percent is more than sufficient to maintain balance in the voluntary portion of the insurance business, where a *nominal* guarantee rate of 3 percent is characteristic. In addition, it is sufficient to maintain price-indexed annuities in the present contractual DB schemes, given that the longevity risk has been properly managed.

An interesting question in the present context is what happens to competition among annuity providers if the whole insurance market has access to and holds long bonds with the same returns. Logically, an investment portfolio that provides a good longevity match between assets and liabilities will inevitably restrict competition among insurance companies. The counterfactual is a situation with portfolios with higher equity content and higher rates of return for customers, but also with more volatility and risk. One can conclude that present Swedish practice enables companies to assume greater risks—and annuity recipients to achieve higher returns— than would be the case if annuity liabilities were more or less exactly matched by long-duration bonds.

Finally, periods with falling interest rates have two important effects on the portfolios of insurance companies. The first is that a lower discount rate increases the present value of a company's commitments—and consequently the required technical insurance reserves—by reducing the possible equity content. Companies' bond portfolios increase in value as coupon rates fall, but this increase will not match the increase in liabilities to the insured, because these liabilities normally have a period of duration of about 22 years, whereas bond portfolios have a period of duration of about 5 years.

In closing, compared, for example, with the United Kingdom, which has a lively public discussion of the need for long-term government debt issuance to create the "matching asset" for private insurance, in Sweden little discussion currently takes place in the insurance community on this issue. Instead, insurance companies seem to be comfortable dealing with the risk of fluctuating values in asset portfolios through the system of balancing with (positive, and when necessary, negative) bonuses, previously described. In addition, as the data mentioned indicate, the occupational schemes are presently running with considerable surpluses, and a negative asset-to-liability balance has been more of a temporary phenomenon than a persistent problem.

PPM Product Provision and Risk Management

As has already been discussed, the PPM is the sole provider of annuity products in the mandatory public financial account scheme. The products that the PPM can provide are specified in law. Participants can choose between single and joint life annuities. Annuities can be traditional with-profits annuities or unit-linked annuities. Lump-sum payments are not among the products offered, nor are phased withdrawals over shorter periods than a whole life. In this respect, the retirement product choice for the individual is much more limited in the mandatory plan than in privately provided individual and occupational insurance plans.

A traditional with-profits annuity is "purchased" from the PPM at retirement and entails closing individual accounts and transferring all balances to the PPM, which invests the funds. This scheme is the PPM equivalent to the traditional insurance alternative within the private insurance framework, which provides a combination of a guarantee and a bonus rate of return. Alternatively, the participant can leave his or her money in market funds and accept a recalculated annuity on an annual basis, which is the unit-linked annuity. These annuities are also handled by the PPM, although the funds are managed by asset managers.

Until April 2007, the guaranteed rate of return was 2.75 percent. In a series of steps during 2007, the PPM changed its policy regarding both the guarantee and the way funds of pensioners should be invested. To enable it to increase its solvency ratio and thereby invest a greater portion of assets in equities, the PPM changed the guarantee to cover only the nominal value of individual balances, meaning that the entire return would be viewed as a "bonus" or profit-sharing segment of investment returns. The PPM hopes this policy will give a better return to policyholders in the long run.

The choice of investment service providers is made by the PPM's board of directors. Money turned over to the PPM at retirement is invested by a public investment company. For the past several years, 73 percent of the assets of annuity holders have been invested in interest-bearing assets and 27 percent in equities. As has already been discussed, insurance companies can by law have a distribution of 75/25 in their technical reserves, but the PPM is allowed a 70/30 distribution. Thus, the share of equities represents what is allowable while complying with the rules regarding technical reserves.

The PPM is not yet in the position where it has free assets (that is, reserves much exceeding the amount needed to cover guaranteed commitments, which it can invest more freely). At the end of 2007, following the switch from a guaranteed rate of return of 2.75 percent on balances to a 0 percent guarantee that covers only the nominal value of balances, the solvency ratio increased from a little over unity (1.04) to about 1.17. The solvency ratio rose further to 1.43 in 2009. Progressively during 2007, the PPM enlisted the services of four private firms to manage its equity portfolio. Its interest-bearing portfolio is still being managed by a publicly owned investment agency that invests other government funds.

Benefits are calculated using unisex life expectancy tables, which is in line with the *Barber* decision of the European Court of Justice regarding benefit calculations in public pension schemes. The life expectancy projections used by the PPM are taken from Statistics Sweden's projections. Statistics Sweden provides two scenarios: a baseline and a low-mortality scenario. In calculating traditional annuities, the model with a guarantee and a bonus, the PPM uses Statistics Sweden's low-mortality scenario, adjusted further by assuming that mortality will be 10 percent lower. The baseline scenario is used in calculating unit-linked annuities, where the participant retains his or her market funds. The difference between the low-mortality scenario and the baseline scenario is substantial, about four years to the year 2050 (table 6.8).

Whereas in with-profits annuities the PPM bears the longevity risk for the guaranteed benefits, it bears no longevity risk in unit-linked annuities.

Table 6.8   The PPM Life Expectancy Assumption

	Life expectancy (years)	
Scenario	2004	2050
Baseline scenario		
Men	77.9	83.6
Women	82.3	86.2
Low-mortality scenario		
Men	78.0	87.5
Women	82.4	89.9

Source: Palmer 2008.

At present, the PPM expects to retain the mortality schedule, determined at age 65, for the remainder of the participant's life. Nothing prohibits changing tables in the future if longevity changes considerably compared to the table values. Within the traditional insurance framework, the insurer—the PPM in this case—has the option of covering negative longevity outcomes for itself by altering the bonus and then setting a new divisor value for newly granted benefits. This option is available to both the PPM and private insurers. Needless to say, in unit-linked annuities, investment volatility is likely to have the greatest effect on the individual benefit outcome.

One issue is not clear in the Swedish legislation: the question of ownership liability. Although the PPM's life expectancy assumptions appear to be very conservative, theoretically life expectancy could possibly outperform this conservative value, or portfolio investment performance might not be sufficient to cover the guaranteed liability. Swedish law prohibits distributing money between cohorts to cover a deficit for any given cohort. In principle, the Swedish government is the owner of the plan administered by the PPM, which implies that the government would be responsible for covering any deficit that might occur, although this liability is not stated specifically in the law.

Regulation of Providers of Insurance Products

Regulation of banking, insurance, and the securities market are all under one roof—the Financial Supervisory Authority (Finansinspektionen, or FSA). The FSA is a public agency. The integration into one supervisory agency is logical, given the development of the financial markets during the past two decades, with integration of insurance into banking and vice versa. The planning and execution of supervision is performed jointly for all financial entities.

The FSA grants the right to establish and operate a financial company in Sweden. From 1999, foreign-based companies can operate in Sweden without establishing a local subsidiary if they register with the FSA. The government sets the framework of principles for operation in Sweden, following EU legislation and regulations.

Quarterly and annual reports, special questionnaires, on-site inspections, and market and specific company analysis provide the basis for supervision. Generally, the focus of supervision is on solvency. Traditionally, quarterly information is processed to examine premium receipts, benefit payments, and portfolios to determine the vulnerability of assets and liabilities to market risks. From 2006, the FSA has introduced a new supervisory instrument, called the *traffic light*, which is designed to provide an early warning signal of the market risks implicit in the asset portfolios of life insurance companies. This instrument is described in greater detail in a separate section later in this chapter.

The FSA summarizes its supervisory role as described in table 6.9.

Generally speaking, the FSA regards insurance companies as presenting much less of a systemic stability risk than banks. Because banks must match liquid liabilities (deposits) with relatively illiquid assets (loans), a rapid fall in deposits is difficult to meet with an immediate adjustment in the stock of loans. The situation is just the opposite for insurance companies, which manage relatively liquid assets that need to match illiquid liabilities.

Table 6.9   Focus of the FSA's Supervisory Role

Role	System functionality	Consumer protection
Supervision of system stability	Supervision of companies' management, financial strength, and risk management to ensure operational stability and adequate risk management	Provision of products with transparent product contents and descriptions that ensure commitments to customers can be understood and met
Supervision of the market	Supervision of how financial actors perform independently and together with the aim of ensuring market efficiency and public confidence in the market	Correct and relevant information and fair treatment of customers

Source: FSA 2004.

The FSA intervenes in the operations of a company if two criteria are met. First, there must be an impending situation or risk that the market cannot handle satisfactorily on its own. Second, the benefits of an intervention must be considered to outweigh the market-efficiency loss implicit in an intervention.

In supervision of insurance companies, the first question asked is whether the company's survival is in danger and whether a risk exists that payments must be canceled. If the answer is yes, then the FSA will interact with the company to achieve a solution to the problem. If a systemic risk exists that is not an immediate solvency problem, the FSA will initiate procedures for restructuring the company—if the company has not already taken the initiative to do so itself. This restructuring is likely to result in a change of ownership through merger or takeover. An immediate solvency problem will require the intervention of the Ministry of Finance and recapitalization through an injection of government funds. In principle, this rule should even hold for the PPM, although the law does not explicitly state that, as has already been mentioned.

Determination of Insurance Solvency

An insurance company is considered solvent if the following are true:

1. Capital base/(0.04 × technical insurance reserves) ≥ 1, where
2. Capital base = value of market assets − technical insurance reserves.

The *technical insurance reserves* are the reserves needed to cover the current guaranteed liabilities to pensioners.

The capital base (expression 2) increases in a rising market and falls in a declining market. Likewise, all else being equal, an increase in technical insurance reserves decreases the capital base. In practice, companies can choose freely any discount rate up to the ceiling established by the FSA. According to an EU regulation, the ceiling is 60 percent of the market rate for long government bonds. If the discount rate falls, then solvency falls with it in the case that companies are forced to use a lower rate because of the fall. An increase in the discount rate increases solvency.

Before 2007, the FSA used the rate on the longest government bond on the market to establish the ceiling. In 2006, this was a bond issued in 2004, maturing in 2020 and carrying a 5 percent coupon. This bond gave a ceiling of 3 percent for the discount rate. Earlier, a lower rate applied, which was based on a bond with a shorter maturity of 11 years. Although market rates began to rise in 2005, the 16-year bond nevertheless remained the measuring rod for establishing the ceiling. According to its stated policy, the FSA will leave this rate only when it sees sufficient evidence for doing so.

Interestingly, in mid-2003, following the fall in the stock market, the solvency ratio for the largest 13 companies was nevertheless relatively high—at 8.7—and by mid-2004 it had improved by even more, reaching 9.7 (FSA 2004). These are high figures compared with an intervention level of unity. This fact indicates that even in the worst years, solvency remained relatively high, even though many companies were compelled to take back previously committed bonuses in response to the fall in the equity market, as has been discussed already. However, for one of the largest insurance companies, SPP, the ratio was only 1.18 in late 2004, and it was below 2 for two other relatively large companies. As a result, the FSA required more and more frequent information from these companies during the crisis period.

Companies that come close to the insolvency level lose considerable potential to invest in equities when the market turns up, putting them in a worse situation to compete with other providers. In fact, the companies that were close to the solvency level after the fall in the equity market in the initial years of the new century and that were forced to reduce bonuses to savers and pensioners were punished by a fall in business in 2004. For example, SPP's sales of new voluntary insurance fell by 65 percent from mid-2003 to mid-2004 (FSA 2004).

During the 2008 global financial crisis, the solvency ratio of the largest nine life insurance companies fell from about 20 in December 2007 to as low as 8 in December 2008, but it has since recovered to about 17 in December 2009. The solvency ratio of occupational pension funds was lower, falling from 17 to 4 and then recovering to 11 over the same period, but it was still comfortably higher than unity. The solvency ratio of mutual companies fluctuated between 1 and 5, but no company had a solvency ratio below unity in December 2009 (FSA 2010).

An important question recently debated in the insurance community in Sweden is what discount rate should be applied to determine the value of technical liabilities. Until 2007, the choice was left up to the individual insurance company, albeit with a ceiling, as indicated. Thus, companies choosing a higher rate had a smaller liability and more room for free investments. In addition, the FSA has observed that some companies used a higher rate than the reigning rate on government bonds during 2006. The FSA responded by issuing a new regulation at the end of 2006. This regulation requires companies to use a risk-free discount rate beginning in 2007. The rate used is to be an average of the rate of return on government bonds and the swap rate; the latter is included to extend the portfolio of instruments on which the discount rate is based.

One of the arguments used in issuing this new regulation was that it is important for all companies to use the same rate, which among other things facilitates comparability, although at the expense of leaving the freedom to choose an even lower rate. If the aim, in addition to specifying a risk-free rate, were for all companies to use exactly the same rate, then it would be practical for the FSA to compute this rate and inform all companies of the resultant value. Instead, the FSA has left the individual company to calculate the risk-free rate, which in practice opens the door to some variation depending on the method of calculation used. Because this procedure conflicts with the FSA's specified goal, one can reasonably predict that this procedure is likely to be replaced by a standard calculation supplied by the FSA.

The Traffic Light Supervisory Tool

In 2006, the FSA introduced a new supervision instrument called the traffic light system, which is based on experience of the application of a similar instrument in Denmark. All insurance companies are covered by the traffic light system since January 2006, and the PPM is covered since January 2007. The traffic light system is intended to provide an advance warning of a company's vulnerability before the insolvency level is reached.

The traffic light system is designed to test the stress tolerance of the financial condition of individual companies by requiring them to compute the change in the values of assets and liabilities resulting from assumed declines in interest rates and equity prices. The following tolerance tests are applied (FSA 2005):

- The equity price risk is separated into a risk for domestic and foreign assets. Insurance companies must be able to tolerate a fall of 40 percent in Swedish and 37 percent in foreign equity prices.
- Companies must be able to tolerate a fall of 35 percent in property values.
- The foreign exchange risk that a company must be able to absorb is a 10 percent change in the exchange rate.
- Companies are required to calculate whether their net interest exposure (the difference between the interest sensitivity of assets and liabilities) is long or short. For a short position, the company is required

to calculate the effect of a fall in the rate of interest. For a long position, the company is required to compute the effect of an increase in the rate of interest. The tolerance levels tested are

○ Nominal Swedish krona interest rate: +/– 30 percent of the 10-year rate
○ Real Swedish krona interest rate: +/– 30 percent of the longest real interest rate
○ Nominal euro interest rate: +/– 25 percent of the 10-year euro rate
○ Nominal interest, other currencies: +/– 30 percent of the 10-year rate for the largest portfolio asset denominated in another foreign currency
• The credit risk (increase in spread) that a company must be able to absorb is the greater of a 100 percent increase or an increase of 50 basis points.

The net outcome is calculated as the square root of each risk raised to the power of two, including correlation components. Whether an insurance company receives a red light or a green light depends on the net result of this calculation. The traffic light system is seen as a complement to the solvency test and the other data collection and supervisory tools used by the FSA.

Concluding Remarks

Major reforms, including structural reforms of the financial market in the 1980s and the public pension system in the 1990s, were important prerequisites to the development of today's thriving private insurance market in Sweden. The financial market reforms of the 1980s and early 1990s did away with a regime characterized by quantitative portfolio investment regulations and, above all, opened the market from 1993 for unit-linked insurance, which made possible coupling the emerging private investment fund market with insurance.

The first step in the reform of the public pension system was to abolish the pay-as-you-go survivor benefit for widows, beginning with women born in 1945 and later. This change led to an immediate increase in the percentage of women purchasing private pension and life insurance products. Most important, however, was the reform of the public mandatory pension system itself from DB to DC. The transformation of the public commitment to a DC framework led to the conversion of the major occupational supplementary benefit schemes from predominantly DB to predominantly DC. Previously unfunded occupational schemes for public sector employees at all levels of government became (largely) prefunded. In addition, all occupational arrangements for private sector employees became prefunded.

The conversion to FDC schemes led to a considerable injection of long-term financial savings into the Swedish financial market. Contributions to the PPM scheme amount to just about 1 percent of GDP, while those to the private voluntary and occupational schemes equal about 4 percent of GDP. These contributions are on top of a mandatory pay-as-you-go (NDC) scheme that costs about 11 percent of GDP. The overall Swedish commitment to pensions amounts to 16 percent of GDP, and about one-third of this commitment is prefunded. The evidence from Sweden is, thus, that a strong welfare commitment can be maintained even with a more-pronounced prefunding profile. The data on expected future replacement rates for full-career workers support this conclusion.

Furthermore, Sweden's experience indicates that, even in the more-advanced economies, the conversion to financial pension schemes can contribute to developing the financial market. The PPM's FDC scheme within the public mandatory system was modeled on unit-linked insurance, providing the opportunity for individuals to make their own portfolio choices during both the accumulation and the payout phases. Private individual voluntary insurance and occupational group insurance also offer unit-linked products as an alternative to traditional insurance, and that alternative has become popular in recent years.

Despite the large number of companies now offering funds in the PPM system, this study reveals that funds owned by the seven largest insurance companies manage the majority of total PPM assets not held in the default fund. The same companies account for almost all the occupational and private insurance business. Thus, despite the large number of insurance companies and fund managers, the Swedish market is highly concentrated and is dominated by only a few companies. However, the presence of some 40 insurance companies and more than 80 fund managers is a healthy sign and suggests that, despite the dominance of the larger groups, many companies still operate successful businesses within this environment.

The analysis in this study of data on the sources of income of pensioners shows that both occupational and private insurance provide an important source of income in the earlier years of retirement for current pensioners. Sweden has no data on the distribution of insurance benefits by types of products. The aggregate data suggest, however, that 5- and 10-year withdrawals of occupational and private voluntary benefits are the preferred options. The data indicate that life annuities from occupational and personal pension plans are not important income sources for present older pensioners. However, this finding may reflect the fact that for a long time the public benefit, with an occupational supplement, was viewed as providing sufficient income.

Two major issues relate to the bearing of longevity and investment risks. A DC scheme based on a unit-linked approach shifts the investment risk during the accumulation phase to the individual. If the individual chooses to manage his or her own funds during the payout phase, with payments being recalculated every year, both the investment and longevity risks are shifted to the individual, because funds remaining on the account balance at the end of the year are divided up according to a given annuity factor. In this sense, this product form is ideal for the insurer, which then provides investment fund options and earns money on charges for these management services.

Likewise, 5- and 10-year withdrawal products eliminate the longevity risk from insurance companies and transfer it to workers. However, if the insurance product is a traditional insurance product, which in Sweden means that the insurance provider guarantees a specific rate of return, an investment risk remains. Nevertheless, as has been discussed here, 10-year bonds are a common form of debt finance for the Swedish government, so in principle, insurance companies have access to a matching asset.

If, however, the participant chooses a traditional insurance annuity, the insurer must bear both the longevity and the investment risk for the guaranteed benefits. In principle, the investment risk could be more easily managed if a matching asset to hold were available in insurance company portfolios. In practice, the Swedish government has not accommodated such a demand. Nonetheless, this issue is not seen as important, judging by the absence of a public debate on it. Hence, insurers are confronted with matching assets to liabilities without the convenience of having a single matching asset.

The Swedish model for traditional insurance provides a guaranteed plus a bonus rate of return during both the accumulation and the payout phases. If the ratio of assets to pension liabilities—including the guarantee—goes below unity, correction entails reducing bonuses granted earlier. The PPM also adopted this model for its traditional life annuity. The bonus is based to a large extent on the returns on the portion of the insurance provider's portfolio that is invested in equities, and given that companies compete through bonus offerings, they are competing on the basis of their investment outcomes.

The guarantee and bonus system assists the provider in managing both the longevity and the investment risk. Both risks are shared with participants because the effects of underestimating life expectancy and volatility of investment returns can be offset by reducing the size of the bonus. The advantage of this system is clear. It enables the insurance company to increase the returns offered to participants by taking on more risk. The disadvantage is that in the worst case, where the provider must create balance between assets and liabilities by reducing the size of a previously announced bonus, this action is not so easy to communicate to plan participants. This feature could be made more transparent through clearer advance information to the participants on the nature of the mode—that is, to make more explicit the nature of the contract.

In 2006, the FSA introduced a new tool for measuring the risk of insurance portfolios. Called the traffic light system, this tool is designed to illuminate the degree of risk in the insurance provider's investment portfolio in relation to the provider's pension liabilities. In addition, whereas prior to 2007 insurance companies were free to choose the discount rate (up to a ceiling) applied in evaluating liabilities, from 2007 they must use a risk-free rate determined as an average of the government bond and swap rates. Judging by these recent events, one can easily conclude that the present trend in Sweden is toward creating a stricter regulatory framework, albeit while still maintaining the guarantee and bonus system.

Notes

1. The new rules cover earnings of people born in 1938 and later, with a gradual transition from 4/20th and 16/20th of the FDC of a new and an old pension, respectively, for people born in 1938, to 19/20th and 1/20th of a new and an old pension, respectively, for those born in 1953.

2. There are many references to the Swedish NDC scheme. A generic NDC scheme is presented in Palmer (2006), whereas Holzmann and Palmer (2006) include an anthology of papers dealing with the various aspects of NDC schemes, with numerous cross-references to the Swedish case.

3. Account balances of people who die before the minimum retirement age of 61 are distributed annually on a birth cohort basis to the survivors in the cohort.

4. Contributions have an employee and an employer component. The individual pays the employee component of sickness, parental leave, and unemployment compensation.

5. The ABM is asymmetric, adjusting for negative but not positive imbalance. However, positive adjustment occurs following a negative adjustment up to

the level that would have obtained with normal indexation in the absence of downward adjustment of liabilities.

6. Contributions had been collected and placed in aggregate in an account at the National Debt Office since 1995.

7. Sweden has long established several AP (*allmänna pension*, or national pension) funds that are responsible for managing the reserves of the public pension system. They are set up as buffer funds and currently include five funds, AP 1 through 4 and AP 6. (AP 5 was proposed but never implemented because of fierce political opposition from large corporations.) They collectively managed SKr 827 billion in 2008, representing 25.7 percent of GDP.

8. The ITP plan has established a centralized administrating unit, known as Collectum, that replicates the role of the PPM for its members. It maintains worker accounts and offers a choice of investment funds and insurance companies for the services covered by the plan.

9. If the real rate of growth is 2 percent per year, the relation between the average benefit and the average wage will decline by about 25 percent, reducing a ratio of 75 percent to 55 percent.

10. This decline was offset by an increase in public saving—through the partial funding of the scheme (Markowski and Palmer 1979; Palmer 1981).

11. The three banks are Skandinaviska Enskilda Banken, Handelsbanken, and Swedbank.

12. Inflation was higher with a factor of at least four to five in the 1980s, before the crisis in 1992, when undisciplined wage cost increases were traditionally managed by devaluing the krona (beginning in the late 1970s). The success since 1992 of fixing monetary policy on the rate of inflation with a floating exchange rate—and given Sweden's poor history of labor cost discipline—has presented a strong reason for Sweden to remain outside the euro currency union. Many, though not all, Swedish economists support this position.

References

Berg, Lennart 1983. "Konsumtion och sparande: En studie av hushållens beteende" [Consumption and saving: A study of household behavior]. PhD thesis, Uppsala University, Uppsala, Sweden.

Eklöf, Matias, and Daniel Hallberg. 2006. "Estimating Retirement Behavior with Special Retirement Offers." Department of Economics, Uppsala University, Uppsala, Sweden.

Frennberg, Per, and Björn Hansson. 1995. "An Evaluation of Alternative Models for Predicting Stock Volatility: Evidence from a Small Stock Market." *Journal of International Financial Markets, Institutions, and Money* 5 (2–3): 117–34.

FSA (Financial Supervisory Authority). 2004. "Finanssektorns stabilitet 2004" [The financial sector's stability 2004]. Finansinspektionen Rapport 2004:9, FSA, Stockholm.

———. 2005. "Trafikljuset och en modernare tillsyn: Remissförslag" [The traffic light and modern supervision: Referral proposal]. FSA, Stockholm.

———. 2010. "Försäkringsbarometern: Solvenskvoterna fortsätter stiga" [Insurance survey: The solvency ratios continue to rise]. FSA, Stockholm.

Gottfries, Nils, Torsten Persson, and Edward Palmer. 1989. "Regulation, Financial Buffer Stocks and Short-Run Adjustment: An Econometric Case Study of Sweden, 1970–1982." *European Economic Review* 33 (8): 1545–65.

Holzmann, Robert, and Edward Palmer, eds. 2006. *Pension Reform: Issues and Prospects for Non-financial Defined Contribution (NDC) Schemes.* Washington, DC: World Bank.

Johannisson, Inger. 2003. "Tax Deferred Pension Saving in Sweden." Department of Economics, University of Gothenburg, Sweden.

Markowski, Aleksander, and Edward Palmer. 1979. "Social Insurance and Saving in Sweden." In *Social Security versus Private Saving,* ed. George M. Von Furstenberg, 167–228. Cambridge, MA: Ballinger.

Palmer, Edward. 1981. *Determination of Personal Consumption: Theoretical Foundations and Empirical Evidence from Sweden.* Stockholm: Almqvist & Wicksell International.

———. 1985. *Household Saving in Sweden and Its Composition: An Empirical Analysis.* Stockholm: Liber Förlag.

———. 2002. "Swedish Pension Reform: How Did It Evolve and What Does It Mean for the Future?" In *Social Security Pension Reform in Europe,* ed. Martin Feldstein and Horst Siebert, 171–210. Chicago: University of Chicago Press.

———. 2006. "What Is NDC?" In *Pension Reform: Issues and Prospects for Non-Financial Defined Contribution (NDC) Schemes,* ed. Robert Holzmann and Edward Palmer, 17–34. Washington, DC: World Bank.

———. 2008. "The Market for Retirement Products in Sweden." Policy Research Working Paper 4748, World Bank, Washington, DC.

Swedish Social Insurance Agency. 2008. *Orange Report: Annual Report of the Swedish Pension System 2007.* Stockholm: Swedish Social Insurance Agency.

CHAPTER 7

Denmark

The Benefits of Group Contracts with Deferred Annuities and Risk-Sharing Features

The Danish pension system includes a modest universal social pension with a supplement for low-income pensioners and near-universal participation in occupational and personal pensions that are primarily based on defined contribution plans. The annuity market is well developed: 40 percent of annual contributions are allocated to the purchase of deferred life annuities, and immediate life annuities are also purchased at or even after retirement. Term annuities are also widely used. However, detailed comprehensive data on the rate of annuitization are lacking. In addition, the lack of detailed data on both projected (ex ante) and declared (ex post) bonuses impedes calculation of money's worth ratios for the different types of annuities.

Distinct features of the Danish pension system include (a) the widespread use of profit-participating contracts with minimum guaranteed benefits and regular declaration of bonuses, covering both the accumulation and payout phases, and (b) the extensive use of group deferred annuity contracts. Risk-sharing arrangements aim at distributing the

---

This chapter is a summary and update, prepared by the editors, of the paper by Carsten Andersen and Peter Skjodt on "Pension Institutions and Annuities in Denmark" (Andersen and Skjodt 2007).

investment and insurance risks between the pension institutions and their members, covering both active and retired workers, while avoiding transfers across different cohorts of members. In recent years, the Danish pension industry has adopted fair value accounting of both assets and liabilities, decomposition of technical provisions between guaranteed benefits and bonus potential, and use of a zero-coupon yield curve to determine their value.

Although the regulatory framework is not yet formally risk based, implementation of risk-based supervision is well advanced following the introduction of the traffic light system with regular periodic stress testing. The new approach has resulted in greater emphasis on asset liability matching and hedging strategies by pension institutions and a shift in investment policies in favor of foreign bonds and long-term swap contracts.

The main objective of this chapter is to assess the adequacy and efficiency of risk-sharing arrangements and risk management practices in the Danish pension and annuity market. The next section considers the overall structure of the pension system and reviews the relative role of different pension institutions. It also discusses the asset allocation and investment performance of different institutions. The section that follows reviews the types of retirement products that are offered in Denmark, reports on the level of annuitization and targeted replacement rates, and examines the extensive use of risk-sharing arrangements. The chapter then looks at the regulation and supervision of providers of pension services and risk management. It places particular emphasis on the growing reliance on risk-based supervision, the use of market valuations for both assets and liabilities, the application of the traffic light system, and the growing emphasis on asset and liability management and use of hedging facilities. The last section offers some concluding remarks.

The Danish Pension System

This section provides an overview of the Danish pension system, including the two public pension schemes, as well as occupational and personal pensions.

Public Pension Schemes

The public pillar covers two schemes that are administered by public sector institutions and aim to provide universal or near-universal benefits. The main scheme is unfunded and financed from general tax revenues, but the main supplementary scheme is financed from employer and employee contributions and is fully funded.

Denmark was one of the first countries to introduce a public retirement pension system. The original scheme, which was introduced more than 100 years ago, targeted the "worthy needy," but over time the system has expanded to become a universal scheme. The social pension is paid to citizens and noncitizens who are over 65 years old, subject to a residency test and proportionality rule. It is also subject to a clawback provision; the clawback amounts to 30 percent of the excess over a specified threshold level of income. The threshold is set by government decision and amounts to the relatively high level of about 75 percent of average earnings. In addition to the social pension, a supplement is paid to low-income pensioners. This supplement is also subject to a 30 percent clawback provision, but the threshold for calculating the excess income that is subject to the clawback is set at a much lower level of about 15 percent of average earnings.

Nearly 870,000 people received social pension benefits in 2008, which corresponded to 16 percent of the total population or 30 percent of the labor force. The average combined benefit from the social pension and the supplement amounted to 27.5 percent of the average wage or 30 percent of per capita income. The total cost of the social pension absorbed 4.7 percent of gross domestic product (GDP) in 2008, corresponding to 8.3 percent of the wage bill. These figures include pension supplements paid to low-income pensioners. The basic social pension, without any supplements, amounted to less than 20 percent of the average wage.

The social pension represents by design a much higher proportion of income for low-income groups that also have less education. Evidence shows that the social pension represents more than 60 percent of the income of unskilled retired workers, about 40 percent of the income of skilled retired workers, and less than 20 percent of that of more highly educated workers.

The projected aging of the Danish population is expected to raise substantially the cost of the social pension scheme. According to official projections by the Ministry of Social Affairs, the cost will rise to 6.5 percent of GDP in 2020 and 7.8 percent in 2037. If the wage bill continues to correspond to close to 60 percent of GDP, this increase would imply a payroll tax of 13 percent if the scheme were to be financed from payroll taxes.

The ATP and Other Statutory Supplementary Schemes

Because the level of the social pension was rather modest, the authorities introduced in 1964 the Labor Market Supplementary Pension

(Arbejdsmarkedets Tillaegspension, or ATP). Initially, the ATP applied to employed people only, but it was later expanded to cover people on parental leave and recipients of sickness and unemployment benefits. Coverage is optional for the self-employed and for recipients of disability pensions or early retirement benefits.

The ATP is funded two-thirds by employer and one-third by employee contributions that are subject to relatively low ceilings (the maximum amounted to 3,240 Danish kroner [DKr] per year in 2009), corresponding to about 1 percent of the average wage.[1] ATP contributions are not related to income but are set as fixed amounts. These levels depend on a few broad categories that have been defined on the basis of the number of working hours. For people on transfer incomes, contributions are split between the transfer recipient and the government (one-third and two-thirds, respectively).

Benefits are also subject to a low ceiling. The maximum annual pension for 65-year-old pensioners with a full contribution record amounted to DKr 23,000 per year in 2009, which was equivalent to 36 percent of the basic social pension and less than 8 percent of the average wage. However, the average pension to new 65-year-old retirees amounted to DKr 14,500 in 2009. Benefits used to be based only on the total size of contributions, irrespective of when they were made, but now investment returns are also taken into account.

Benefits take the form of life annuities. Before 2008, they were calculated at an interest rate of 2 percent but with the possibility of bonus payments from accumulated investment reserves.[2] In 2008, the calculation of benefits changed. A new system was introduced that sets the deferred annuity benefit each year on the basis of long-term interest rates prevailing in the bond and swap market. Bonus payments are declared each year and aim to maintain the real value of pensions. Bonus payments reflect both the investment performance and the longevity experience of the ATP and are made to both cash pensions and accumulated balances (Vittas 2008).

ATP coverage increased rapidly over the years. The total number of member accounts exceeds the total labor force, reflecting the temporary exit of economically active people from the labor force. The number of ATP pensioners has increased steadily relative to the number of recipients of the social pension. It reached 80 percent of all pensioners in 2008. It is projected to reach 98 percent when the extension of ATP membership to universal participation reaches maturity.

The limited role played by the ATP is highlighted by the size of contributions and benefits relative to GDP. Contributions and benefits respectively amounted to 0.41 percent and 0.48 percent of GDP in 2008. Total annual contributions amounted to 0.74 percent of the wage bill in 2008. However, because the ATP was created in 1964 and has universal coverage, its total assets have grown steadily and now exceed 32 percent of GDP.[3] The ATP is one of the largest financial institutions in Denmark.

Three other statutory supplementary schemes have been created over time to supplement the benefits obtained from the social pension and the ATP. The most important was, until recently, the Special Pension Savings Scheme (Særlige Pensionsopsparing, or SP), which was introduced in 1998 to dampen economic activity and increase savings. However, contributions to the SP were suspended for 2004 and 2005. The suspension was later extended to 2007. In 2009, SP participants were allowed to withdraw their balances, and the scheme will be closed down in 2010.

The third supplementary scheme in terms of importance is the Employees' Capital Fund (Lønmodtagernes Dyrtidsfond, or LD), which was introduced in 1977. It aimed at changing the then prevailing highly inflationary practice of automatically adjusting wages and salaries to cost-of-living increases. The LD froze these cost-of-living adjustments in a special pension scheme, which involved creating individual accounts, investing the saved amounts, and paying out the accumulated capital as lump sums on retirement.

The LD has not received any contributions or new members since 1980. About half its members have retired by now, but about 1 million workers still have LD accounts. The scheme is managed by LD Pensions, a public sector institution that is similar to the ATP. The total assets of LD correspond to less than 2 percent of GDP.

The fourth supplementary scheme is a narrow voluntary scheme, known as the Supplementary Labor Pension (Supplerende arbejds-markedspension, or SUPP). SUPP was introduced in 2003 for people who had taken early retirement prior to that year and who wanted to increase their future pension income by saving through tax-favored accounts.[4] The scheme covers about 250,000 people, representing 7 percent of the population between 18 and 65 years of age.

The pension provider for SUPP can be freely chosen among ATP and private pension institutions (although not all of the latter participate in SUPP). One-third of contributions are made by the pensioners themselves and two-thirds by the government. The benefits are similar to those of the ATP: either a life annuity or a lump sum, depending on the size of the account balance. The rate of contribution is subject to a maximum of about 3 percent of the early retirement benefit.

Occupational Pension Plans

Occupational pension plans were first introduced in the 19th century. The first plan covered civil servants, but over time other privileged sectors, such as banking, insurance, and utilities, also created pension plans for their employees. Coverage expanded gradually during the 20th century but received a major boost in the late 1980s and early 1990s as a result of collective bargaining and political support through the offer of tax incentives.

Denmark, like most members of the Organisation for Economic Co-operation and Development (OECD) and unlike Australia and Switzerland, has not enacted a mandatory occupational pension pillar, but coverage is extensive and reaches almost 80 percent of wage earners. Participation is compulsory without discrimination in those industries and companies where a pension plan has been created.

The vast majority of occupational pension plans are defined contribution plans, and they also offer death and disability benefits. Most schemes offer minimum guaranteed benefits with additional bonuses that depend on performance and involve the use of group annuities. Pursuant to the legislation, unisex criteria are applied for the calculation of benefits under group annuities, even though women have a longer life expectancy than men. In addition, participation in standard occupational pension schemes, including life and disability insurance, and group annuities is not subject to health screening.

Because occupational pension plans have been established by collective bargaining rather than through a government-mandated program, terms and conditions vary widely, reflecting among other things industry- or sector-specific factors. This variety adds to the complexity of the Danish pension system and makes its analysis very dependent on the availability of detailed data. However, the high fragmentation of the system among a large number of pension plans has impeded the compilation of detailed information on the design and structure of different pension plans as well as on their performance.

Three main types of institutions participate in the second pillar. Corporate pension funds cover the employees of single companies but play a marginal and declining role. Many of them are actually runoff schemes, having been closed to new members and even to new contributions. Thus, pension funds as known in several other OECD countries— that is, closely linked to a sponsoring company—play a marginal role in the Danish market. Multiemployer pension funds are created as member-owned pension institutions and cover industrywide plans, such as nurses.

Life insurance companies are the most important group of institutions. They are established as shareholder-owned joint stock companies—some on a commercial basis (with shareholders demanding a return) and some on a noncommercial basis.

Life insurance companies typically manage employer-specific plans, which are negotiated with the employers concerned and cover all people employed by them. Although they have different ownership structures, life insurance companies and pension funds are subject to identical accounting, reporting, and other regulatory rules, and strong competition exists between pension and insurance companies. Banking institutions play a small part in the second pillar.

Life insurance and multiemployer pension funds have the lion's share of the market for occupational pensions. Corporate pension funds have a small share of the market, whereas banks receive about 15 percent of total contributions.

Contributions to occupational pension plans have increased steadily over the past 10 years or so. Their annual growth rate was remarkably stable, ranging between 10 and 12 percent in nominal terms, whereas during the same period (1995–2008) inflation averaged 2 percent per year. The strong performance of contributions is reflected in their growing level relative to GDP, which more than doubled from 2.36 percent in 1995 to 5.23 percent in 2008 (table 7.1).

The increase in contribution amounts is partly because of expanding coverage and partly because of a gradually rising contribution rate. Although contribution rates (like many other features of pension plans) vary considerably among different schemes, the average contribution rate for schemes covered by the labor agreement between the Danish

Table 7.1   Contributions to Occupational Pension Plans

Contributions	1995	2000	2004	2008
Contributions (DKr billion)	23.80	41.52	62.92	90.89
Contributions (% of GDP)	2.36	3.21	4.29	5.23
Contributions to annuities (% of total)	59.8	57.2	50.1	42.0
Contributions to phased withdrawals (%)	9.9	23.1	35.1	47.0
Contributions to lump sums (%)	30.3	19.7	14.7	11.0
Contributions to life insurance companies and pension funds (%)	85.8	89.6	89.0	85.5
Contributions to banks (%)	14.2	10.4	11.0	14.5

Sources: Data provided by Statistics Denmark, Central Customs and Tax Administration, and Danish Insurance Association.

Confederation of Trade Unions and the Danish Employers' Confederation crept upward from 1 percent in 1993 to over 10 percent in 2006.

Occupational pension plans offer a variety of retirement products, ranging from deferred and immediate (at retirement) life annuities to term annuities (which are equivalent to phased withdrawals) and lump-sum payments. Most plans offer this choice of products. Plans differ in the degree of flexibility and choice they allow to their members. In some cases, the premiums for term life and disability insurance are allowed to vary with commensurate changes in the size of the related benefits, but otherwise all contributions are directed to group life annuities. In other plans, members have broader choice between the different retirement products. Members are free to choose additional life or term annuities at any time, but once an annuity has been chosen the contract is not reversible.

In the case of occupational pension plans, 42 percent of contributions were allocated to deferred life annuities in 2008 (table 7.1). The 2008 pattern represented a significant relative decline in the importance of life annuities, which absorbed about 60 percent of contributions in 1995. Allocations for term annuities (phased withdrawals), which run for between 10 and 25 years, absorbed an increasing proportion of total contributions. They rose from about 10 percent in 1995 to 47 percent of total contributions in 2008. In contrast, contributions allocated to lump-sum payments fell from about 30 percent to 11 percent of the total. To a large extent, this decrease reflected changes in tax provisions, which sought to discourage the use of lump sums on retirement. Lump sums and phased withdrawals can be converted into life annuities at any time. Hence, data based on the allocation of contributions understate the actual share of life annuities.

A relatively recent feature of the Danish pension industry is the offer of unit-linked products. This change has been prompted by the reduction in guaranteed investment returns and a growing preference of plan members to invest in high-return and high-risk assets. However, the proportion of annual contributions that is allocated to unit-linked products is still small, at less than 10 percent of the total.

Personal Pensions

Personal pension plans constitute the third pillar of the Danish pension system. They are offered by banking, insurance, and pension institutions and are established on a voluntary basis by people who are not covered by occupational pension schemes or who wish to obtain additional coverage. As in most countries, personal pension plans benefit from tax advantages that emulate the fiscal benefits conferred on occupational pension schemes.

Contributions to personal pension plans have grown at a more modest rate over the past decade. In 1999, they suffered a large decline, but otherwise they kept pace with the growth in national income. They amounted in 2008 to 1.27 percent of GDP (table 7.2), at about one-third the level of contributions to occupational pension schemes. Total contributions to the second and third pillars were close to 6.5 percent of GDP, or about 11.5 percent of earnings.

Allocations to life annuities absorbed a small part of personal pension contributions at close to 15 percent. As in the case of second-pillar contributions, a major shift has occurred away from lump-sum payments and in favor of term annuities. This trend reflected changes in the tax treatment of lump-sum payments. Banking institutions play a bigger part in personal pension plans than in second pillar plans, accounting for 65 percent of total contributions. The relatively greater success of banks in personal pension plans may be explained by their stronger presence in the retail financial services market and the preference of some people for savings rather than insurance.

Asset Accumulation and Investment Performance

With expanding coverage, rising contribution rates, and positive real investment returns, the total assets of the pension system increased from DKr 847 billion in 1995, corresponding to 83 percent of GDP, to DKr 2,533 billion in 2008, or 146 percent of GDP (table 7.3). That figure is comparable to, if not higher than, the levels found in the Netherlands, Switzerland, and the United Kingdom and suggests the existence of a strong capital base for financing the pensions of retiring workers over the coming decades.

Table 7.2   Contributions to Personal Pension Plans

Contributions	1995	2000	2004	2008
Contributions (DKr billion)	15.58	16.21	19.93	22.02
Contributions (% of GDP)	1.54	1.25	1.36	1.27
Contributions to annuities (% of total)	11.8	15.2	15.1	13.1
Contributions to phased withdrawals (%)	20.2	37.6	49.3	55.3
Contributions to lump sums (%)	68.1	47.3	35.6	30.9
Contributions to life insurance companies and pension funds (%)	40.8	44.2	41.7	34.1
Contributions to banks (%)	59.2	55.8	58.3	65.9

Sources: Data provided by Statistics Denmark, Central Customs and Tax Administration, and Danish Insurance Association.

Table 7.3   Pension Assets

Assets	1995	2000	2004	2008
Total pension assets (DKr billion)	847.2	1,507.2	1,822.1	2,533.0
Total pension assets (% of GDP)	83.1	116.5	124.8	145.8
ATP (% of total)	15.2	16.4	16.9	22.2
SP (% of total)	n.a.	1.4	2.5	1.8
LD (% of total)	4.3	4.1	3.2	2.4
Life insurance companies (% of total)	41.8	43.1	44.5	44.1
Multiemployer pension funds (% of total)	17.2	17.9	18.6	15.6
Corporate pension funds (% of total)	4.0	2.9	2.2	1.7
Banks (% of total)	17.5	14.3	12.2	12.2

Sources: Statistics Denmark and Danish Financial Supervisory Authority.
Note: n.a. = not applicable.

The relative shares of different pension institutions have been remarkably stable. LD, corporate pension funds, and banks—and more recently multiemployer pension funds—suffered some decline in their market shares while ATP and life insurance companies experienced increases.

Pension institutions used to invest heavily in Danish bonds, especially Danish mortgage bonds, which enjoyed a higher yield over government securities while being considered as highly safe. However, during the course of the 1990s, a shift toward Danish and foreign equities had taken place. As an example, in 1998, the ATP invested 55 percent of its assets in Danish bonds, 26 percent in Danish equities, and 10 percent in foreign equities. Life insurance companies had more conservative portfolios because of the guaranteed elements of the products they offered, with Danish and foreign equities absorbing 25 percent of total assets in 1998.

However, the global decline in equity prices and a stronger emphasis on risk-based supervision induced a reconsideration of those investment policies. By 2004, ATP direct investments in equities, both domestic and foreign, fell to 18 percent of total assets and those of life insurance companies fell to 12 percent. For life insurance companies and pension funds, direct equity investments decreased to 15 percent of total assets. They increased their use of investment funds, which invest in diversified portfolios and may also incorporate various risk-hedging elements. All types of institutions increased substantially their investments in foreign bonds, seeking higher yields and benefiting from the stability of the exchange rate between the Danish krone and the euro. They also increased their use of derivatives, especially long-term swap contracts in the euro market, to hedge their long-term liabilities.

The investment performance of different types of pension institutions was broadly similar. In a competitive market, where each company decides its own investment policy, some will perform above and some below market average, but for practical purposes, the performance of the different groups of institutions should be considered very similar.

Average investment returns on total assets from 1995 to 2008 amounted to 6.7 percent for the three largest groups of institutions (table 7.4). With inflation averaging less than 2 percent over this period, investment returns were substantially positive in real terms. All types of institutions achieved higher returns in the late 1990s.

Returns in the second subperiod were affected by the global collapse of equity prices and the large fall in interest rates, whereas returns in the more recent period suffered from the global financial crisis of 2008. The ATP achieved a better performance in the more recent period because of its very extensive use of hedging facilities.

Pension institutions in Denmark suffer when interest rates fall, because the vast majority of mortgage bonds that represent a substantial part of their assets are callable and because borrowers refinance their mortgages when rates are falling. Falling interest rates and the embedded call option of mortgage bonds also affect the financial solvency of pension institutions because the increase in the value of their long-term liabilities is not matched by a corresponding increase in the market value of their holdings of long-term bonds.

The growing use of long-term swap contracts has aimed at hedging pension liabilities and insulating pension institutions from the impact of changes in interest rates. Nevertheless, most pension institutions experienced significant financial strains during the global financial crisis of 2008, mainly because of their large investments in mortgage bonds. Such institutions suffered from increased credit risk and a widening spread of their yields over government bonds.

Table 7.4   Investment Returns

Pension type	Return (%)		
	1995–99	2000–04	2005–08
ATP	9.9	5.5	9.0
Life insurance companies	10.4	4.5	3.5
Multiemployer pension funds	9.8	4.1	3.5

Sources: Danish Financial Supervisory Authority, LD Pensions, and ATP.

The operating expenses of pension institutions, at least for those institutions for which detailed data are available, are comparable to those of similar institutions in other continental European countries and significantly lower than those prevailing in Latin American private pillars. The operating costs of the pension accounts held with banks are not published, but they are probably close to those of retail mutual funds and thus somewhat higher than those of life insurance companies and pension funds.

Benefiting from economies of scale because of its large size and also from its compulsory nature, the ATP reports very low operating costs, again replicating the experience of similar institutions in other countries. In general, public sector institutions have lower expense ratios than private sector ones. The main reasons are the nature of the public schemes as compulsory schemes and the offer of standardized products without the possibility of adjustment to individual demands. Administrative expense ratios were stable or even declined over time. In contrast, investment expense ratios rose for all types of institutions, probably reflecting the greater intensity of investment policies and the more active search for improved returns.

Despite the grave concerns that have been expressed in recent years about the solvency and investment performance of pension institutions in light of their long-standing guarantees, the overall performance of most types of pension institutions has been quite satisfactory. Investment returns have been substantially positive in real terms and have exceeded the guaranteed returns, while operating costs averaging 43 basis points for all pension institutions are low by international standards.

Like the retail financial markets of most countries around the world, concentration in the market for pensions and annuities is on the high side. However, because of new entries in the market and the growth of some of those pension institutions that were established as part of labor market agreements, the share of the top five companies fell from 70 percent of total premiums in 1995 to 53 percent in 2008. This low level of concentration implies a contestable market. In fact, individual institutions experienced significant changes in their market shares as well as rankings.

Retirement Products, Replacement Rates, and Risk Sharing

This section describes the retirement products offered in Denmark, looks at the level of annuitization and targeted replacement rates, and analyzes the use of risk-sharing arrangements.

Retirement Products

Retirement products include life annuities, term annuities, and lump-sum payments. Two distinct features of the Danish pension system include (a) the widespread use of profit-participating contracts with minimum guaranteed benefits and regular declaration of bonuses, covering both the accumulation and payout phases, and (b) the extensive use of group deferred annuity contracts. Recent years have seen an increase in unit-linked annuities with or without guarantees.

Traditional annuities offer minimum guaranteed benefits for both the accumulation and the payout phases. The minimum guarantees are effectively embedded options that members and policyholders have the right to exercise if market rates fall below the guaranteed rates. Pension institutions create appropriate reserves to cover the guaranteed benefits and then distribute bonuses to members depending on the performance of their funds. The distribution of bonuses is based on the so-called contribution principle to prevent unjustified and distorting transfers across different groups of members.

The maximum guaranteed technical rate was set at 4.5 percent per year in the early 1980s, was reduced to 2.5 percent in 1994, and was reduced further to 1.5 percent in 1999. The new rates apply to new contracts. New contributions made to old contracts are subject to their original guaranteed rates. However, such contributions are not unlimited but are subject to rules specified in the relevant plans or contracts. The setting of minimum guaranteed returns has reflected the evolution of market rates, especially the yields on 10-year government bonds (figure 7.1).

The use of deferred group annuities commits workers to a life annuity at the time of making their contributions at a preset minimum conversion factor that reflects the guaranteed minimum interest rate and prudent estimates of future longevity. Annuity payments are augmented by bonus payments if the actual investment performance exceeds the guaranteed return or if longevity experience is lower than projected.

This type of policy prevents the problems of adverse selection and provides guaranteed minimum benefits, while allowing participation in any future superior performance. However, its success depends on the equitable distribution of bonuses between shareholders and different cohorts of policyholders and requires strong confidence in the integrity of the management of pension institutions.[5] Deferred group annuities with guaranteed benefits also lack flexibility and expose pension institutions and their members to difficult adjustment decisions when investment

Figure 7.1   Guaranteed Interest Rates and After-Tax Yield to Maturity on a 10-Year Government Bond, 1988–2005

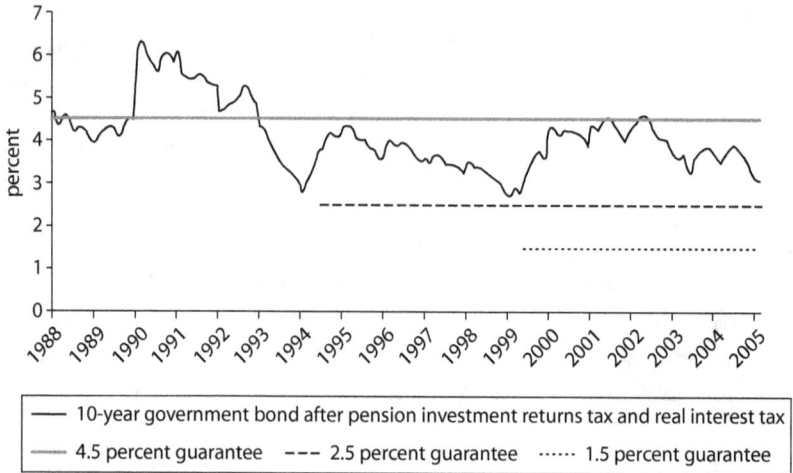

Source: Andersen and Skjodt 2007.

performance and longevity experience weaken the ability of institutions to maintain the level of promised pension benefits.

The benefits provided in collective labor agreements include survivor benefits to the heirs of contributing workers in cases of early death as well as disability pensions in cases of incapacitation. These types of benefits are based on calculations of actuarial probabilities reflecting previous experience as well as projections and expectations. Benefits also include annuities with a minimum number of guaranteed payments as well as immediate life annuities, which are purchased at the time of retirement (or even later).

Group contracts are generally specified in collective labor agreements. These contracts aim to provide for minimum life annuity benefits to complement the pension benefits from the public schemes and also include survivor and disability benefits. Participating employees and their dependents are not subject to individual health screening, but costs and benefits depend on group experience. Pursuant to legislation, group annuities, like occupational pension schemes, are calculated on the basis of unisex rates. In contrast, individual contracts are not based on unisex rates and are subject to health screening.

Collective labor agreements vary in their specific terms and especially in the extent to which they allow for nongroup benefits, such as term annuities (phased withdrawals), lump sums, and unit-linked policies. Term annuities are extensively used. For premiums to be deductible from taxable income, payments must be spread over at least 10 years but may run for up to 25 years. However, benefits cannot be paid after the pensioner reaches the age of 85. Lump-sum payments are also possible if their use is provided in the pension contract or collective labor agreement that governs pension benefits. Their use has declined in recent years, but they are still the preferred form of benefit when accumulated balances are low.

Tax considerations also affect the choice of retirement product. In general, contributions are deductible from taxable income, whereas benefits are subject to tax. The only exception is the special labor market tax of 8 percent, which is levied on contributions but not on benefits.[6] As in some other countries with advanced occupational pension systems, such as the Netherlands, South Africa, and Sweden, in Denmark, the investment income of pension institutions is subject to income tax at a flat rate of 15 percent. Other than the ceiling that is imposed on annual contributions to lump-sum contracts, only a few other ceilings exist on pension saving, but the application of a 15 percent tax on investment income acts as a disincentive to excessive saving through pension contracts for pure tax-avoidance purposes.

Lump-sum payments used to be favored by the tax system because they were subject to a flat tax rate of 40 percent that was lower than the marginal income tax rates applied to annuity payments and phased withdrawals of high-income earners.[7] Probably lump sums were also favored simply because many pensioners preferred to be able to decide on the use of their savings at retirement. Reductions in the value of the tax deductibility of premiums paid to lump-sum schemes—for people paying the highest marginal rate of income taxation—have reduced the tax attractiveness of lump-sum payments, which explains the declining share of new premiums that are allocated to lump-sum contracts. However, generally speaking, the progressive nature of the Danish income tax system continues to confer benefits to tax deferral through pension saving.

Level of Annuitization

No data are available on the distribution of payouts among the different types of benefits, probably because of the young age of pension system universality. Although occupational pension schemes have existed for a very long time, their expansion to near-universal coverage is a relatively recent phenomenon. The new coverage has not reached maturity yet, and few data are available on the conversion of term annuities and lump-sum payments into life annuities.

The availability of data for the allocation of contributions to different contracts is explained by tax considerations: the rate of tax deductibility depends on the identification of premiums by category of payout profile. Because of the lack of data on payouts, no direct indication exists of the level of annuitization. However, because contributions to deferred life annuities have accounted for 50 percent or more of total contributions, one can argue that the level of annuitization is at least 50 percent and may be significantly higher if account is taken of the possibility of additional purchases of life annuities at retirement or even after retirement. In contrast, the growing popularity of term annuities, which reveals a preference for higher incomes during the first 10 years of retirement, suggests that the actual level of annuitization would be unlikely to be much higher.

Replacement Rates

Money's worth ratios are difficult to calculate in the Danish system because of the extensive reliance on bonus payments. An ex ante calculation would need to be based on assumed rates of future performance and bonus declaration, whereas an ex post calculation would require a considerable amount of detailed data on actual bonus payments. However, although money's worth ratios are not calculated, considerable effort is devoted in Denmark to calculating current and future replacement rates.

These rates are also based on assumptions about future performance and bonus payments, but they take into account all types of pension benefits and even allow for tax payments. Two reports, one from the Ministry of Economic and Business Affairs (2003) and the other from the Danish Pension Council (2005), provided details of current and expected replacement ratios. Although the two reports adopted slightly different methodologies, their basic results were broadly similar.

The average replacement rate is expected to increase in the future irrespective of education (and income). For people with a lower level of education, the replacement rate will increase from 80 percent in 2000 to almost 100 percent in 2045, whereas for highly educated people, it is projected to reach a little less than 90 percent in 2045 (figure 7.2). The reason for the rise in replacement rates is the expanding coverage of occupational pensions, which will affect, in particular, the lower-income groups. For all groups, private pensions will play a more important role in

Figure 7.2   Average Expected Replacement Rates for Different Groups of Education, 2000 and 2045

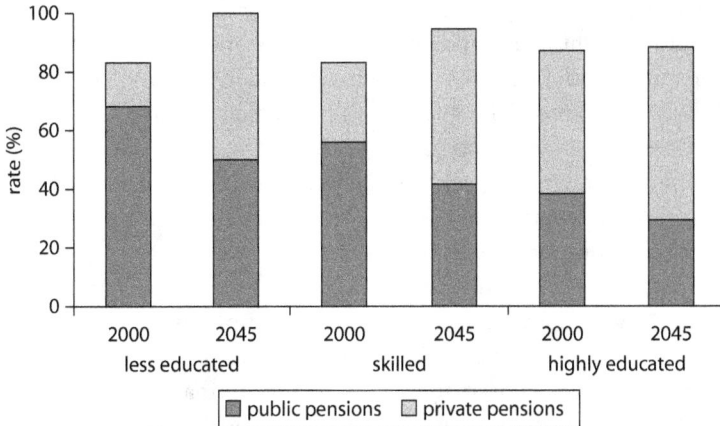

Source: Andersen and Skjodt 2007.

the future, but the social pension will still represent the major source of income for pensioners with modest incomes in 2045.

Risk-Sharing Characteristics

One of the most interesting features of the Danish pension system is the extensive use of risk-sharing arrangements. These arrangements take several distinct but complementary forms. First is the social pension scheme, which provides minimum benefits with considerable additional payments for low-income pensioners. It is financed on a pay-as-you-go basis from general tax revenues. Second, extensive use is made of group contracts, including deferred group annuities, under the quasi-mandatory occupational pension plans that are covered by collective labor agreements. Third, minimum guaranteed benefits are offered for the accumulation and payout phases by both the second and third pillars. Fourth, the system is based on the management and distribution of bonuses in accordance with the so-called contribution principle, which tries to prevent transfers across groups of participants. Both shareholder-owned joint stock companies and member-owned mutual institutions compete for pension business and are subject to identical rules regarding buildup of reserves and declaration of bonuses.

The size of the benefits allocated to members depends on the size of individual contributions, the investment income from accumulated assets, the operating costs of the plans, and the net results of insurance risks arising from the offer of life, disability, and longevity insurance. When employees join a plan, all future premiums, including those emanating from future pay raises as part of labor market agreements, are taken into account in calculating the level of guaranteed benefits. Even in the payout period, benefits that are not provided as lump sums are covered by the guarantee. The guaranteed benefits are computed by making projections that may extend for 60 years or longer, considering both the accumulation and payout phases. The risks to the pension institutions that provide the guarantees are potentially very large and necessitate the use of highly conservative assumptions.

The guaranteed benefits are calculated according to actuarial techniques, taking into account a number of assumptions concerning future interest rates and insurance risks as well as expected costs. The assumptions are made on a conservative basis. Under normal circumstances, the realized results will show a surplus, most of which must be given during the lifetime of the pension contract to the insured in the form of regular bonuses.

The bonus policy is decided by the pension institutions. Life insurance companies and pension funds compete to offer the best bonuses to their customers. However, the freedom to establish the individual institution's own bonus policy is subject to restrictions. The so-called contribution principle sets clear limits on the use and release of realized surplus. The offer of minimum guaranteed benefits does not imply the transformation of the Danish pension system into a defined benefit system because the use of highly conservative assumptions allows the declaration of large bonuses under normal circumstances.

Bonuses are often distributed to policyholders by increasing the guaranteed benefits. However, the guarantees on the bonuses themselves are given at the guaranteed rate prevailing at the time of bonus declaration and not at the rate that was guaranteed at the inception of the contract. Thus, for most pension plans, the investment and longevity risks are shared between the pension institution concerned and the members. The risk that the realized investment return will be lower than the guaranteed rate is borne by the pension institution, whereas the risk of low investment returns but above the guaranteed floor is shared with the insured. In the same way, insurance risks, including longevity risk, are shared between the pension institution and the insured. The insured are guaranteed a minimum level of lifelong pension benefits, but a prolongation of the mean lifetime will result in lower pension benefits as long as they are above the guaranteed minimum level.

The guarantees are based on all technical elements: interest rate, insurance risks, and costs. Hence, a surplus in one of the technical elements reduces the risk of the pension institution in the other elements. The technical rates, including assumptions on insurance risks, such as mortality and disability tables, must be notified to the supervisory authority before they can be used. The supervisor has the power to set aside the notified tables and demand a more cautious practice by a particular pension institution. But the supervisor does not provide any guidelines or benchmarks concerning mortality or disability tables. These matters are left to individual pension institutions to determine on the basis of their particular experience, but they are subject to notification to the supervisor. Traditionally, the Danish pension institutions use population tables that do not incorporate projections of longevity improvements. They use different techniques to correct for such improvements, and many of them consider introducing cohort tables.

The continuing prevalence of pension contracts with the relatively high minimum guaranteed return of 4.5 percent has forced pension institutions to invest in a cautious way to lower their investment risks. However, this kind of investment policy is likely to result in lower returns over the longer run. This outcome implies that choosing a guarantee for the pension benefits could produce lower pension benefits. Realization of this possibility has led to a growing demand for products without guarantees or with a lower level of guarantees. In the Danish market, a large variety of such products has been developed in recent years—in both pillar 2 and pillar 3 schemes. Market supply is now much more diverse and allows customers to select the products that suit their personal characteristics.

In some pension schemes, conditional guarantees have been introduced—that is, guarantees under which the interest rate and thus the guaranteed benefits can be reduced in certain extraordinary circumstances. Such circumstances are defined in the contracts and depend on external events, such as changes in the market interest rate. The aim of such contracts is to provide the individual member of a pension scheme the maximum security of fixed minimum benefits under ordinary market conditions and at the same time allow the pension scheme to optimize its investment policy.

Other products have been introduced without any guarantee or with a low guarantee, normally a zero-rate guarantee, which most often is a guarantee that workers will at least not lose the principal amount of their investments during the whole saving period, although they may still suffer losses from inflation. Another type of zero-rate guarantee is a "water-level" guarantee, in which interest, once earned, can never be lost again. These products typically offer customers a choice between a few investment categories with different risk profiles, but the actual investment management is left to the company. This option gives customers a choice to adjust their investment risk to their age or other aspects of their economic situation.

The demand for unit-linked products has grown considerably in recent years, although it has not reached the levels found in other European countries. Unit-linked products offer customers a choice of investment funds with varying policies as well as a choice of fund managers. However, most of the unit-linked products used in Denmark carry some sort of protection against investment risk, usually a zero-rate guarantee. In addition, most customers have opted for products where fund managers determine the investment policy. Thus, a fair interpretation of the Danish unit-linked market would be that customers have not chosen unit-linked products because of the investment choice but rather because of the higher degree of transparency that these products offer. This option represents a partial move away from extensive risk sharing—a partial correction that may be fully justified in light of the large fall in guaranteed returns.

In sum, the main features of the risk-sharing arrangements in the traditional annuity policies are that pension institutions assume the investment and longevity risks up to the level of guaranteed benefits, but in the declaration of periodic bonuses these risks are shared by participants. In the case of unit-linked products, the investment risk is borne by individual members, reflecting their choice of instrument, but the longevity risk is shared among participants. In deferred group annuities, the investment and longevity risks are shared among both active and retired workers, although special emphasis is placed on avoiding transfers across different cohorts (for instance, with regard to contracts that are issued at different levels of guaranteed benefits).

Regulation and Supervision

Like providers of all financial services, pension institutions are subject to extensive regulation, the aim of which is to protect the interests of policyholders and members of pension plans and to promote a competitive and efficient market for pension saving products, during both the accumulation and payout phases.

Solvency and Investment Rules and Stress Testing

Denmark is a member of the European Union (EU), and its legislation is therefore based on EU directives for solvency, accounting, and freedom of services across borders. However, as a general principle, EU directives are minimum directives. They provide broad guidance and leave ample room for detailed provisions to be determined by national authorities.

All pension institutions, whether they are established as life insurance companies or pension funds, are subject to the Financial Services Act (the main law governing all financial services) and to all secondary legislation established as a consequence of this act. Therefore, they are all subject to the same legislation on the contribution principle, to the same investment and solvency rules, to the same accounting framework, to the same stress-testing requirements, and so on. Any differences primarily mirror institutional differences; that is, pension funds have no external shareholders and do not pay dividends and hence, in contrast to commercial life insurance companies, they are not subject to company taxation rules.

Like the accounting rules and the general approach to regulation of insurance activity in Denmark, the solvency rules for Danish life insurance companies and pension funds are identical. The solvency requirements for life insurance amount to 4 percent of the technical provisions plus a requirement on the sums insured—totaling approximately 5 percent of technical provisions. Under the fair value accounting rules, the technical provisions represent the sum of the guaranteed benefits, the bonus potential on future premiums, and the bonus potential on premiums paid.

However, the current solvency rules are not risk based. The required solvency margin is only reduced to 1 percent when the institution does not bear the investment risk, as, for example, in unit-linked products that are offered without any guarantees. If the product in question contains *any* guarantee on the return, meaning that the insurer bears some of the investment risk, the solvency requirement is as described previously. Thus, a contract with a guaranteed return of 0 percent implies the same solvency requirement as a contract with a guaranteed return of 4.5 percent—notwithstanding that the latter contract clearly exposes the insurer to a larger risk.

The solvency requirement has to be met with available capital at least equal to this requirement. *Available capital* is defined to include shareholders funds—assets less liabilities—with some additions and reductions, especially regarding subordinated loans and special bonus provisions. The latter belong to policyholders but count as part of regulatory capital under certain conditions.

On the asset side, quantitative limits apply. Restrictions apply, especially on the share of assets that can be made up of so-called risky assets, notably equities. Moreover, quantitative limits are applied to reduce concentration risks. For example, quantitative limits apply to the possible exposure to *one* issuer of mortgage bonds or the proportion of total assets that might be invested in the securities of just *one* company or a group of closely related companies.

Although quantitative limits still apply, a gradual move has occurred over a number of years toward regulation based more on the prudent person principle. This principle implies that greater emphasis is placed on prudent behavior by each pension institution's monitoring and controlling of risk, rather than on specific quantitative limits.

Over a longer time span, the share of assets that can be invested in risky assets, such as equities, has been increased. In 2001, the proportion of assets covering technical provisions, which could be invested in risky assets, was raised from 50 to 70 percent. The reason for the increase was that some institutions had reached the former ceiling of 50 percent and still wanted more freedom to invest.

The increase, however, was not granted without conditions. It was accompanied by a political wish that the actual share of risky assets in the portfolio should be considered against objective criteria, in the sense that the share of risky assets should be based on an assessment of the company's risk-weighted capital.

These objective criteria were implemented in terms of the so-called traffic light system borrowed from the banking sector (a political aim was to ensure that identical investment risks in different financial subsectors would imply the same solvency requirement). Since the introduction of the traffic light system with its regular, periodic stress testing, the share of risky assets (equities) has steadily fallen, mainly because of adverse market developments. The flexibility in the current investment regulation is so great that asset allocation strategies are probably influenced more by internal asset and liability considerations and capital rules (like the traffic light system) than by investment rules and limitations per se.

Valuation Rules on Assets and Liabilities

The Danish accounting rules for life insurance companies and pension funds are based on fair values. All assets must be measured at their market value by using observable market prices or by using a valuation technique in the case of inactive markets. For the majority of assets—such as shares and bonds—there is an active market where the assets are traded, giving rise to observable market prices. For property, an economic model is used to provide an estimate of the market price. For the remaining assets—such as unlisted shares—a best estimate of fair value must be used.

For the valuation of liabilities, a major obstacle is the absence of an active market where insurance and pension liabilities are traded and where an observable price can be determined. In Denmark, the Market Value Committee recommended the decomposition of technical provisions into several components, reflecting the guaranteed rates of return:

- The *guaranteed benefits*, which measure the difference between the market value of the benefits guaranteed according to the terms of the insurance and pension contract and the market value of the future premiums to be paid
- The *bonus potential on future premiums*, which measures the market value of the excess return over the guaranteed benefits that will arise from the future premiums
- The *bonus potential on premiums paid*, which measures the market value of the excess return over the guaranteed benefits that arise on premiums that have already been paid.

Furthermore, the *collective bonus* measures the value of bonuses that have been allocated to policyholders as a group but that have not yet been allocated to individual policyholders.

The sum of guaranteed benefits, bonus potential on future premiums, and bonus potential on premiums paid constitutes the technical provisions, which form the base for calculating the solvency requirement. The collective bonus is not a part of the technical provisions and is, therefore, not taken into account in computing the solvency margin.

The calculation of technical provisions must be based on

- The best estimate of relevant underwriting risks (that is, mortality, morbidity, and the like)
- The best estimate of market costs (administration costs) for which the insurance policies, on average, could be administered on conditions governing the market
- A discount rate prescribed by the supervisor.

Hence, technical liabilities must be reported at their best estimate. No general assumptions are used. The life insurance companies and pension funds must base measurement of their liabilities on their best estimates and take into account any projected developments. In addition to the best estimates, a risk margin must be added.

One important assumption when measuring technical liabilities is the assumption about mortality. The supervisor does not stipulate any mortality table to be used. Each pension institution is allowed to use its own best estimates of mortality, although the assumption is subject to scrutiny by the supervisor.

If assumptions—for example, mortality assumptions—turn out to be unfavorable for the pension institution because improvements in life expectancy have not been properly taken into account, then this risk must be borne by the institution and the policyholders in accordance with the terms of the underlying contracts. Although the supervisor keeps a close eye on the key assumptions behind the calculations, ultimate responsibility does not rest with the supervisor or the government, but with the management of the pension institution. Any losses arising from underestimating future improvements in longevity must be shared with policyholders.

Guaranteed benefits are increased in accordance with the contracts. The collective bonus acts as a buffer—in relation both to fulfilling the guarantees and to absorbing any losses. The collective bonus is not, strictly speaking, a residual, because each institution must assess the need for declaring a collective bonus in conjunction with a requirement to release surplus to the individual policyholders at reasonable terms over the contract period. The need for a collective bonus, naturally, is quite dependent on the guarantees given: the higher the level of guarantees, the higher the need for a collective bonus.

Market Values and the Choice of Discount Rate

An important feature of the measurement of liabilities at fair value is the choice of an appropriate discount rate. The Market Value Committee concluded after lengthy discussion that the discount rate should not reflect the actual asset composition of individual pension institutions. Only one discount rate should obtain, equal for all actors in the market. Given that conclusion, the committee debated whether the rate should be a so-called risk-free rate of interest or whether it could include some kind of credit risk. In the latter case, the discount rate would reflect the credit standing of a high-quality bond.

Another conclusion was that the discount rate should be a market interest rate with the same term and in the same currency as the liability.

In other words, the rate was to be based, in principle, on a yield curve, so as to ensure that in the discounting of future cash flows, the rate used was equal to the point (maturity) on the market yield curve that was equal, at the time of calculation, to the time period until the payment date for the payment in question.

At the time of the introduction of the new fair value accounting rules, pension institutions were not, however, immediately prepared to apply maturity-dependent discount rates, nor were they able to do so in practice. Under the rules in force at the time, pension institutions had been using discount rates that were independent of the maturity of liabilities. The new guidelines gave companies the option to decide whether to use a single rate (flat rate) or a zero-coupon yield curve. Although rules were established for calculation of the flat rate, no rules were initially specified for determination of the yield curve for companies opting to use it rather than a flat rate.

The flat discount rate was determined as the average of the yield on three government bonds, weighted to ensure that their maturities correspond to 10 years—with the addition of a premium commensurate with the spread between a 10-year swap rate and a 10-year government bond yield. The accounting rules also stipulate that an adjustment for risk and uncertainty should be made. This adjustment for risk and uncertainty could be made in the form of a deduction from the discount rate corresponding to 5 percent.

Over time, some pension institutions showed interest in applying a yield curve to the measurement of insurance liabilities. However, in the guidance from the supervisor about the appropriate discount rate, the details of applying a yield curve were left for the institution in question to decide and to notify the supervisor.

A special task force was then appointed to study the issue. It recommended that the yield curve should be determined on the basis of the euro swap rate but with an allowance for a spread to reflect the difference between Danish and euro rates. The recommendations of the task force were accepted, and starting on January 1, 2005, the Danish supervisor started publishing the yield curve on a daily basis on its home page. The yield curve is delivered to the supervisor by the Danish National Bank, which has contracted with an international investment company to supply the underlying data and technical expertise to simulate the zero-coupon bond yield structure. Pension institutions had the option to use a flat discount rate until the end of 2008, but since January 2009, use of the yield curve has been compulsory.

The determination and use of the risk margin were also modified. In principle, each company should assess and justify the size of the premium for risk, uncertainty, and value of guarantees, and the risk premium should be taken into account in determining cash flows, rather than as a deduction in the discount rate. The new accounting rules do not contain the 5 percent deduction method. The companies may still notify the supervisor that the 5 percent will be applied, but now they must argue in the notification why its application is appropriate. Moreover, the deduction does not have to take place in the discount rate but can be applied to the cash flows. This change represents a further move toward refining the life insurance accounting rules in the direction of fair values. Whereas the discount rate should be uniform across the industry, the premium for risk and uncertainty is not uniform.

Profit Participation and Market Discipline

The fair value accounting rules enable management to better monitor the risks of the insurance portfolio and to provide better and more relevant information for users, the media, and the public. The benefits of this accounting system, however, go further than merely providing better accounting information. The fair value accounting rules also have real economic effects. In this regard, the possibility of using the bonus potential on paid-up premiums to absorb losses also implies that the asset allocation can be better optimized for contracts carrying relatively low risk.

An important issue in profit-participating contracts is the way in which the different life insurance companies and pension funds divide the result obtained in a given year between policyholders and shareholders. It is a focus of attention in the media and an important parameter affecting the competitive environment among the companies. To improve market transparency and comparability, the supervisor has issued a guidance document on market discipline and notification of rules related to the equity's share of the realized result in life insurance companies and pension funds. The focus point is the risk premium awarded to shareholders.

The annual result must be divided between policyholders and shareholders so that the part accruing to the portfolio of insurance contracts is reasonable in relation to the manner in which the portfolio contributed to this result. Pension institutions are required to submit to the supervisor the rules and the assumptions applied in calculating the part of the annual result that accrues to its equity.

In the notification, each institution must divide the equity part of the result into one part related to the return on equity and one part reflecting the extent of the risk incumbent on equity. It must also explain the rationale for the particular allocation. The aim of this regulation is not to establish maximum ceilings on the risk premium to be allocated to shareholders but to force management to consider the risks facing equity holders and thus ensure that the remuneration of both policyholders and shareholders is fair and based on clearly specified criteria.

An institution has no obligation to follow the specified guidelines. However, if the notification of the risk premium to the supervisor follows the guidelines, the supervisor will be less likely to challenge the institution and ask for additional explanations. If the notification does not follow the guidelines, the supervisor will study the notification to evaluate whether the allocation of the result is fair to policyholders.

The notification must be in place before the beginning of the accounting year. Among other things, the notification must specify (on a comparable basis) how much extra return could be awarded to the insured if the equity was not rewarded with a risk premium. The company must specify the assumptions behind the calculation of the risk premium in two categories:

- Risks that are not specific to the company in question
- Risks that are related to the business plan and strategy for the specific company.

The first category includes financial risks, biometric risks, and risks related to cost assumptions. If, for example, a company has issued contracts over the long term, guaranteeing lifelong benefits, these actions might expose its equity capital to a relatively large risk when life expectancy increases (compared to a company where increasing life expectancy might lead to reduced benefits). Risks in the second category could be risks related to the investment strategy and reinsurance program.

The notification must also specify the amount of the equity risk premium that will not be transferred to the equity capital because the annual result is not expected to be sufficient. A larger part to owners than to policyholders may be distributed only to own funds, when this larger part plus the amounts distributed to the insurance portfolio can be covered by the result for the year. If the result for the year is insufficient to allow distribution to own funds, the company may rectify the situation in future years from future profits.

In the course of a given year, a company is not allowed to change the principles and assumptions governing the calculation of the risk premium if it is to stay within the scope of sufficient market discipline. However, at the end of each year, the notification to the supervisor must be renewed; that is, the company must consider whether the notification and the arguments for the size of the equity risk premium that it is using still apply.

No later than eight days after board approval of the way in which a given year's result will be allocated to policyholders and shareholders, the institution must notify the supervisor as to the *actual* risk premium awarded to equity. Hence, the expected and actual risk premiums to equity can be compared and any difference explained.

Experience is still quite limited about whether the intent of the guidance on market discipline—to force companies to consider the risks that they are facing and to enable the market to discipline the size of the risk premium attributed to the equity—has actually been realized. The rules have applied for only a few years, and they have been amended a couple of times.

Clearly, however, introducing transparency into the complex issue of how to calculate a reasonable reward to the risk of the equity in life insurance companies and pension funds is difficult. Many factors influence the size of this risk, and different companies have different strategies for the risk premium.

So many companies are active in the market that even the seemingly easy task of presenting an overview of the rules and assumptions for calculating the risk premium across companies poses practical challenges. However, such practical difficulties can be overcome for those really interested in understanding the issue of risk premiums across the industry.

Consumer interest in this issue is very limited for obvious reasons. Pensions are difficult to understand, and technical issues, such as equity risk premiums, do not attract the attention of the average consumer. Instead, the question of fairness of the allocation of the realized result between policyholders and shareholders has been a hot issue both in the media and in the ongoing competitive struggle among the companies.

In the media, particular attention has been paid to those companies having relatively high equity risk premiums. Risk premiums have been compared across life insurance companies and pension funds, and those companies with relatively large risk premiums have been accused of allocating too much to shareholders—that is, of breaching the principle of fairness, which is the whole essence of the contribution principle. The claim has been that companies awarding high risk premiums to the equity are paying off shareholders with funds belonging to policyholders. The reasoning is that the risk premium is a payment (a cost) transferred from policyholders to shareholders, which must be taken into account when comparing costs across companies.

Care must be taken about this reasoning, however. Different companies and pension funds have different needs. Some companies have no need and do not wish to build up their available capital (to match the solvency requirement) through the profit and loss account. Other companies must make a return to external shareholders that over time is sufficient to attract shareholder capital. Others are growing fast and wish to meet an increasing capital requirement through policyholders' own funds, which in the guidance are treated like equity.

Moreover, the requirement that a risk premium may be distributed only to own funds, when this larger part plus the amounts distributed to the insurance portfolio can be covered by positive results for the year, creates volatility in the risk premium. Amounts that the equity capital has actually earned but that cannot be allocated to the equity because of insufficient results are transferred to a "shadow account." They are gradually released when future years' income allows. Hence, in a given year, a part of the risk premium to the equity may relate to unpaid risk premiums in earlier years.

The use of the shadow account is one reason the risk premium allocated to shareholders in a given life insurance company or pension fund—and the consideration whether that risk premium is reasonable—must be viewed over a number a years. The underlying volatility of financial markets, which shows up in the accounts under fair valuation, is another reason.

Finally, the risk premium is not a cost borne by policyholders and used for the remuneration of the equity. The risk premium is a payment to a factor of production—the capital at risk. The shareholders (including policyholders if they are contributing to the risk capital with special bonus provisions) are contributing to the company being able to bear those risks that create an income that allows a risk premium to the equity. The risk premium represents an *allocation* of profits, not a transfer from policyholders to shareholders.

There is no doubt, however, that the guidance has served its purpose of forcing insurance companies and pension funds to consider what risk their equity is facing and what the price for running this risk should be. Over time and with forthcoming amendments to the guidance, one may expect that this important insight will also be introduced to other users of the guidance, not least the media. Also, by relying on transparency and competition instead of strict quantitative limits on the risk premium to the equity, the guidance on market discipline rests on a sound approach that is well in line with the approaches to risk, accounting, and solvency that international bodies such as the European Commission are aiming for in these years.

The Traffic Light System

The supervisor introduced the traffic light system in 2001. The aim was to ensure that companies hold sufficient reserves to cover possible adverse market developments. The requirements were imposed on all life insurance companies and pension funds—not just those exceeding the former quantitative limit (50 percent) on the share of risky assets.

The stress testing is divided into two scenarios: yellow and red. When a company does not fall into one of those two categories, it is deemed to be in a green-light situation; hence, its capital base is adequate when measured against its potential to absorb losses from possible adverse market developments.

Both tests measure the capital strength against scenarios that are possible but have not occurred at the time the stress is performed. Measurement and reporting is done every half year.

The yellow scenario is possible but unlikely, whereas the red scenario is more likely (though it still is only a plausible scenario). The colors indicate a serious matter if the plausible scenario poses capital problems (red light), whereas the problem is less serious if the rather unlikely scenario (yellow light) poses capital problems.

Soon after the introduction of the traffic light system in the Danish life insurance and pension business, financial markets were hit by severe turmoil. Life insurance companies and pension funds suffered huge losses on the shares in their portfolios. Likewise, the fall in interest rates to unprecedented levels created problems, because the dominant proportion of contracts outstanding were written with a guaranteed rate of return.

In this situation, a large number of institutions were in the yellow-light scenario and some were in the red-light scenario. For one company, the situation turned out to be so severe that it encountered real problems in fulfilling the solvency requirement, and it was taken under special supervision by the authorities.

The traffic light system forced life insurance companies and pension funds to consider the risks to which they were exposed. The proportion of shares in the portfolios of pension institutions was reduced, and financial instruments were bought to provide cover against further declines in the level of market interest rates. The supervisor reacted reasonably to the results of the traffic light stress testing. Companies facing the red light were asked to reduce their risks. However, the supervisor did not interfere with management decisions and did not force the sale of specific assets. Companies in the yellow-light scenario were able to rectify their situation without undue intervention from the supervisor.

The traffic light system created better awareness by the management of life insurance companies and pension funds of the risks that they were facing. Although it continues to be improved, the system influenced the monitoring of risks in the insurance business. Moreover, it contributed to the growing trend of relying on products with lower or no guaranteed returns.

The traffic light system, as well as risk-based supervision in general, faces a difficult policy dilemma. It requires pension institutions to assess their resilience to declining market values without making any allowance for the long-term nature of pension business. Even at times when market values are at historically low levels, pension institutions are required to test their capital base against further substantial declines in market values. Although this dilemma has no easy answer, excessive reliance on the traffic light system runs the risk of forcing institutions to adopt overly conservative investment policies to the detriment of investment returns. Risk-based supervision needs to evolve further to achieve a more efficient trade-off between stability and efficiency.

Risk Management

The main risks faced by pension institutions are investment and longevity risks. They also face credit and counterparty risks as well as operational risks. These last three have grown in importance in recent years as a result of the increasing complexity of financial products.

In Denmark, the risk exposure of pension institutions is limited by the widespread use of profit-participating policies that offer minimum guaranteed benefits with regular declarations of bonuses. Institutions assume the investment and longevity risks up to the level of the guaranteed benefits. In the declaration of bonuses, these risks are shared among the participants. Profit-participating annuities are popular with participants because they avoid the inflation risks of fixed nominal annuities as well as the low returns of fixed real annuities. They allow participation in higher market returns in equities and other assets, although they expose pensioners to greater volatility in returns.

In the Danish context, the main financial market risk for pension institutions is the risk of declining interest rates. As long as the market interest rate remains a safe distance above the minimum guaranteed rate, the risk of falling market rates affects the declaration of bonuses only and is thus borne by customers. However, when market rates come very close to or fall below the guaranteed levels, pension institutions face a serious risk of capital erosion and even insolvency.

A market risk arises from falling interest rates as well as from rising interest rates because of the fair value accounting rules, according to which the assets are valued at market prices and the liabilities are valued at estimated market prices. The capital loss of assets caused by an increase in the interest rate is not offset by a capital gain of liabilities, because according to the accounting rules, the decrease of the reserves for guaranteed pensions is balanced by an increase in the required reserves for future bonuses. However, the change in the composition of liabilities—with heavier reliance on bonus potentials when interest rates increase—creates a loss-absorbing buffer. Therefore, the risk of low or falling interest rates is more pervasive because of the guaranteed benefits built into most contracts.

Risk management is further complicated by the presence of large investments in mortgage bonds that enjoy embedded call options. These options allow borrowers to refinance their mortgage loans at a preset price when rates are falling and deprive pension institutions of high-yielding assets when the value of their long-term liabilities increases because of the fall in market interest rates.

A mismatch of the duration of assets and liabilities forms a special challenge for pension institutions. As a rule, the duration of liabilities is much longer than the duration of assets or even the duration of derivatives available on the market. Asset-liability management is totally based on market instruments because the Danish government does not supply the market with long-term instruments dedicated to closing the duration gap between the assets and liabilities of pension institutions.

Most pension institutions responded to the financial market risks by reducing their equity portfolios (risks are in large part caused by the very fall of equity prices); replacing short-duration bonds with long-duration ones, especially foreign bonds; and engaging in extensive hedging operations, mostly through the use of long-term interest rate swaps in the more liquid euro market.[8] Although such policies ran the risk of "locking in the losses," generally accepted wisdom was that pension institutions could not afford to suffer additional losses and endanger their financial solvency. All these developments have been in response to the changing market conditions and the gradual introduction of risk-based supervision.[9]

Credit risk attracted considerable attention during the global financial crisis of 2008. First, mortgage defaults increased significantly. This situation resulted in a much higher credit risk premium and a substantial widening of the yield differential between mortgage and government bonds. Second, the failure of several global financial institutions heightened concern about exposure to counterparty risk, especially in the growing area of long-term interest rate and credit default swaps.

The extensive government intervention and support that were provided on a global scale mitigated the potential adverse effects of the growing exposure to counterparty risk. But the widening yield differential between mortgage and government bonds provided a vivid manifestation of the difficult policy dilemma mentioned in the last paragraph of the section describing the traffic light system. Taking account of the long-term nature of pension business and to prevent large sales of mortgage bonds in a declining market, the authorities allowed pension institutions to use, on a temporary basis that was later extended for a further year, the mortgage bond yield curve for valuing their pension liabilities. This measure was a temporary and ad hoc solution to a very serious problem. Whether a more permanent solution can be found for this very important policy dilemma remains to be seen.

The insurance risks—such as longevity, disability, and early death—are shared between insurance providers and the insured. As long as the realized result is better than the assumptions made for the technical reserves, changes result in higher bonuses; thus, the risks are on the side of the customers. But if the realized result turns out worse than assumed for the calculation of technical reserves, providers bear the risks. In general, however, pension institutions use conservative estimates of future longevity and other insurance risks, and thus these risks are in practice shared among policyholders. Because of this history, little attempt has been made to use market instruments, such as derivatives or longevity bonds, to hedge insurance risks.

Concluding Remarks

In many ways and at various levels, the Danish pension system is robust and well designed. First and foremost, the Danish pension system provides a basic cover for pension needs to virtually the entire population through the tax-financed, pay-as-you-go schemes in pillar 1, supplemented by the fully funded ATP, which—although not part of the public welfare system—shares several characteristics with public schemes. The broad coverage ensures that pensioners do not end up in poverty, even if they have insufficient private savings.

Second, the Danish pension system has a multitude of pension institutions providing pillar 2 schemes. These institutions represent funded pension schemes that have been negotiated as part of labor market agreements. Over the past 20 years or so, these schemes have been widened to cover almost 80 percent of wage earners, who contribute 10 percent—and often much more—of their salary for pension purposes. The schemes are fully funded, and the obligations to provide future pension incomes are isolated from the companies where the employees earn their salary. Risk sharing, therefore, does not involve the companies of the employees. This aspect is a very important advantage compared to the pension systems of many other countries.

Third, in pillar 3, each individual has the possibility to align his or her intentions for future life as a pensioner with his or her present income stream and to purchase additional coverage in the case of early death or disability.

By relying on these three pillars, the Danish pension system combines the strengths of each pillar while limiting their weaknesses. For example, the tax financing in pillar 1 schemes does lead to some economic inefficiency (through the creation of tax wedges); however, this problem would be much more severe if the pension system was totally based on pillar 1. Support seems enthusiastic for the additional pension provision in pillars 2 and 3, and over the years a large proportion of pay raises has been used to increase pension contributions in pillar 2.

The funded nature of pillars 2 and 3 also strengthens the trust in and support of the system. Clearly, a risk exists that future pension income could be taxed more heavily than foreseen when contributions were made; however, the real values of any promise of future pension income depend on the size of future real national income (production). The Danish case provides some evidence that funded pension schemes are able to gather support among the working population and pensioners and probably more so than a system relying more heavily on future taxpayers to provide future pension income.

In Denmark, the demand for pension benefits has for several years been concentrated on contracts with guaranteed benefits. Pension institutions have issued contracts with guarantees, which imply that over time a certain investment yield must be obtained. For this system to work, reserves are built up in years of high investment yields, and these reserves are used in years with lower or negative yields to smooth out the increase in the benefits of the policyholders. Over time, each policyholder will obtain a market yield, but the smoothing of yields between policyholders and over time has been seen as an integral part of the risk-sharing mechanism.

This system has come under strain in recent years because of falling interest rates and turbulence in stock markets, not least after the events of September 11, 2001. When life insurance companies and pension funds guarantee future benefits, they are not able to optimize the long-term relationship between expected returns and benefits. The cost of the guarantees attached to traditional pension products in terms of lower average yields has been widely recognized in recent years.

Hence, new products with no or very limited guarantees have gained market share. The products include unit-linked insurance, but product development is taking place at a rapid pace. New products that fall between unit-linked insurance and more traditional products (in the Danish market) seem to be entering the market with great success.

The growth of products with no or limited guarantees—based on the yield obtained being attributed to policyholders in each year—also satisfies wishes expressed by politicians. They want the pension market to become more transparent for the individual. Whether consumers also have this need—especially considering the long-term nature of pensions and the importance of providing pensions for future generations instead of merely achieving short-term individual influence on asset allocation—remains to be seen.

The increasing market share of new products also reflects a market trend toward more freedom of choice for the individual. This trend has been seen for many years regarding individual choice of benefits of insurance coverage. Thus, the widow's pension used to be a mandatory part of an ordinary occupational pension scheme, but today members of many occupational schemes can individually select a widow's pension. In recent years, this demand for more freedom of choice has widened to include individual influence on investment policy. Therefore, the increased market share of new products can also be seen as a demand for individual freedom of choice.

The menu of retirement products is moving toward more flexibility, evidenced by more variable annuities (as in unit-linked products) and more combinations. The political authorities and legislators have promoted these trends and have supported the resulting decline in the share of guaranteed products. This change has been possible, not least because the Danish pension system contains first-pillar benefits that provide protection against longevity and market risk.

As in every country, the activities of life insurance companies and pension funds are tightly regulated. The Danish regulatory and supervisory system has several forward-looking elements. Accounting rules require market valuation of both assets and liabilities. In such an environment, unrealized and realized gains and losses are not distinguished; they all go through the profit and loss account, they are taxed, they are distributed to policyholders and shareholders, and they count equally for solvency purposes. The application of market accounting rules on the liability side is a major Danish achievement and should serve to inspire many other countries.

The accounting environment serves to strengthen and buttress the risk-sharing features of life insurance and pension business in Denmark. All gains and losses are recognized and shared between policyholders and shareholders—and among policyholders—according to the contribution principle. The accounting framework prevents gains and losses from being hidden and reveals the underlying risk profile of the different contracts.

Risk sharing is, therefore, quite transparent in the Danish system. Liabilities and losses cannot be hidden through artificial accounting measures, nor can risks be turned over to third parties. The effect of positive and negative market events is shared between policyholders and shareholders, thus not imposing strains on other actors in the economy.

Because of the well-developed risk-sharing mechanisms and reliance on funded schemes in pillars 2 and 3, issues that are very important in many other countries are less important in Denmark. The funded system, coupled with the use of market values and market-based information, requires, for instance, that changes in longevity (and other factors) be taken into account. When longevity increases, the actuaries must ensure that liabilities are adjusted properly, and the technical assumptions governing the pension products must be reconsidered. Hence, the system provides incentives and requirements to react when important underlying factors change.

In the case of unfunded pillar 1 schemes that are subject to political decision making, however, changes in longevity will require political intervention only over a longer time span. Therefore, the pressure on politicians today to secure the long-term sustainability of the public pillar is limited. Thus, the risk exists that the need for such changes may be hidden for years, which is less likely in pillar 2 and 3 schemes. Although the public pension system does not run an insolvency risk like schemes in pillars 2 and 3, a risk of intergenerational conflict is inherent in the public pension system.

The regulatory framework governing the private pension system has, over the years, gradually been changed. Today, the supervisory focus is on gathering market-based evidence and strengthening incentives to control and monitor risks. Also, market discipline is being enhanced through the release of market-based information. Market forces and market discipline, emphasizing the responsibility of management, are seen as more effective than regulation through laws, limits, and requirements. Although regulation is in many ways quite intense—also seen from a cost perspective—the basic premise to rely on incentives, risk control, and management responsibility must be seen as a major advantage of the Danish pension system.

Notes

1. The contribution amounts are adjusted from time to time.

2. This benefit form was introduced in 2002. Before 2002, benefits were calculated with a 4.5 percent rate of interest.

3. Netting out liabilities to other credit institutions lowers this ratio to 26 percent of GDP.

4. Workers and employees receiving early retirement benefits after 2003 are mandated to contribute to the ATP.

5. The fact that these annuities are governed by collective labor agreements may explain their broad acceptability and may also have mitigated the need for extensive regulation and supervision.

6. The special labor market tax is not imposed on investment and transfer income. It is a regular tax that is not earmarked for any particular purpose.

7. Before the tax rules were changed, contributions to lump-sum schemes were deductible at the marginal rate of up to 58 percent, but lump-sum benefits were taxed at a maximum rate of 40 percent. After the change in the rules in 1999, the maximum tax deduction of contributions to lump-sum schemes was limited to 43 percent (that is, it no longer applied to the top tax bracket of 15 percent).

8. The response of pension institutions to the financial turmoil and the growing use of derivatives are analyzed in some detail in Ladekarl and others (2007).

9. A detailed account of the evolution of risk-based supervision of pension institutions in Denmark is provided in Van Dam and Andersen (2008).

References

Andersen, Carsten, and Peter Skjodt. 2007. "Pension Institutions and Annuities in Denmark." Policy Research Working Paper 4437, World Bank, Washington, DC.

Danish Pension Council. 2005. *Pension Contributions, Replacement Ratios, and Mortality*. Copenhagen: Danish Pension Council.

Ladekarl, Jeppe, Regitze Ladekarl, Erik Brink Andersen, and Dimitri Vittas. 2007. "The Use of Derivatives to Hedge Embedded Options: The Case of Pension Institutions in Denmark." Policy Research Working Paper 4159, World Bank, Washington, DC.

Ministry of Economic and Business Affairs. 2003. *Increased Freedom of Choice in Pension Saving*. Copenhagen: Ministry of Economic and Business Affairs.

Van Dam, Rein, and Erik Brink Andersen. 2008. "Risk-Based Supervision of Pension Institutions in Denmark." Policy Research Working Paper 4540, World Bank, Washington, DC.

Vittas, Dimitri. 2008. "A Short Note on the ATP Fund of Denmark." Policy Research Working Paper 4505, World Bank, Washington, DC.

CHAPTER 8

Chile

*Building a Robust Market for Fixed
Real Annuities*

Chile's market for retirement products has its origins in the pension
reform that was implemented in 1981 and involved the gradual replacement of the old public pay-as-you-go system with a new private and fully
funded system operating on a defined contribution (DC) basis. In the new
system, workers can choose freely among different pension funds managed by dedicated pension fund administrators (*administradoras de fondos
de pensiones*, or AFPs). Workers contribute 10 percent of their wages to an
individual account up to a specified ceiling.[1] They also pay about 2.2 percent of their wages to AFPs, part of which is used to pay for disability and
survivorship insurance, while the remainder covers the operating costs
and profits of fund administrators.

At the time of retirement, workers use their accumulated balances
either to make phased withdrawals (PWs) from a pension fund or to purchase a life annuity from an insurance company. Lump-sum withdrawals
are allowed only under strict conditions. Workers with disabilities are
entitled to a disability pension, and the dependents of deceased workers

---

This chapter is based on Rocha and Rudolph (2010), which provided a summary and
update of the book by Rocha and Thorburn (2007), *Developing Annuities Markets: The
Experience of Chile.*

and pensioners are entitled to a survivor's pension. Both disabled pensioners and survivorship pensioners can also choose between life annuities and PWs.

Because of the restrictions on payout options and the absence of either a universal or an earnings-related public pension, demand for life annuities has been strong, especially by middle- and high-income workers.[2] The demand for life annuities has been stimulated by the conditions that have been applied to early retirement and by the provision of generous recognition bonds for past contributions. The growth of the new pension system and the development of the market for retirement products have been supported by a robust regulatory framework and by the provision of several important government guarantees that cover both the accumulation and payout phases.

This chapter provides an overview of the development and performance of the market for retirement products in Chile. The chapter summarizes the main findings of the book by Roberto Rocha and Craig Thorburn (2007), *Developing Annuities Markets: The Experience of Chile*. It also provides a timely update of Chilean developments in view of the major reform of the Chilean pension system in 2008.

The next section offers a brief summary of the overall structure of the system, reviews the types of government guarantees, and sets out the conditions for retirement. The following section then focuses on the menu of retirement products and reviews the demand for different products. This section also looks at the performance of different retirement products, targeted replacement rates, the level of annuitization, the use of risk-sharing arrangements, and the regulation of marketing. The penultimate section discusses the prudential regulation of life insurance companies and pension fund administrators and the evolution of risk management in those institutions. The last section offers some concluding remarks.

Overall Structure of the Pension and Retirement System

This section describes the structure of the pension system in Chile, the evolution of the life insurance sector, and the market for retirement products. It also reviews the government guarantees that apply and the conditions for retirement in Chile.

The AFP System

The AFP system was made mandatory for new entrants into the labor force starting in 1981 and voluntary for existing workers, but most

workers opted to switch to the new system because they received generous recognition of their accrued rights (in the form of recognition
bonds issued by the government) and enjoyed a reduction in contribution rates. By 2008, the number of active contributors was 4.5 million
workers, or the equivalent of about 63 percent of the labor force, as
shown in table 8.1. This coverage ratio is much higher than the Latin
American average of 28 percent, although still low by comparison with
the Organisation for Economic Co-operation and Development
(OECD) average of about 90 percent. In 2008, the government implemented reforms aimed at increasing the coverage of the mandatory
funded pillar and strengthening the solidarity of the Chilean pension
system. These reforms are expected to reduce the coverage gap of Chile
compared with other OECD countries.[3]

The number of pensioners under the new system has increased significantly, reaching 694,000 in 2008, the equivalent of 15 percent of the
number of contributors and 47 percent of the number of total pensioners, as shown in table 8.2.

Contributions and total assets in the AFP system have grown rapidly.
Annual contributions have amounted to nearly 4 percent of gross domestic product (GDP), reflecting the labor income that is covered by the
pension system. Total assets reached 26 percent of GDP in 1990 and 65
and 53 percent in 2007 and 2008, respectively. On average, AFPs have
achieved high investment returns but have also suffered from relatively
high operating fees.

Table 8.1   Coverage in the Chilean Pension System, 1990–2008

Year	AFP contributors	Employment	Labor force	Contributors/ labor force (%)	Contributors/ employment (%)
1990	2,642,757	4,539,040	4,896,680	54	58
1995	2,961,928	5,206,650	5,596,630	53	57
2000	3,196,991	5,366,570	5,993,550	55	60
2004	3,477,500	5,946,430	6,607,650	55	61
2005	3,784,141	6,170,340	6,798,410	56	61
2006	3,956,992	6,271,850	6,802,750	58	63
2007	4,329,412	6,448,860	6,944,390	62	67
2008	4,572,327	6,641,570	7,203,230	63	69

Sources: Data provided by Superintendency of Pensions and Institute of Pension Normalization.

Table 8.2   Number of Pensioners in the Old and New Pension Systems, 1990–2008

Year	Pensioners in old system	Pensioners in new system	New pensioners/ AFP contributors (%)	New pensioners/ total pensioners (%)
1990	894,359	57,119	2.2	6.0
1995	872,946	190,400	6.4	17.9
2000	878,297	343,965	10.8	28.6
2005	882,175	574,011	15.2	39.4
2008	795,305	693,929	15.2	46.6

Sources: Data provided by Superintendency of Pensions and Institute of Pension Normalization.

The Insurance Sector

The increase in the number of pensioners from the AFP system has led to a strong demand for both annuities and PWs and fast growth of the Chilean insurance sector in the past decade. As shown in figure 8.1, total insurance premiums increased from 2.7 percent of GDP in 1990 to about 4.0 percent of GDP in 2001 to 2003. This growth was followed by a decrease to levels of about 3.2 percent in 2006 and a subsequent recovery to levels of about 4.0 percent. The evolution of insurance premiums has been driven primarily by the life sector, and fluctuations in life business have been driven in turn by the expansion of the annuity business. The tightening of the early retirement conditions in 2004 explains the reduction in premiums written by life insurance companies between 2004 and 2006. As the old-age annuity market matures, the total premium is expected to recover in the future.

The expansion of the insurance sector is also reflected in its total assets, which grew from about 5 percent of GDP in the mid-1980s to about 20 percent of GDP in 2003. With the exception of 2008, where figures are volatile because of the effect of the financial crisis, the ratio of total assets of insurance companies to GDP has remained relatively stable since 2003. As shown in figure 8.2, the assets of the insurance sector are still smaller than the assets of the pension sector. The increase in the ratio of insurance assets to pension assets between 1990 and 2003 was followed by decreases in this ratio to a level similar to that prevailing in 2009. This declining trend is partially explained by regulatory changes that tightened the requirements for early retirement.[4]

Chile has the highest level of life insurance premiums relative to GDP in Latin America and compares well with high-income OECD countries. As shown in table 8.3, life insurance premiums are three times the Latin American average and about two-thirds the OECD average. This result is essentially due to the large size of annuity and PW premiums, which

Figure 8.1   Insurance Premiums in Chile, 1990–2008

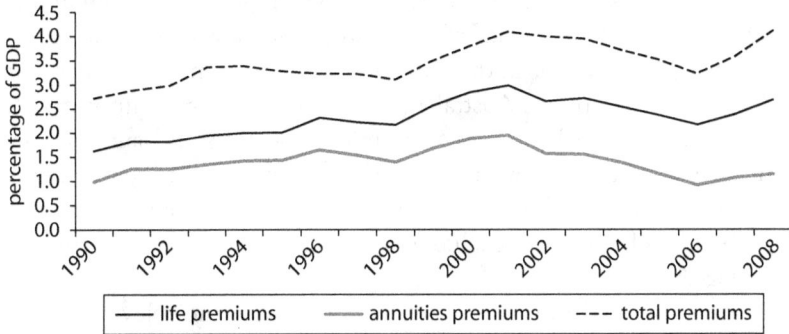

Source: Data provided by Superintendency of Securities and Insurance.

Figure 8.2   Pension and Insurance Assets, 1990–2008

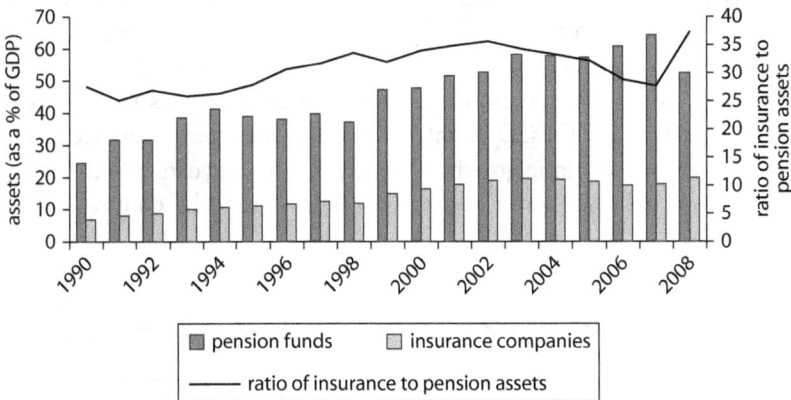

Sources: Data provided by Superintendency of Securities and Insurance and Superintendency of Pension Fund Administrators.

Table 8.3   Insurance Premiums in Chile, Latin America, and the OECD, 2007–08

| | Percentage of GDP | | | | | |
| | Chile | | Latin America | | High-income OECD | |
Type of insurance	2007	2008	2007	2008	2007	2008
Total insurance premiums	4.1	4.5	2.6	2.6	7.7	7.5
Life insurance	2.7	2.9	1.0	1.0	4.7	4.5
of which PW in AFPs[a]	0.5	0.5	n.a.	n.a.	n.a.	n.a.
Nonlife insurance	1.4	1.6	1.6	1.7	3.1	3.0

Sources: Data provided by Swiss Re and Superintendency of Pensions.
Note: n.a. = not applicable; OECD = Organisation for Economic Co-operation and Development.
a. Estimated.

amounted to about 2.4 percent of GDP and almost 70 percent of life premiums.[5] The lack of accurate information on annuity and PW premiums in OECD countries does not allow a direct comparison, but the size of annuity and PW markets in the OECD is known to be much smaller than in Chile. For example, in Australia (a country with a mandatory, private DC pension system like Chile's) premiums on PWs and annuities are equivalent to only 0.8 percent of GDP and 16 percent of life premiums. In the United States, the share of single immediate life annuities is only 7 percent of life business, excluding variable annuities in the accumulation stage.[6]

Comparing total insurance assets in Chile with the relevant benchmarks yields similar conclusions. As shown in table 8.4, the ratio of insurance assets to GDP in Chile is about four times larger than the Latin American average, and the difference is primarily because of the large volume of annuity assets in Chile. The ratio of insurance assets to GDP is still smaller than the OECD average, but the share of annuity-related assets is probably larger than in most OECD countries (a straight comparison of annuity assets is not possible because of the lack of information). Moreover, combining pension and insurance assets places Chile at the same level as many OECD countries and indicates that insurance assets in Chile should continue growing strongly in coming years because these amounts include pension accounts that will need to be converted into

Table 8.4   Assets of Insurance Companies in Chile, Latin America, and the OECD, 2006

Type of company	Assets (as a % of GDP)		
	Chile	Latin America	High-income OECD[a]
All insurance companies	18.6	4.8	55.4[b]
Life insurance	17.6	—	47.4[c]
Nonlife insurance	1.0	—	10.4[d]
Pension funds	61.0	15.1	39.0
Insurance plus pension funds	79.6	19.9	94.4

Sources: Data provided by Asociación Internacional de Organismos de Supervisión de Fondos de Pensiones, Axco Insurance Information Services, OECD, Superintendency of Pensions, and Superintendency of Securities and Insurance.

Note: — = not available; OECD = Organisation for Economic Co-operation and Development.

a. High-income OECD excludes Chile, Hungary, Mexico, Poland, the Slovak Republic, and Turkey.

b. This figure excludes New Zealand.

c. This figure excludes Belgium, the Czech Republic, Iceland, the Netherlands, New Zealand, Portugal, Spain, and Sweden.

d. This figure excludes Belgium, the Czech Republic, Iceland, the Netherlands, Portugal, Spain, and Sweden.

annuities and PWs at retirement.[7] All in all, the data indicate that the Chilean market for retirement products is already large by international standards and should continue to expand in the coming decades as the second-pillar pension system matures.

The Structure of the Market for Retirement Products

Chile has adopted a competitive decentralized institutional structure for its retirement market. Only institutions specializing in pension fund administration and life insurance are authorized to offer retirement products. These institutions are established as profit-seeking commercial undertakings. There are no not-for-profit mutual groups, and central agencies offering common services to all competing institutions have only a very small presence.[8]

Strong competition exists among a small number of AFPs in the accumulation market and among a larger number of insurance companies in the annuity market.[9] The competitive environment has resulted in large marketing costs, mostly taking the form of high commissions paid to agents and brokers. However, a growing consolidation of the two markets (which is much more pronounced among pension administrators), the threat of regulation, and the adoption of informal agreements among competing institutions in the two main segments of the market have recently resulted in a major containment of marketing costs.

The potential role that central agencies can play in collecting contributions, paying benefits, and maintaining accounts—all activities that are characterized by large economies of scale—has been considered but not adopted in Chile; however, more intensive use of electronic payment systems is expected in the future.[10] On one hand, competitive decentralized asset management structure would stimulate innovation and efficiency, which are essential for attaining high investment returns. On the other hand, centralized administration lowers operating costs because of scale economies and avoidance of high marketing costs, while the centralized offer of life annuities could benefit from using a larger customer base and thus more efficient risk pooling.

The structure of the pension and life insurance sectors evolved very differently in the past 20 years. As shown in figure 8.3, the pension sector became very concentrated during the 1990s, with the number of AFPs declining from 20 in the 1980s to 8 between 1990 and 2000 and to only 6 more recently. This reduction in the number of participating institutions was reflected in a sharp increase in concentration ratios. As shown in figure 8.4, the three largest AFPs increased their combined market

Figure 8.3   Number of Life Insurance Companies, Annuity Providers, and AFPs, 1990–2008

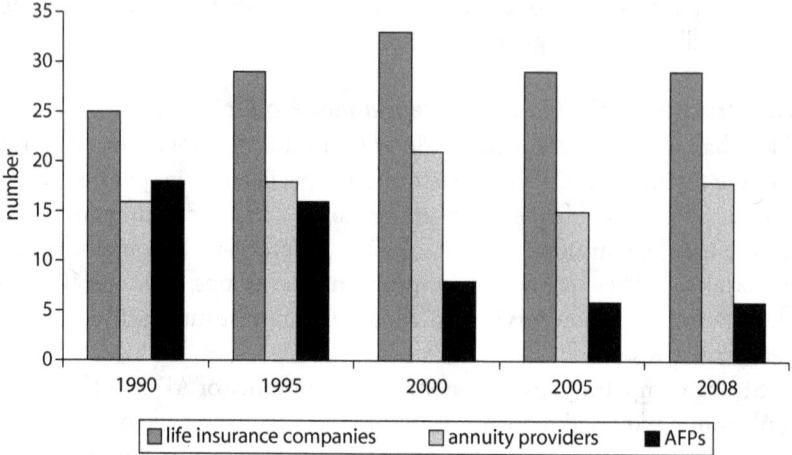

Source: Data provided by Superintendency of Securities and Insurance.
Note: AFP = administrador de fondo de pensión, or pension fund administrator.

Figure 8.4   Market Concentration Ratios in Pensions and Annuities: Herfindahl Ratio and Share of Three Largest Firms, 1988–2005

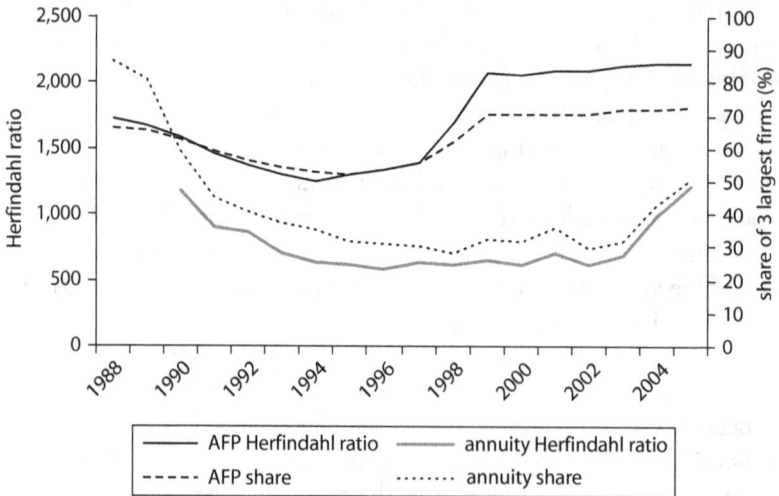

Sources: Data provided by Superintendency of Securities and Insurance and Superintendency of Pensions.

share significantly and now account for more than 70 percent of total assets. The increase in the Herfindahl index is even more pronounced.[11]

By contrast, the fast increase in the number of annuity contracts in the 1990s attracted new entrants to the life insurance market, increasing the total number of life insurance companies to 33 by 2000, 21 of which were providing annuities. At that time, foreign participation was substantial, accounting for two-thirds of total capital. The annuity market was very concentrated in its early stages—by the end of the 1980s, the share of the three largest firms in the annuity business amounted to 87 percent. The increase in the number of participants in the 1990s led to a continuous decrease in concentration ratios, and one decade later the share of the three largest firms had declined to less than 30 percent (about 10 percent each).

The past decade has been characterized by the active entry and exit of companies from the annuity segment. The annuity market is highly competitive and operates with thin intermediation spreads and relatively low returns on equity. The electronic quotation system for annuities introduced in 2004 has contributed to greater transparency and price competition, opening room for some firms to gain market share and encouraging others to leave the market. These factors have resulted in an increase in concentration ratios, whether measured by the three-firm concentration ratio or the Herfindahl index. However, the annuity sector in Chile today still remains more competitive than the AFP sector, whether measured by the number of participants or by concentration ratios. Also important is that life insurance companies that decide to exit the annuity market can enter the market again if the conditions prove attractive; that is, the annuity market not only remains less concentrated than the AFP market but also looks more contestable. In 2008, 29 life insurance companies were operating, 18 of which were offering annuities. Some life insurance companies with a small market share in the segment of mandatory savings for retirement have found more profitable business in the less competitive market of voluntary savings.

Government Guarantees

Because participation in the pension system is mandatory for all new workers, the state has provided four types of guarantees. The first two apply to the accumulation phase and include a minimum relative return guarantee and a guarantee of coverage against disability and death risks. The minimum relative return guarantee involves the obligation of AFPs to ensure a minimum return relative to the industry's average. If the AFP cannot honor this obligation with its capital and *encaje*,[12] it is subjected to supervisory intervention, and the government provides the required resources to raise the return to the minimum level. The second guarantee ensures that workers remain properly covered against disability and death risks, in case the insurer defaults in its obligations.[13]

The third and fourth guarantees apply to the retirement phase and include a recently introduced solidarity pension pillar, which includes a basic solidarity pension (*pensión básica solidaria*, or PBS) and a pension solidarity supplement (*aporte previsional solidario*, or APS) and a guarantee against the bankruptcy of annuity providers.

In 2008, the government introduced amendments to the pension system aimed at strengthening the solidarity pillar. Before these amendments, the poverty protection system included two programs: (a) the Care of Elderly Pension (Pensión Asistencial de Ancianidad, or PASIS), which was a means-tested benefit given to poor elderly people who were not receiving any sort of pension, and (b) the minimum pension, which was offered to pensioners of the private pension funds who fulfilled minimum requirements of eligibility, including a minimum of 20 years of contributions. The government found that the then-existing structure of PASIS and the minimum pension did not provide incentives for low-income individuals to contribute and that the coverage was limited.

The new solidarity pillar serves as an alternative to improve the coverage of the pension system and to improve the retirement benefits of low-income individuals with limited capacity to contribute to the pension system. Because the support of the solidarity pillar is linked to the amount of contributions to the pension system, low-income individuals always have incentives to contribute to the funded pillar. The old PASIS was replaced by a noncontributory PBS of approximately US$150 (75,000 Chilean pesos [Ch$]) per month in 2009. It will be paid to all aged people with no pension of their own. The benefit initially covered 40 percent of the poorest individuals, but it will be gradually extended to 60 percent of the poorest population by 2011 (table 8.5). The APS was also introduced as a top up for pensions to all aged persons who are in the lowest three quintiles (60 percent) of the income distribution and have a pension from the private system. The APS will be equal to the PBS but subject to a clawback provision of eventually 29.4 percent of the private pension (not the total income) of eligible pensioners. The APS will be exhausted when the private pension equals 3.4 times the PBS in steady state. This level is known as the maximum pension with solidarity support (*pensión máxima con aporte solidario*, or PMAS). Between 2010

Table 8.5   Benefits Included in the 2008 Amendments to the Pension Law

Date	PBS (Ch$)	PMAS (Ch$)	Coverage target (%)
July 2009	75,000	120,000	45
September 2009	75,000	150,000	50
July 2010	75,000	200,000	55
July 2011[a]	75,000	255,000	60

Source: Data provided by Superintendency of Pensions.
a. Initially these changes were expected to take place in 2012, but they were modified by law in 2009.

and 2011, the PMAS will increase gradually from approximately US$300 to approximately US$500 per month (figure 8.5).[14] After 2012, these benefits will be indexed to price inflation.

The 2008 amendment to the pension law addressed one of the major concerns of the Chilean pension system, which was the problem of coverage of self-employed workers. The new law gradually extends mandatory coverage to self-employed workers. In the first stage, self-employed individuals are encouraged to contribute to the pension system by establishing the payment of contributions in their default option in the annual declaration of taxable income. Suggested rates are set at 4, 7, and 10 percent of the taxable income for 2012, 2013, and 2014, respectively. During the transition period, which lasts until 2014, self-employed individuals have the option of not contributing to their pension fund, but they need to actively make such a request. Starting in 2015, self-employed individuals will be required to contribute to the pension system at a rate of 10 percent of their taxable income (the same rate that applies to dependent workers). According to Berstein and others (2009), this measure is expected to increase pension coverage by more than 1 million workers.[15]

The fourth stage is a guarantee in the case of insurance company failure. If a self-employed worker's annuity provider defaults, the government covers 100 percent of his or her annuity up to the PBS and 75 percent of the amount above this level up to a maximum of UF 45 per month (approximately US$1,900).

The Conditions for Retirement

Workers can retire at the normal retirement age of 65 for men and 60 for women. Early retirement is allowed if a sufficient balance has been accumulated in a worker's account. Before 2004, this balance was defined as that needed to generate a pension equal to at least 50 percent of the worker's average real wage over the preceding 10 years as well as

Figure 8.5   Chile's Solidarity Pillar

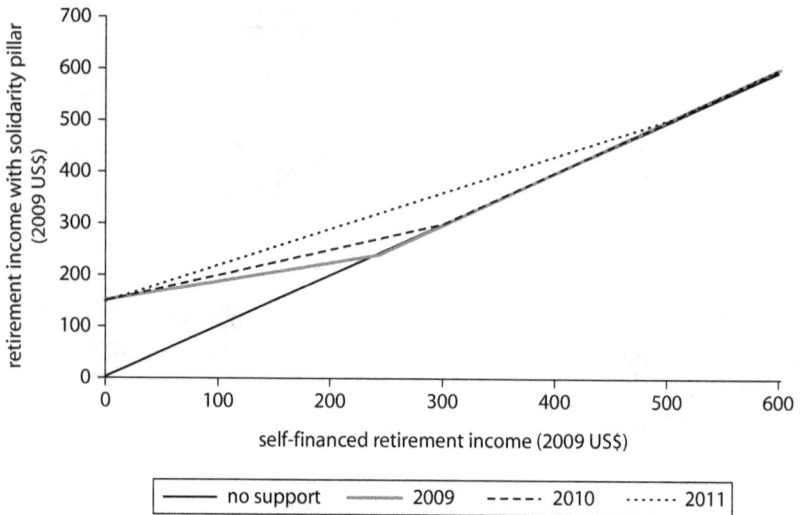

Source: Data provided by Superintendency of Pensions.

at least 110 percent of the minimum pension. The 2004 amendments to the pension law raised these parameters to 70 percent and 150 percent, respectively, and introduced a stricter definition of the average real wage, excluding periods of no contributions. The 2008 amendments to the pension law maintain the 70 percent of the real average wage requirement but replace the minimum pension requirement with an 80 percent of the PMAS requirement.[16]

The changes in the parameters in 2004 were introduced in reaction to the rapid growth of the number of early retirees and the concomitant decline in the average age of retirement. As tables 8.6 and 8.7 show, by 2004 roughly 540,000 workers had retired under the new system, the proportion of early retirees had increased to more than 40 percent of the total, and the average age of retirement had declined by three years among early retirees. Early retirees outnumbered normal-age retirees by 65 percent. Early retirement in Chile does not necessarily imply withdrawal from the labor force, and the average pension of early retirees is higher than the average pension of normal old-age retirees, because their incomes are higher (table 8.8). Nonetheless, a concern arose that the retirement rules were too liberal, that many workers were encouraged to retire early by insurance brokers, and that there was a risk of low

Table 8.6   Breakdown of Pensioners by Type of Retirement, 1985–2007

Year	Total	Normal old age		Early retirement		Disability plus survivors	
		Number	% of total	Number	% of total	Number	% of total
1985	7,609	2,647	34.8	n.a.	0.0	4,962	65.2
1990	57,119	23,876	41.8	5,790	10.1	27,453	48.1
1995	190,400	55,591	29.2	69,537	36.5	65,272	34.3
2000	343,965	93,152	27.1	132,221	38.4	118,592	34.5
2004	540,342	134,207	24.8	221,201	40.9	184,916	34.2
2005	574,011	148,096	25.8	229,033	39.9	196,882	34.3
2006	606,342	163,223	26.9	233,384	38.5	209,735	34.6
2007	642,064	179,146	27.9	239,790	37.3	223,128	34.8

Source: Data provided by Superintendency of Pensions.
Note: n.a. = not applicable.

Table 8.7   Average Retirement Age by Type of Retirement, 1988–2007

Type of retirement	1988–90	1991–95	1996–2000	2001–03	2004–07
Old age	65	65	65	64	64
Men	67	67	67	66	66
Women	63	62	62	62	62
Early retirement	58	57	56	55	54
Men	58	57	56	56	56
Women	56	55	54	53	53

Source: Data provided by Superintendency of Pensions.

Table 8.8   Average Monthly Pensions by Type, 1990–2007

Period	Period average (UF)				
	Old age	Early retirement	Disability	Survivorship	Average pension
1990–94	5.6	9.5	7.4	2.7	5.7
1995–99	6.1	9.8	7.7	3.2	6.8
2000–04	6.8	10.2	8.2	3.7	7.4
2005–07	7.7	10.7	9.1	4.7	8.2

Source: Data provided by Superintendency of Pensions.

replacement rates in the future, with possible fiscal consequences through access to the minimum pension guaranteed (MPG), which was the PBS predecessor.[17]

The stricter retirement conditions introduced in the 2004 amendments to the pension law were successful in reducing the proportion of early retirees from 41 percent to 37 percent of the total retirees from

2004 to 2007, respectively. Early retirees accounted for 18 percent of the increase in the number of all pensioners, underscoring the effect of the tighter restrictions. In addition, because the average retirement income of old-age retirees grows at a faster pace than that of early retirees, opting for early retirement becomes relatively less attractive (table 8.8). The sustained increase in retirement income of old-age retirees is one of the clear indicators of the maturity of the pension system.

After medical examination, workers with disabilities are entitled to a full or partial disability pension, depending on the severity of their condition. Partially disabled pensioners need to be recertified after a period of three years, but fully disabled pensioners do not require recertification.[18] Unlike old-age and early retirement pensions, disability pensions are determined according to a defined benefit formula and amount to 70 percent of the average real wage of the worker in the 10 years preceding the disability. Survivor pensions are defined as 50 percent of the average wage of the worker who dies before retirement. This amount is paid to the surviving spouse; each surviving child under 21 years of age receives an additional 15 percent. In the early phase of the new pension system, most pensioners were disability and survivor pensioners with few old-age retirees. This pattern was expected because most retiring workers in the early 1980s preferred to stay in the old system. The share of disability and survivor pensioners has recently stabilized at about one-third of the total.[19]

The Menu and Performance of Retirement Products

Retiring workers can take a partial lump-sum payment subject to strict conditions and can also choose from three basic retirement products: a phased withdrawal, a life annuity, and a temporary withdrawal (TW) combined with a deferred life annuity. This section briefly describes these products. Before 2004, workers could take a partial lump sum if they met strict conditions—namely, the remaining balance had to be sufficient to finance a pension equal to at least 50 percent of the average real wage of the worker in the 10 years preceding retirement and 110 percent of the MPG. In 2004, the first condition was raised to 70 percent and the second to 150 percent of the MPG. In 2008, the second condition was replaced by a requirement to reach 80 percent of the PMAS. Relatively few workers drew partial lump sums, and the amounts were generally considered small. After the change in the rules, the incidence of early retirement was substantially reduced.

The basic condition for buying a life annuity at the normal retirement age is that it must be higher than the PBS.[20] Workers who do not meet this basic condition must use a PW at the PBS level from their own account until the balance is exhausted. The 2008 amendments to the law introduced an additional actuarial factor in the calculation of the PW to account for the risk of longevity. Use of the actuarial factor will require pensioners to have enough resources until they reach 105 years of age to receive an income equal to at least 30 percent of the first PW or 30 percent of the reference annuity.[21] As shown in figure 8.6, the introduction of an actuarial factor in the calculation of PWs will reduce the probability of receiving an income lower than the PBS and, consequently, the contingent liability of the government. This amendment was introduced because of the moral hazard incentives for individuals who preferred PWs to take advantage of the fiscal subsidy through the MPG or PBS when the retiree ran out of resources for earning the minimum pension. Because the attractiveness of PWs will decrease compared to life annuities, demand for PWs likely will come mostly from retirees with low life expectancy who are interested in leaving bequests.

Figure 8.6   Phased Withdrawals under the New Pension Law

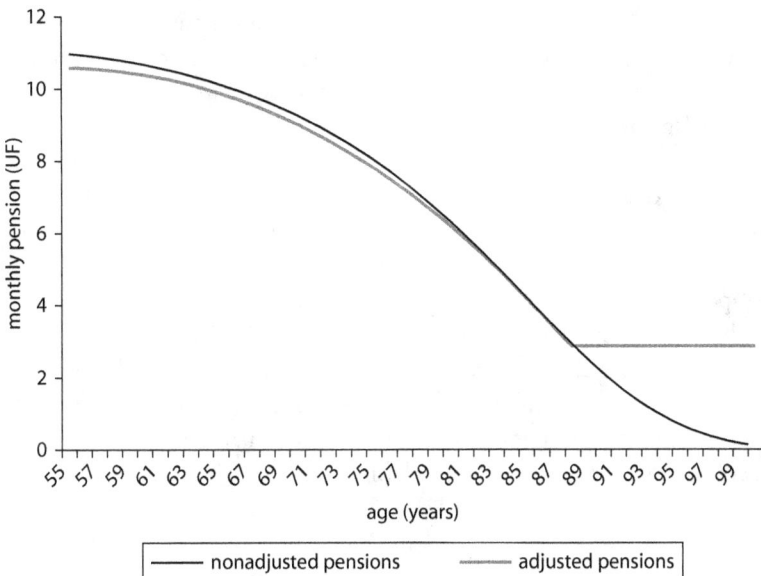

Source: Data provided by Superintendency of Pensions.

Annuities are provided by life insurance companies and are freely priced according to age, gender, and market conditions—particularly the level of interest rates. Workers can choose any of the licensed companies at retirement. Until recently, all annuities were fixed and indexed to prices (fixed real annuities) and denominated in UFs. The 2004 pension law introduced other options, including combinations of PWs and fixed real annuities as well as combinations of variable and fixed real annuities in the case of higher-income people. Married couples have to buy joint life annuities. The reversion rate for joint life annuities is 60 percent for the surviving dependent beneficiary. Annuities with a guaranteed period of payment are optional. They entitle the surviving spouse to receive the same level of annuity as the main beneficiary during the guarantee period.

In the PW option, the individual balance remains in the AFP and is drawn according to a formula that takes into consideration life expectancy and the possibility of triggering the PBS. In the past, PW holders had no choice of fund: their balances were invested in the same diversified portfolio of assets as active workers. Before 2008, PW holders were allowed to choose from three different funds, which were differentiated according to the maximum share of equities that they could hold—40 percent, 20 percent, and 0 percent, respectively (active workers had access to two additional funds, which could hold more equities). From 2008, PW holders are allowed to choose from the five different funds offered by AFPs, under the condition that the contributor have enough resources to finance a pension equivalent to the value of the PMAS and that the calculated pension be at least 70 percent of the real wage over the past 10 years. At the end of each year, PW payments are recalculated on the basis of the residual balance and the drawdown formula. PW holders can decide to draw less than the formula, provided it is at least equal to the PBS, but not more. PW holders can also switch to a life annuity at any time during retirement, provided that the annuity exceeds the PBS. After the death of the main beneficiary, the spouse continues receiving the PW payments, and following his or her death, the residual balance goes to the heirs as a bequest.

TWs involve a fixed drawdown for a predefined number of years (most commonly one year), followed by a deferred life annuity. The market for deferred annuities for periods longer than two years has not developed. The size of the two types of payouts is defined jointly at the time of retirement, and the balance is split accordingly between the AFP and the selected insurance company. The TW payout cannot be lower than either the PBS or the eventual annuity and cannot be higher than twice the level of the eventual annuity. TWs differ from PWs in that they involve a deferred annuity and can be considered an annuity for all practical purposes.

These three retirement products have different strong and weak features and appeal to workers with different needs and risk profiles. Fixed real annuities provide protection against inflation, investment, and longevity risks but do not allow bequests, unless the annuities are guaranteed. The holder is subject to the risk of bankruptcy of the annuity provider, although this risk is reduced by the annuity guarantee. PWs allow their holders to share the gains in the capital market. If returns are high, PW payments may even increase in the initial years. They also allow bequests. However, PWs expose holders to investment and longevity risks. PW payments decline over time and eventually reach the PBS level. Introduction of the actuarial factor in the calculation of the PW reduces the probability of reaching the PBS level. TWs offer the possibility of larger initial payouts in the early years, combined with longevity insurance when the deferred annuity is received.

The Demand for Retirement Products and Level of Annuitization

The number of retirees choosing annuities has increased considerably in the past 20 years. As shown in table 8.9, only 3 percent of the number of pensioners chose annuities in 1985, whereas in 2007 this percentage increased to 58 percent (including the small number of TW holders). Excluding disability and survivor pensioners, the share of retirees who selected annuitization reached 71 percent. No data are published on the size of accumulated balances that are used for PWs, and thus no data are published on the share of accumulated balances that is annuitized. However, this proportion is also likely to be close to 70 percent.

These numbers imply one of the highest levels of annuitization in the world. The average annuity payment is significantly higher than the average PW payment, as shown in table 8.10, indicating that the average income of the annuitant population is higher. The average TW payment is much higher, reflecting a segment of higher-income annuity holders.

Table 8.9   Breakdown of Number of Pensions by Type of Instrument, 1985–2007

Year	Total	PWs Number	% of total	TWs Number	% of total	Annuities Number	% of total
1985	7,609	7,373	96.8	0	0.0	236	3.2
1990	57,119	36,696	64.2	148	0.3	20,275	35.5
1995	190,400	98,699	51.8	6,803	3.6	84,898	44.6
2000	343,965	147,532	42.9	6,632	1.9	189,801	55.2
2005	557,712	214,239	38.4	6,917	1.2	336,556	60.4
2007	626,405	252,095	40.2	8,578	1.4	365,732	58.4

Source: Data provided by Superintendency of Pensions.

Unlike other countries, such as Denmark and Sweden, Chile has very detailed and comprehensive data on the use of annuities (table 8.11). Most annuities are joint life, reflecting the regulation that forced married men to take this type of annuity.[22] The share of deferred annuities in the flows of annuities increased slightly from 20 to 30 percent, but the period of deferment has remained short, about one year. The short period of deferment helps explain the low share of TWs in the total stock of retirement products.

The share of guaranteed-period annuities is large, and most of these annuities are guaranteed for periods of 10 to 15 years or even longer. The strong demand for guaranteed-period annuities reveals a voluntary insurance or income-smoothing arrangement within the family unit as

Table 8.10   Average Pensions by Instrument, 1990–2007

Period	Period average (UF)			
	PWs	Annuities	TWs	Average pension
1990–94	3.8	7.5	25.0	5.7
1995–99	4.8	7.5	23.4	6.8
2000–04	5.0	7.9	26.7	7.4
2005–07	5.4	9.5	26.7	8.2

Source: Data provided by Superintendency of Pensions.

Table 8.11   Types of Annuities Issued in March 1999, 2002, 2003, 2004, and 2005

Type of annuity	March 1999	March 2002	March 2003	March 2004	March 2005
Total number of annuities issued	937	1,517	1,193	1,490	1,391
Number of joint annuities	670	1,069	823	973	763
Number of deferred annuities	199	331	307	409	419
(% of total)	(21.2)	(21.8)	(25.7)	(27.5)	(30.1)
Number deferred for 12 months	164	275	238	322	315
Number of guaranteed annuities	708	1,191	948	1,153	1,093
(% of total)	(85.6)	(78.5)	(79.5)	(77.4)	(78.6)
Number guaranteed for 10 and 15 years	666	1,088	846	1,016	912

Source: Data provided by Superintendency of Securities and Insurance.

well as a preference for bequests. The main beneficiary accepts a lower payment in exchange for maintenance of the same payment to the surviving spouse during the guaranteed period (when the guarantee expires, the payment is reduced to 60 percent of the main annuity). If both die, the heirs keep receiving the payments during the guaranteed period. In the case of single annuities, payments go directly to the heirs during the guaranteed period.

A very strong association exists between annuitization and early retirement. As shown in panel a of figure 8.7, approximately two-thirds of normal-age retirees use PWs, and only one-third purchase annuities. By contrast, 90 percent of early retirees buy annuities, and only 10 percent use PWs (panel b of figure 8.7). From the point of view of the retirement product (panel d in figure 8.7), 60 percent of all annuitants are early retirees, and only 15 percent are normal-age retirees (the remainder are retirees with disabilities and survivors). If retirees with disabilities and survivors are excluded, the share of early retirees in the number of annuities increases to 80 percent.

The high rate of annuitization and its relation to early retirement is the result of several factors. First, restrictions on lump-sum payments increase the demand for all retirement products, including annuities.

Second, the absence of a front-ended public pillar benefit before 2008 implies that middle- and higher-income retirees who use PWs are substantially exposed to investment and longevity risks. These retirees have no other stable source of retirement income and can experience a large erosion of the real value of their pensions if they take a PW. Therefore, they may find the protection provided by life annuities attractive. Although the introduction of the solidarity pillar has multiple benefits for low- and middle-income individuals, it is unlikely to change this behavior because the value of the PBS is only 46 percent of the value of the old MPG.[23] Moreover, these retirees tend to be early retirees precisely because only higher-income retirees can meet the conditions for early retirement.

Third, low-income workers whose benefits were close to the old MPG found PWs more attractive because they could enjoy any high returns in the early stages of retirement without being exposed to downside risk. If returns proved weak, they would receive the old MPG anyway. The introduction of the actuarial factor in the calculation of PWs in the 2008 amendments to the law and the reduction in the level of the minimum pension are likely to reduce this preference for PWs. In general, PW holders tend to be lower-income workers retiring at the normal age, precisely because they cannot meet the conditions for early retirement. The PW

Figure 8.7   Shares of Phased Withdrawals and Annuities, 1990–2007

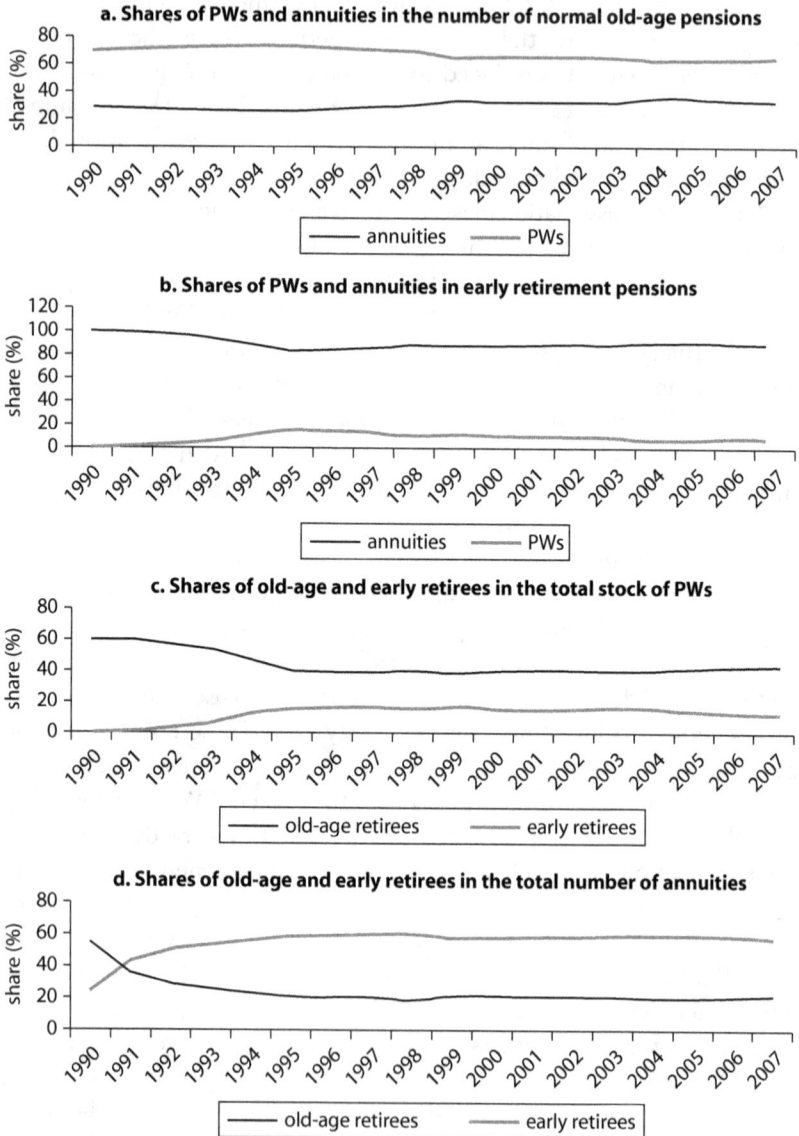

Source: Data provided by Superintendency of Pensions.

population also includes low-income workers who are forced to take PWs because of their very small balances.

Finally, the marketing of retirement products has been one-sided. AFPs focus on the accumulation phase of the pension business and do not market PWs actively. In contrast, life insurance companies depend on the annuity business and have marketed their products aggressively. Insurance brokers obtain their income from commissions on annuity premiums. They target their marketing efforts primarily to higher-income workers, frequently encouraging these workers to retire early and annuitize. Brokers do not receive any commission from a client or provider in the case of the client taking a PW.[24]

The Performance of Phased Withdrawals

The pension market has been extensively examined in the literature. Most researchers conclude that AFPs have generated high real returns on managed funds but have charged—and still levy—high operating fees to contributors. As of May 2008, at the bottom of the financial crisis, gross and net real returns have averaged 9.2 percent per year and 6.2 percent per year, respectively, since the creation of the system in 1981, well above the average annual rate of growth of real wages of 2 percent over the same period. At the same time, the difference of 3 percentage points between gross and net investment returns reflects the high fees that have been charged. This difference reflects the high costs and very high profit margins during this period. In the past 15 years, with the sole exception of 2008, AFPs have always earned real returns on equity (ROEs) above 20 percent, and in some years, the average ROE reached 50 percent.

AFP operating costs and fees have declined significantly in the past 20 years but still remain high. In 2007 to 2008, total fees amounted to 1.0 to 1.3 percent of assets, including fees of about 64 basis points paid to foreign asset managers.[25] Fees paid by pension funds to international mutual funds have decreased from about 100 basis points in 2003 to about 64 basis points in 2009. By comparison, the average costs of U.S. occupational pension funds of similar size are about 0.5 percent of assets. The average fees of U.S. mutual funds of similar size are about 1 percent of assets, but these funds include equity funds with high turnover. Bond funds and equity funds with low turnover have much lower fees.[26] These figures indicate that an opportunity still exists for reducing operating fees, costs, and profit margins in the AFP sector.

The 2008 amendments to the law required that new entrants should be allocated to the pension fund that levies the lowest fees. In January 2010, through an open bidding process, the Superintendency of Pensions selected the AFP that offered to charge the lowest fee to its contributors. This fee was approximately 24 percent lower than the weighted average of the fees charged by the AFP industry.

The AFP market has generally performed better for PW holders than for active contributors, because pensioners earn the same rates of return as active workers in the three portfolios in which they are allowed to invest but are charged much lower fees. Although the multifund regime, created in 2002, allowed active workers and PW holders to choose between five and three different portfolios, the 2008 amendments to the law allow retirees with higher expected retirement income to choose among the five pension funds as well. At the same time, PW holders are charged much lower fees for the management of their accounts. AFPs do not maintain a sales force for the promotion of PWs and charge a fee of only 1 percent on PW benefits paid, an amount that is designed to cover just marginal administrative costs. AFPs have been able to generate high returns on equity, but these returns are derived from the accumulation phase, not the payout phase.[27]

The Performance of Annuities and Money's Worth Ratios

Assessing market performance in the annuity market involves the use of more elaborate indicators, given the different nature of annuity contracts and their very long duration. One indicator that is commonly used is the money's worth ratio (MWR), defined as the ratio of the expected present value of benefit payments to the annuity premium. This indicator measures how much the annuitant receives back for the premium paid. A ratio equal to 1 is usually interpreted as an actuarially fair annuity. Table 8.12 provides information on MWRs for all annuities issued in March 1999, 2002, 2003, 2004, and 2005.

As shown in table 8.12, the average MWR was slightly lower than 1 in 1999 and has been above 1 since then, indicating that Chilean annuitants have generally received good value for their premiums. However, the dispersion between the maximum and minimum ratios has been wide, amounting to 40 percent in some years and suggesting that some annuitants may have obtained less favorable terms. Average MWRs are lower for younger retirees, consistent with the greater investment and longevity risks involved in annuities with longer durations. MWRs are lower for joint annuities by comparison with single annuities, consistent with their longer duration as well.

MWRs are higher for larger premiums, indicating that insurance companies are willing to pay higher annuity rates for larger balances, just as banks pay higher interest rates for larger deposits, because unit costs are lower and profit margins are higher in these cases. MWRs of single female annuities are higher than those of single male annuities, despite their longer expected duration. This result may be partly caused by the higher average premium in the case of single females. MWRs of guaranteed

Table 8.12   Average Money's Worth Ratios for Annuities Issued in March of 1999, 2002, 2003, 2004, and 2005

Annuity characteristics	March				
	1999	2002	2003	2004	2005
All cases	0.978	1.080	1.036	1.064	1.062
Maximum	1.148	1.222	1.181	1.276	1.223
Minimum	0.755	0.872	0.872	0.876	0.706
Male, age 55	0.981	1.081	1.056	1.036	1.042
Male, age 65	0.996	1.098	1.066	1.042	1.067
Female, age 55	0.994	1.105	1.056	1.060	1.064
Female, age 60	1.021	1.120	1.066	1.074	1.083
Joint life (male age 65, female age 60)	0.998	1.089	1.058	1.062	1.069
Premium up to UF 1,000	0.980	1.078	1.045	1.068	1.067
Premium above UF 3,000	0.997	1.099	1.047	1.075	1.071
Nonguaranteed	0.990	1.092	1.045	1.071	1.073
Guaranteed	0.974	1.076	1.033	1.062	1.059
Without deferment	0.979	1.079	1.035	1.063	1.061
With deferment	0.974	1.080	1.036	1.067	1.064

Source: Rocha and Thorburn 2007, annex 1.

annuities are lower than those of nonguaranteed annuities, because long guarantee periods change the time path of payments and increase duration. Finally, the MWRs of deferred annuities are higher than those of nondeferred annuities, but the difference is marginal.

The availability of a large data set on individual annuities in Chile has allowed the formal testing of these relationships.[28] Annex 1 of Rocha and Thorburn (2007) contains a detailed analysis of MWRs. This analysis shows that MWRs have been positively and significantly related to the age of the annuitant and the size of the premium—and negatively and significantly related to the length of the guarantee period. It also shows that annuities with longer expected durations have lower MWRs than annuities with shorter expected durations and that larger premiums get better value on average than smaller ones. This finding is consistent with the view that insurers are concerned with the higher reinvestment and longevity risks presented by long durations and, in the case of size, the effect of fixed expense loadings is more significant in the Chilean market than attempts to differentiate mortality between annuitants of different income levels.

At the same time, the analysis shows that nearly 40 percent of the variation in individual MWRs is not explained by these individual characteristics. The wide dispersion between the highest and lowest annuity is intriguing and is especially wide for lower premiums, indicating that market search may be more inefficient among lower-income retirees. Further examination of the data set reveals that annuitants with the same characteristics, such as age, premium, and gender, frequently receive materially different annuities.

Comparing average MWRs in Chile with those estimated for other countries suggests that Chilean annuitants have generally received a better deal than annuitants in other countries, especially considering that Chilean annuities are indexed to inflation. As shown in tables 8.12 and 8.13, average MWRs in Chile are higher than the average nominal MWRs estimated for other countries, which range from 0.9 to 1.0. The differences are striking in the case of inflation-indexed annuities: buyers of indexed annuities in the United Kingdom receive a much lower annuity value of 86 percent of the premium, and they pay a charge of about 5 percent of the premium to obtain inflation protection. The cost of inflation protection in the United States is even higher, amounting to more than 20 percent of the premium. This result is explained, at least in part, by the larger supply of inflation-indexed instruments in Chile, including not only indexed government bonds, but also other higher-yield, fixed interest instruments that allow providers to hedge inflation risk while obtaining more attractive returns.[29]

Although the differences between MWRs of inflation-indexed annuities in Chile and MWRs of such annuities in other countries can be reasonably explained, other differences cannot be easily interpreted. For example, the relationship between MWRs and age is negative in the case

Table 8.13   Average Money's Worth Ratios in Selected Countries

Annuity characteristic	Australia	Canada	Switzerland	United Kingdom	United States
Nominal annuities					
Male, age 55	—	—	—	0.921	0.934
Male, age 65	1.013	0.981	1.046	0.908	0.927
Female, age 55	—	—	—	0.928	0.937
Female, age 65	1.002	0.976	1.037	0.907	0.927
Joint	0.988	0.980	0.985	—	0.929
Indexed Annuities					
Male, age 55	—	—	—	0.867	—
Male, age 65	—	—	—	0.854	0.822
Female, age 55	—	—	—	0.876	—
Female, age 65	—	—	—	0.857	0.782
Joint	—	—	—	—	—

Sources: Brown and others 2001; James and Song 2001 as cited in Rocha and Thorburn 2007, annex 1.
Note: — = not available.

of the United Kingdom and the United States, quite the inverse of the Chilean case. As mentioned before, the positive relationship in the Chilean case can be explained by the higher reinvestment and mortality risks associated with annuities with longer expected durations. The same factor also explains the lower MWRs of joint annuities in Chile; of note is that joint annuities have similar or lower MWRs than single annuities in other countries as well. Therefore, the inverse relationship between MWRs and age in the U.K. and U.S. cases probably reflects factors specific to those countries.[30]

Market performance can also be measured by the relationship between the annuity rate (defined as the internal rate of return on the annuity) and the risk-free rate. As shown in figure 8.8, the average annuity rate measured by the RV-04 mortality table tracked the interest rate on 10-year central bank bonds reasonably well during the 1990s, with the difference between the two rates averaging 0.7 percent annually in that period.[31] It would be tempting to conclude that retired workers could have obtained a better deal by investing directly in risk-free bonds, but this conclusion would need to be modified considering the costs and the risks to retirees, especially their exposure to longevity risk.

In 2001, the difference between the two rates inverted, and the annuity rate has exceeded the risk-free rate since then. This negative difference between the risk-free rate and the annuity rate is unusual. For example, Brown, Mitchell, and Poterba (2001) calculate the internal rates of return on U.S. annuities and obtain rates ranging from 5.9 to 6.5 percent per

Figure 8.8   Average Annuity Rate and Risk-Free Rate, 1993–2009

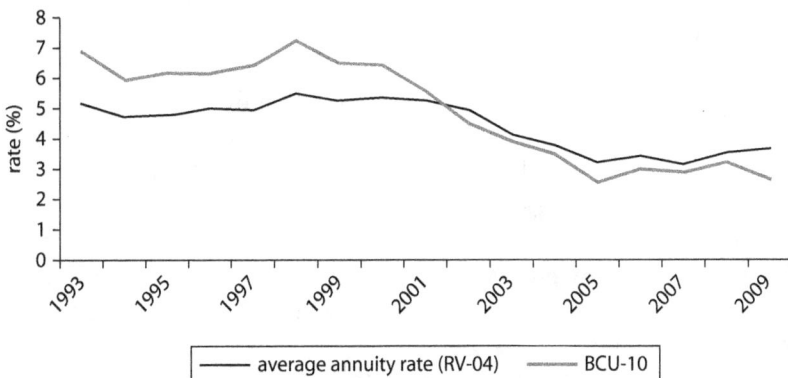

Sources: Data provided by Superintendency of Securities and Insurance and Central Bank of Chile.

year, lower than the yields of 10- and 30-year Treasury bonds—which were 7.1 and 7.3 percent per year in the same period. James and Song (2001) performed the same exercise for several countries and obtained similar results.

The average MWRs estimated for March 1999, 2002, 2003, 2004, and 2005 are consistent with the movements in the two rates. The MWR is slightly lower than 1.0 in 1999, consistent with a slightly higher risk-free rate, and higher than 1.0 in the following years, consistent with a higher annuity rate. In general, MWRs are higher in the period after 2002, when the annuity rate has exceeded the risk-free rate. The MWRs for 2004 and 2005 are similar, consistent with a stable relationship between the two rates. This chapter has not estimated MWRs for previous years, but the relationship between the two rates suggests that MWRs were lower in the 1990s and increased significantly after 2000. All in all, these results suggest that annuitants in Chile in the mid-2000s were receiving better value for their premiums and are also receiving a better deal, on average, than annuitants in other countries.

Replacement Rates

Despite the collection of massive amounts of data, Chilean statistics do not contain information on the replacement rates achieved by retiring workers. Projections of replacement rates are based on assumptions regarding the length of active work and retirement lives, the average rate of wage growth, and the average rate of net investment returns. Assuming an active life of 40 years, a retirement life of 20 years, an average growth rate of 2 percent, and a net investment return of 5 percent would produce a replacement rate of 60 percent of the final wage for a 10 percent contribution rate. If the net investment return is 3.5 percent, the replacement rate will amount to 38 percent.

Chile closed down its old social security system and until recently did not operate a public pillar. The introduction of a solidarity pillar in 2009 is an implicit zero or first pillar that tops up pensions if they fall below the PMAS. The law sets the amounts of the PBS and PMAS, which are expected to reach about US$150 in 2009 and US$500 in 2011, respectively. Both pensions will be indexed according to inflation.[32] The solidarity pillar was designed to provide income support not only to low-income individuals, but also to an important proportion of middle-income households.

Replacement rates benefited from the high investment returns that were achieved in the first 29 years of the new system's operation and from the generous terms of recognition bonds provided to members of the old system who switched to the AFP system. In the early years of the new system, most people receiving pensions were recipients of disability and survivorship pensions. They received defined benefits financed from compulsory group disability and term life insurance. Early retirement and old-age pensions accelerated in the mid-1990s. Early retirement pensions, which accounted for about 40 percent of all pensions between 1995 and 2004, obtained replacement rates of around 50 percent because this rate was a regulatory requirement. The AFP system was successful in making possible early retirement at high replacement rates for short active lives and long retirement lives. Because early retirement age was on average 9 years lower than normal retirement age, early retirees would have an average active life of 31 years and an average retirement life of 29 years. With a growth rate of 2 percent and a 10 percent contribution rate, a net investment return of 6.5 percent would be needed to generate a replacement rate of 50 percent of the final wage. Such a net investment rate was close to the average net return achieved over this period. The replacement rates of normal old-age retirees were probably much lower than those of early retirees but significantly higher than the old MPG level.

Risk-Sharing Arrangements

The Chilean retirement market does not make use of risk-sharing arrangements. Retirement risks are assumed either by providers or by pensioners, depending on the type of product. Holders of PWs assume the investment, inflation, and longevity risks as well as the credit and bankruptcy risks. However, some of these risks are mitigated by the strong conduct and prudential regulation of AFPs and the provision of government guarantees in case of institutional failure. The MPG or PBS covers some of the longevity risk of PW holders because the government assumes the responsibility to pay the MPG (now the PBS) for life once the account balance of a PW holder has been exhausted.

Fixed real annuities transfer the investment and longevity risks to annuity providers, whereas the inflation risk is covered by the extensive use of inflation-indexed financial instruments. An important shortcoming of fixed real annuities is that their holders are prevented from participating in the higher returns that can be obtained from equities and real estate. Thus, the protection against investment and inflation risks comes at a potentially high cost. In Chile, the level of real interest rates has been high for most of the past 29 years, reflecting the effect of anti-inflationary policies in the early 1980s and the slow reduction of risk premiums that has affected all countries in the Latin American region. Risk premiums have occasionally increased in response to regional financial crises. Hence, the annual real rates of return on inflation-indexed annuities have not been low. During the period from 1990 to 2002, they fluctuated between 4.88 and 5.73 percent. However, real rates experienced a drastic decline in 2003 and 2004, when they fell to 3.33 percent.

The decline in real interest rates in the mid-2000s underscored the exposure of retiring workers to the annuity rate risk or annuitization risk. In fact, available data show that the annuity conversion factor has declined steadily over the years. It fell for old-age annuities from 8.46 percent in 1998 to 7.31 percent in 2003. The corresponding levels for early retirement annuities were 7.35 and 6.28 percent.[33]

Profit-participating annuities with guaranteed benefits and annual bonuses are not found in Chile. In these policies, which are widely used in some OECD countries (for example, Denmark and Sweden), annuity providers assume the investment and longevity risks for the guaranteed benefits, but these two risks are shared among participants for the annual bonuses. Variable (unit-linked) annuities were authorized in 2004 to be used in combination with fixed real annuities, but these products have not been developed. In unit-linked annuities, the individual pensioner bears the investment risk, but all annuitants share the longevity risk. Profit-participating and unit-linked annuities avoid the timing of annuitization risk and also permit participation in higher long-term returns from equities and other real assets. However, regular payments are exposed to the risk of significant fluctuations.

Marketing Regulation

The marketing of the two main payout options, PWs and life annuities, is highly asymmetrical. AFPs focus on the very profitable accumulation phase of the pension business and adopt a passive marketing stance on PWs. PWs are mainly used by workers with low balances who cannot purchase an annuity above the MPG or PBS level. Workers with balances that were slightly higher than the old MPG level but with a potential financial advantage in choosing a PW also chose PWs. The introduction of the actuarial factor in the calculation of PWs is expected to reduce the demand for PWs from this latter group. The actuarial factor makes the PWs relatively less attractive compared with annuities. People in this group will be able to obtain a higher level of income by using annuities rather than PWs. For tax reasons, very few high-income and large-balance workers use PWs.

The commission income that AFPs can raise from offering PWs is very limited. A modest fee of about 1 percent of benefit payments is charged on all PW holders just to cover operating costs, whereas the fees during the accumulation phase, excluding premiums for term life and disability insurance, still amount to close to 15 percent of contribution amounts. The profits from the accumulation phase have been very large because, although operating costs have declined with the growing maturity of the pension system, the reduction of operating fees has lagged considerably.

In contrast, life insurance companies engage in very active marketing of annuities, using employees and company agents as well as independent brokers. They have strong incentives to market annuities, which represent the core of their business. Independent brokers account for 40 percent of sales, and agents and employees account for the remaining 60 percent. Brokers and agents play a part not only in the choice of the annuity option but also in the decision to retire early. Brokers have influenced the early retirement decision by emphasizing the potential access to two incomes (since "early retirement" does not imply exit from the labor force) and immediate access to any excess funds. Brokers have also offered assistance with the handling of recognition bonds and the considerable amount of paperwork involved.

During the 1990s, when commissions paid to brokers reached very high levels of 5 to 6 percent of the value of the annuity contract, brokers reportedly offered kickbacks to their clients, effectively increasing the amount of funds that early retirees could withdraw as lump sums. Commission rates have fallen since then to 2.5 percent or less, and this practice is no longer used. Commission rates are built into the annuity price and are not charged directly to consumers or even disclosed to them. The decline in commission rates is attributed to the threat of regulation and was brought about by an informal agreement among life insurance companies. A similar informal agreement among pension companies has lowered commissions paid to agents for attracting new customers to AFPs during the accumulation phase. Account switching among AFPs was a major policy issue at that time.

Regulators were concerned during the 1990s with the bias in favor of early retirement, the dispersion of annuity prices, the high level of commissions, and the spread of illegal marketing practices such as the cash rebates. New rules were adopted in the 2004 revision of the pension system: the conditions for early retirement were tightened, a cap of 2.5 percent was imposed on annuity commissions, banks were allowed to participate in the distribution of annuities, the menu of retirement products was expanded by allowing use of PWs or variable annuities in combination with MPG (or higher) fixed real annuities, and a new electronic quotation system was introduced. In 2008, a new cap of 2.0 percent was imposed on annuity commissions.

The new quotation system, known as the Pension Consultations and Offers System (Sistema de Consultas y Ofertas de Montos de Pensión, or SCOMP), has attracted particular interest because it represents an attempt to reduce the influence of brokers in the selection of annuities. The aim is to enhance the quality of information available to consumers as well as to enable direct access to a full range of annuity quotations. Quotations are solicited through SCOMP participants, and SCOMP validates the personal data of the workers concerned. SCOMP receives quotations from insurers and also calculates the PW and sends this information to the applicants. Workers can select one of the offers made within 15 days or seek another offer outside SCOMP, but only from an insurer who made an offer under SCOMP. The offer made outside SCOMP must be better than the first offer. In addition to the quotation system itself, a list of all potential retirees, including those reaching normal retirement age and those eligible for early retirement, is prepared and circulated to all SCOMP participants (brokers or advisers, insurance companies, and AFPs). This information reduces further the influence of individual brokers. However, workers who object to the circulation of their personal data can have their names removed from this list.

The new quotation system became effective in August 2004. Early experience showed an increase in the average number of quotations, an increase in price competition because the final selection of provider has been closely associated with the ranking of quotes, and a reduction in commissions to 2.2 percent. However, early experience has also shown an increasing concentration in the annuity market.

The regulation of marketing activity in the annuity market is extensive. Independent brokers have to pass a certification test administered by the supervisory agency as well as a basic "fit and proper" test. Most applicants take a 120-hour course on annuities. Licensed brokers are legally obligated to represent their clients and generate their income from commissions on the sale of annuities. They are not permitted to accept volume-related remuneration from insurers. However, they are not required to disclose the level of commissions they receive from different insurers.

Brokers have strong incentives to influence their clients toward both an early retirement decision and a selection of an annuity in favor of a

PW. Before 2004, retiring workers were required to obtain at least six annuity quotes from the market before making their selection. These quotes had to be presented to their pension companies, which were not allowed to release the funds and transfer them to an insurance company unless these quotes were presented. The requirement of a minimum number of quotes was motivated by a concern for disclosure and transparency. It was aimed at preventing pension companies from directing retiring workers to affiliated insurance companies. However, though sensible, the regulation was not effective in preventing the emergence of high dispersion in annuity prices and broker manipulation of the process. Brokers often directed customers to the insurance companies that offered the highest commissions.

The 2008 amendments to the pension law replace brokers with pension advisers, who are subject to stricter eligibility requirements. Although licensing requirements have been challenging for most of the applicants, these pension advisers are expected to be self-regulated. Currently, pension advisers have not created an association that may act as a self-regulatory organization to impose a code of ethics on its associates. Whether this upgrade creates a change in the behavior of the market remains to be seen.

Regulation and Supervision

This section looks at the sustainability of MWRs, the prudential regulation of life insurance companies and AFPs, and the evolution of risk management in those institutions.

The Sustainability of Money's Worth Ratios

An important question that arises in Chile is whether the high MWRs that have been observed in recent years can be sustained in the future. Annuity providers could, in principle, pay high annuity rates and still achieve positive spreads by investing in higher-yielding assets. Table 8.14 indicates that the industry has shifted toward higher-yielding mortgage-backed securities and corporate bonds since 1995. As interest rates decreased during most of this decade, individuals prepaid their balances, and insurance companies lost an important part of their mortgage bond portfolios. Banks developed alternative instruments for housing finance, and life insurance companies increased their share of bonds issued by banks and alternative instruments such as mutual funds, investment funds, and foreign investments. The move toward corporate bonds since 2000 is particularly noteworthy, with the share of these instruments

Table 8.14   Portfolio of Life Insurance Companies, 1991–2008

| | Share of total assets (%) | | | | | |
Portfolio asset	1991	1995	2000	2003	2005	2008
Government sector	38.3	40.3	28.7	17.6	15.0	9.0
Financial sector	23.0	28.4	45.1	37.6	32.4	33.8
Mortgage bonds	13.9	18.6	24.2	18.8	11.9	7.9
Mortgage-backed securities	3.0	6.0	10.1	10.1	9.6	11.9
Other financial instruments	6.1	3.8	10.8	8.7	10.9	14.1
Company sector	29.0	22.1	15.3	33.4	38.4	35.5
Shares	8.9	10.2	3.4	2.9	3.5	2.0
Bonds	20.1	10.7	10.7	29.3	34.8	33.4
Real estate	7.8	7.7	7.4	7.3	7.9	10.7
Other assets	2.0	1.5	3.6	4.1	6.4	11.1
Total assets	100.0	100.0	100.0	100.0	100.0	100.0

Source: Data provided by Superintendency of Securities and Insurance.
Note: December values in 1991–2008, with the exception of June values in 1995.

increasing from one-tenth to one-third of the portfolio. These instruments are also indexed and pay a higher yield than government and Central Bank of Chile bonds, thereby allowing providers to match their liabilities while extracting a higher return.

Annuity providers may have been able to extract a higher return adjusted for credit risk, because annuities are much less liquid than government or Central Bank of Chile bonds and probably pay a liquidity premium. Providers may be able to extract this premium because of their much longer investment horizon. Moreover, providers have only held bonds issued by banks and corporations with very good credit standings—usually rated AA and higher and sometimes with specific credit enhancement features, which allow them to maintain credit risk at relatively low levels.

This pursuit of higher yields has been observed in other countries as well. For example, the Teachers Insurance and Annuity Association–College Retirement Equities Fund, which is the largest annuity provider in the United States, holds privately issued fixed income instruments offering higher yields to match its fixed annuities, including a large share of less liquid instruments bought through private placements. The Chilean situation is different not because of the shift toward fixed income instruments issued by the private sector, but because these instruments are also inflation indexed, thus allowing providers to match their indexed liabilities while extracting higher yields.

Figure 8.9   Annuity Rate, Adjusted Annuity Rate, Central Bank Bond Rate, and Corporate Bond Rate, 1993–2009

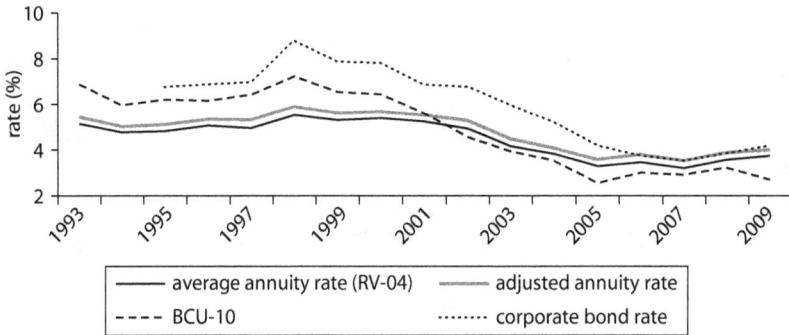

Sources: Authors' estimates and data provided by Central Bank of Chile, Superintendency of Securities and Insurance, and Superintendency of Pensions.

Although this portfolio strategy has apparently succeeded in preserving positive financial spreads, the spreads have narrowed dangerously in the second half of the present decade. As shown in figure 8.9, the marginal return on the fixed income portfolio, measured by the corporate bond rate, largely exceeded the annuity rate every year until 2006 (with the difference amounting to about 100 basis points after 2001), but these margins have become extremely narrow in the past few years. This spread is thin considering the need to cover all costs and risks and still generate a positive return on equity.

Providers' costs include the commissions paid to annuity brokers and all operating costs. As shown in figure 8.10, commissions averaged 3 percent of the premium in the early 1990s, increased continuously to almost 6 percent at the end of the decade, and then decreased sharply to levels of about 2 percent. The increase in the 1990s reflected the practice of charging higher commissions and providing an informal (and illegal) cash rebate to retirees. This cash rebate amounted de facto to a partial lump sum and proved a popular marketing device, but it was also inconsistent with the intention of the law and prompted a reaction from policy makers, who at the end of 2000 submitted a draft new pension law to the Chilean legislature that, among other things, capped broker commissions and proposed the new electronic quotation system. Although the law, which imposed a 2.5 percent cap on fees, was passed only in 2004, the threat of the law and political pressures induced a change in behavior, as indicated by the sharp decline in fees in 2001.[34]

Figure 8.10   Commission Rates, 1991–2008

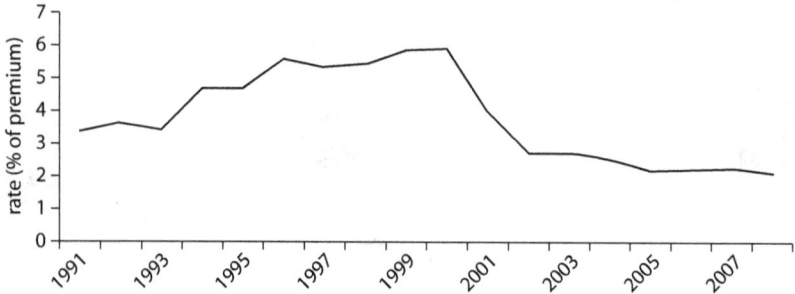

Source: Data provided by Superintendency of Securities and Insurance.

The commission cost has added about 30 basis points to the annuity rate, as shown by the adjusted annuity rate line in figure 8.9, reducing the intermediation spread commensurately.[35] In addition, providers also need to cover their operating costs, which in 2008 amounted to about 2.2 percent of assets, implying a negative spread overall. As shown in figure 8.11, although the largest life insurance companies have reduced their operating costs and may continue reducing them further, the overall market has increased them. However, if cost ratios decline to 0.6 percent, which is the lowest cost ratio among OECD countries, prospective profit margins would appear to remain unattractive even for the five largest life insurance companies.

The analysis of MWRs and intermediation spreads suggests that at least some annuity providers may have experienced losses from the annuities issued between 2002 and 2005. These losses have not resulted in immediate financial problems for the companies because of the strong capital and reserve buffer that accumulated in previous years as a result of the strict capital regulations implemented in the early 1990s. However, the analysis also suggests that the high MWRs offered in 2002 to 2005 probably cannot be sustained, because they would imply further erosion of capital, at least for some companies.

The question arises as to why profit-maximizing companies have issued life annuities with such thin financial margins. Underpricing of these annuities is unlikely to have been caused by outdated mortality tables, because most companies seem to have sufficient technical capacity, including well-trained actuaries. More likely, companies have priced their annuities counting on a future increase in interest rates from the low recent levels. The intermediation spreads shown in figure 8.8 do not

Figure 8.11   Administrative Costs of Life Insurance Companies, 1991–2008

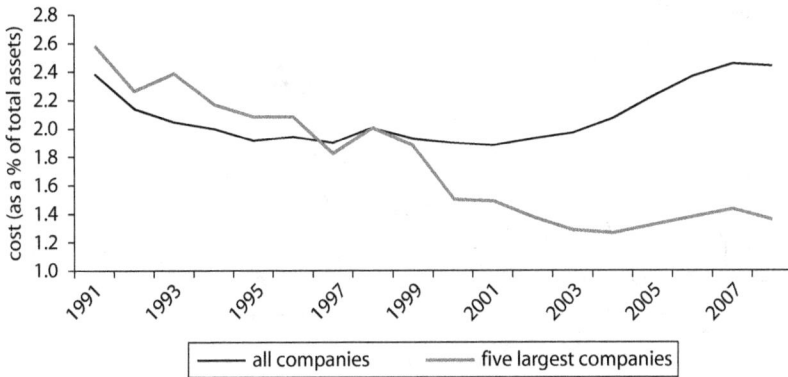

Source: Data provided by Superintendency of Securities and Insurance.

capture the spread earned over the entire life of the annuity contract because assets have a shorter duration than liabilities. If interest rates increase (above the levels implicit in the current yield curve), margins earned on currently issued contracts would increase as well.

The possibility also exists that some companies are deliberately adopting aggressive pricing strategies to drive competitors out of the market, thus gaining market share. Industry participants acknowledge that intermediation margins have been thin and returns on equity low, and that is probably why some life insurance companies have decided to exit the annuity market in recent years. Although the industry has become more concentrated and the possibility that the annuity market will undergo a process of consolidation similar to that observed in the pension sector in the 1990s cannot be entirely discarded, some life insurance companies have found a profitable business in the provision of voluntary savings for retirement. Because it is more heterogeneous, less transparent, and therefore less competitive, smaller life insurance companies can compete in the voluntary savings market.

The differences between the degrees of competitiveness of the pension fund and insurance sectors are also reflected in the reported ROEs of AFPs and life insurance companies. As shown in figure 8.12, while AFPs have generated ROEs above 20 percent and in some years even above 50 percent, life insurance companies have earned much lower ROEs, despite bearing much higher levels of risk.

The ROEs of the two sectors are not directly comparable year by year, because the returns of pension funds and the ROEs of AFPs reflect a

Figure 8.12   Returns on Equity of AFPs and Life Insurance Companies, 1997–2008

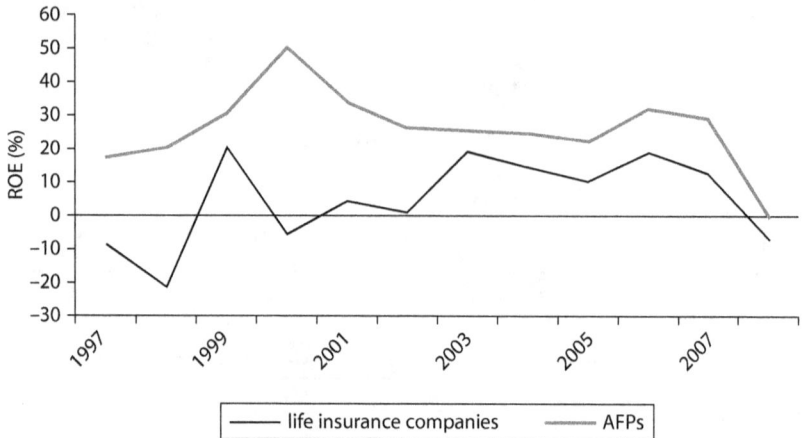

Sources: Data provided by Superintendency of Securities and Insurance and Superintendency of Pensions.

mark-to-market valuation, whereas the portfolios of insurance companies are valued by a combination of book and market values, largely book values. Moreover, the accounting ROEs of annuity providers are affected by a strict capital rule that imposes large provisions when the company sells an annuity that leads to accounting losses at the point of sale. However, the two indicators are more comparable over longer periods of time, and the numbers indicate clearly a more competitive annuities industry.

Prudential Regulation

Chile is the first country in the world that has mandated the use of retirement products with regular income streams over the expected life of beneficiaries (either in the form of life annuities or life expectancy PWs). As a result, it has introduced a rigorous regulatory regime on providers of retirement products to minimize the bankruptcy risk faced by pensioners. It has also introduced state guarantees to protect pensioners against provider insolvency as well as aberrant behavior.

The capital regulation of pension companies includes a stipulated minimum capital that rises with the number of beneficiaries but is generally low and does not act as a barrier to entry. For an APF with 10,000 members or more, the minimum capital amounts to UF 20,000, or about US$840,000. A more stringent capital requirement is the obligatory reserve (*encaje*) of 1 percent of the value of assets under management.[36]

The *encaje* is required to be invested in units of the fund to ensure an alignment of interests between the pension companies and their members. The *encaje* is designed to support the minimum relative rate of return guarantee that Chilean AFPs are required to observe. The guarantee initially specified that the average real rate of return of any company could not be lower than 50 percent of the average of all AFPs or the average return minus 2 percent over the preceding 12 months. In 2002, the period of calculation was extended to 36 months and was applied to each of the five funds that AFPs were then required to offer, while the spread below the average was differentiated by type of fund, being higher for the more volatile A and B funds (4 percent) and lower for more conservative funds (2 percent). The *encaje* and the minimum relative return guarantee are intended to protect workers from aberrant managers. They have been effective in forcing AFPs to stay close to the average of the industry. The guarantee has never been called.

AFPs do not suffer from any mismatching between their assets and liabilities because the value of liabilities is by definition equal to the value of assets. The only other capital regulation concerns the valuation of assets, which are required to be mark-to-market. Because most assets have to be invested in instruments that are traded on public markets, asset valuation is relatively straightforward, but challenges arise in the valuation of instruments such as derivatives and private equity funds.

The capital regulation of life insurance companies is far more complex. Because long-term annuity business dominates the balance sheets of life insurers, the valuation of assets and liabilities and the regulation of any mismatches between them play a critical part in determining the capital adequacy of life insurers. Chile introduced the *calce* reserve rule to regulate asset and liability mismatches.

The first step in *calce* is to calculate the asset and liability cash flows for 10 different maturity brackets. The asset flows depend on the characteristics of particular instruments, but the liability flows need to be expressed in actuarial terms, allowing for the survival probabilities of the main and contingent beneficiaries. Regulators specify the life tables used for calculating the survival probabilities. The tables used to be based on data from the early 1980s (RV-85) but were replaced with the more up-to-date RV-04 tables in 2005. Insurance companies are free to use their own life tables for pricing annuities but have to use the standardized tables for the *calce* rule.

Asset and liability cash flows for each maturity bracket are then compared. A matching factor of 1 is used if asset flows are equal to or exceed the liability flows; a value of less than 1 is assigned to any bracket in which liabilities exceed assets, implying an increased capital requirement. Data for 2004 show that the matching factor, known as CP in Chile, was close to 1 for brackets 1 to 7, ranging up to maturities of 16 years, but fell drastically for higher brackets, reaching a low of 0.203 for the highest bracket, which covers maturities of 29 years or longer.

The third step is to calculate the basic financial reserve, which is given by the discounted value of matched and unmatched liability flows. Matched liability flows are discounted at the market rate of interest that prevailed at the time each contract was issued, whereas unmatched flows are discounted at a technical rate of 3 percent that is prescribed by the regulators. The market rate is the same for all companies but varies by contract depending on its time of issue.

The fourth step is to calculate the basic technical reserve, which involves discounting liability flows by the rate of interest used in determining the annuity pricing of each contract. The technical rate of discount not only is different for each company, but also is different for each contract in each company. However, the basic technical reserve for each contract cannot be lower than the corresponding basic financial reserve.

The *calce* reserve is then obtained as the difference between the basic technical reserve and the basic financial reserve. Companies are required to show on their balance sheet the basic financial reserve and the *calce* reserve. The basic technical reserve is not shown but is used for determining the size of the *calce* reserve.

This complicated approach was used because insurance regulation was based on projected asset and liability cash flows rather than on market values. Insurance companies were not required to use mark-to-market asset valuation, partly because the companies followed a buy-and-hold approach and held debt instruments to maturity (Rocha and Thorburn 2007, 123, 135). The insurance regulators are now taking steps to introduce risk-based supervision that will focus on market valuation of assets and use of market rates of interest for valuing liabilities.

It is not clear how the *calce* rule will be modified or whether it will be discarded completely in favor of the full market valuation and traffic light system that has been introduced in Denmark and other continental European countries as well as in several Anglo-American countries. Despite its shortcomings, the *calce* rule played a useful role in forcing insurance companies to maintain an adequate level of reserves that reflected the degree of asset and liability mismatching. Nevertheless, the dearth of long-term assets with maturities exceeding 16 years—whereas annuity liabilities can run for much longer periods—has exposed insurance companies to significant investment as well as longevity risks.

In addition to maintaining the *calce* reserve, insurance companies were required to operate with a leverage of not higher than 15, which implied a required equity ratio of 6.7 percent. The leverage limit was recently raised to 20, lowering the required equity ratio to 5 percent. However, in the absence of a requirement to use market values for assets and market interest rates for valuing liabilities, the measurement of equity is itself subject to a considerable degree of arbitrary valuation. In addition, an asset sufficiency test was introduced. This test requires a detailed calculation of future asset cash flows, including credit and prepayment risks, and computation of the reinvestment rate that would be needed to equalize asset and liability flows.

The last element in annuity regulation of insurance companies concerns the offer of a government guarantee to annuitants in cases of insurer insolvency. The guarantee covers 100 percent of payments up to the PBS level and 75 percent of any annuity payments above the PBS, up to UF 45 per month (approximately US$1,900). The cost of the guarantee is not prefunded but is covered from general tax revenues. However, the authorities have in place a speedy resolution mechanism that allows early interventions in companies that face financial difficulties.

Risk Management

Risk management has evolved considerably over time in line with the growing maturity of the new pension system. Increasing demand from life insurance companies has stimulated the development of high-yielding, long-term corporate and mortgage bonds. Most fixed income instruments are indexed to consumer prices, whether they are issued by the public sector or the private sector. Fixed income instruments have long maturities, up to 30 years for public sector bonds, mortgage bonds, and corporate and infrastructure bonds.

Despite the ample supply of long-term fixed income and indexed debt instruments, annuity providers are still faced with an overall asset and liability mismatching because the average duration of assets is shorter by three to four years than the average duration of liabilities. Most insurance companies report an average duration of the asset portfolio of 8 years, which is substantially shorter than the average duration of liabilities (11 or 12 years, depending on the clientele).

The absence of derivative instruments has complicated risk management, especially the underdevelopment of long-term interest rate swaps.

Although prudential regulations force insurance companies to maintain higher capital reserves to cover the mismatching at the longer end of the maturity spectrum, insurance companies face a significant reinvestment risk, which is aggravated by the steady decline in long-term real interest rates. By increasing their holdings of corporate and mortgage bonds, insurance companies have increased their exposure to credit and prepayment risks. Prepayment risk, in particular, has risen in response to the fall in interest rates. Insurance companies have invested in equities and real estate to increase the average duration of their assets and have raised short-term debt to lower the average duration of their liabilities, but these strategies have provided limited benefits in asset liability management.

Managing longevity risk has also been a major challenge. Risk-sharing arrangements, whereby longevity risk is shared with annuitants, have not been used in Chile. The use of international reinsurance to cover the long tail of liabilities has been constrained by regulations that require localization of reinsurance assets, while local reinsurance has not been available at reasonable cost. In addition, the industry has had no access to risk-hedging instruments, such as longevity bonds or longevity derivatives. Thus, insurance companies have fully assumed the longevity risk. Estimating future improvements in longevity has proved one of the most challenging tasks of risk management, especially dealing with data limitations in the tail end of the age distribution. Since 2007, the private sector, with the support of the insurance supervisor (the Superintendency of Securities and Insurance) and the World Bank, has tried to launch a longevity bond in Chile, but so far this effort has been unsuccessful.

Insurance companies are required to use life tables prescribed by the regulators for determining their technical and capital reserves and for reporting purposes but are free to use proprietary life tables reflecting their own clientele for pricing and marketing purposes. Although companies are not allowed to ask personal questions on health history, they are allowed to price annuities freely and to differentiate risks by observable characteristics, such as age, sex, level of income, and accumulated account balance of retiring workers (income and financial wealth tend to be well correlated with educational levels, which in turn tend to be highly correlated with life expectancy). Although evidence indicates that insurance companies price their annuities according to the risk characteristics of annuitants, evidence also exists of aggressive pricing and marketing campaigns that result in thin financial spreads and increase the exposure of insurance companies to investment and longevity risks.

AFPs do not bear either investment or longevity risk. These risks are assumed by holders of PWs. The introduction of multiple (lifestyle or life-cycle) funds has allowed a better alignment of investment risks with the risk preferences of retired workers. Workers near retirement and PW holders face restrictions for holding the funds with the riskiest portfolios.[37] However, the short duration of fixed income assets in the conservative funds exposes retiring workers to annuitization risk. Therefore, a fund with a portfolio of long bonds that is better aligned to the pricing of annuities is needed.

Concluding Remarks

The rapid growth of the market for retirement products has its origins in the pension reform that was implemented in 1981. However, the pension reform was a necessary but insufficient condition for development of this market. Other countries (for example, Australia) have also introduced a private mandatory pension pillar but have not experienced such an increase in the number of PW and annuity contracts, especially the latter. The high rate of annuitization is particularly impressive, given the thinness of annuity markets in most countries.

The outcome in Chile reflects a number of additional factors, including restrictions on lump sums, the absence of a front-ended first-pillar benefit, the low level and back-ended nature of the old MPG, and the influence of brokers and sales agents. Restrictions on lump sums have increased the demand for all retirement products, including life annuities. The absence of a front-ended first-pillar benefit and the low level of protection provided by the old MPG have led most middle- and higher-income workers to prefer annuities.[38] PWs are primarily used by lower-income workers, because these workers benefit relatively more from the MPG (now PBS) and also because some of these workers have to use PWs because of their small balances. Finally, insurance brokers have focused their selling efforts on middle- and higher-income workers because their commissions are related to the size of the premium, and they have encouraged these workers to retire early and to annuitize. Which products retirees with retirement income between the PBS and PMAS will select remains to be seen.

Chilean annuitants have generally received good value for their premiums, as indicated by average MWRs on indexed annuities of around 1.04 to 1.06. These MWRs have been high by international comparison. In most other countries, MWRs range from 0.90 to 1.00 for nominal annuities and from 0.80 to 0.85 for indexed annuities in the few countries that offer inflation protection, such as the United Kingdom. The higher MWRs of indexed annuities in Chile are in part because of the availability of a larger supply of financial assets indexed to prices, including higher-yield assets such as mortgage, corporate, and infrastructure bonds. The higher MWRs are also due to the presence of a very competitive annuity market. In recent years, providers seem to have engaged in aggressive pricing strategies, as indicated not only by the high MWRs but also by the very thin intermediation spreads. The high MWRs of recent years may not be sustainable in the long run because they imply very low spreads and profit margins and possibly losses in the annuity business, at least for some companies.

The industry could absorb these losses because of the strong capital buffer accumulated in the 1990s, attributable to the introduction of a strict capital regulation regime early in that decade. However, the continuation of aggressive pricing strategies could lead to further erosion of capital. Therefore, some market adjustments should be expected, leading to some decline in MWRs. The implementation of a new electronic quotation system in 2004 has enhanced price competition and led to further consolidation of the industry, suggesting that these adjustments may be taking place.

The regulatory framework has been reasonable and has supported the development of the market. Product regulation has prevented an early exhaustion of real incomes at retirement. Annuities have been fixed and indexed, and married men have been required to purchase joint annuities. Those features imply relatively lower payments in the early stages of retirement but ensure adequate payments for beneficiaries in later stages. The PW formula follows the same approach, by preventing a depletion of the balance in a finite period of time and distributing payments according to life expectancy. The 2004 pension law introduced new products, but these products are combinations that always include a minimum fixed, indexed annuity, thus ensuring minimum insurance against investment and longevity risks.

Marketing regulation allowed some questionable selling practices during the 1990s but has been tightened with the amendments to the pension law in 2004. Broker commissions have been capped at 2.5 percent of the premium. More important, an innovative electronic quotation system for annuities and PWs has been introduced. The new system has improved market transparency and seems to be producing positive outcomes: retiring workers have selected annuities on the basis of the best quotes, and broker commissions have declined further to levels below the cap.

The regulation of providers has supported the sound development of the market. Strict capital rules introduced in the early 1990s penalized mismatches of assets and liabilities and provided a capital buffer that has proved essential for the stability of the industry. The capital buffer weakened over time because of the failure to account for the improvements in mortality rates in the past 15 years. This regulatory failure affected not only capital regulation but also product regulation. It was addressed in 2005 through the adoption of an updated mortality table and an asset sufficiency test that should enhance transparency and market discipline.

The government provides guarantees to retirees, but the regulatory framework contains elements that should prevent excessive recourse to these guarantees. The introduction of stricter conditions for early retirement and the actuarial factor in the calculation of the PWs will reduce the potential number of retirees eligible for the PBS. The annuity guarantee has an element of coinsurance that seems reasonable, especially considering that the private pension system is mandatory.

At the same time, some important weaknesses must be addressed in the future. The separation of the accumulation and retirement phases implies that neither pension funds nor annuity providers are effectively maximizing an individual's pension wealth over the entire life cycle. In particular, workers in the preretirement phase are subject to some risks, such as annuity rate risk, that have not been properly addressed. Managing longevity risk remains a particular challenge for annuity providers. In addition, although annuity providers have access to a wider range of financial instruments than providers in other emerging countries to manage market or investment risk, they still face a duration mismatch problem that needs to be continuously addressed. Providers also lack access to a wider range of risk management tools, such as derivatives and reinsurance.

The Chilean experience provides many lessons for other developing countries. The most important lesson concerns the feasibility of developing a market for retirement products from a low initial base. First, the provision of PWs and annuities to workers with disabilities and survivors enabled an early and rapid start to the market for retirement products, attracting new providers into the market. Second, the Chilean approach to product regulation is appropriate for countries that expect the new second pillar to play a major role in retirement provision and social protection. The restrictions on lump-sum payments increase the potential demand for all retirement products, including annuities. A PW formula that is based on life expectancy prevents a very premature exhaustion of funds. The imposition of both fixed annuities indexed to inflation and joint annuities for married couples contributes to preventing an early exhaustion of funds and poverty in old age. The introduction of new products, such as variable and adjustable annuities, should require a minimum fixed annuity component that provides investment and longevity insurance.

Countries that have preserved a large first pillar and introduced only a modest second pillar can adopt more liberal product regulation, because in those cases, the exposure of retiring workers to investment and longevity risks is more limited. However, very liberal rules for lump sums can hinder significantly the development of the market for retirement products, especially the market for life annuities. The appropriate policies in this area will vary significantly from country to country. In some cases, continuing restrictions on lump-sum payments but also adopting a more liberal approach to the design of retirement products may be appropriate. For example, the regulation of PWs may be more liberal, allowing designs that enable a faster withdrawal of funds. Likewise, variable and adjustable annuities may be introduced without the obligation of a fixed annuity component.

Access to long-term instruments, including inflation-indexed bonds, and freedom to price annuities on the basis of proprietary life tables have been essential elements of the success of the annuity market in Chile. In addition, robust marketing regulation to ensure market transparency, free choice, and informed decision making by retiring workers has played an important part. The new electronic quotation system has improved transparency in the market for retirement products and has ensured that retirees effectively get the best quotes.

Chilean regulators have addressed reinvestment and longevity risks by imposing strict capital regulations on providers. The capital rules introduced in 1990 were innovative and were based on the extent of asset and liability mismatching. This approach to capital regulation enabled the early buildup of a strong capital buffer that has proved very important for the sound development of the industry. The production of appropriate mortality tables to be used for regulatory purposes is also of central importance. Finally, ensuring that bankruptcy rules protect the interests of annuitants in the case of insurance company failure and offering a government annuity guarantee with a reasonable element of coinsurance by annuitants are further essential components of a sound regulatory framework.

Notes

1. Since the creation of the AFP system, the ceiling has been set at 60 *unidades de fomento* (UFs). The UF is a unit of account that is indexed to prices and is widely used in the valuation of contracts and tax parameters (the UF was

equal to approximately US$42 in December 2009). When initially set, the ceiling amounted to six times the average wage, but it has since declined to about three times the average wage.

2. In 2008, the government introduced a noncontributory solidarity pillar to alleviate problems of poverty in old age.

3. In February 2010, Chile was accepted as a new member of the OECD.

4. The true ratio is higher than 28 percent, because insurance assets are measured by a combination of market and book values, whereas pension fund assets are measured at market values. Because of decreases in the value of pension fund assets and a steady increase in the value of insurance assets, the ratio in 2008 increased to 38 percent.

5. In Chile, PWs are provided by pension funds, and the PW premiums (the initial balance) are not reported. The PW premium was estimated and included in table 8.3 to allow for international comparisons. The PW premium was estimated assuming a ratio of the average payout to the average premium similar to that observed for annuities.

6. Premiums on variable annuities are large, but these products are mostly in the accumulation stage and may not be converted into actual life annuities at retirement. See, for example, Brown, Mitchell, and Poterba (2001).

7. However, in Chile, the total assets of pension and life insurance institutions are smaller relative to GDP than in several OECD countries (for example, Australia, Canada, Denmark, the Netherlands, Sweden, Switzerland, the United Kingdom, and the United States), mainly because labor market coverage of the pension system is so much smaller than in those countries.

8. An example is the Pension Consultations and Offers System (SCOMP), which plays the role of information clearinghouse, collecting and communicating electronic quotations in the market for annuities.

9. The PW market is handled in a passive way by AFPs.

10. The institutional framework has inhibited action in this area.

11. Attracted by high profit margins, the number of AFPs had increased during the second half of the 1980s from 12 to 20 before the recent trend of consolidation. The latter has been stimulated by the importance of scale economies and the failure of most new entrants to attain critical mass.

12. See the section titled "Prudential Regulation" for a discussion of *encaje*.

13. Since 2009, a syndicate of insurance companies insures disability and survivorship. All pension fund members are charged the same fee.

14. Conversion into U.S. dollars uses an exchange rate of Ch$500 per U.S. dollar.

15. This measure does not apply to workers who as of January 1, 2002, were older than 50 and 55 years for women and men, respectively.

16. This 80 percent requirement becomes effective in 2012.

17. The 2008 amendments to the law replaced insurance brokers with pension advisers, who are required to pass a stricter examination administered by the pension and insurance supervisors.

18. The exemption from recertification for fully disabled pensioners was introduced in the 2008 amendments to the pension law.

19. Although disability and survivor pensions play a critical role in any pension system, they involve specific issues that require a separate examination and that are beyond the scope of this report. The focus of this chapter is on old age and early retirement.

20. Before 2008, the life annuity had to be higher than the MPG. Because the MPG was substantially higher than the PBS, whether insurance companies will be interested in selling life annuities to pensioners with low pension assets or whether the insurance companies will charge a premium for serving low-income retirees remains to be seen.

21. The *reference annuity* is the value of an annuity an individual would receive on the earlier of his or her retirement and the official retirement age.

22. Since 2008, this requirement is imposed on married women as well.

23. As of July 1, 2009, the value of the MPG was Ch$163,000, and the value of the PBS was Ch$75,000.

24. James, Martínez, and Iglesias (2006) provide an insightful analysis of the demand for PWs and annuities in Chile. As noted before, the 2008 amendments to the law replaced brokers with pension advisers.

25. Because of excessive charges paid by pension funds on international mutual funds in the past, regulation requires these fees to be reported regularly.

26. Collins (2003) and the Investment Company Institute (2004) provide a detailed analysis of costs and fees of pension and mutual funds in the United States.

27. The 2008 amendments to the law allow pension advisers to charge a commission for advising retirees to take PWs.

28. Other researchers have computed MWRs for other countries on the basis of a smaller number of annuity quotes than the actual annuities issued.

29. Chilean providers probably succeed in extracting an increase in returns adjusted for risk because of, among other things, the existence of a liquidity premium in higher-yield bonds.

30. Brown, Mitchell, and Poterba (2001) report the negative relationship between MWR and age for the United Kingdom and the United States but do not provide a clear explanation for that outcome.

31. Until 2005, insurance companies had to report their average annuity rates using an outdated mortality table, the RV-85. During 2005, annuity rates were calculated and reported with both the RV-85 and the recently built RV-04. Past annuity rates were recalculated with the RV-04 on the basis of the

relationship between the two rates in 2005. This calculation resulted in an average increase of 60 basis points in the annuity rate. The interest rate is the PRC-20 (20-year Central Bank indexed bond rate) for the period from 1993 to 2005 and the BCU-10 (10-year Central Bank inflation-indexed bond rate) for the period from 2003 to 2009. Both instruments have the same duration.

32. The laws involved are Laws 20.255 and 20.366.

33. Annuity conversion factors are smaller for people who retire at a younger age because annuity payments will need to cover a longer period of retirement life.

34. Walker (2009) examines the relationship between the annuity rate and the risk-free rate and concludes that the threat of the new pension law did produce a change in behavior.

35. The commission rate is transformed into an interest rate (that is, capitalized) by calculating the difference between the internal rates of return of an annuity with the gross and the net premiums.

36. The *encaje* was initially set at 5 percent of assets, but this level was found to be excessive and was quickly lowered to the current level.

37. The 2008 amendments to the law allow pensioners to use the riskiest funds under certain conditions.

38. The introduction of the solidarity pillar in 2008 is unlikely to affect the behavior of middle- and high-income workers.

References

Berstein, Solange, Pablo Castañeda, Eduardo Fajnzylber, and Gonzalo Reyes, eds. 2009. *Chile 2008: Una Reforma Previsional de Segunda Generación* [Chile 2008: A Second-Generation Pension Reform]. Santiago: Superintendencia de Pensiones.

Brown, Jeffrey R., Olivia S. Mitchell, and James M. Poterba. 2001. "The Role of Real Annuities and Indexed Bonds in an Individual Accounts Retirement Program." In *The Role of Annuity Markets in Financing Retirement*, ed. Jeffrey R. Brown, Olivia S. Mitchell, James M. Poterba, and Mark J. Warshawsky, 107–52. Cambridge, MA: MIT Press.

Collins, Sean. 2003. "The Expenses of Defined Benefit Pension Plans and Mutual Funds." *Perspectives* 9 (6): 1–20.

Investment Company Institute. 2004. "The Cost of Buying and Owning Mutual Funds." *Fundamentals* 13 (1): 1–23.

James, Estelle, Guillermo Martínez, and Augusto Iglesias. 2006. "The Payout Stage in Chile: Who Annuitizes and Why?" *Journal of Pension Economics and Finance* 5 (2): 121–54.

James, Estelle, and Xue Song. 2001. "Annuity Markets around the World: Money's Worth to Annuitants." CeRP Working Papers 16/01, Center for Research on Pensions and Welfare Policies, Turin, Italy.

Rocha, Roberto, and Heinz Rudolph. 2010. "A Summary and Update of Developing Annuities Markets: The Experience of Chile." Policy Research Working Paper 5325, World Bank, Washington, DC.

Rocha, Roberto, and Craig Thorburn. 2007. *Developing Annuities Markets: The Experience of Chile*. Washington, DC: World Bank.

Walker, Eduardo. 2009. "Los Mercados de las Rentas Vitalicias en Chile: Competencia, Regulación, ¿y Miopía?" [Annuity Markets in Chile: Competition, Regulation, and Myopia?]. *El Trimestre Económico* 76 (1): 145–79.

Index

Boxes, figures, notes, and tables are indicated by *b*, *f*, *n*, and *t*, respectively, following the page numbers.